Big M̄oose Lake in the Adirondacks

"Camping on Big Moose Lake, not a building on the shore. A solitary trapper shanty-ing at the other end of the lake. Wolves howling in the wilderness."

ENTRY IN THE DIARY OF
A. AUGUSTUS LOWE-1867

Big Moose Lake
in the Adirondacks

THE STORY OF THE LAKE, THE LAND, AND THE PEOPLE

THE BIG MOOSE LAKE HISTORY PROJECT COMMITTEE

Jane A. Barlow, Editor

with contributions from

Mark Barlow	Arthur Hostage	Edith Pilcher
Frank Carey	Joy Waldau Hostage	Mary Ann Simpson
William S. Dunn	Annette J. Lux	Barbara Kinne Wheeler
Janet Stone Holmes	Wanda Kinne Martin	

THE BIG MOOSE LAKE HISTORY PROJECT/SYRACUSE UNIVERSITY PRESS

First Edition 2004
04 05 06 07 08 09   6 5 4 3 2 1

Title page: *Lake View Launch, Big Moose Lake, by Henry M. Beach.*
Courtesy of Frank Carey.

Facing page: *Signatures of early Big Moose residents.*
Courtesy of Wanda K. Martin.

The paper used in this publication meets the minimum requirements of
American National Standard for Information Sciences—Permanence of
Paper for Printed Library Materials, ANSI Z39.48–1984.∞™

Library of Congress Cataloging-in-Publication Data

Big Moose Lake in the Adirondacks : the story of the lake, the land, and the people /
The Big Moose Lake History Project ; Jane A. Barlow, editor ; with contributions from
Mark Barlow ... [et al.].— 1st ed.
      p. cm.
  Includes bibliographical references and index.
  ISBN 0-8156-0774-1 (alk. paper) — ISBN 0-8156-0799-7 (pbk. : alk. paper)
  1. Big Moose Lake (N.Y.)—History. I. Barlow, Jane A. II. Big Moose Lake History Project.
  F127.H5B54 2004
  974.7'61—dc22   2004004331

Manufactured in the United States of America

G. H. Higbe

H H Coney

Francene A Higby

James Macallister

Wm Hart

Chas Williams

Danforth R Ainsworth

Dana Bissell

Edward J. Martin

Chas. A. Martin

Richard Crage

George A Burdick

Frank J. Martin

Margaret Rose

Asa J Williams

Earl W Coney

Walter Dunn

Arthur Burtch

Frank Day

Alice J. Martin

Fred Williams

Romaine F. Kinne

Ernest LeFountain

Harry Kellogg

Frank Veery

Contents

Illustrations

3 *Making a Living at Big Moose Lake*

4 Ventures from Outside the Lake

5 Private Homes and Camps Before World War II

The Big Moose Lake History Project Committee

JANE A. BARLOW, the senior editor, is an archaeologist, now retired. She worked for many excavation seasons in Cyprus and spent one year there as a senior Fulbright scholar. She is a coeditor of *Cypriot Ceramics* (Philadelphia, Pa.: Univ. of Pennsylvania Museum of Archaeology and Anthropology, 1991), a coauthor of *Alambra: A Bronze Age Town in Cyprus* (Jonsered, Sweden: Paul Åströms Förlag, 1996), and the author of numerous articles in archaeological journals. She has taught at Cornell University and at Smith College. Since 1956, she has spent at least part of every summer at Big Moose Lake, having been lured there by her husband, Mark Barlow.

MARK BARLOW was imprinted during his childhood with an affinity to Big Moose Lake by frequent trips to visit his aunt and uncle, Lillian and Romaine Kinne. Before retiring, his professional career was in education at both the secondary and university levels. After renting a cottage at Big Moose for several seasons, in 1962 the Barlows bought what may be the oldest cottage on the lake, located on Crag Point.

FRANK CAREY's family was one of the first at the lake, arriving even before William Seward Webb bought the land. Although his family sold the camp in 1938 after the death of his grandmother, Frank has returned to the lake regularly and recently bought a camp on nearby Twitchell Lake. He is an avid postcard collector and a railroad buff. He and William L. Scheffler have recently published *Big Moose Lake New York in Vintage Postcards* (Charleston, S.C.: Arcadia Publishing Company, 2000).

WILLIAM S. DUNN is a Big Moose native. He lived at Big Moose Lake until he entered the armed service in early 1943. After college, he spent his career working for the United States government. Now living in North Carolina, he has lately researched his family origins and written countless letters giving the authors invaluable details of his early recollections.

JANET STONE HOLMES was carried by boat in a pack basket to the family camp on the North Shore that was originally the store for the Bissell and Yousey Lumber Company. She is an expert botanist and provides a long perspective on life at the lake.

JOY WALDAU HOSTAGE has been coming to Big Moose Lake since she was an infant. Her husband, ARTHUR, joined her after they were married. She shares with her brother Roy the family camp in West Bay. She and Arthur also own one of the Higby Point cottages.

ANNETTE J. LUX has been a summer resident since 1969, when her husband, who has been at the lake since childhood and who is an expert hunter and fisherman, introduced her to Big Moose Lake. An avid canoeist, Annette is the founder and commodore of the Big Moose Canoe Crew.

WANDA KINNE MARTIN has lived at Big Moose Lake all her life except for four years spent in Utica at business school and at work. She married Howard Martin, son of E. J. Martin, founder of the Waldheim. She is now retired from many years of managing the personnel and finances of the resort. The recent discovery in an attic of Wald-heim correspondence and business records has turned her into an indefatigable researcher, and she has produced much valuable information not only about the Waldheim but also about other hotels and residents on the lake.

EDITH PILCHER is a professional writer and historian, author of three Adirondack histories and nearly two dozen magazine articles. Her books include *Castorland* (Harrison, N.Y.: Harbor Hill Books, 1985), *Up the Lake Road* (St. Huberts, N.Y.: Adirondack Mountain Reserve, 1987), and *The Constables—First Family of the Adiron-dacks* (Utica, N.Y.: North Country Books, 1992). She was a founder and the first chairman of the Adirondack Research Library in Schenectady, which is now affiliated with the Association for the Protection of the Adiron-

dacks. Her current job at the library is chair of collection development and newsletter editor. During summers she resides at the end of East Bay.

MARY ANN SIMPSON, a retired schoolteacher and an East Bay summer resident, has made herself an expert on the Big Moose Property Owners Association, poring over the organization's minutes and correspondence, which go back to 1926.

BARBARA KINNE WHEELER is a sister of Wanda K. Mar-tin and also a Big Moose native. Until her marriage in 1949, she lived at the lake and witnessed the transition from prewar to postwar conditions. She was the postmas-ter at Apulia Station, New York, until her retirement in 1989 and is now a summer resident.

Preface

THE REVEREND PERCY B. WIGHTMAN, founder of the Big Moose Property Owners Association, suggested in 1931 that "facts, traditions and persons having to do with the beginning and early life of the lake be collected for preservation," but at the time his advice was not taken. During the 1980s, William Judson began to amass family photographs from around the lake and their accompanying stories to be used for a videotape on the lake's early history. Unfortunately, he died unexpectedly in 1990 without completing his plans.

A morsel of news that circulated at an after-church coffee hour in the summer of 1995 galvanized a few people into action. Word that two longtime residents of Big Moose Lake had moved to nursing homes struck a small group of summer and year-round lake residents with the realization that we as a community were in imminent danger of losing irreplaceable stories and history. The Big Moose History Project Committee soon became a reality. A number of us not only hastened to interview those who had moved away but also began to search for other material. We sent out a questionnaire to property owners asking for stories about their camp and for any records they would like to share. Many residents of the lake cooperated beyond our wildest expectations, as did the Town of Webb Historical Association and the Adirondack Museum at Blue Mountain Lake.

Memoirs, diaries, and photographs from Henry Bruyn, Peter Bruyn, Katharine Wightman Hadden, Emma Dart LeSure, Grace Vander Veer McDonough, Elizabeth Kreitler Singleton, Mary Alden Covey Williams, and others poured out of trunks and desks. Longtime residents or visitors such as Charles Adams, Barney and Betty Barnum, C. V. Bowes, Clinton Getty

Dr. Percy Wightman (1871–1958). Undated photograph; courtesy of Elizabeth K. Singleton.

and his family, Bonnie Bennett, Arnold Drooz, William Gordon, Ray Hanlon, Harry and Lynda Kellogg, William Lux, Philip Martin, Dennis McAllister, members of the Wertz family, and assorted Colpitts/Menand relatives allowed us to interview them or gave us notes about their families, their businesses, or their pastimes at the lake. Still others—Libby Barlow, Frank Carey, Lucy Newman Craske, Donald F. Dew, William S. Dunn, James Harland

William Judson (1922–1990), first collector of Big Moose Lake photographs. Undated photograph; courtesy of Sarah Judson Dew.

Higby, Joy Waldau Hostage, Bonnie Hubbell, Christine Lozner, William Lux, Grace Collins McCullough, Elizabeth Traverse, Hamilton White, Ida Ainsworth Winter, and more—wrote recollections on specific subjects or gave us access to previously written accounts. Wanda Kinne Martin discovered three large bushel baskets of Camp Waldheim records, ledgers, diaries, and business correspondence in an attic that had been undisturbed for fifty years. Other Martin letters appeared later after the death of a family member. Edith Pilcher conducted meticulous research in state documents regarding lumbering, the Hamilton-Herkimer county line, and the Adirondack Park Agency.

An archive of Big Moose oral histories done in 1984 by Karen Taussig-Lux, a professional folklorist with Big Moose connections, turned up at the Adirondack Museum. Jerold Pepper, the museum's librarian, produced not only historic maps but also hotel registers, camp architectural plans, and other unexpected treasures. Caroline Welsh, curator of the Adirondack Museum, assisted with material on David Milne. Peg Masters, Town of Webb historian and former director of the Town of Webb Historical Association, found obituaries, photographs, articles, and artifacts for us. Those working on the *Big Moose Lake History Project* labored to organize this avalanche of unpublished material.

In the summer of 1999, the history project committee arranged for a group of people who had attended the one-room schoolhouse on the lake in the late 1930s to gather at the Big Moose Property Owners Association Center to share their reminiscences about their life at Big Moose Lake sixty years ago. Mary Alden Covey Williams came from New Hampshire, Bill Dunn from North Carolina, Wanda Kinne Martin from her home on the lake, her sister Barbara Kinne Wheeler from Apulia Station, New York, and Harry Kellogg Jr. from Old Forge. Helen Strife and Bill Wilcox, who had lived at Big Moose Station, joined them. Ida Ainsworth Winter, from Big Moose Station, participated as well. All told stories about their teachers, their social life, the food they ate and how it was preserved, ice harvesting, and many other experiences. More than 175 people attended and were mesmerized by the stories and anecdotes that the principals related. The interest shown that evening in the history of the lake convinced the committee to gather all the archival material into a book.

Major inspiration for this volume came from forest ranger William Marleau, whose book, *Big Moose Station,* published posthumously in 1985, is a lively personal account of the growth and decline of the railroad village that was the lifeblood of Big Moose Lake. His story inevitably spills over a bit into lake history, but, in the same way that he carefully limited his stories to Big Moose Station, we have respected similar boundaries. Stories or hints of stories that came from him are acknowledged in the endnotes.

Another seminal source is William S. Dunn, son of one of the four Dunn brothers who figure prominently in many incidents. Bill Dunn's memory is phenomenal, and he has generously shared with us in voluminous correspondence the dramatic story of his family's arrival at Big Moose Lake as well as his recollections of life at Big Moose Lake before World War II.

Members of the committee volunteered to undertake specific projects. These often required extensive research—digging through property records at the Herkimer County and Hamilton County courthouses; sifting through piles of notes, letters, and record books from lake residents; and exploring the rich resources of both the Town of Webb Historical Association in Old Forge and the Adirondack Museum at Blue Mountain Lake. There were taped interviews with both Bertha Dunn and Bob McAllister, who have since died. There was extensive follow-up with those who had submitted the original questionnaire and with many who had not. Committee members who wrote the various sections are not named as authors unless their contributions are personal memoirs written in the first person.

Many residents contributed to the illustrations. After the discovery of Bill Judson's collection of old photographs, Richard Widdicombe presciently preserved them and made them available. The postcard collections of Frank Carey and Wanda Kinne Martin have been especially valuable as well. Jill Binyon Kurtz supplied drawings for the section on ice harvesting and for the Disappearing Propeller boats.

All of these activities were coordinated by Jane Barlow, who agreed to be the senior editor.

The penultimate drafts were reviewed and revised by Scott Shindell, a professional writer, teacher, and journalist, who summered as a youth at Big Moose and now regularly visits his family's summer home on Crag Point. Scott volunteered to help us organize the book, enliven the narrative, and clarify our sometimes murky writing. His labor of love has improved the book immensely.

We are also grateful to the staff of the Syracuse University Press, particularly to Mary Selden Evans, Mary Peterson Moore, and Michael W. Rankin, who gave us encouragement and support throughout the entire enterprise.

This book has been eight years in the making. The committee recognizes that more has been written about some topics than about others. It is not that some topics are more important, but, as the reader will note, original sources existed for some topics but were missing for others. The committee has been conscientious in its effort to be accurate. We hope that errors will be brought to our attention so that they can be corrected in a revised edition. Correspondence should be addressed to Jane Barlow (summer), Big Moose Lake, Eagle Bay, New York 13331, 315-357-2926 or (winter) Box 254, Shutesbury, Massachusetts 01072, 413-259-1391. In addition, we invite you to record your own Big Moose history in the space provided in the back of the book. Although there are variations in spelling that occur in primary sources, we have tried to be consistent within the book. Early writers were often casual, even about their own names.

The book is composed of history gleaned largely from original sources, recollections from those who lived through the adventures and incidents described, and accounts about or by contemporary lake residents who relate their own stories. It is, therefore, a mixture of conventional history spiced with quotations of people who were there and of reminiscences that give a more immediate flavor of personal experience.

Although many of the memoirs and much of the written material had to be condensed in order to keep the book within a manageable size, the original materials (including information written by contemporary residents) will be archived at the Adirondack Museum or the Town of Webb Historical Association. In the process of condensing, we attempted to place greater emphasis on the earlier history of the lake. The endnotes contain references to the primary sources so that anyone who wishes may pursue a subject further.

In addition to the people mentioned above, we are most grateful for the help of Olga Adams, Adirondack Museum at Blue Mountain Lake, Diane Bowes, Harrison Bicknell Jr., Robert Binyon, Francis Carey, Sr., Elizabeth Casscells, Barbara Dietze Colose, Kathleen Dexter, Sarah Judson Dew, Spartacus DeLia, the late Phyllis Strack Dietze, Barbara Dix, Faith Wertz Eastwood, Hazel Ellsworth, Hunter W. Finch, Grace Quimby Flock, Andrew and Barbara Getty, Ray Hanlon, Thomas Hartz, Ann Dunn Hall, John Isley, Molly Menand Jacobs, John Judson, Gordon Kellogg, Harry and Lynda Kellogg, Katherine S. Kingsford, Nelle Menand Knox, Charles Kreitler, Doris Lederer, Frances Leonard Lepper, Donald Lux, Edward Legere, Howard Littman, Paul and Rainy Littman, C. Robert McCoy, Rae Harvey Marcy, Donald Mawhinney, Jon Martin, David Milne Jr., Gail Murray, Cheryl A. Nevelizer, Andreé Dennis Newton, the late Robert Jeffress Page, Roger and Nancy Martin Pratt, Diane Dunn Ritz, William Rosenfeld, George Rote, William Scheffler, Carolyn Seamans, Gilbert Smith, Robert and Elizabeth Smith, Michael Tarbell, Town of Webb Historical Association, Robert Van Slyke, Elizabeth Traverse, John Vander Veer, Helen Weltman, Richard Wenner, Justin White, Martha Bruyn Widdicombe, Jane Wilson, and Betty York.

A SPECIAL THANKS

We are grateful to those whose support made the publication of this book financially possible: Jane and Mark Barlow, Marie and Spartacus DeLia, Joy and Donald F. Dew, William S. Dunn, Bill, Ann, Liz, and Katie Scheffler, and Wanda K. Martin.

Introduction

FOR CENTURIES, Big Moose Lake was simply an oddly shaped fragment in the vast mosaic of Adirondack lakes. By a quirk of geology, it lay far from the main water routes. Indians from along the Mohawk River found abundant game and fish in the area, but the growing season was too short and the soil too thin for them to raise corn or establish settlements. After the English and the French pushed the Indians out of their hunting grounds, a few sportsmen and commercial hunters filtered into the region. Land speculators, who did not know what the Indians knew, envisioned prosperous farms but failed to attract settlers. In the early nineteenth century, well-to-do hunters and fishermen discovered that men who knew and loved the woods were willing to guide them up the rivers, around the swamps, and over the mountains where they could enjoy rugged recreation while leaving the bothersome logistics to others.

Late in the nineteenth century, a few intrepid wives agreed to share the adventures. Some of the guides established permanent camps that later became hotels. However, it took a capitalist and entrepreneur to envision the possibilities of summer resort and camp opportunities, if only access to the mountains could be made easier. William Seward Webb, working against almost impossible odds, built a railroad that cut through the Adirondacks from south to north, ignoring the traditional water corridors. A railroad station appeared near Big Moose Lake.

After the railroad was completed in 1892, commercial opportunities blossomed. Teamsters, who had come to help lay the rails, now found work with loggers or helped in road construction.

Guides expanded their skills to become builders of comfortable camps and hosts to families who could now enter the wilderness without making an arduous journey by buckboard, foot, and guideboat. Many guides developed specialized skills in carpentry, masonry, blacksmithing, boat maintenance and repair, and dozens of other crafts.

The prosperous hunters and fishermen from the cities brought their wives and children. Some stayed in hotels where services and amusements—ranging from maid service and meals to water activities, horseback riding, and evening entertainments—were provided. Others, preferring more privacy, commissioned their own camps and arrived with or hired cooks, handymen, chauffeurs, and boatmen. Many families stayed for the entire summer, with the railroad making it possible for husbands to commute to cities and join their wives and children on weekends.

Neither those who came for holidays nor those who lived at the lake year-round could have survived without the other. During the first part of the twentieth century, outside services simply were not available. The local residents offered expertise that was needed throughout the winter. Camps were cleaned and opened in the spring, closed and secured for the winter, and sometimes opened again for winter parties. Icehouses needed to be filled. Snow piled up on roofs and had to be shoveled. Wood was cut and stacked in woodsheds. Boats and, later, motors were stored. Docks were built and repaired. Hotel keepers had additional chores—maintaining livestock; making, buying, or repairing lighting, kitchen equipment, boats, and furniture; planting and caring for gardens; building roads; advertising for or corresponding with their guests; hiring help; and keeping financial records. Some hotels opened early for fishermen and stayed open through the hunting season or even all winter.

At Big Moose Lake, friendship and respect developed between the year-round residents and those who came for the summer. Later, many local residents and businessmen became members of the Big Moose Property Owners Association, participating in decisions that affected the lake. Common interests, such as defending the area against careless logging, maintaining lake water levels, preserving water quality, and ensuring boat safety, brought residents together.

Year-round residents led an isolated life in the winter. In some cases, mothers lived with their children on "the outside" so that the youngsters could attend school. A one-room school was eventually established, but when students in the early days reached high school they had to abandon their education or, if their parents could afford it, board in another town. Amusements centered on the church, social events at one another's houses, or community jobs such as ice harvesting.

Recreation for summer visitors evolved from the traditional hunting and fishing to porch sitting and scenery viewing to trail hiking to participating in or cheering for hotel-sponsored baseball games and eventually to sophisticated water sports.

Several disastrous fires aroused community spirit (and community fund-raising efforts) that resulted in ever more technologically oriented safety services—a volunteer fire company with a truck and a fire boat to reach camps without road access, and later an ambulance manned by certified emergency medical technicians.

A few celebrities found the lake—an artist, an actress, a journalist-playwright, and, of course, Chester Gillette, whose tragic adventure inspired Theodore Dreiser's *An American Tragedy*.

Over the years, Big Moose Lake changed. The automobile arrived, making access to the lake easier. Vacations became shorter. After World War II more people were able to afford second homes. New camps were built and camps changed ownership more often. Hotels found their clientele declining, went out of business, and sold their cottages to individuals. The population of the lake grew from about 65 families and hotels before World War II to nearly 150 today. Most families feel that the lake is an anchor that is central to the lives of those who spend time on its shores.

Description of Big Moose Lake

BIG MOOSE LAKE is one of the most beautiful lakes in the Adirondacks, stretching some four miles in length, with an irregular shoreline and four scenic bays. Its inlet, a long and broad marshy area of great contrasts, is fed by brooks and streams from the outlets of neighboring ponds. The shores are lined with cedar trees, spruce, balsam, and towering white pines. Although windstorms and acid rain have diminished their vigor in recent years and

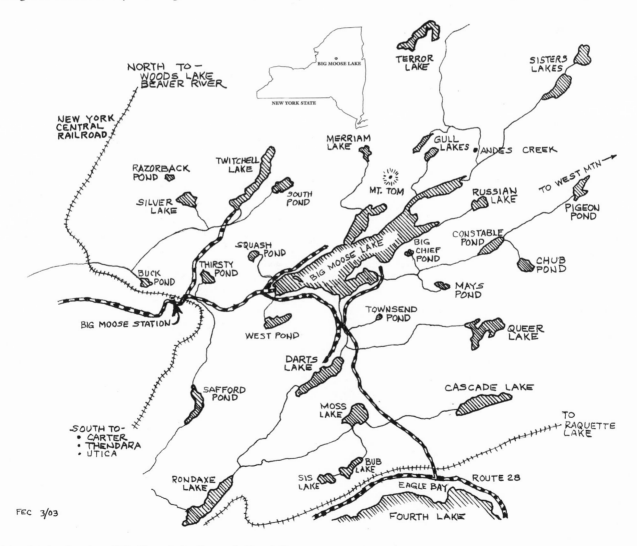

Map showing location of Big Moose Lake. Drawn by Frank Carey.

felled some of the taller trees, the lakeshore still appears largely verdant at the start of the twenty-first century.

Because of its relative obscurity and location away from major road and river corridors, Big Moose Lake has not undergone the extensive development that characterizes many other lakes in the region. It is traditional to retain screening trees on private properties and to stain buildings a dark color that blends in with the background scenery. Few commercial or public facilities are located on the lake. Beyond the perimeter, the surrounding hillsides are part of the Pigeon Lake Wilderness Area, state-owned land governed by the "forever wild" restrictions in the New York State constitution. At the eastern end of the lake, some of the shoreline is also state-owned. Over the past 150 years, the lake has been fortunate in attracting hotel keepers, visitors, and property owners who value its natural beauty.

Elusive otter still frolic along the shores; loons congregate in sociable groups, hooting and fishing, particu-larly in late summer; and beaver maintain lodges and dams in the wilder sections. Bear and deer frequent the area, and even an occasional moose wanders by. Although the lake waters are now acidic, they are by no means dead. They support a large population of bullheads, perch, and sunfish that tempt the loons, and some lake and brook trout have survived now that the acidity is beginning to return to more normal levels.

Big Moose Lake covers 1,268 acres and reaches a seventy-foot depth near the eastern end. It lies mostly in Herkimer County, but a survey at the beginning of the twentieth century disclosed that the eastern end and the Inlet lie in Hamilton County.

Seasonal and full-time residents alike have a strong affection for and deep appreciation of Big Moose Lake. This feeling is perpetuated by generations of children and grandchildren who form the same attachments, strengthened by community activities, strong friendships, and often marriages with other lake families.

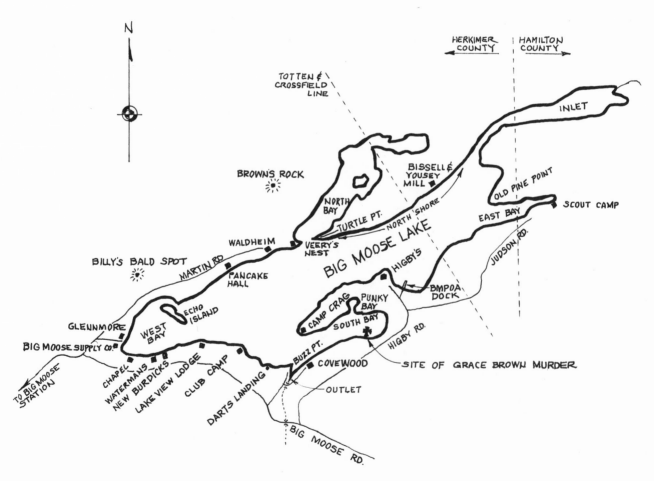

Map of Big Moose Lake. Drawn by Frank Carey.

Big Moose Lake in the Adirondacks

1 *The Intractable Wilderness*

Beginnings

THE FOUR HUNDREDTH ANNIVERSARY of Christopher Columbus's discovery of America, October 12, 1892, also marked the most significant event in the history of Big Moose Lake. The day was clear and unseasonably warm, with the autumn colors of the hardwoods well muted. On a railroad bed less than one-half mile from the Twitchell Creek trestle, dozens of jubilant railroad workers cheered an assistant engineer as he readied himself to drive the spike that would complete Dr. William Seward Webb's Adirondack and St. Lawrence Railroad. The engineer missed twice and broke the handle of the spike hammer.[1] It took the efforts of a Mohawk Indian and of Seth Rozon,[2] a resident of Big Moose Station, to complete the job. As of that day, a railroad ran through the Adirondacks. Twelve days later, on October 24, trains started scheduled runs from Herkimer on the Mohawk River to Malone on the Canadian border, with connections to New York City and Montreal.

For more than three-quarters of a century, others had tried to penetrate the Adirondacks with railroads. Some efforts were successful, some were aborted after only a few miles of construction, and others were abandoned before a shovel had even touched the ground. But Webb's railroad was the first to run through the Adirondacks—in every respect a singular accomplishment, given the imposing geology of the Adirondacks.

The great geologic dome of the Adirondacks was shaped by a hot spot beneath the earth's surface 50 mil-

Centennial painting of Dr. William Seward Webb's train crossing the Twitchell Creek trestle, 1992. Courtesy of Robert B. Partridge, artist.

1

Roosevelt Rock, an erratic on the northern shore of the main lake, 1999. Photograph by Mark Barlow.

lion years ago. Later the climate grew colder, and countless glaciers scrubbed and gouged the land, leaving behind ancient rivers. They in turn receded, creating innumerable lakes among the mountains. Like the Fulton Chain of Lakes, Big Moose Lake, with its sister lakes, Dart's and Rondaxe, is a remnant of an ancient river system that has long since disappeared.

The retreating glacial ice also left behind sand and gravel moraines (one at the base of Dart's Hill on the Eagle Bay-Big Moose Road), as well as *erratics* (huge boulders scattered through the woods and on the shores).

The warming climate that caused the glaciers to retreat also changed the area's vegetation and wildlife. Fish and game could now survive, and this fact brought Indians from the Mohawk Valley north in search of food. No evidence of permanent Indian settlements in the central Adirondacks has yet been discovered, but there is abundant evidence that they hunted and fished in and around the Fulton Chain.[3] No doubt there had been temporary Indian camps in the Big Moose area, but they left no traces. The only indication of an Indian presence near the lake is two arrowheads found in 1961 at Cascade Lake. Experts at Cornell University identified them as belonging to the nomadic Owasgo Indians, who roamed the Adirondacks in the early seventeenth century.

Although the Iroquois Indians appreciated the Adirondacks as excellent hunting grounds, Europeans, most notably the English, the French, and the Dutch, who were looking only for agricultural land, turned up their noses at the wilderness. One mapmaker noted, "This country by reason of mountains, swamps, and drowned lands is impassable and uninhabited."[4]

However, trade quickly developed between the Indi-

ans and European settlers. The white men were eager to buy furs, especially beaver pelts, which until the 1840s were in great demand in Europe for men's hats.[5] The cold climate of the mountains stimulated the animals to grow thick fur of particularly fine quality.

When the region's rich natural resources at last became obvious to some, the Adirondack wilderness became part of colonial America and later of the young United States. A few white men who had previously bypassed the region began to follow the Iroquois paths in search of game and profits. Nevertheless, as historian Joseph Grady wrote, "The average [white, Mohawk Valley] settler, interested only in agricultural land, pictured the area as an interminable jungle of alternating swamps and peaks, the severity of its tempests and climate inimical to health, and the ferocity of its brute inhabitants an actual menace to life. In fact the beautiful Adirondacks were snubbed and ignored as a piece of totally undesirable property."[6]

EARLY LAND SPECULATORS

When newcomers to America at last awoke to the idea that land in the north country might be valuable, the governments that held the land were poised to make a profit. Big Moose Lake chanced to lie at the boundary of two major land grants. The first, the Totten and Crossfield Purchase of more than one million acres, was being negotiated with the British crown when the American Revolution intervened. Many of the backers of this purchase were loyalists who soon fled to Canada. The colony of New York claimed the wild land (which had already been surveyed) and in 1785, in an effort to dispose of it, divided it into fifty townships to be sold. The eastern end of Big Moose Lake lies within one of those townships, number 41. The Totten and Crossfield Line crosses East Bay and the North Shore, and it is still used in land records and on geodetic survey maps.

The second land grant was a later tract formed in 1792 and known as the Macomb Purchase. In that year, Alexander Macomb, purchaser of six of the Totten and Crossfield townships, joined with two other speculators, William Constable and Daniel McCormick, and persuaded the struggling State of New York to sell nearly four million acres at the bargain rate of eight pence an acre. This property, the Macomb Purchase, lay west of the Totten and Crossfield Line and included in its vastness all of the western end of Big Moose Lake. This purchase, together with Township 41, made Macomb the owner of all of Big Moose Lake.

However, Macomb, whose financial dreams were beyond his means, eventually landed in debtor's prison. Nearly two million acres of the Macomb Purchase, including not only the Moose and Beaver River Valleys but also a large part of the Fulton Chain of Lakes, were conveyed to William Constable. Within six months, Constable sold more than one million of those acres to Samuel Ward, and less than two years later Ward sold 210,000 acres to James Greenleaf.

James Greenleaf had arranged to buy a cargo of tea from John Brown, a wealthy merchant from Rhode Island after whose family Brown University is named. Brown owned a clipper ship, and his son-in-law, John Francis, acting as his agent, accepted partial payment for the cargo in cash and negotiated a mortgage on Greenleaf's Adirondack land for the remainder of the debt. Within this acreage, now called Brown's Tract, lay Big Moose Lake.

Brown first divided the 210,000 acres into eight townships, giving each the name of a virtue. He named Township 8, which includes much of Big Moose Lake, Regularity. Township 7, the site of Old Forge, became Economy. The other townships were Industry, Sobriety, Enterprise, Unanimity, Frugality, and Perseverance. John Brown made a noble attempt to develop the tracts into viable investments, seeking to develop permanent settlements and to convert the wilderness into farms. He was among many who thought the Adirondacks could be tamed and made into good farm land, but his efforts came to naught. The few settlers he did induce to come found the land inhospitable.

John Brown died in 1803, and his heirs struggled for almost fifty years under the burden of taxes on land that seemed to resist development. His son-in-law, Charles Herreshoff, who did his best to establish a mine and iron works in Old Forge, became so discouraged that he committed suicide.

HUNTERS AND TRAPPERS

While the land lay unexplored and unclaimed, hunters and trappers used it both for recreation and for profit. The most notorious of the early hunters and trappers was Nathaniel Foster, a veteran of the Revolutionary War, whose sister, Zilpha, had been abducted by the Algonquins. Although she was later returned unharmed, Nathaniel Foster developed a lifelong hatred of Indians. Foster ranged throughout much of Brown's Tract, exercising his legendary marksmanship and even leaving his name temporarily attached to a lake (now named Dart's Lake). He conducted a vendetta against Peter Waters, a young Mohawk Indian known as Drid, finally ambushing him as he rowed a party of two through a narrow spot at the south end of First Lake. Drid's death resulted in a trial in Herkimer, but Foster was acquitted of murder. Drid's grave, which had been carefully tended by Maurice Dennis, an Abenaki Indian who lived in Old Forge for many years, was recently discovered when the footbridge was built near the Old Forge dam in 2000.

The Constable brothers, William, John, James, and Stevenson (grandsons of the William Constable who had once owned the land), loved the wilderness and made many hunting and fishing trips to the area over the course of forty years. After two decades of summer camping at Raquette Lake and finally finding the visitors there too numerous, the brothers and their guide built the first

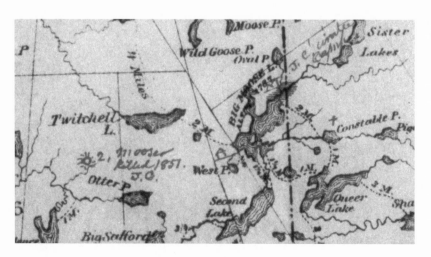

A section of the 1881 Seneca Ray Stoddard map, with handwritten notes by John Constable showing a winter camp at the Inlet, a campsite on West Bay, and the spot where he killed two moose. The shape of Big Moose Lake is inaccurate. Courtesy of Edith Pilcher.

cabin on Big Moose Lake about 1870. Unfortunately, we do not know where it was located, but it might have been in South Bay or East Bay. There they would have had easy access to their favorite hunting locations at Constable Pond or Constable Creek. Evidence of the existence of this cabin comes from E. R. Wallace's *Guide to the Adirondacks*, first published in 1872: "The Constable families, of Constableville, N.Y. and New York City, so long identified with the woods—most enthusiastic admirers of forest life—have constructed a model cabin on the shores of this lake."[7]

The Constables' favorite guide was William Higby ("Higby the Hunter") from Watson, a relative of James Higby, the first settler on Big Moose Lake. There is no record of a land purchase, and probably the cabin was gone by 1876 when Jim Higby built Pancake Hall, commonly considered to be the first structure on the lake. (The full story of the Constables' ventures into the wilderness is told in Edith Pilcher's book, *The Constables: First Family of the Adirondacks*.)[8]

In 1851, John Constable killed two moose between Twitchell Lake and Otter Pond. Bill Marleau vividly describes the event in his book *Big Moose Station*:

> After butchering the two animals, Constable hung the bull's horns in the crotch of a large soft maple on the edge of the swamp. The flaming foliage formed a perfect outline against the golden tamarack background. The horns remained in the maple tree for many years . . . The early surveyors, guides, trappers, and sportsmen referred to the area as the "Big Moose Swamp." Shortly after the railroad was built [some forty years later] the tree fell over. But the name stuck and the railroad station built there was called Big Moose Station.[9]

In 1857, twenty years after the Constables' first exploratory trip, a group of friends from Utica, all of whom had at one time or another ventured into Brown's Tract to hunt and fish, met for dinner one night and organized themselves into a recreational club. They called themselves the Northwoods Walton Club after Isaak Walton, the seventeenth-century fisherman and author of *The Compleat Angler*. The prime mover of the group was General Richard U. Sherman, father of James Schoolcraft Sherman, who became vice president of the United States under William Howard Taft. General Sherman had made his first trip to Brown's Tract in 1853. The isolation and beauty of Big Moose Lake drew him frequently. Maps began to refer to the lake as "Sherman Lake" because of the general's prominence as a distinguished citizen of New York State and the frequency with which he visited. An example is the 1862 map "Headwaters of the Moose and Black Rivers," by William S. Taylor and S.H. Sweet, where Sherman Lake is vaguely recognizable as Big Moose Lake. This may be the first map to show bodies of water that can be identified as Big Moose Lake, Dart's Lake (called Foster's), and Rondaxe Lake (called Landon). Before this, Big Moose Lake was known simply as the Third Lake of the North Branch, while Dart's Lake was called Second Lake and Rondaxe, First Lake.

The 1862 map also marks the location of a Northwoods Walton Club shanty, built in 1857, on the northern shore of Big Moose Lake about where Pancake Creek enters. A pamphlet published by the club offered a caution: "The North Branch Lakes are celebrated sporting grounds, but they are to be reached only by severe effort by land and water, and none should undertake to visit them except those inured to the hardships of the wilderness."[10]

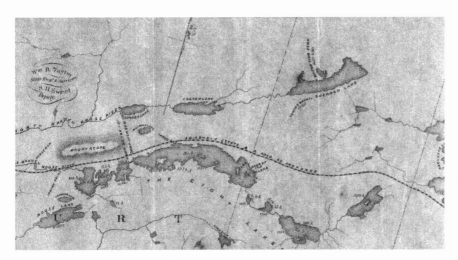

Early map, "Headwaters: Moose and Black River," (detail) showing Big Moose Lake, then known as Sherman Lake, 1862. Courtesy of the Adirondack Museum.

SURVEYORS AND ADVENTURERS

In 1867, the name Big Moose Lake at last appeared on a map. Cartographer Dr. William W. Ely's map showed the lake, although the shape is unrecognizable. Nearby Dart's and Rondaxe Lakes are not labeled at all.

Not long after the end of the Civil War, the Reverend William H. H. Murray, minister of the Park Street Congregational Church in Boston, published *Adventures in the Wilderness or Camp-Life in the Adirondacks.*[11] Murray had been fishing and hunting in the Adirondacks for some years, and in the book he wrote about his adventures and encouraged others to participate in these wholesome sports. Thousands of ordinary people were seduced by Murray's presentation of the alleged redemptive qualities in nature, and they headed for the mountains en masse. Most, however, were physically and psychologically ill equipped for the challenges of life in the woods, and they were often shocked by the harsh realities they faced. The press referred to them as "Murray's Fools." However, in spite of this label and all the inconveniences they endured, their belief in the salutary effects of nature and its treasures took hold and endured.[12]

In 1876, Verplanck Colvin, the superintendent of the New York State Adirondack Survey, reached Big Moose Lake in his travels and experienced something of the challenges of the woods. He wrote in his journal,

> Night had already settled in when we launched our canoes on the waters of the Great Moose Lake. A fierce northwest wind drove the scud in wild, fierce eddies around us, while the icy snow, driven before the blast, stung our faces. Shivering, we hurriedly bestowed our baggage and instruments within the boat, to which we were about to entrust ourselves . . . The seas grew higher and more threatening, but the fearless guides bent to their work with undaunted gallantry, . . .[At last] the wind grew less boisterous, the foaming billows turned to glossy rollers, and the prow grated on the gravel beach.[13]

Eventually, Big Moose Lake moved past the surveyors' notes and into guidebooks. E. R. Wallace wrote in his 1876 *Guide to the Adirondacks,* "This most beautiful and secluded sheet (4½ x 1 [miles]), furnishes, it is said, the best June fishing in the Wilderness, and there is no scarcity of venison here."[14] In another edition in 1896, he added, "Both speckled and salmon trout abound in its cold deep waters. The wide and deep inlet of the Two

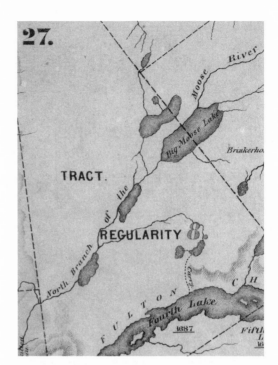

Section of "Map of the Adirondack Wilderness," by William Watson Ely, 1867, showing "Regularity," Township 8 of Brown's Tract, which encompasses much of Big Moose Lake. Courtesy of the Adirondack Museum.

Sisters P[onds], and navigable for 1 and ½ miles, swarms with large speckled trout; and the broad marshes lining its course form a vast feeding ground for deer."[15]

NEW OWNERS OF THE LAKE

John Brown's descendants finally found a buyer for the tract on which they had been paying taxes since 1803. In 1850, Lyman R. Lyon of Lewis County agreed to pay eleven cents an acre, six cents above the going price, for all the Brown holdings. Lyon may have been betting that the new Black River Canal would bring prosperity to the area. (It did not.) More likely, he was speculating that the charter that New York State had recently granted to the Sackets Harbor and Saratoga Railroad Company would give him the chance to sell the land at a handsome profit. The railroad would have provided the first east-west route through the Adirondacks. Dr. Thomas C. Durant, a major player in the construction of the transcontinental Union Pacific Railroad, became president of the railroad. He changed the name to the Adirondack Company.

Lyon lost his bets. At some point between 1862 and 1867, an arrangement regarding the land was negotiated between Lyon and Durant's Adirondack Company. Whatever the deal, it went sour. On August 27, 1867, the Supreme Court of Herkimer County "ordered and directed [Lyon] to release and grant claim to Adirondack Co. [all the lands] . . . including *all of tws #8*."[16] Together with Township 41, the Adirondack Company now owned all of Big Moose Lake.

New York State had granted extensive tax advantages to Durant's Adirondack Company on condition that the railroad line from Saratoga to Sackets Harbor be completed in ten years. Construction of the railroad had stalled. By 1870, less than one-half the distance had been completed. In 1872, New York State took a mortgage on some 32,000 acres of Adirondack Company land in Herkimer County (which included most of Township 8) but foreclosed on it in 1881.[17]

Durant remained president of the company until his death in 1885. His son, William West Durant, succeeded him as president and immediately started to look for a buyer of the company. Somehow he managed to remove 350,000 acres of the company's holdings, ostensibly for himself. But within three months, New York State took title to the acreage that Durant had acquired. The state, in turn, quickly sold the land to the Adirondack Timber and Mineral Company, a company formed solely for the purpose of buying land.

Exactly how all this land had remained under William West Durant's control for so long is a mystery. The story of land owned and land exchanged, mortgages taken and mortgages foreclosed, taxes excused and taxes defaulted is virtually impossible to unravel, given the often casual records of more than one hundred years ago. Craig Gilborn's book *Durant*[18] and Barbara McMartin's *The*

Great Forest of the Adirondacks[19] deal with such intricacies, but they do not resolve them.

Guides, Early Visitors, and First Settlers

The first visitors at Big Moose Lake arrived at an attractive piece of unoccupied land around a lake full of fish surrounded by woods inhabited by deer, bear, and other animals. The land seemed to belong to nobody. The actual owners were either too far away or too busy to care about it, or else it belonged to New York State, a distant and impersonal entity. Fishermen and hunters who came to the lake were led through the wilderness by guides, men who not only knew where fish and game were to be found but who also knew how to make their clients comfortable. The first actual settlers of the land, moreover, had no legal claim, paid no taxes, and were technically squatters.

GUIDING

As men from the cities were drawn to the Adirondacks, they soon discovered that they needed help negotiating the woods. Rugged individuals who lived in the wilderness and who had spent time trapping or hunting found that they could turn their skills and knowledge of the rivers and mountains to making a profit. Guiding became a way to make a living, but it was not an easy life.

A guide usually had his own territory where he knew the habits of the fish and the deer. Guiding a party of sportsmen began well before their arrival. First, the guide would hike alone to the camping spot carrying a sixty-five-pound pack basket filled with provisions. He would follow this with a second solitary trip, this time carrying a

Guide Danforth Ainsworth, Jr. (with rifle) and a hunting party, ca. 1915. Courtesy of Ida Ainsworth Winter.

E. J. Martin's hunting camp at Sister's Lakes, ca. 1910. Courtesy of Wanda K. Martin.

seventy-pound guideboat. By the time the sportsmen (or "sports," as the guides called them) arrived on the scene, they would be led to the camp carrying only fishing tackle, guns, and their personal gear. The guide built the shelter—often a bark-covered lean-to—cut the spruce boughs for bedding, split the wood, built the fire, and did the cooking. Many guides took only minimal food supplies such as flour, tea, salt, sugar, and bacon, depending on the catch of the day for the main course. Whiskey was always included in the provisions.

When the sports were settled, the guide might organize a drive by getting some of the party to beat their way through the woods making as much racket as possible to push deer toward waiting hunters. In the early days, hounds were sometimes used to chase deer into the water so that hunters could shoot the exhausted animals when they struggled to the shore. A nighttime technique, called "jacking," was to fix a bright kerosene lamp on a pole in the bow of a canoe. A deer feeding at the edge of the water would stare into the light while the guide silently paddled close enough to allow the sport to get a good shot. Bill Dart used to tell about taking a green hunter out jacking deer.

> They were moving slowly and silently along the shore when suddenly right overhead a hoot owl let loose. The man jumped, yelled, and shot off his gun. [Bill], in the stern of the boat nearly fell in the lake, he laughed so hard. The hunter said, "What was it, Bill?" [Bill] said, "just an owl," and started to turn the boat around. The man asked where he was going. "Back to camp." "Can't we go on?" asked the hunter. [Bill] said, " 'Tain't no use. All the deer around here are in the next county by now."[20]

Both jacking and hounding were later outlawed on the initiative of the guides themselves.

As time went on and guides found it practical to work within the areas they knew best, they built tent platforms or enclosed shanties. They stashed cooking pots and even cookstoves nearby to save carrying heavy loads along the trail. Even guideboats or canoes might be concealed in the underbrush, ready for use when needed.

JAMES HIGBY AND HENRY COVEY

It was in just this way that James Higby became one of the first two settlers on Big Moose Lake, arriving about 1875.

James Henry Higby, ca. 1890. Courtesy of the Adirondack Museum.

As a young guide to the area, he would bring his clients to a sandy point on the north side of Big Moose Lake, where a small stream entered the lake.

Most of what we know about the early life of James H. Higby—usually called Jim—comes from descendants of his first marriage.[21] Jim's son from his second marriage, Roy, says little about his father in his autobiography[22] and nothing at all about his father's first marriage.

Jim Higby was born in 1842 in Watson, New York, a town in Lewis County to the west of Herkimer County. During the Civil War he served in the 142nd New York Volunteer Infantry, most of whose members were from Herkimer and Hamilton Counties.[23] The 142nd was part of the Sixth Corps of the Army of the Potomac, which General Ulysses S. Grant sent to Virginia's Shenandoah Valley in late summer 1864 to "lay waste the bread basket of the Confederacy." The unit also fought at Little Round Top at Gettysburg. When the Civil War ended, Jim and a brother traveled around the country for a while. Roy Higby tells the story of his father being asked in Chicago by the brother of General Custer to enlist in the general's troops, the same troops that were annihilated at Little Big Horn.[24]

After his travels, Jim returned to New York State and took a job driving the stagecoach between Boonville, New York, and the Moose River Settlement. Later, he worked in Thendara in a number of capacities for Otis Arnold, whose hostelry was the first in the Fulton Chain region. By 1870, Higby had become a surveyor's helper to Verplanck Colvin and a guide on Fourth Lake. As a guide, his travels often took him to Big Moose.

On January 13, 1872, Jim married Ella Amy Chase, also from Watson, New York. He also became close friends with his brother-in-law (Ella's sister's husband), Henry Covey. Ella had tuberculosis and could not live the rough life of a settler, so she and the children lived in Utica for many years. Eventually, they moved back to Watson so that Ella's parents could care for them until she died.

While his wife remained in town with their children, Jim Higby continued his guiding activities. As his reputation grew, he became much sought-after as a guide in the Fulton Chain and Big Moose areas.

When Jim Higby settled at Big Moose, about 1875, there were more than 250 permanent residents of the Town of Wilmurt, from which the Town of Webb was

JIM HIGBY'S FIRST FAMILY

Some of Jim Higby's contemporary descendants were unaware until recently of Higby's first family. In the autobiography published in 1974 by Roy Higby, Jim's son,[51] Roy makes no mention of Jim's first wife, Ella Chase, who had borne him not only a daughter, who died at age six, but also a son, Elmer Eugene. "E. E.," as he was known, was born in Utica in 1873 and was raised there by his mother. Ella lived in Utica with the children because she was too ill with tuberculosis to come to Big Moose. She died in 1887 after fourteen years of marriage.

According to a genealogy of the Higbys,[52] Elmer joined Jim in the woods as a young boy and helped his father with guiding. In 1898, E. E. joined the army and was sent to the Pacific as part of the Philippine campaign of the Spanish-American War. There he contracted not only yellow fever but also the tuberculosis that would later ravage his own family.[53] When E. E. was thirty, he helped his father fight the 1903 forest fire.

E. E.'s first wife, Linda, died of consumption in 1899, just before her twenty-sixth birthday. He then married

Anna O'Donnell in 1904 and had three children by her: Grace, Elmer Eugene "Gene," and James Edwin. Tuberculosis would eventually leave these children orphaned. Their mother, Anna O'Donnell Higby, died of the disease in 1915. Two years later, in 1917, their father succumbed to the same malady—but only after marrying his third wife, Caroline Clark, who had been Anna's nurse. The two boys went to the Masonic Orphanage in Utica. The eldest child, Grace (1905–73), was also tubercular but recovered. She spent two years in a cottage on the Higby Camp property with her stepmother, Caroline Clark.[54]

James E. Higby, one of the boys who had been sent to the orphanage, later became the father of James Harland "Hal" Higby of Wilton, Connecticut, who has returned to the Waldheim at Big Moose every summer since 1980. Oddly, Roy Higby never mentions this part of his family in his book; in fact, he mentions few of his relatives. Long after Roy's death in 1990, some of his grandchildren were surprised to learn of their great-grandfather's first family and their descendants. Apparently no one had ever mentioned them before.

Pancake Hall, ca. 1879. Courtesy of Wanda K. Martin.

later carved. There were even hotels, or at least hostelries, from the Arnold House in Thendara to Baker's Hotel at Saranac Lake, an early watering hole. But to "settle" may have meant little more than building a four-sided cabin that was useable, if not always inhabited, year-round.

Among those Higby introduced to Big Moose Lake was Billy Dutton. In 1876, Higby built Dutton what Grady described as a "pretentious bark shanty" [25] on the northern shore of the main lake, where Pancake Creek enters. (Recently, a gazebo has been erected near the spot.) This structure, named Pancake Hall in recognition of Higby's dexterity with the griddle, was little more than a framework of poles, roofed and sided with spruce bark. A similar camp, an open shanty called Camp Germantown, was built nearby for a group of Philadelphians who were friends of Dutton. [26] Pancake Hall, however, soon proved to be inadequate, and in 1880 Dutton asked Higby to build a more substantial camp to replace it, on the island between West Bay and the main lake.

When Dutton made this request, Higby asked his friend and brother-in-law, Henry Covey, to join him in the construction. Covey, a journeyman and a blacksmith, agreed to help. Covey hiked to Big Moose from his home in Glenfield, New York, on the Tug Hill Plateau, probably following the Independence River to its headwaters near what is now Big Moose Station and then walking from there to the lake. When he arrived at the shore of the lake, opposite the island where the Dutton camp was to be built, his whistles and yells raised no response, so, without hesitation, he took off his clothes and swam over. "Yes sir, I arrived from Lewis County without a stitch," he was fond of repeating.

William Dutton became the lake's first regular visitor. He was a successful piano and organ builder from Philadelphia, a plump, benign little man with a flowing white beard. [27] "For ten happy summers" relates the historian Joseph Grady,

> "Billy" Dutton, as guides and other residents on the lake privately referred to the genial organ builder and woods lover, occupied his island camp, entertained guests from New York and Philadelphia, many of whom were well known vocal and instrumental artists, and enjoyed himself with a sense of contentment that few vacationists have surpassed. He ate Jim Higby's pancakes, drifted hours at a time in a small canoe (said to be the first ever brought to the lake by a white man), or sprawled dreamily on the bald rocky crest of the ridge that towers high above the lake's western shore line. His fondness for this exalted perch was well known in the eighties, and the crest became known at that time as "Billy's Bald Spot." The name still clings to the crest . . . and sojourners on the lake still follow the old trail up the ridge to view the expanse of the lake and forest that stretches away in three cardinal directions from the bald spot. [28]

The camp that Higby and Covey built stood on the island for many years. When the Harvey family owned the island, it was still in use as a children's playhouse. Eventually, however, it decayed, became dangerous, and was torn down. After his summers at Big Moose, Billy Dutton disappeared from Big Moose history. Some say that he craved more solitude and moved north to wilder areas near Cranberry Lake.

Billy Dutton's camp on Echo Island, ca. 1950. Courtesy of Rae Harvey Marcy.

Emma Covey with Earl and Clarence, ca. 1880. Courtesy of Ann Dunn Hall.

Meanwhile, Ella Higby died in April 1886, leaving Jim a widower. Their son Elmer, then fifteen years old, came to live at Big Moose with his father, who by this time had built a permanent building, the first on the lake.

Most of what we know about Henry Covey, Higby's friend and fellow builder, is contained in the biography of his son, *The Earl Covey Story*, written by Earl's wife, Frances Alden Covey.[29] Henry was born in the town of Croghan in Lewis County, New York, on April 11, 1850. While growing up in that area, he did considerable hunting and trapping along the Beaver River with Jim Higby.

In 1876, he married Emma Chase, the attractive red-haired younger sister of Ella Chase, Jim Higby's wife. She was barely sixteen at the time. They lived in Glenfield, New York, where Covey's blacksmith shop was located.

The construction of Dutton's camp on Echo Island was Henry's introduction to Big Moose Lake. He liked the lake and the surrounding Fulton Chain area so much that he decided he would settle somewhere in the area. Covey built an ingenious portable camp of boards fastened together with hooks and eyes. He soon brought his wife, Emma, and their two sons, Clarence and Earl, to this camp, which he set up first on Fourth Lake and later on Third Lake in the Fulton Chain. Earl Covey recalls his "father guiding . . . and away most of the time. A great deal of [his] time was spent at Big Moose." Henry, like Jim Higby, had a reputation as a reliable and competent guide.

In 1880, Henry Covey settled permanently at Big Moose, choosing the rugged point of land known as Crag Point that extends into the lake toward West Bay. Covey built a small camp to accommodate hunting and fishing parties. Henry's wife, Emma, never lived at Big Moose. Like her sister, she was a consumptive, and she stayed in Old Forge where she could be assured of the nursing care she needed. Emma Covey died in 1890, three years after her sister. Sadly, two years later Covey's elder son, Clarence, died as well, drowning at the age of sixteen in a boating accident off Turtle Point, near the entrance to North Bay.

Both Higby and Covey had become widowers, each with a son. Each would eventually remarry and carry on with a new life. Their base camps were to grow into hotels.

Dart's Camp, 1906. Courtesy of Wanda K. Martin.

Bill and Mary Dart, ca. 1920. Courtesy of Wanda K. Martin.

Bill Dart's bull and stone boat, 1906. Courtesy of Wanda K. Martin.

WILLIAM DART

From 1875 to 1880, Jim Higby was the only person living on Big Moose Lake year-round. At the end of that five-year period, Henry Covey had established himself on Crag Point. Their nearest neighbor, although not a resident of Big Moose Lake, was William Dart, who had first come into the woods in 1872. As his daughter tells the story,

> He set out to trap for a season with several other young men. They told him that they would each make $100 over expenses, come spring. Sometime later the others pulled up and decided to leave for home. One of the boys said, "How about it, Bill? Coming with us?" Father shook his head and drawled, "I came here to make $100 and I'm going to stay until I do." And . . . he always added, "I've been here ever since." [30]

While spending several years trapping and guiding out of the Forge House in Old Forge, Dart built a base camp

in 1879 on a point on what was then known as Second Lake (later Dart's Lake). He took his fishing and hunting parties there and stayed at the camp in winter when he was trapping. In the winter of 1887 he became ill. His daughter continues, "If one of his friends, Philo Wood, whose trap line crossed his had not noticed that Father's traps had not been tended to, he would not have survived. Wood went to his camp and found him. The last wood he had was on the fire, and his food was almost gone. That was the last winter he spent alone. In May he went out of the woods to find a wife and on July 9, 1888, Father married Mary Kronmiller." [31]

Bill Dart enters Big Moose Lake history frequently. His hotel opened in 1888 and became well known for the fresh food from its garden and Mary Dart's excellent cooking. Later, the camp drew guests with small children who wanted fresh milk from the cow Bill kept. In the late 1890s, Bill Dart's portable sawmill was also much in demand. Henry Covey used it occasionally at Camp Crag, and Jim Higby rented it to build his second camp in 1900.

Club Camp, ca. 1880. Courtesy of Wanda K. Martin.

In the early years, Bill purchased a bull, which he tamed with great difficulty. He used it to pull a stone boat from a spot on Big Moose Lake called Dart's Landing (between Buzz Point and the Stag's Leap camp). The stone boat carried guests' luggage and other goods that had come by rail and traveled to Dart's Landing by steamboat. The bull would also pull a buckboard, although probably only far enough to allow the guests riding in it to have their pictures taken.[32] Besides Jim Higby, Henry Covey, and Bill Dart, others were gradually drawn to the woods.

CLUB CAMP

In 1878, two years before Higby and Covey built Dutton's island camp, a group of sportsmen (mostly from New York City) had engaged Edwin "Jack" Sheppard, another well-known guide in the area, to build a camp for their private use. Sheppard and fellow guides Richard Crego, Bart Holliday, and John Van Valkenburgh together erected a building near the southern shore camp now known as Tojenka. They called this structure Club Camp.

Jack Sheppard did not live on Big Moose Lake, but he had done a great deal of guiding in the area and built his own camp for his "sports" on the south shore of the Inlet. This structure is identified on the 1876 map drawn by Verplanck Colvin, whom Jack Sheppard had assisted (as had Jim Higby) when Colvin was surveying the area.

Sheppard had come to the Fulton Chain for health reasons in 1855. Later, when the Civil War broke out, he enlisted in the 117th New York Volunteers and served until the end of the war before returning to the Fulton Chain. In addition to his guiding and construction endeavors, he owned and operated the first steamboat on the Chain of Lakes. Sheppard was also a studious man and acquired a private library. He also apparently loved solitude, because eventually he became "discouraged by the advent of the railroad" and "left the Adirondacks in 1893 for points west."[33]

On July 18, 1900, the *Adirondack News* carried an article titled "An Interesting Camp" with the further subtitle, "Some of the Thrilling Accounts of Hunting Experiences on the Walls of Club Camp, Big Moose Lake."[34] The jocular spirit of Club Camp comes through clearly in the graffiti found on the walls.

Club Camp members made their own arrangements with guides to lead them into the woods and take care of

AN INTERESTING CAMP.

Some of the Thrilling Accounts of Hunting Experiences Which Are Written On the Walls of Club Camp, Big Moose Lake.

Now that the great Adirondack wilderness is every year being thronged with people eager for rest and recreation, and new camps and cottages are constantly being built, a peculiar interest centers about the old camps—the camps that were built before the days of the fast trains and steamers through this wilderness and that could reveal many wonderful tales of hunting and fishing that will never again be surpassed or probably equalled in this region.

In the year 1877, when Mr. Dutton, with Mr. Higby for guide, first came to fish in Big Moose Lake, the camp known as Club Camp was completed. It was built on the south shore of Big Moose. The club was organized in 1879, and in that year there are records of visitors entertained at the camp. Season after season this camp was occupied by enthusiastic members of the club. The best guides always accompanied them on their hunts, and the walls and doors, written over with interesting accounts, testify to their great success.

Perhaps one of the most striking of these accounts is the following, written in the early years of the club's existence, and when bear were still numerous:

"Sept. 26, 1880. Martin Van Buren killed in single combat, unaccompanied by a guide, a black bear weighing 346 pounds in the West Bay. Witness of the fearful struggle, W. P. Talboys." The Martin Van Buren here spoken of was the grandson of the president of that name.

As showing that the killing of bears was then almost as common as the killing of deer now may be noted the following account: "Sept. 30, 1880. W. Remsen, jr., killed a black bear in the West Bay, accompanied by Ed. Arnold, guide. It was rainy and not a good day for bears either. This, therefore, was the only bear killed this day."

As many of the visitors to this region know the thermometer often takes sudden falls, much to their inconvenience, but it is seldom, if ever, the change is so decided as is noted in this entry: "Oct. 3, 1881—Temperature 65 degrees. Oct. 5, 1881—Temperature 22 degrees. Gosh!"

Column from The Adirondack News, *July 18, 1900. Courtesy of Town of Webb Historical Association.*

their needs. As time went on, some Club Camp members brought their families. The Woodburys, for instance, came in 1893, and others who later built camps of their own on the lake are known to have been early visitors. T. P. Kingsford, who later built Tojenka, bought the Club Camp in 1902. The camp burned in about 1903. Shortly afterward, George Davidson, a guide who became caretaker for Kingsford, built a model of the log camp. The model is still in the possession of the Hubbell family. It shows a substantial building with three wings attached to a central block that probably held common living and dining space. The flat area where the camp stood is close to the line between the present DeLia and Hubbell properties.

THE BROWN'S TRACT GUIDES' ASSOCIATION

Many guides like Ed Arnold and Jack Sheppard, who led Club Camp members on their expeditions, became affiliated with The Adirondack Guides' Association, which was established in Saranac Lake in 1891. The group strove to set standards and to secure fair pay for difficult and dangerous work. However, woodsmen from the western and central Adirondacks came to feel that there was not enough focus on their local concerns. Ken Sprague relates, "Approximately twelve of them withdrew from the group to form their own guild-like organization, the Brown's Tract Guides' Association, on March 8, 1898. It first met in Boonville, by invitation . . . Contrary to what the name implies, membership included guides from the entire Central Adirondacks." [35]

Guideboat builder Dwight Grant hosted the first meeting of the Brown's Tract Guides' Association in his boat shop in Boonville, and he is said to be the father of the organization. Membership requirements, in addition to being a United States citizen, were to have lived in the Adirondack region for five years and to have been a reliable and well-equipped guide for three years. Dick Crego (who guided for Theodore Page) was the first president and Artemis Church was secretary and treasurer. Charles Martin of Big Moose served on the executive committee. The association championed the efforts to protect the wilderness status of the Adirondacks. It backed the law against hounding and against deer-jacking.

THIS Association has been formed to secure a better enforcement of the game laws; to secure to the sportsman and tourist competent and reliable guides, and to maintain a uniform rate of wages.

A guide to become a member, must be a citizen of the United States, a resident of the Adirondacks for five years, a guide of at least three years' experience, and in all ways well equipped and reliable.

Each guide will have a card of membership of the year, showing that he is a member of the Association and in good standing.

In granting this certificate all Active Members are deemed in honor pledged to assist Associate Members whenever practicable.

The uniform rate of wages of guides is fixed at three dollars per day and their ordinary expenses.

The cover of the Brown's Tract Guides' Association handbook, together with its Statement of Purpose of the Brown's Tract Guides' Association, ca. 1900. Courtesy of Gilbert Smith.

The association also led the effort to restock the area with the almost-extinct beaver. Once ubiquitous in the Adirondacks, the beaver had been practically wiped out because of the popularity of the pelts for making hats. Efforts to restore the moose were also undertaken. An experiment to introduce the wapiti (an elk-type animal) proved to be a failure.

The Adirondack guide who adhered to the standards set by the Brown's Tract Guides' Association was the knight-errant of the forest. He respected the forest and its inhabitants, making it available to sportsmen and tourists through his role as a guide. The guides' steeds were their cedar guideboats painted a camouflaging dark green and black; their lances were their rifles; and their code of chivalry consisted of valor, dexterity of arms, honor, and courtesy. Besides leading parties to the best hunting or fishing grounds, a good guide saw to the needs of the members of the party, providing shelter, cooking the meals, cleaning up, rowing the guideboat, and shouldering and transporting it between lakes on the carries. Guides were also expected to entertain the group with tall tales around the campfire.

In 1898, the stated purposes of the Brown's Tract Guides' Association were "to secure better enforcement of the Game Laws of the State of New York, to secure to the sportsman and tourist competent and reliable Guides, and to maintain a uniform rate of wages of Guides."[36] (The usual fee for a guide at that time was three dollars per day.) Among the men from the Big Moose area listed in 1907 as members were Dan Ainsworth, Jr., Eugene Barrett, George H. Burdick, H. H. Covey, Earl W. Covey, Richard Crego, William Dart, Eugene M. House, Low S. Hamilton, C. V. Joslin, Charles Martin, Gil Puffer, John J. Rose, and George W. Smith.[37]

On a later list provided by Roy Higby, which he titled "Big Moose Guides, 1870–1910," the following are also mentioned: Ed Martin, Frank Martin, Charles Wood, Billy Stevens, Jim Higby, Dave and Carson Conkey, Will Woodward, Arthur Burtch, Nelson Dunn, and Reuben Brownell.[38] More Big Moose guides' names are found in a complete listing of Adirondack guides in Brumley's *Guides of the Adirondacks: A History,* among them Rodney Ainsworth's brother Richard, Edgar Hobart, William Jarvis, A. MacEdward, J. W. Morris, Willis C. Van Skoik, Reuben Brownell, and Francis Young.[39]

But the wilderness was changing. Dams that were built to provide water depth for the steamboat lines killed the trees and destroyed the beauty of the riparian locales.

Guides watched with uneasiness as the steamboat itself whittled away at their livelihood, replacing the strong arm of the oarsman. The independent guides found the reputations of the official Adirondack guides sullied by some of the less-committed hotel guides (those who were on the payrolls of the hotels). The Brown's Tract Guides' Association disbanded in 1913, the Adirondack Guides' Association in 1952.

The State of New York began the mandatory licensing of guides in 1924, imposing much more stringent requirements for qualification. Guides were required to have skill in small boat handling (which most already had) and the ability to swim (which many did not).

In 1935, after mandatory licensing was well established in New York, Gurth Whipple wrote,

> The latter-day guides are like the latter-day saints; they can't compare in genuineness with the old orthodox patriarchs; they are a different race. Their hunting ground is no longer a free domain; they can no longer take game at will and build camps wherever their fancy dictates. They are all regimented, registered, licensed and badged, which proclaims to the public that they are qualified persons. The old-timers would rest uneasy in their graves if they knew this. No member of that gnarled and woolly coterie could ever be mistaken for anyone else. He needed no badge and no government mandate to designate his business or support his qualifications.[40]

In the 1970s, new regulations were put in place,[41] and in 1987 still more stringent conditions became necessary for licensing.[42]

An article in the *Rochester Times-Union* in July 1988 featured Rodney Ainsworth in "An Old Guide's Campfire Tales." Rodney, then age eighty-three, is quoted, "All the old guides are gone . . . Them were the good old days. Worked hard, drank good liquor."[43]

PRIVATE CAMPS

Within a year or two after the completion of Club Camp, Jack Sheppard and Richard Crego built two more camps.

The first was a cabin put up about 1880 for a man named Frank Williams from New York City. It sat on land south of the entrance to the Inlet now known as Deerlands Peninsula. In a booklet published in 1927 by the Big Moose Property Owners Association, it was identified as the third permanent structure on the lake.[44] However, historian Joseph Grady in his 1933 book calls it the fourth structure.[45]

Frank Williams named his camp Lakeview. But as far as we know he was not related to Charles Williams, who later built Lake View Lodge. A genealogy of Charles Williams's family shows no direct relationship, although Charles did have a younger brother named Frank, born in 1876 and therefore too young to have owned a camp in 1882.

Frank Williams rented his camp to various parties, including two gentlemen from New York City who left a diary behind when the property changed hands. Bill Marleau in his history of Big Moose Station quotes from the entries in those diaries between 1882 and 1885. They record a prodigious amount of fish caught.[46]

Sheppard and Crego's second building was a camp for Mr. and Mrs. F. C. Moore on the southern shore near the entrance to South Bay. Called Fern Spring, it was owned by F. C. Moore of New York City, president of the Continental Insurance Company. Moore built before official records were kept, but one of the first owners, Edward O. Stanley, described the camp as having existed in 1888. It may have been constructed a little earlier, however. Originally there were three buildings plus an icehouse and a woodshed. The main building was located just south of where the present manse is located. Stanley and three friends who had been regular visitors to Club Camp purchased the land on which it stood from William Seward Webb in 1898 and became legal owners and taxpayers. The original Fern Spring camp survived until 1938, when it was torn down to be replaced by the Chapel manse that took over its name.

An early camp on Turtle Point at the entrance to North Bay, later the site of the Retter house, belonged to a man named Hamlyn, about whom nothing is known. His name appears on the back of a Retter family photograph (see illustration on page 183) and in a brief article in the *Adirondack News.*[47]

At some time in the 1880s, still another Williams (Irvin), unrelated to either Frank or Charles, settled on the adjacent peninsula at the head of the lake. Irvin Williams was a prominent citizen of Utica, descended from Roger Williams, founder of Rhode Island. He later became well known as the inventor and manufacturer of a locomotive headlight. In the days before electricity, a light that would not be extinguished by the rush of air generated by a speeding train was no easy challenge.

When Williams was in his early twenties, he began tinkering in his father's machine shop to try to improve upon the feeble light from the lanterns then used by the railroads. He secured three patents for locomotive headlights, the last in 1862, which was "a circular hollow wick burner to burn coal oil or gasoline."[48] Although the device worked well in the shop, Williams was determined to test it. Paul C. Willard, quoted by Walsh in *Vignettes of Old Utica,* describes his travails:

> [He] received permission to ride from Utica to Rome on the cowcatcher of the locomotive . . . One important and ominous string was attached—he was to go at his own risk . . . When night came, he risked everything, even his life, on the railroad . . . Often the sensitive flame died under the terrific lashing of wind that beat on the locomotive. Day after day Williams made changes and improvements and night after night he was rewarded by seeing the light beams lengthen on the silvery rails . . . [Finally] With blackened hands, he unleashed the lamp from the smokestack for the last time, shook the cinders from his clothing and returned home.[49]

Williams began to manufacture the headlight, a "burner placed in a copper, silver-plated reflector about two-feet in diameter . . . the whole enclosed in a sheet metal case with a round, glass-covered window in front."[50] The business expanded, merged with others, and eventually became the leading headlight company in the United States (see illustration on page 173).

Early seasonal visitors such as Irvin Williams as well as James Higby, Henry Covey, Bill Dart, and members of Club Camp were all squatters who settled on land that seemed to belong to nobody. Although their holdings were technically under the control of, if not solely owned by, William West Durant, their occupancy was never challenged until Dr. William Seward Webb took title to the land that surrounded Big Moose Lake in 1891.

Penetrating the Wilderness: Webb's Railroad

Big Moose Lake is located in the Town of Webb, not the Town of Durant or the Town of Brown, and for good reason. As important as Durant and Brown were as landowners, neither could match the achievements and the impact of Dr. William Seward Webb.

William Seward Webb was born in New York City on January 31, 1851, into an old and distinguished American family. As a child, he was educated at a military school

Dr. William Seward Webb at Ne-Ha-Sa-Ne, 1902. Courtesy of the Adirondack Museum.

and from there went on to Columbia University. After two years at Columbia he left to study medicine in Vienna, Paris, and Berlin. He then returned to enter the College of Physicians and Surgeons in New York City, graduated in 1875, and practiced medicine in New York City for a few years.

In 1881, Webb married Eliza Osgood Vanderbilt, the only daughter of William H. Vanderbilt, the railroad baron. At that time, medicine was not a highly regarded profession nor was it a lucrative one. Under the strong influence of his father-in-law, Webb left his practice for Wall Street, forming the financial firm of W. S. Webb & Co.

Eventually, and probably with the help of his father-in-law, Webb became president of the Wagner Railroad Company, a firm that manufactured sleeping cars. About that time, Webb decided to build a railroad through the Adirondacks, a project that many had attempted but none accomplished.

The building of this railroad is recounted by Charles H. Burnett in his book *Conquering the Wilderness: The Building of the Adirondack and St. Lawrence Railroad by William Seward Webb.*[51] Burnett had worked closely with Webb and vividly tells about the difficult access to the Adirondacks in 1890, when Webb was negotiating the various rights-of-way: "after a century of effort, backed

by the resources of the State and private capitalists, the great heart of the Adirondack region was accessible only by the most primitive means of transportation. Its mountain ranges, its forests, and its lakes had proved an impassable barrier to the construction of highways, canals, and railroads and vast sections were without any means of approach except by trail and packbasket."[52]

Emma Lesure, in her reminiscences, tells how her father, William Henry Dart, made his way in the early 1880s to the small lake where he had established Dart's Camp. From Fulton Chain (later Thendara), he traveled to a point about halfway up Fourth Lake, where he headed overland to Bub's Lake. From Bub's he went on to Moss Lake, and then over the end of South Mountain to Second Lake, now called Dart's Lake. Anyone heading for Big Moose Lake would have continued across Dart's Lake and followed the north branch of the Moose River upstream.[53]

Indeed, the Utica and Black River Railroad only went as far as Boonville. By 1888, the People's Line took the traveler on a buckboard over a crude wagon road to Fulton Chain (Thendara), stopping at the Moose River Settlement, which was located near what is now McKeever.

Later, the traveler rode from the Moose River Settlement to the place now called Minnehaha on the Peg-Leg Railroad. This narrow-gauge rail line operated for only three years, from 1889 to 1892. The initial plans were to use horses to draw the cars on wooden rails, thus avoiding the danger that sparks from a locomotive might start forest fires. Before operation began in 1889, the horses were replaced with a small locomotive but the wooden rails were retained. In 1891 the roadbed was improved in order to support a larger locomotive, an open-sided car

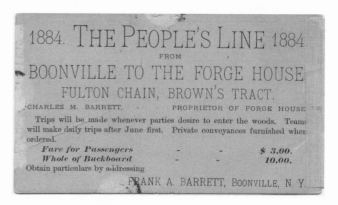

Advertisement for the People's Line, 1884. Courtesy of the Big Moose Property Owners Association.

The Peg-Leg Railroad engine, ca. 1890, running on wooden rails. Courtesy of the Town of Webb Historical Association.

with chairs for twenty-five passengers and a baggage car. In rainy weather the wooden rails became saturated with water and were wet and slippery. Whenever the train reached a slight incline, it invariably stalled, and all hands were invited to get out and help to push the train up hill. The line ran along a branch of the Moose River to a dam and lock at Jones Camp (Minnehaha) near Little Rapids. There, the traveler boarded the steamboat *Fawn* for the trip to Fulton Chain, where the boat docked in front of the residence of William and Julia deCamp on Birch Street (west of Van Auken's Tavern).[54] From that location, transportation was available to Old Forge and Fourth Lake.

By 1891 the journey from Fourth Lake to Big Moose Lake would have passed through land owned by Webb and ended at the lake, which he then owned in its entirety.

On May 11, 1891, Webb purchased 350,000 acres of land from the Adirondack Timber and Mineral Company. This tract encompassed all of Township 8 in Brown's Tract and included all of Big Moose Lake except the eastern end, which, as part of an earlier purchase of a portion of the Totten and Crossfield Township 41, was already part of Webb's holdings.

There is little doubt that Webb bought this land because he saw the lumbering and mining possibilities in the Adirondacks. He was equally aware of the public's growing interest in resorts and knew that building an Adirondack railroad was the key to both opportunities.

SURMOUNTING OPPOSITION

Webb, however, had several obstacles to overcome. While he owned much of the area through which his railroad would pass, a considerable amount of land was still controlled by New York State. To build his railroad, Webb would need the permission of the State Land Commission and the State Forest Commission, and he knew that such permission would not be forthcoming without active debate. In addition, Webb was battling lawsuits and other obstructive maneuvers by competing railroad companies. Added to all of these problems were major public-relations issues that arose as soon as Webb's intentions to build a railroad became known.

At the time, the public was becoming increasingly concerned about the future of the Adirondacks. Many people had become alarmed at the desecration of the wilderness, first by loggers who had no strategy for controlling their cutting in a way that would foster natural reforestation, and second by the many forest fires caused by sparks coming from coal-burning locomotives that were now pushing deeper into the wilderness.

In 1890 the Adirondack Park Association was organ-

Peg-Leg Railroad car, ca. 1890, with chairs for the passengers and a corduroy loading platform. Courtesy of the Town of Webb Historical Association.

The steamboat Fawn, *ca. 1890. Courtesy of the Town of Webb Historical Association.*

ized "with the avowed purpose of stimulating public sentiment in favor of the preservation of the Adirondacks and urging upon the State Legislature the desirability of acquiring the greater part of that beautiful wilderness and making of it a State park."[55] On May 26, 1891, the executive committee of the association met to discuss Webb's plans for a railroad through the Adirondacks. The day before, the president of the association had met with Webb, who had assured him that he (Webb) had "no intention whatever of injuring the Adirondack region. On the other hand he, as a large property holder there, was deeply interested in protecting it from devastation. [Webb] proposed to institute a system of forestry on his own property, and for that purpose had offered an expert in forestry $5,000 a year to go there and take charge."[56]

When the *New York Times* reported on this meeting the following day, the headline read, "Soft Spot for Webb, Adirondack 'Defenders' Reconciled to his Scheme."[57] The day after that, Martin Burke, a member of the Adirondack Park Association, in a letter to the *New York Times*, resigned in protest, asserting that "a bill [before the New York State legislature] whereby a state park might be made . . . was unfairly defeated in committee before it could come before the people. So nearly, however, was it successful that the railroads became alarmed, and at once en-

deavored to push their lines to a successful termination before we could again approach the Legislature."[58]

The *New York Times* continued to campaign against the railroad and stated that "there were enough expressions of opinion heard in the business portion of this town to convince any doubting committee member that the people generally want the Adirondack forests preserved in their natural state and without any railroad trimmings."[59] Public sentiment had undoubtedly been aroused.

It was true that lumbering enterprises had been despoiling the area, but Webb did not believe that there needed to be a contradiction between lumbering and preserving the wilderness. On the contrary, he was convinced that intelligent lumbering practices would enhance natural reforestation to the benefit of the Adirondacks. This was no idle gesture designed to placate critics.

The expert whom Webb had hired for the generous salary of $5,000 a year and placed in charge of his own lumbering operations was Gifford Pinchot, a man with impressive forestry credentials. As a youth, Pinchot had developed a keen interest in forestry and had traveled to Germany to study, there being no forestry schools in America at that time. Upon his return, Webb's father-in-law, William Vanderbilt, had hired Pinchot to manage Biltmore, the Vanderbilt estate in North Carolina. (Much later, Pinchot was to become chief of the Division of Forestry in the U.S. Department of Agriculture.) Pinchot's ideas on scientific forestry later proved to be better in theory than in practice (see chapter 4, pages 115–16), but he did arouse in Webb a true devotion to preserving the forests and encouraging regrowth.

Meanwhile, in spite of the public outcry, work on the railroad continued. Logistical headaches were always present. In order to complete the line as quickly as possible, Webb had engaged eight independent construction engineers who were each responsible for a different section of the line. Managing the work was not always easy. For example, a Herkimer-to-Poland line already existed, but it was narrow gauge and had to be replaced with standard-gauge track. Many of the other sections required new construction. On a section north of Remsen to Thendara, supplies had to come overland from Boonville to the Moose River Settlement, then on the Peg-Leg Railroad to Minnehaha, and then by boat to Thendara. Each engineer had to ensure that supplies, equipment, and laborers were available when needed.

The labor force, which the engineers hired from distant

regions of the country, was also a source of problems. Laborers came from many different ethnic backgrounds and included African Americans, Chinese, Slavs, St. Regis Indians, and French Canadians. Serious ethnic antagonisms often arose among them. Some were also ill prepared for the climate and the hardships. Nonetheless, Webb's tenacity ensured that the railroad would be completed.

Webb's expectations for his workers were sometimes unreasonable, but at the same time he earned a reputation as a just and fair employer who genuinely cared about his men. At one point, a rumor circulated that work crews were being treated badly by the bosses. Webb heard the rumor and was concerned enough to visit the crews, unannounced, and to sleep and eat with the men in order to learn for himself whether the rumors were valid. They were not.

Burnett reported that "The Doctor made frequent trips over the work, traveling on foot, handcar, or construction train as opportunity afforded. He knew every engineer, every contractor and sub-contractor by name. He never failed to stop and shake hands with them . . . He was generous to a fault . . . He was loved and respected by everyone on the job. As one of the engineers expressed it, 'There was not a man on the line but would stand on his head for the Doctor.' "[60] This universal respect was later acknowledged when a large part of the then Town of Wilmurt changed its name to the Town of Webb.

In spite of all the problems, the railroad was completed in an astonishing eighteen months, and Webb began to sell some of his vast holdings. "Tourists, buyers of private camp sites, hunting and fishing clubs, hotel builders and lumbermen came tumbling into the western Adirondacks in Webb's wake . . . remote forest retreats blossomed into thriving summer resorts."[61]

Consistent with his respect for the natural qualities of the Adirondacks, Webb included a stipulation in each deed that significantly proscribed how the land could be used: "the lands and premises above conveyed shall be used solely for permanent forestry, hotel, camp or cottage purposes and shall not be used for commercial, agricultural or manufacturing purposes; that all trails and ways of communication across and over said lot and premises above conveyed shall forever remain free and open to the People of the State of New York." Deeds also contained a further qualification: "failure to adhere to these terms will make ownership null and void and owners shall from henceforth be divested of all title to said premises." The

The Big Moose Railroad Station, 1894. Courtesy of the Big Moose Property Owners Association.

document is now known as the Webb Covenant and can be found in every deed to property on Big Moose Lake today.[62]

THE RAILROAD IN ACTION

After only one year of operation, Webb's Adirondack & St. Lawrence Railroad was leased to the New York Central and Hudson River Railroad and the line's southern terminus moved from Herkimer to Utica. It was the beginning of a new era. The railroad advertised the convenience of its rail service, and travelers soon began to come to the Adirondacks from Boston, New York City, and the American West. Passengers would reach Utica and then change to the Adirondack line. A timetable published in early 1893 shows one train per day running in each direction and offering passenger service to Big Moose, which was then just a flag stop.

Soon, camps and hotels were advertising the convenience of rail travel, while, in turn, the New York Central Railroad was promoting rail travel by advertising the beauty of the Adirondacks and the joys of the woods. A 1910 promotional brochure had this to say: "The beauties of the Adirondack Mountains are beyond words to describe. Paddling or rowing over the limpid waters at the foot of mountains clad in their forest verdure of pine, balsam, and birch, and breathing the pure air that imparts new life with every breath is an experience never to be forgotten and will always linger as one of memory's most cherished legacies." The railroad also provided detailed

Ticket for the New York Central and Hudson River Railroad dated May 30, 1898. Courtesy of William L. Scheffler.

information on local hotels, including hotels and camps on Big Moose Lake. One New York Central brochure printed several views of the Glennmore Hotel.

By 1910, rail travel had increased significantly. A timetable from that year shows ten trains serving Big Moose. All of the northbound and three of the southbound stops were scheduled stops, while the others were flag stops. By 1919, all were scheduled stops. By the 1920s, the New York Central even offered a Friday evening overnight sleeper during the summer months. It left New York's Grand Central Station in five sections (five separate trains), all following one another, to the Adirondacks. Each train had ten to fourteen cars and could carry 350–400 passengers.

The railroad also brought regular freight service to Big Moose. Not only could local timber be taken directly to cities without the difficulty and expense of floating it down streams, but also hotel and camp owners could order supplies and materials to be shipped directly by rail to Big Moose.

By the 1920s, with people flocking to the Adirondacks, demand for accommodations skyrocketed, construction at Big Moose Lake increased dramatically, and the community that we know today began to take shape.

2 *Hotels and the Birth of a Resort Community*

A SURPRISING VARIETY of hotels sprang up at Big Moose Lake. The earliest began as simple accommodations for fishermen and hunters and evolved gradually into larger hostelries. Some were small, containing as few as seven guest rooms. Others turned into elaborate complexes with central dining rooms, guest rooms, cottages, and numerous outbuildings that housed boats, amusement spaces, libraries, stables, and other features for the enjoyment of guests. Early growth was succeeded by gradual decline as the automobile drew vacationers in a variety of different directions.

Big Moose had a total of eight hotels of various types. Not all flourished at the same time, but all of them were in existence before World War II. William Scheffler and Frank Carey have published a book that shows in postcards all of the hotels including both exterior and interior views.[1]

In addition to these eight there were some small enterprises that functioned as adjuncts to larger hotels (Alice and Charlie Martin's home that took Waldheim guests) or were very small, often short-lived establishments (Warren Richards's abortive effort to operate the Charles Martin house as a small resort, the Barnums' guest house at the Ogden camp).

Beginning in the 1920s, automobiles became more common, and the nature of vacations began to change. Better roads and road maps enabled people to travel from one spot to another rather than spending their entire holiday in one place. Businesses began to give their employees paid vacation time. The prosperous clientele who spent a month or two at hotels could travel to more distant destinations or even to Europe. More people wanted and could afford their own private cottages. Change pro-

gressed slowly throughout the 1930s and even during World War II. However, after the war the lake saw rapid development, many new private camps, and the precipitous decline of the hotels.

A few hotels have survived, each adapting in a different way to changing demands and tastes. The Waldheim retains its kitchenless cottages and caters to families who prefer "American Plan" eating (three meals a day). Covewood maintains housekeeping cottages. The Big Moose Inn features its dining room and keeps only twelve guest rooms. The Glennmore Hotel has transformed itself into the Glenmore Bar and Grill (with a few rooms) in a building that was part of the original Glennmore complex. The following section relates the story of each hotel in the order in which they were built or established: Camp Crag, 1880; Higby Camp, 1891; Lake View Lodge, 1898; the Glennmore, 1899; Burdick's Camp (later Waterman's, and still later the Big Moose Inn), 1903; the Waldheim, 1904; Camp Veery (later Veery's Nest), 1923; and Covewood, 1924.

Camp Crag, the First Hotel on Big Moose Lake, 1880

One day in 1898, Henry H. Covey received a letter dated May 13 from Edward Burns, the manager of Dr. William Seward Webb's sizeable land holdings. Webb owned Big Moose Lake and all of the land around it—including Crag Point, the peninsula on which Covey lived as a squatter and operated his Camp Crag resort, which he had opened in 1880. The intent of the letter was clear: purchase the land or leave.

Webb was in the process of surveying and subdividing

W. SEWARD WEBB, Prop'r.   EDWARD M. BURNS, Manager.

NE-HA-SA-NE PARK.

MANAGER'S OFFICE.

HERKIMER, N. Y. May 13, 1896.

H. H. Covey, Esq.,

    Big Moose, N. Y.

Dear Sir:-

        I have your letter of May 11th, which but for an unexpect-
ed delay would not have reached me until after I had departed for
Salt Lake City, for which point I am about to take the train at this
writing.

        The matter of settlement with reference to your rent will
have to remain over until my return, which will be in the course of
two or three weeks.   Provided we agree upon a purchase price
within the next sixty or ninety days I will agree to rebate the
rent.

        It is Dr. Webb's purpose to lay out Big Moose Lake into camp
and hotel sites as soon as Mr. Wood can undertake the work after
which prices will be determined upon and we can then negotiate with
reference to a purchase, but his experience in depending upon those
he has allowed to occupy the land to look out for his interests has
been such that he has instructed me that I must collect rents hereafter.   It is susceptible of proof that those who occupy Dr. Webb's
lands in some cases are quite as active in furnishing information to
and looking out for the interests of those who are antagonistic to
Dr. Webb, as his own paid agents are in caring for his interests.

        I shall make it a point to communicate with you as soon as I
return.

            Yours respectfully,

                        Manager.

Letter from Webb's manager, Edward M. Burns, to Henry H. Covey regarding the purchase of the Crag Point property, 1896. Courtesy of the Adirondack Museum.

Drawing of pit sawing; artist unknown. Courtesy of the Sorting Gap, Tupper Lake, N.Y.

tenoned in place. The logs were then shaved flat so that a deck could be built on top. Workers then "pit sawed" logs, an economical and time-efficient technique—economical because it avoided the cost of milled lumber and time efficient because shelters could be built quickly. (See illustrations on pages 23, 60, and 89.)

Roy Higby describes the pit saw. "A pit saw looked very much like an ice saw, about six feet long but with handles at both ends. A log would be rolled onto an elevated platform and placed in a crevice, fastened in place by two iron prongs. A chalk line would then be snapped the length of the log, and with one man on the ground pulling the saw downward and the other on the top pulling it up, they would split the log lengthwise."[2] A half log could do the work of a whole log.

his land into lots that he intended to sell, and every squatter on the lake received this letter. Some left, but Henry Covey found that the price Webb was asking was fair. He bought not only the land upon which he was living and running his business, thus making his occupancy of Crag Point legal, but also another one hundred acres in South Bay. Camp Crag was now secure.

ARCHITECTURE

Camp Crag was a classic early Adirondack resort. All of its original buildings were constructed from materials available in the woods and made by hand. No power tools. No bulldozers. No lumber brought from outside. It is an example of the region's traditional palisade style of architecture. Immigrants (perhaps from Normandy, France) may have brought this style to Canada and subsequently south across the St. Lawrence River and into New York State.

To construct a building in the palisade style, a platform was first built with logs that had been mortised and

Edward J. Martin and Danforth Ainsworth, well-known personalities on Big Moose Lake, pit sawing at Camp Crag, ca. 1900. Courtesy of Robert and Elizabeth Smith.

Edward J. Martin, left, and Danforth Ainsworth, ca. 1900. Courtesy of Wanda K. Martin.

Harter Cottage and boardwalk at Camp Crag, ca. 1915. Courtesy of Mark Barlow.

Logs were stood on end to form the walls, then connected at the top with a timber that became the top plate. This structure was sometimes referred to as *poteaux sur sole* (stakes on a sill).[3] Unlike standard modern construction, the standing logs functioned as the building's supporting frame. The bark-covered outer side became the exterior finish, while the smooth inner side became the interior walls. The spaces between the standing logs were covered on the inside with thin boards called battens and on the outside with trimmed, narrow branches. Often they were further chinked with sphagnum moss.

Henry Covey was resourceful and self-reliant, and he never considered using an outside contractor. He did all the building himself, along with the help of his son, Earl, and a few dependable neighbors.

GROWTH OF THE HOTEL

Undoubtedly, Covey first built a simple structure for his family. Soon after, he constructed a larger main building with a living room, a central dining hall, a kitchen, and some guest bedrooms. Gradually he added cottages that he scattered along the shore of the main lake and into South Bay, each with a spacious living room and bedrooms but no kitchens. All were connected by a board-walk. Additional buildings followed, including icehouses, woodsheds, outdoor privies, and a large boathouse on the South Bay side of the Point where guests arrived by steamboat. Camp Crag also featured a general store located in the main building, from which many lake residents, both year-round and summer, purchased supplies.

Camp Crag's stationery and letterheads boasted of the camp's special features, including fresh milk, daily mail, and telephone. Later brochures mention spring water that was piped from across South Bay under the lake to Crag Point, hot and cold running water, and indoor bathrooms.

Henry Covey was very protective of his guests. There was no road to Crag Point, and he would have none built. Covey was convinced that his guests wanted privacy and quiet. He would not even permit the steamboat that delivered groceries and mail to camps on the lake twice every day to blow its whistle when near Crag Point. "It might disturb the guests," he is reported to have said.

Photograph of Camp Crag from a letterhead, 1896. Courtesy of Mark Barlow.

Camp Crag office and general store, ca. 1910. Courtesy of Mark Barlow.

A verse by an unknown author found in an old Camp Crag brochure describes the ambience sought by Henry Covey.

> Come to the mountains, tired heart
> And from thy worries dwell apart;
> Here golden afternoons are long,
> And voices ripple into song,
> And vexing cares are swift forgot,
> And fret and hurry harass not;
> . . . .
> Here the long days are calm and sweet
> And earth and heaven nearest meet—
> Come to the mountains, weary soul,
> And let their healing make thee whole!

Such tranquility was not easily achieved, and Covey was well known as a demanding boss. His daughter-in-law, Frances Covey, in her biography of her husband, Earl, said that Henry was one who "worked without thought of sparing himself and he expected his employees to do the same. If they did not, or if they incurred his displeasure in any way, they received from him a tongue lashing which they did not soon forget."[4]

Covey was also particular about his guests' behavior. Dr. George H. Longstaff, the longtime owner of the Moss Lake Camp for Girls, remembers Camp Crag as "a rustic masterpiece [with] an extremely affluent clientele that bowed to the whims of its proprietor. Henry Covey set his own code of behavior for his guests, which included not allowing women to smoke, to wear jewelry or make-up or to dress in anything but the most proper attire of the period."[5] James Schoolcraft Sherman, vice president of the United States under William Howard Taft and the son of the General Sherman who had come to Big Moose Lake in the 1850s with the Walton Club, was among the celebrities who vacationed at Camp Crag.

In August 1910, the *Utica Sunday Tribune* described Camp Crag as "An Exclusive Resort in the Adirondacks. . . , in the wildest part of the North Woods, one thousand feet above sea level and surrounded by some of the most beautiful scenery in mountain vastness. The Proprietor of Camp Crag has no motor boats to disturb the peace and quiet of the place. No musical instruments are allowed at the resort. Dogs are barred and no intoxicants are to be secured at the camp."[6] This last prohibition is curious. In 1962 the purchaser of one of the camp's outlying cottages found dozens of early vintage

Henry H. Covey, ca. 1900. Courtesy of Ann Dunn Hall.

beer and wine bottles in about six feet of water off the shore, all within tossing distance of the cottage porch.

RESTRICTED CLIENTELE

Anyone of whom Covey did not approve did not stay long. In fact, some people never got to stay there at all. In addition to those appealing features of the camp that were described on the letterheads and in the brochures, some prohibitions began to appear. As early as 1907, if not before, the prohibition "No Hebrews or Consumptives Taken" was added. Covey had earlier lost his wife and sister-in-law to the virulent tuberculosis bacillus, and it is understandable that he would want to exclude consumptives from his resort. The fear of this highly infectious disease was palpable throughout the Adirondacks. Fresh air and rest were the only cures available at the time, yet many who were afflicted and who could afford to seek the healing qualities of the mountains were nonetheless denied accommodations for fear of infecting others.

Reprehensible, yet far from unusual, was Covey's anti-Semitism, a sentiment that was blatant at most Adirondack resorts. Indeed, Camp Crag was not the only hotel at Big Moose Lake that barred Jews. Some resorts expressed it openly, as Covey had done. More often, the anti-Semitism was stated more subtly by such language as "undesirables," "the right people," or "gentile guests only." Clearly, the extreme bias that permeated American society at that time had reached the North Woods.

In 1890, Henry Covey's wife, Emma, lost her debilitating fight with tuberculosis and died. Two years later, Henry married his late wife's former nurse, Margaret Rose, who became a devoted wife, a steady helpmate, and a hard worker at the expanding Camp Crag.

BUSINESS OPERATIONS

Henry Covey was a successful businessman. Two years after he had purchased Crag Point and the land in South Bay from Webb, Covey bought an additional 155 acres, much of it lying west of South Bay and extending into West Bay. While he could not be called a speculator on the

grand scale of a John Brown, a William West Durant, or a William Seward Webb, Covey did make more than a few profitable sales around the lake to families seeking to build vacation homes.

Henry Covey also invested in the stock market. His portfolio included many mining companies in the far West as well as U.S. Steel and the Southern Pacific Railroad. Records contained in the archives at the Adirondack Museum reveal that some of the dividends from his investments were not insignificant.

ARRIVAL OF THE DUNN FAMILY

Covey was also a meticulous record keeper. What would serve solely as a guest registration book for most hotels became a daily diary of life at Camp Crag.[7] His register contained the temperature and general weather conditions, financial transactions (including expenditures by Mrs. Covey), the comings and goings of guests, evidence of wildlife, records of construction, renovation and repair around the camp, bits of gossip about neighbors—almost anything that came into his mind.

One enigmatic entry in the register stands out because the story behind it came to light only in 1995. It is the entry for October 16, 1908. It reads, "Janet & 4 boys came last night." "Janet" was Janet Dunn, whose four sons and their descendants were to become a major presence on Big Moose Lake.

Janet and her sons arrived by an unusual route. On the night of October 14, 1908, the weather forecast for the Adirondacks and northern New England was for light, variable winds from the Northwest. Seasonal temperatures were predicted, although the Ohio Valley could expect its first heavy frost. The moon was half full. In the middle of that night a large rowboat with three adults and three children pushed off from Stanley Island, just offshore from Summerstown on the Canadian side of the St. Lawrence River.

Charles Rose, Henry Covey's employee (and his wife's brother), had arranged to meet one of his sons-in-law, J. R. Duquette, the owner of the Algonquin Hotel on Stanley Island. Together they helped Charles's daughter Janet and three of her children into the boat and rowed it across the St. Lawrence River to a remote spot between Fort Covington and Hogansburg, on the American side. The landing place was only a short distance from the New York-Ottawa branch of the New York Central railroad that went from Ontario, Canada, to Tupper Lake, New York.

Janet's husband, Stephen Dunn, had been operating a farm near Summerstown, Ontario, when he contracted tuberculosis. He died in 1907. Janet had contracted the disease while nursing him. She soon realized that she was unable to run the farm and rear her four sons, Nelson, the eldest at about eleven, followed by Charles, Walter, and Edward. Certain that she had only a short time to live, she decided to take the boys to her parents, Charles and Catherine Rose at Big Moose. The clandestine operation was necessary because the U.S. government had recently passed a law that prohibited entrance into the country of anyone with tuberculosis. Janet had no alternative but to conceal her journey from the authorities. The three older boys came with her in the boat. As the story is pieced together, Edward Dunn, barely a year old and likely to be dangerously noisy, did not come in the boat. It was probably one of Janet's sisters, Catherine or Elizabeth, who went to Summerstown and brought him over the border by train. They all met near Hogansburg and went by rail to Tupper Lake and then on to Big Moose.

Janet Rose Dunn arrived with her family at the Big Moose station on October 16, 1908. The story has been handed down in the Dunn family that eleven-year-old Nelson was carrying baby Eddie as they alighted from the train coach.

This drama was never revealed to the people at Big Moose, including the descendants of the four boys, until William Dunn, the elder son of Nelson Dunn, went to Ontario in 1994 in search of his roots. He located the old family farm and found that the owner at that time was the grandson of the executor of Stephen and Janet Dunn's estate. He remembered his grandfather telling about the "poor, sickly, destitute widow crossing the river at night." Although Nelson Dunn was old enough to remember the trip, he undoubtedly was sternly cautioned not to breathe a word of the story lest the U.S. government find out and send them all back to Canada on illegal-entry charges. Walter and Charles were probably too young to remember any of the details, and Edward was only an infant.

The four boys were raised by their grandparents, fondly called Grandma and Grandpa Rose by everyone in the Big Moose community, and by Margaret, the unmarried sister of Janet Dunn, affectionately known to all as Aunty. Charles and Catherine Rose had come to the United States from Summerstown around 1903 to work for their grandson Edward Duquette, who had purchased the Hess Camp on Fourth Lake. In 1905, young Duquette was killed when the acetylene generator used for lighting the hotel exploded. (It was rumored that the generator had been sabotaged by a disgruntled employee.) Duquette's widow immediately sold the hotel, and the Roses lost their jobs.

Instead of returning to Summerstown, the Roses went to Big Moose Lake to work for Henry Covey at Camp Crag, where Charles Rose's sister Margaret was now Henry Covey's wife. The Roses lived in what became known as Rose Cottage, built by Covey on land that he owned. It stood at the corner of the Eagle Bay Road and what is now the Covey Road.

Sixteen months later there was another brief entry in Covey's Register: "Janet['s] death occurred this P.M. 11:10." Janet had lived only a short time after her arrival.

Henry's careful records reveal that his relationship with the Dunn family did not preclude keeping track of Janet's expenses. Entries in her account included "88 oranges @ 2[cts]," "3 pairs long pants @ $2.50," etc. Curiously, there is also a debit for "15 weeks board (for 3 boys) per week @ $3.00." All the evidence that has come down

Charles and Catherine Rose, ca. 1915. Courtesy of Ann Dunn Hall.

Rose Cottage, ca. 1920. Courtesy of William S. Dunn.

through the Dunn families indicates that Janet and the boys always lived at Rose Cottage and never at Camp Crag. That is understandable, because Henry Covey was adamant that there be no consumptives at Camp Crag. Charging board for the boys is difficult to understand. Henry Covey had a reputation of being exceedingly frugal. Perhaps these charges were a way to compensate for the free rent of the Dunns in Rose Cottage.

The entries continue after Janet's death under "Dunn Estate." They include matter-of-fact delineations of expenses associated with her death—the undertaker's bill, telegrams, and rail tickets to Canada. In addition to such sundries as "1 pair mittens," "1 stick shaving soap (Nelson)," "1 pair suspenders (Nelson)," the charges for board for the boys continued for almost a year after Janet's death. Why they suddenly stopped is as much a mystery as why they ever existed in the first place.

During this time the estate accumulated a substantial debt. Nelson started to work in the kitchen of Camp Crag as a helper at age eleven, although his earnings were minimal. By April 1911 he was making $26 a month. Two years later Nelson's brother Charlie started work at $26 a month, and by then Nelson was earning $38 a month. Covey's register records the payments that Nelson, Charlie, and occasionally their grandfather Charles Rose made to the account. By February 1914, all debts were discharged.

Henry Covey had given the Roses the use of the cottage and space in the adjacent barn in which he kept the horses and carriages used to transport guests in the summer, as well as space for a garden. Grandpa Rose kept a cow and some chickens, and he also raised pigs. Trout and venison, both plentiful at the time, were other important food sources. The Roses were not paid a salary, although Aunt Margaret did earn money from waiting on table and from tips. Grandpa Rose guided hunting and fishing parties and did chores for guests at Camp Crag and other hotels and camps on the lake. He also cut fuel wood on the land near Rose Cottage. Grandma Rose died in 1919 and Grandpa Rose in 1920.

BUSINESS CONTINUES, DECLINING YEARS

The Camp Crag registers from 1913 to 1922 have been lost, but there is no doubt that Camp Crag continued to

Margaret Rose, known as "Aunty," ca. 1920. Courtesy of Ann Dunn Hall.

be popular and that Henry himself enjoyed the respect and affection of many people. However, beginning in the early 1920s, ill health began to affect both Margaret and Henry.

The register for the last year of Camp Crag's operation, 1922–23, has been preserved and contains many entries of interest. By then, Henry Covey was in his seventies and spending a good deal of time at his desk. He recorded the weather meticulously. A national weather bureau would not have been more complete. He often wrote his entries in the third person. At other times, someone else in the camp office made the entry. A few examples illustrate the style:

> May 22, [1922,] Temp—44—above, Clear wind south. Michel and the other Boys Puting seeds in garden today[.] Mr C. dictating mail in the AM. and Plumbing office Wash Room and Repairing same[.] Got water turned on just Before Supper time. Pretty Hard work as He was not feeling very well all Day[.] Wrote the Beecher Family. Had some Important Mail, answered most of it. Had a very large exhibition of Black Bass between the office docks today. Hundreds of them basking in the warm sun with the whole of back fin out of water.

Earlier that month:

> May 2, Mr Thompson caught a fine brook trout— Elmer caught five salmon. Mr C caught a nice brook trout off front dock.

> May 3, Mr. Ralph Thompson caught a 7½# lake trout in South Bay.

> May 4, Caught 3 lakers, and 2 brook trout one of the lake trout weighed 6¾ lbs.

> May 5 . . . caught some fine fish today ranging from 5¾# to 8½#. Mrs. Thompson caught a good fighter taking nearly ¾ hour to land him.

In that last year of the register, Covey made frequent references to successful fishing parties all over the lake and wrote as well about deer, moose, bear, beaver, and even the absence of wild rice.

By 1922, neither Henry nor Margaret was in good health. The register frequently reports "Mr C not feeling good today" or "Mrs. Covey remained in bed today." It

also becomes clear that the two were having difficulty accomplishing the work necessary to keep the place going. In addition, Henry was becoming increasingly forgetful.

An entry for Saturday, September 23, 1922, is particularly interesting: "Temp 49. Clear. Wind west. Mr Covey went to see and talk with Mr. Milligan in reference to the Place [Camp Crag?] and Earl and the other Partys Must know what to Depend upon." From this and other entries, it becomes apparent that Henry Covey was seriously considering selling his property. In fact, his son Earl had already made an offer to purchase Camp Crag, an offer that his father had tentatively accepted. However, when Edward P. Morse, a frequent guest at Camp Crag and the new owner of the Hermitage near Queer Lake, heard that the property was for sale, he made a higher offer. Earl walked to the Hermitage to explain to Morse his own interest in his father's property. In the end, Henry rejected his son's offer and accepted that of Morse. The record is not entirely clear, but it appears that the transaction was for $40,000. Earl was bitterly disappointed.

To be sure, business at Camp Crag had declined in recent years, and many of the stocks in Covey's portfolio (especially those in mining companies) had lost much of their value. He had to consider his financial security in old age and that of his ailing wife. The extent of the difference

Margaret and Henry Covey, ca. early 1920s.
Courtesy of William S. Dunn.

between Earl's offer and that of Morse will never be known, but on Friday, November 3, 1922, the camp register recorded, "Mr. and Mrs. Covey . . . returned tonight from Utica. Transacted business with Mr. Morse. Sold Camp Crag Property Real Estate to Mr. Morse. All that part from the Point on which Camp is situated around to the Kelsey Property [lot #69] on South side of South Bay."

Christmas of that year brought Henry many greetings from former guests at Camp Crag. His entry in the register for December 22, 1922 reads,

> Temp—23 above Cloudy wind Southwest. Water coming on top of ice more or less all over the lake this AM. Michel Treading snow on our road across [the lake] to Darts Landing. This AM snowed a trifel but not to much for good Roads, Received Sevril Christmas Greetings from old Guests which seems very Pleasant to Receive their Greatly Esteemed Remembrances and Kind Words, but also makes me sad to think I can no longer administer to their Comforts and Pleasure on account of Sale and Retirement from my Place CAMP CRAG.

Three weeks later, on January 18, 1923, a poignant entry reads,

> Temp—4 Below, wind South and Blowing quite Hard. Excitement Running High Here this AM as we are Moving last loads to Rose-wood Cottage from Camp Crag which Has been our Consistent Home for over (40) Forty Years. Selected Sight [site] and Location for the original Camp Crag on May 3rd, 1880, and built the original Camp that spring.

And so in January 1923 Henry and Margaret Covey moved to Rose Cottage, now vacant after the deaths of Charles and Catherine Rose. Margaret Covey did not live there long, however. Her health continued to fail, and she died during the summer. Henry stayed on alone in Rose Cottage.

At that time, Earl, widowed since September 1920, and his new wife, Frances Alden, were living in a house that Earl had built at Big Moose Station. Earl would look in on his father when he was going back and forth to the Station. However, he was building a new house next to a small stream on the eastern boundary of property that would ultimately become Covewood Lodge. The following spring, the new house was completed. Earl named it the "Henry Covey Cottage," and Henry moved in with his son and daughter-in-law. By this time, Henry Covey was very frail and declining rapidly. He could not remain alone. On October 12, 1924, Henry Covey died in his sleep at the age of seventy-four.

CAMP CRAG'S NEW OWNER

The new owner of Camp Crag, Edward Morse, was an industrialist and a multimillionaire. He never intended to operate the property as a summer resort. In fact, the January 23, 1923, issue of a Utica newspaper reported—under the headline "Covey Disposes of Camp Crag Property"—that "Morse would remodel the camp for his own private use."[8]

Morse could afford to live in a comfortable resort without sharing it with paying guests. He had come to the United States from Nova Scotia, Canada, as a young man. The small repair shop he started in Brooklyn at the age of twenty had grown into the Morse Dry Dock and Repair Company. It was not only the largest dry dock serving the Port of New York and critical during World War I, but it also was said by the *New York Times* to be the largest in the world.

There is no evidence that Morse spent much time at Camp Crag. In fact, he returned to his native Nova Scotia, where he was building a $250,000 mansion. On August 26, 1930, he suffered a heart attack while supervising the construction of his new house and died before medical attention could reach him.

In a way, Morse lives on. Owners of property on Crag

Excerpt from the Camp Crag register, January 18, 1923. Courtesy of C. V. Bowes.

Point have, in the abstract of their deeds, a copy of Morse's Last Will and Testament, wherein he left all of his Big Moose property to his wife and children, with the exception of his son Edward whom he disinherited. Many years earlier, the son had sued his father to recover certain profits that he alleged were due to him under an agreement made when he had become general manager of the dry dock plant. The son won the suit, and Morse apparently considered that he had already received his share of the estate.

At some point between 1923, when Morse bought Camp Crag, and 1930, when he died, the main building of Camp Crag vanished. It has always been assumed that a fire destroyed the building, yet no one alive today can recall ever hearing about such a major fire. Some have suggested that there is a mystery surrounding it. In 2000, William Dunn wrote, "I cannot recall my mother or father ever discussing this event even though both had been very close to H.H. and Margaret Rose Covey. In retrospect, this now seems rather curious to me. I have often thought about this, and I can't help but wonder if there wasn't something undesirable about this event that they just did not want to discuss or wanted to forget."[9] On May 1, 1931, less than a year after Morse's death, his widow sold Crag Point and his land around South Bay to Robert Guy Harry of Schenectady, New York.

A SPECULATOR AND CHANGING TIMES

Guy Harry, as he was called, was indeed a latter-day speculator. He bought the property with the intention of selling it for the construction of summer camps on Crag Point and around South Bay. On May 25, 1931, he formed the Big Moose Camp Sites Company, Inc. of Old Forge, conveying to it the land starting from lot 76 and continuing around South Bay to Punky Bay. However, Harry retained ownership of the Crag Point parcel under his own name. The Big Moose Camp Sites Company eventually sold land in Punky Bay to Donald W. Salisbury, then president of Sun Oil, who built what is now the Watkins-Zorge camp, and to C. Ray Harvey from Boonville, who built the present Hadden camp in South Bay.

Harry's only sale on Crag Point was to Edward Winslow Kane on September 26, 1931. About the time that Kane bought, Harry published a brochure extolling the special features of Crag Point: "Entire peninsula nearly a mile of shore line . . . Virgin timber, ample spring water piped across South Bay from mainland . . . A location unsurpassed in the Adirondacks, for exclusiveness and scenery, reached only by private trail, boat or plane. Inaccessible to the public. . . . a real bargain at $25,000."

As attractive as this sounded, Harry could not have sought to sell property at a less auspicious time. The country was in the middle of the Great Depression, and there were no buyers for land on Crag Point. Eventually, Harry's personal financial situation deteriorated to the point that he and his family were forced to spend the winter of 1933–34 in what had been the caretaker's house on the Point.

The Great Depression was soon followed by the start of World War II, and hard times continued for the Harry family. Even if some people now had the money to purchase land for a summer camp, gasoline rationing made it impossible to get there. The property sat empty during the war. On September 27, 1951, J. Ross Paltz from Syracuse, New York, bought all of the land on Crag Point that Robert Harry owned. He intended to develop the Point further, and so began the Camp Crag community that exists today.

Camp Crag sale advertisement, 1931. Courtesy of Wanda K. Martin.

Higby Camp, 1891

The most vivid account of the beginning of the Higby Camp, the second hotel on the lake, comes from Francena Higby, the second wife of Jim Higby, in a handwritten document titled "Life of F A H."[10] Francena's adventurous spirit is evident in her account of the events of November 1891:

> 2 of our neighbors while calling asked Jim if he expected to guid[e] next summer. He said probably. I spoke up, asked if he thought we coul[d] make it pay to go to B[ig] M[oose] & keep boarders. He replied "I know we coud. Would U like to go?" I answered *Yes* (the start of H[igby] C[amp]) Next day while at Old Forge Election he hired 2 or 3 men to work with. Next day we came to B M. I to cook. Men first cut logs & built a fair sized Ice house & laid foundation for L S [lake side?] Cottage. Got many things as could ready for Spring. Went back to Sperryville for the winter[11]

In March of that year, Jim and Francena Higby had traveled to Big Moose Lake to clean and prepare for rental the log cabin that Jim had built about 1877. Jim used the cabin at the lake for the parties he and his son Elmer (by his first wife) guided on fishing and hunting trips. At the end of April, Jim and Francena then went to Fourth Lake, where Jim put up a small board cottage in only eleven days, while the couple lived in an open Adirondack camp.

Francena's enthusiasm for living in the woods is even more remarkable considering that she was without her right hand. When she was a child she lost her right arm

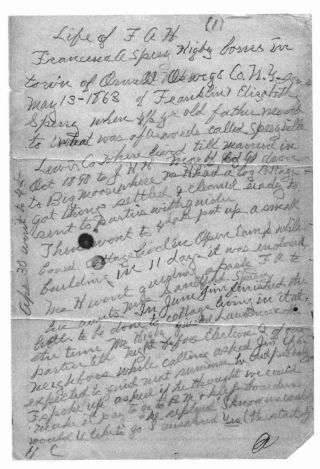

First page of the autobiography of Francena Higby, written ca. 1936. Courtesy of Phyllis Strack Dietze.

below the elbow in a sawmill accident, an incident she does not mention in her four-page autobiography.

Francena was born in 1863 in the town of Orwell, in Oswego County, New York. When she was four and one-

Cover of an early Higby Camp brochure, ca. 1902. Courtesy of William S. Scheffler.

Francena Higby, who lost her lower right arm as a child, rowing a guideboat, ca. early 1900s. Courtesy of Donald Lux.

half years old, her parents, Franklin and Elizabeth Sperry, moved to a Lewis County town later called Sperryville. As an adult Francena taught school until, at age twenty-seven, she married Jim Higby, a man twenty-one years her senior. There is no doubt that Jim, having lost his first wife to tuberculosis, was looking for a helpmate, and he certainly found one in the energetic and cheerful Francena. Jim was in much demand as a guide, no doubt a circumstance that made him eager to move to Big Moose permanently and "keep boarders."

Francena and Jim spent the first four winters of their marriage back at Francena's hometown of Sperryville, but in 1892, the summer after the momentous decision was made, the couple was back at Higby Camp where they were building the cottage and

serving meals to *Dr. Webb* and men of [whom?] we bought our land, nearly 100 acres. A party of 3 from NY came in Aug for month. Hunters and fishermen most [of] that summer. Next Spring, '92, my cousin Addie Buts [Addie Butts later became Earl Covey's first wife] who was with me 2 or 3 summers went in with me.[12]

In spite of her handicap, Francena was never daunted by any task. She continues: "I used to help cut wood. Saw till tired, rest while Jim split at it again. In fall when alone would go hunting with Jim, enjoyed it very much."[13]

The year that her son, Roy, was born, Francena describes as "1893 Our Eventful Year." She evidently had extra help, but the couple was certainly living in wilderness conditions. "An elderly woman came in to cook for me. Had a tent for guests. 2 girls came on Aug 1. My dear son [Roy, born August 1, 1893] arrived & my Dear husband to care for all 27 guests. Nurse came that night. That fall after a successful summer we went out happy."[14] It is not clear whether the nurse arrived before or after the baby.

The next year, 1894, "Charlie Wood and wife went in with [us]. Mr Covey met us with his team . . . put my box of Hens on. I sat on top [of the box of hens] with Roy in arms to start another successful season as 1894 proved to be."[15]

Francena was a small, active woman with a quick, charming smile.[16] She must have been a lively companion for her husband:

> For eight weeks [during the first summer] I saw a dress on no one but myself. We finally brought a cow, the first

First Higby Camp, ca. 1898.
Courtesy of Wanda K. Martin.

Bill Dart's portable saw, ca. 1900. Courtesy of Robert and Elizabeth Smith.

one in the woods, to Big Moose in the spring of '94 and trained her to draw wood. Year by year we added on to the first little settlement, till we had a fine camp.[17]

Then went out for my last winter as we had builded up a larger 12 [?] room [house] & had 2 men & wives with us while putting on an addition. Bad thunder storm. Our Cook & R[oy] were both knocked down. R was lifeless. We worked over them till all right.[18]

Roy Higby, in his book *A Man from the Past,* refers to the lightning incident.[19] His uncle, D. B. Sperry, and his father had brought the first telephone line to the area, and Roy had been playing near it when lightning struck. The lack of access to medical care or advice was a problem that the isolated residents of the woods undoubtedly worried about but still met with stoicism.

When the Higbys started their camp, they provided board bunks with straw-filled mattresses for beds. "This was followed by kerosene lamps, sagging coil springs, and still straw mattresses or occasionally, for which extra was charged, a featherbed made by mother from chicken feathers."[20]

The camp gradually grew, until in 1900 the couple decided to put up a large building—34 feet by 72 feet, and three and one-half stories high. Two years later, they added a two-story, 11-foot-long ell on the west end. Francena writes about the plans: "I drew them. My brother D. B. Sperry figured out stairs and what amount lumber we would need to build. Mr. H. got Bill Dart to move his portable sawmill up this side of Constable Creek near Sand Beach, and there they cut down trees, sawed the Lumber for the largest log bld in the country."[21]

It was indeed an impressive building, and, like most of the other buildings on the lake at the time, was made entirely from materials available on the spot.

During this era many people who later became familiar figures on the lake worked for the Higbys, no doubt learning much about the hotel business. A photograph of the staff taken on the front steps of the first Higby Camp shows E. J. Martin, Hattie Brown (head waitress and later wife of E. J. Martin who built the Waldheim), Gertrude Oakley (later Ainsworth), Jim Higby, young Roy and his sister Lila Higby, Caroline Brown (sister of Hattie Brown), and others.

At some time during the first decade of the twentieth century, Jim Higby sold the camp he and Francena had worked so hard to build. Two hints led to solid evidence found in the Herkimer County Courthouse. First, a note on the back of a photograph owned by Sarah Judson Dew states that, according to information given to Bill Judson (Roy Higby's son-in-law), the picture shows "Jim Higby in front of fireplace at camp that is now Rutherford's. Camp was built by Jim Higby and family stayed there when they sold Higby Club in 1904 and took it back two years later."[22] Second, J. Rowbottom, a Waldheim guest, has an old but undated envelope with this return address: "Higby Camp, George A. Franke, Prop., F. C. Hall,

Higby Camp, ca. 1906. Courtesy of Wanda K. Martin.

Higby Camp staff, ca. 1899. Standing, left to right: Jim Higby, Frank Higby, Willie Glenn, Caroline Brown, Mr. Conkey [unknown first name], Gertrude Ainsworth, two unknown girls, and E. J. Martin; seated on rail, unknown boy; seated, left to right, unknown boy, Elmer Higby, Roy Higby, Lila Higby, two unknown girls, Hattie Brown, unknown boy, and chef. Courtesy of Wanda K. Martin.

Mgr." (Unfortunately, the two-cent stamp has no visible postmark.) However, investigations at the Herkimer County Courthouse turned up a deed recording on November 15, 1909, a sale *from* "George A. Franke, single, of Toronto, Canada" *to* James H. Higby, transferring 65 8/10 acres extending from lot 140 to lot 148 along the shoreline of Big Moose Lake.[23] These lots include lots 145 and 146, on which the main hotel buildings stood, and toward the end of the document the "appurtenances for the use and occupancy of the hotel and cottages" are specifically mentioned. Both parties agreed to a mortgage of $20,000. Although there is no deed showing when James Higby sold the property to Franke, it was not unusual at the time for such transactions to be unrecorded. It seems certain that James Higby sold the hotel a few years before 1909, perhaps because the new building that

Jim Higby in his later years, ca. 1912. Courtesy of Wanda K. Martin

went up in 1900 and its extension in 1902 were too heavy a financial strain.

In any case, the Higbys were able to buy back the original property and to resume operations. The camp continued to grow in the number of both buildings and patrons. In 1913, Jim Higby died, and Francena ran the hotel with her son, Roy, who was only twenty at the time of his father's death. His two younger sisters, Lila and Lora, were teenagers at the time.

Francena was a very religious Methodist. On Sundays her children were expected to read only Sunday School papers or the Bible. Of course, guests bought the Sunday papers. Phyllis Dietze remembers her mother, Lora (the youngest of Francena's three children), telling her that she managed to read the "Katzenjammer Kids" and other comic strips as well as other forbidden things.[24] When Lora went to college it was to a Methodist institution, Syracuse University.

In 1916, Roy Higby married Frieda Strack, and together they gradually began to take over more management responsibilities. Roy's sister, Lila, married Harry Jones of Utica in 1920. Roy's other sister, Lora, married Frieda's brother, Eric Strack, in 1923, and lived in Amsterdam, New York.

Things went well for Roy and Frieda until disaster struck on June 19, 1921. At 8:00 A.M. Roy noticed a small fire in the rear of the building. Although the hotel had recently installed a fire line, the line broke, and the Higbys were forced to watch helplessly while the fire consumed the hotel and twelve other buildings.

It was a terrible loss, but the family was determined to carry on. They put in kitchen and dining facilities over the boathouse, improvised an office, and rented out the cot-

Ruins of the Higby Camp following the fire of 1921. Courtesy of Ann Dunn Hall.

tages that remained. Roy soon began planning a new main building that, at 80 feet by 160 feet, was much larger than the old one. The guests continued to come.

The new hotel began to take on a more sophisticated character. Although still called the Higby Camp, it was advertised as "a private club for select patrons who desire privacy without ostentation." A brochure that circulated in the 1920s states, "The management reserves the right to prohibit the presence of persons who would in any way be injurious to the business. . . . Hilarious night parties are forbidden . . . Persons with pulmonary affections [*sic*] are not accepted as guests. Gentile trade is solicited."[25] Later in its history, in the mid-1930s, Higby Camp became the Higby Club, a change that allowed it to be even more selective in its clientele.

The new main building, three and one-half stories high (as was the second building), was not built of logs but of shingled dimensional lumber. There was a spacious lounge and a large dining room and kitchen. The hotel had wide Adirondack verandas and sleeping porches for many of the rooms, but few private baths.

More cottages were gradually added to the six or seven that had escaped the fire, until they lined the lakeshore. One lakefront cottage that did not burn is the last surviving building put up by Roy's father, James Higby. Erected in 1898 in the palisade style, Comfort Cottage earned its name because its privy was a "two holer." Helen Weltman (of Burlington, Vermont) purchased the cottage with her husband in 1979. After his early death in 1983, Helen Weltman restored much of the camp to its original state and was recognized in the year 2000 by the Adirondack Architectural Heritage Association.

The Higby Club featured a four-piece orchestra at dinner and dancing (formal dress required for the ladies) on Wednesday and Saturday evenings. At one time, four tennis courts were available, although Roy, an excellent tennis player himself, sacrificed the court near the store in

Construction of the New Higby Camp, later to be called Higby Club, 1922. Courtesy of Richard Widdicombe.

The Higby Club, 1949. Courtesy of Wanda K. Martin.

order to install a putting green. Golf and riding were also available, although not on the premises. There were manicured lawns, colorful flower gardens, a gift shop, a snack bar, a theater/playhouse (for games of table tennis, pool, or cards, musicals, or dancing), and a library. Inside the playhouse were murals painted by Donald Lux (whose wife was Roy's niece) depicting some of the regular guests, individually identifiable, at play.

As Frieda took over more responsibilities, Francena gradually retired but continued to help. For many years in the 1920s and into the late 1930s, she ran the store. She was also very active in community organizations such as the chapel and the Willing Workers. Francena was a skilled seamstress, well known for her quilts. More than one person has said of her, "What anyone else could do with two hands, she could do as well or better with one."

As Francena became older, she left the management of the hotel to others, although she continued to live at the club. She died in 1951, a much-respected member of the lake community, at the age of eighty-eight.

There are stories that during Prohibition liquor was available. In 1936, after Prohibition ended, Roy added a cocktail lounge, which his Methodist mother, Francena (who strongly disapproved of alcohol), entered only once, just before it opened.

Phyllis Strack Dietze, Roy's niece, remembers playing with slot machines when she was a child.[26] The New York State trooper in Old Forge, who was responsible for enforcing laws against gambling, would thoughtfully telephone beforehand to announce that he was planning to make a visit, allowing time for the game room to be locked. There are rumors that in the end, the machines

Comfort Cottage, the sole remaining cottage built by Jim Higby, 1990. Courtesy of Helen Weltman.

were hastily consigned to the bottom of the lake, perhaps because of a change in law-enforcement personnel.

Business improved during World War II and for a short time afterward. Many guests stayed for two weeks or a month, and some remained for the entire summer. During this time, the Higby Club complex spread over many acres.

Water activities were very popular. Ray Hanlon was the last of the boatmen in charge of water activities. He not only managed the boathouse and the fleet of boats but also taught waterskiing and swimming, organized regattas, and generally took care of the beach for many years. He started at the job as a young man in 1946, continued throughout the intervening years, and now summers with his wife in a cottage on the former Higby property.

After the war, Roy's daughter Patricia married William Judson, son of Marguerite Judson who owned a camp on the North Shore. Bill was active in helping to run the hotel for several years. His genial personality made him many friends. Of the three Judson children, Lanny, Christine, and Sarah, only Sarah (now Sarah Dew) has remained at the lake as a summer resident.

In the 1950s, times began to change. Automobiles, rather than trains, became the popular means of travel. Guests took shorter holidays, and families began to drive to a variety of vacation spots. It was also possible again to travel abroad. The hotel business began to decline.

Bill Judson looked around for other things to do. He spent several winters at a resort in Scottsdale, Arizona. Eventually, he undertook to develop the Higby property that stretched along the eastern shore beyond the Higby Club. Putting in a road (the Judson Road) that led to hitherto inaccessible property, he sold land and built and sold some cottages. In 1981, he also built a house next to the property owners' dock, where he and his wife lived year-round. Bill died in 1990 at the age of sixty-seven after a short illness, and Pat died a year later.

Roy Higby, always a rather single-minded character, continued to operate the Higby Club for years after it became evident that there was little demand for large hotels where guests stayed for extended periods of time. He was a familiar figure—muscular, bald, and wearing glasses perpetually hanging from one ear. Finally, in 1973, Roy closed the hotel and began selling the cottages to individuals, who then installed kitchens and converted them to housekeeping cabins. No one wanted to buy the main building.

After selling the rustic furniture and other furnish-

The controlled fire that demolished the main lodge of the Higby Club, 1978. Courtesy of Barbara K. Wheeler.

ings, Roy turned the building over to the Big Moose Volunteer Fire Company for a controlled practice fire. In November 1978, after careful planning, the Big Moose Fire Company, with the help of companies from nearby towns, burned the hotel to the ground. They burned the second floor first, so that the walls fell toward the center of the building and made a minimum of mess. In an up-

Howard Martin and Roy Higby watching the burning of the Higby Club's main lodge, 1978. Courtesy of Barbara K. Wheeler.

Frieda and Roy Higby, ca. 1950. Courtesy of Sarah Dew.

stairs room, Bill Judson lighted the ceremonial match that resulted in an instructive and sadly spectacular blaze.

Roy and Frieda Higby continued to live in West Lodge, on the side of the property that faced the main lake. Frieda died in 1982. Roy continued to live in West Lodge with the help of a caretaker until he died in 1990 at the age of ninety-seven.

Lake View Lodge, 1898 | *Hamilton White*

Charles Williams knew a good thing when he saw it. When he was about thirty years old, he saw that teamsters

Hamilton White of Syracuse, New York, is a summer resident of Lake View and is now the owner of a cottage in the Lake View Subdivision.

would be needed to work on the construction of William Seward Webb's Adirondack and St. Lawrence Railroad, and he left his family's large farm in Watson, New York, to work for Webb. He soon became head teamster.

After the railroad was completed in 1892, Williams saw the possibilities in Webb's offer to become caretaker at Ne-Ha-Sa-Ne, Webb's private estate several miles north of Big Moose Station. He accepted Webb's offer, and while working for Webb between 1892 and 1896, Williams managed the boardinghouse for Webb's employees and for the lumbering crews working on Webb's scientifically managed forest. This experience in the hotel business showed him yet another "good thing"—an opportunity to build and operate a resort that would later be known as Lake View Lodge.

Williams may have approached Webb with his idea. In any case, Webb must have thought highly of Williams, for he offered him free land on Twitchell Lake or, for $1,000, a stretch of property on the south shore of Big Moose Lake (lots 27–31). Williams chose the Big Moose property and lost no time in starting construction of the third hotel on the lake. He later invested $3,000, buying additional land that increased his holdings (lots 1–26, 32–33, and 376–77).

Williams was an impressive figure. He stood straight and tall, six foot two inches in height, and weighed more than two hundred pounds. His penetrating eyes would cast a formidable stare, and he spoke short, direct sentences in a deep, booming voice. He was a shrewd judge of people and of horses, and he demonstrated an aggressive and keen business judgment. He had the reputation of being good at everything he tried.

Williams had foreseen the influx of vacationers and sportsmen that the railroad was bound to bring to Big

Cover of Lake View Lodge brochure, 1925. Courtesy of William S. Scheffler.

AINSWORTH CAMP, 1894 | *Ida Ainsworth Winter*

Although the Ainsworth Camp was located at Big Moose Station and not on Big Moose Lake, the Ainsworth family had close ties to the lake. They first arrived in the Big Moose area in 1895 when Danforth R. Ainsworth, Sr., moved from the Moose River Settlement. The first dwelling was a rough cabin not far from the recently completed railroad.

Life was hard, but the small family made it through the rigorous winters with the help of strong determination and good health. Soon they erected a three-storied house with split-spruce siding on the north side of the railroad near a stream, the outlet from Thirsty Pond. A few neighbors also made this area their home. Almost everyone had a garden, raised chickens, sometimes owned a cow or two, and maybe even pigs. The Ainsworths always had a team of horses that were used for lumbering and ice harvesting.

The family began taking boarders and called themselves Ainsworth Camp. It was an advantage to be near the railroad, but in the early years guests did not provide enough income. Lumbering was a thriving business at that time and it supplemented the family coffers. Also, Danforth Ainsworth trapped, hunted, and fished for his family. He and his son, Danforth Jr., guided "city sports" for hunting and fishing, working side by side. Queer Lake, Terror, and the Sisters Lakes were favorite spots to take their parties. Also, Dan spent many a day guiding on Big Moose Lake and smaller lakes nearby.

In 1904, Danforth Ainsworth Jr. married Gertrude Oakley, who came from the Constableville area. Both had worked for Bill and Mary Dart at their hotel on Dart's Lake and also at hotels on Big Moose Lake. Gertrude had been employed by H. H. Covey, Jim and Francena Higby, and E. J. and Hattie Martin, as well as by the Darts. The hotel business seemed to prosper more every year. Because the Ainsworth Camp did not serve alcohol, schoolteachers (who were expected to lead exemplary lives) and lawmen were regular boarders in the early days.

By about 1912, a much larger building containing the office, the dining room, and eight guest rooms was built to the east. The original spruce-sided building was moved farther from the road in 1921 and a new fully winterized shingled building was built in front of it. Four small cottages supplemented the rooms in the main houses. Early in the 1920s, Dan Ainsworth Jr. bought the property from his parents (who later moved to California) and continued to expand Ainsworth Camp. Soon, a tennis court became part of the complex, and in 1926 a cement-sided swimming pool (very unusual for the time) was built, fed by the stream that ran next to the main building.

Dan and Gertrude Ainsworth had five children: Rodney, Richard, Lula, Dorothy, and Ida. The family sustained several tragedies in the span of a few years. In 1926, Dorothy, the wife of Ralph Osgood, a teacher at the Lake School, perished along with her baby girl from carbon monoxide fumes in a house on Big Moose Lake. In September 1930, when he was fifty-two years old, Dan drowned in Big Moose Lake while on his way to prepare camp for a hunting party, and in 1931, his daughter Lula died of tuberculosis after sanitarium treatment failed to help her.

After her husband's death, Gertrude was left alone to

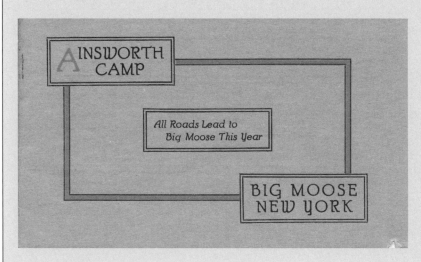

Cover of an early brochure for Ainsworth Camp. Courtesy of Ida Ainsworth Winter.

The main lodge at Ainsworth Camp, ca. 1908. Courtesy of Ida Ainsworth Winter.

run the hotel. She bolstered the family income by taking in washing, cleaning houses, and making quilts, which sold in those days for $25 each. Richard, her second son, never married and stayed on to help run the business, which continued for many years. He too was much sought after as a guide and knew his craft.

The eldest son, Rodney, married Rose Betzing in 1929 and was not involved in the Ainsworth Camp after that date. Rodney worked most of his life in the Big Moose area. He was often employed by the state to build lean-tos, trails, and bridges. He also worked for many years at the Higby Club and was very much a part of life on the lake. In 1953 he and Rose bought a house on the Covewood Road, and Rodney continued to work in many capacities, especially as a highly respected guide and builder, until he died in 1989.

Ida, the youngest, was born at Big Moose Station and has lived there most of her life. She married Robert C.

Winter in the Big Moose Chapel in 1949. After living briefly in the Syracuse area, the couple moved back to Big Moose and in 1955 purchased the hotel from Ida's widowed mother, operating it as Ainsworth Lodge until 1970. Ida has been active in Big Moose Lake community organizations, especially the Chapel. Their three children, Nancy, Virginia, and Robert, are now all working elsewhere. In 1992, Ida and Bob Winter sold part of the hotel property and built a home of their own nearby, where Ida, whose husband died in 1995 and who is now the only remaining member of her generation, still lives.

All of the family have deep roots in this north country and have always been active in community and civic organizations. Much of the lumber used in the building of the Big Moose Community Chapel was harvested from Ainsworth land. Danforth and Gertrude were charter members of the Chapel and worked diligently to help make the Chapel a reality.

Moose Lake, and he envisioned a hotel more luxurious than the two hotels then standing, Camp Crag and Higby Camp. Both of these establishments had been built in the palisade style using material available in the surrounding woods. They had opened before the railroad had been completed, and both depended for business on those fishermen and hunters who were hearty enough to undertake the long and arduous journey over roads that were little more than crude paths cleared through the forest.

Lake View Lodge, on the other hand, was designed for a clientele that sought comfortable travel and genteel recreation. It was the first hotel on the lake to be built with

milled lumber. In contrast to the two earlier rough-log establishments, the new hotel was in the "Folk Victorian" style. It was a simple, three-story wood-frame building embellished with Queen Anne-style decorative details along the rooflines of the upper and lower porches as well as on the cornices. The horizontal tongue-and-groove siding was painted yellow with gray-green trim, which contrasted smartly with the red tin roof. The original building also had an ell that projected toward the lake, with porches on the first and second stories that faced the water.

Opened in 1898, Lake View Lodge boasted thirty-two bedrooms, most with in-room washbasins. Shared

Charles Williams in front of fireplace at Lake View Lodge, ca. 1925. Courtesy of Frank Carey.

Lake View Lodge, 1901. Courtesy of Wanda K. Martin.

bathrooms were provided for the guests. Williams warmed the structure with steam heat and three fireplaces, and he planned to keep the hotel open year-round. The hotel had a number of modern amenities, including the first telephone on Big Moose Lake. Spring water was brought in from Pancake Creek on the north side of the lake via a pipe that had been installed by making a narrow cut in the winter ice and running a pipeline under the lake. This was a difficult and expensive operation that had to be redone at least three times during the life of the hotel. The water was stored in a large concrete-lined cistern above the main building in order to provide a gravity-fed system for the hotel.[27] This system still exists, although plastic and PVC lines have now replaced most of the old iron pipes.

When the hotel was first built, the main entrance was

from the steamboat dock. Later (probably in the 1920s), a road was built at the rear of the building. The horse-drawn wagons that brought guests from the railroad station drew up near a flower-filled circular garden. A lobby divided one end of the hotel from the other end with entrances on both sides. The spacious sitting room was furnished with Victorian rocking chairs, sheer white curtains, a fireplace, and oriental rugs. Electric lights were added by at least 1924.

In the early years, Williams lost no time in building rustic cottages to accommodate more guests. Many families preferred to be in the cottages rather than scattered about in the main building. The first cottage was built for and named after Charles C. Cook, a Syracuse attorney. It was the only cottage with four bedrooms and a small kitchen, and it was the only one to be considered winterized by the standards of the day. Cook used the camp during all seasons, hunting and fishing throughout the year and vacationing with his family in the summer. Five other cottages followed almost immediately and were probably completed by 1903 or 1904. Some were built at the request of regular guests and were thus named after them.

View of Lake View Lodge from the lake, 1905. Courtesy of Wanda K. Martin.

The Bungalow, an early Lake View Lodge cottage with canvas sides to be let down in inclement weather, ca. 1910. Courtesy of Frank Carey.

Patrick E. Crowley, president of the New York Central Railroad, had an elegant cottage with hardwood floors and walk-in closets designed for his family and named for him. Other cottages, built with spruce slab siding and tin roofs, spread to the west and east of the main hotel. The Owner's House, where Charles and his family lived, was built of milled lumber and stood above the main hotel and slightly to the east. All of the eleven guest cottages were designed with open front porches and fireplaces, and were equipped with wooden iceboxes.

The main dining room faced east and south, so that it captured the morning sun. White tablecloths, changed daily at the noon meal, established an air of formality. The cuisine was considered on a par with the best New York restaurants. Male guests wore dark suits at the noon and evening meals, and women chose between summer dresses or evening attire at dinner.

There were two dining rooms, the main dining room being located off the lobby. The rustic dining room, a freestanding building, was built at the west end of the main hotel, separated from the cottages. This dining room, decorated with deer and moose antlers and designed for the use of the occupants of the cottages, was considered more exclusive. The same central kitchen served both the main dining room and the rustic dining room.

Mrs. Williams closely supervised the waitresses. She sat in a straight chair at the bottom of the stairway that led

PATRICK CROWLEY

One of the original occupants of a rustic cottage at Lake View Lodge was Patrick E. Crowley, president of the New York Central Railroad. Crowley had his own private railroad car, but he often traveled to Big Moose incognito, sitting among ordinary passengers in order to quiz them about the service. When he was expected to arrive in his private car, however, Big Moose residents would gather at the station to see his descent. Crowley was a small man, and a porter would precede him with a portable step. The jovial Crowley would then emerge, eager to meet the waiting locals. He sometimes brought an organ grinder with a monkey for the amusement of the children.

Although there are stories that Crowley had his own railroad turntable at Big Moose Station, the arrangement that enabled his car to turn around was actually a *wye*. A wye is a roughly triangular piece of track (shaped like an upside-down "Y") leading off the main track. The tail of the Y is very long, making it possible for an engine to push a car, along with its own engine, onto the straight tail and then pull it back on to the main line on the opposite leg of the Y. The car is then facing in the opposite direction. Remains of the wye at Big Moose are still visible on the west side of the station running back into the woods, although much of the track was taken up and used for fill at the Kingsford camp.[51]

Crowley and his family—his wife, two sons, and two daughters—would stay throughout the summer. After he retired, Crowley continued to vacation at Lake View, using a wheelchair to move along the sidewalks between his cottage and the hotel.

The boathouses at Lake View Lodge, ca. 1920.
Courtesy of Frank Carey.

from the waitresses' quarters so she could make sure they were properly dressed. The girls wore black and white uniforms and were required to wear stockings even on the hottest days. Joy Waldau Hostage recalls working at the hotel in the early 1940s. She and her friends found that a line carefully drawn with eyebrow pencil down the back of a tanned leg, to imitate the seam of a stocking, would deceive even Mrs. Williams's eagle eye. Because the waitresses, at least up until about 1945, were not allowed to write down the guests' orders, their job became an exercise in memory training. Gracie Quimby Flock recalls carrying large, heavy trays with the main dishes in the center surrounded by covered ceramic "monkey dishes" containing such condiments as olives, celery, and pickles—an exercise in balance and strength.

The complex at Lake View Lodge included many buildings, but the boathouse was among the most important. This large rectangular structure, probably built at

the same time as the hotel in 1898, originally stood with its gable end toward the lake. The first floor housed the hotel's large collection of guideboats and canoes. A roller and dolly system built into the floor enabled the boats to be dragged through two wide barn doors and across the dock to the water. Lake View, along with other hotels on the lake, sponsored or participated in the annual summer water carnival or regatta.

Later, after the boathouse was turned so that its long side faced the lake, two smaller boathouses stood at the south end. One housed the gasoline launch, the *Daydream,* which took guests on expeditions around the lake. "Steamboat Bill" Irwin, whose title derived from the days when he actually did run a steamer,[28] piloted the boat. The *Daydream* was scuttled in 1941, perhaps because she had grown too old. The other boathouse was the home of a boat called the *Begum,* a gift from Minnie Maddern Fiske.

Lake View Lodge launch, ca. 1913.
Courtesy of Frank Carey.

Lake View Lodge with addition, 1926.
Courtesy of Frank Carey.

The second floor of the boathouse housed a recreation hall, complete with a shuffleboard court and a jukebox. It provided space for square dances, for church services held in rotation with other hotels, and for the occasional fund-raising show. The doors, which opened onto the second-story porch, helped to cool revelers on hot summer nights.

In 1926, Williams completed an addition at the east end of the hotel that added another thirty-five to forty bedrooms, most with private baths, as well as two large attic dormitories. In its heyday in the late 1920s, Lake View Lodge accommodated about 130 guests.

The first floor of the addition contained the "new living room," with large windows on three sides and a huge fireplace as its focal point. It became the center for bingo, bridge, parlor games, masquerades, and sing-alongs. Charles Williams himself was an avid poker player, and he often invited guests to his private quarters on the main floor for a game.

Also in the new living room, Frederick Hodges from Blue Mountain Lake set up displays of his photographs. Hodges, a pioneer photographer of the Adirondacks, worked from a kiosk in the lobby. While he did visit other hotels around the Big Moose area, he centered his work at Lake View, spending four or more days each week at the hotel. His work, archived at the Adirondack Museum at Blue Mountain Lake, is the subject of several books.

Like the other hotels on the lake, Lake View entertained guests with group hikes and cookouts. Harold Squires, an attractive man with a white brush cut topping his ruddy complexion, organized these outings. Don Mawhinney, now a Crag Point resident, recalls that Squires always wore a khaki uniform and knee-high boots.[29] He was famous for his "cheese dreams," a kind of grilled-cheese sandwich whose recipe is now lost. Squires spent his winters in New York City, where he worked at various times as a fashion model and as a buyer and manager for various department stores, notably Saks, Bloomingdale's, and Altman's. While at Big Moose, he lived, at his request, in a tent set up on a platform above the Owner's House.

Lake View also provided guides to accompany the guests on fishing and hunting expeditions. At various times the guides included Frank Williams, Charles's younger brother; Dick Crego; Gil Puffer, a well-known registered Adirondack guide who married Ann Williams, one of Charles's younger sisters; Pit Smith; George Burdick; and Billy Stevens. Most guides had their favorite territories, which frequently included an open camp or even a closed, bark-covered shelter. Lake View guides often took their clients to Constable Pond to fish or hunt.

Charles Williams was always fond of horses and kept a stable of seven or eight for his guests. In addition, he, with a partner Bernard "Matt" Sullivan, owned a livery stable in Utica. This establishment provided a place for the saddle horses in the winter, although Williams always kept one or two working teams at the hotel year-round to help with drawing wood and ice. Don Mawhinney recalls riding a white horse in the 1940s called Major, who was proud of his appearance and hated to get dirty. Major used to gallop along the trails until he came to a puddle, where he was likely to swerve without warning, leaving his rider to dodge low-hanging branches or risk falling into the puddle himself.

Fred Williams, Charles Williams's son, developed an extensive network of bridle trails that stretched to Moss

Lake, as far out as Lake Rondaxe, around Dart's Lake, along the Martin Road past the Glennmore and the Waldheim, as well as closer to Lake View along the south shore. Some of these trails were built during the Depression as public-works projects. For many years an annual horse show, usually held at Dart's Hotel, was a feature of the summer. Lake View was the last hotel to maintain a blacksmith shop, which remained usable until at least 1950. In later years, Jean Daiker Johnson, still a resident of the North Shore, was a riding instructor at Lake View.

Among the other amusements was the game of horseshoes, which was very popular among the male guests. Charles Adams remembers that the men frequently wagered on the outcome of the games. Young Charlie was often able to hustle bets at a nickel a point by challenging unsuspecting new guests to games.

Baseball was another recreation for guests and staff alike. Most of the hotels had their own baseball field, and Lake View's was near the place where the Big Moose Fire Hall now stands. Competition ran for the entire summer and was particularly fierce between Lake View and the Glennmore Ghosts. Indeed, rivalry was so intense that young men who sought work for the season at some hotels (Higby's among them) would not be hired unless they were skilled baseball players. Guests were often recruited to play, and the late Hamilton S. White played during the 1930s. About once a summer during the 1930s, an enterprising man would appear, hauling donkeys in a truck. A game of donkey baseball would follow, with players poised to cajole the donkeys around the bases once the ball had been hit. These games always drew large crowds of people ready to shout advice.

A tennis court stood at the top of the hill on the opposite side of the Big Moose-Eagle Bay Road. The cement court, constructed with a wire net and macadam seams between the concrete slabs, is now the property of the Town of Webb and is still in use.

Indoor amusements included pool and table tennis in rooms at the basement level. After Prohibition ended, a bar was built in this area. For the convenience of the guests, a barber shop was located on the same level.

Like the other hotels, Lake View tried to be totally self-sufficient. Cows provided fresh milk and dairy products. Chickens supplied eggs and meat. Pigs were raised and slaughtered. A large garden, located on both sides of the Big Moose Road and maintained by a full-time gardener, provided fresh vegetables in season. The giant icehouse, filled with ice from the lake in winter, helped to preserve food and supplied ice that was delivered daily to the wooden iceboxes on the rear porch of each cottage.

Several woodlots supplied lumber and firewood, which was delivered daily to the cottages. The first lot was on land behind North Bay purchased from L. Warnick Brown (lots 262–302). For a time this area was used also for commercial lumbering. The shell of the old lumber camp still exists and is now on Waldheim property. A second woodlot near Mays Lake was acquired later, probably during the 1930s. Other wood came from properties above the road to Eagle Bay and along the North Branch of the Moose River below Dart's Lake.

Lake View Lodge thrived during the Depression, perhaps because most of the guests were affluent enough or sophisticated enough to weather the economic storm. The hotel was free of debt and continued to attract guests during World War II.

Charles Williams also had business interests elsewhere, including the large livery stable, horse trading, and transportation company of Sullivan and Williams in Utica. In addition he was a founder and director of the Old Forge Bank, along with his son, Charles Frederick (1887–1979), who, in the 1920s, became a partner with his father in the hotel. In the 1930s and 1940s, two families, related by marriage, helped to operate and manage the hotel. George Deis and his wife, Mary Louise, a daughter of Fred, worked along with Perry "Pit" Smith. Smith had arrived as a guide and later married Fred's daughter, Elizabeth, known as Nibs. When Charles Williams died in 1945, his son Fred continued to operate Lake View, with the daughters' families as the active managers.

Fred was a genial host and was well liked. He circulated among his guests dressed in a suit, dress shirt, and bow tie. His voice was gentle and warm, yet commanding. While not as aggressive as his father, he was more as-

Fred Williams, ca. 1930. Courtesy of Lynda Kellogg.

tute in business management. Among other activities, he was a lumber specialist.

Fred also was very much involved in community affairs. When the first community schoolhouse, behind Burdick's Hotel, burned in 1918, Fred arranged for Lake View sleighs or carriages to provide bus service to take the children to the school at Big Moose Station. For fifty years he sat on the local school board.

Along with his father, Fred Williams was active in the Town of Webb and the Herkimer County Republican Party. Through his political connections, he was able to bring public-works projects into the area to provide off-season employment. By donating land behind the hotel, he persuaded the Town of Webb to build a ski hill for children. (Alice Martin is said to have had a hand in this venture.) He was also a partner in the real estate firm that developed McCauley Mountain. Fred was influential in getting the county to improve the road between Eagle Bay and Big Moose, dealing with the persistent problem of frost heaves and potholes caused by the underlying stone and corduroy base, and straightening the curves at Kingsford's Hill and the Cascade corner. A section where the road widens for parking for the trail to Sis and Bub Lakes was often called "the Fred Williams Memorial Highway."

After World War II, as roads improved and automobiles came into common use, guests who had once come to the hotel for a month or for the whole summer remained for shorter periods of time or spent their vacations touring the countryside. Fred's son-in-law, George Deis, and his daughter Mary Louise managed the hotel during the postwar years. Nevertheless, business at Lake View gradually declined, as it did at most large hotels in the Adirondacks.

In 1957, when he was about seventy years old, Fred Williams concluded that changing lifestyles foreshadowed a difficult future for Lake View Lodge. He called in Charles Vosburgh, an auctioneer from Boonville, who conducted an auction over the weekend of July 4–5. The cottages, boats, and most of the barns and outbuildings were sold. Fred retained the Owner's Cottage (now called Williams) and some of the barns and land. At a second auction in the early 1960s, the hotel and everything but his own cottage were sold.

In 1960, his first wife having died, Fred married Olive S. Freeman, a newspaperwoman from Utica who was active in the Republican Party. The couple spent time at the cottage until Fred's death in 1979 at the age of ninety-two.

The new owner of the hotel operated it for only a short time, after which it reverted to Fred Williams. Barney and Betty Barnum of Dart's Lake then purchased it from Fred and ran it for two years. They, too, found that it was not a viable enterprise. Not only had vacation habits changed, but also the Barnums found it difficult to attract local residents to the dining room, because Williams had previously reserved the restaurant for Lake View guests.

After the Barnums sold the hotel, the building may have passed through other hands before O. W. Hubbell, a businessman and owner of the Tojenka camp, bought it. Hubbell sold the hotel to Edward and Janis Legere of Scotia, New York, in the winter of 1968–69. Legere, with a friend, anticipated using the building as two private camps. Legere later bought out his partner, and for a time his daughter and son-in-law used part of the west end of the hotel. The westernmost section of the original building has now been torn down, and Legere owns the entire structure. The 1926 addition, although partially remodeled in the interior, remains almost intact. Recent changes include the terracing of the front lawn to make it easier to maintain and to enhance the lakeside appearance. The cottages and various outbuildings are also now in the hands of private owners, who have formed an association to maintain the roads and common areas.

The Hotel Glennmore, 1899

THE EARLY YEARS

No pretense of woodsiness here. No bark-covered half-logs or pine-needle trails leading to rustic cottages. The Hotel Glennmore's main building was blatantly modern and utilitarian for its time—a clapboard-sided structure that rose five stories above the lake and dominated the end of West Bay.

The green lawn in front of the hotel was dotted with hydrangea bushes. Concrete sidewalks made walking easy—ideal for ladies in high heels. A macadamed road circled a formal flowerbed, at the center of which rose a flagpole floating an American flag. Not what anyone would call a classic Adirondack camp, but, because of its location at the end of the station-to-lake road, the Glennmore was the "downtown" of Big Moose Lake during its heyday in the 1920s and 1930s. Vacationers from around the lake would tie up at the public dock to buy necessities

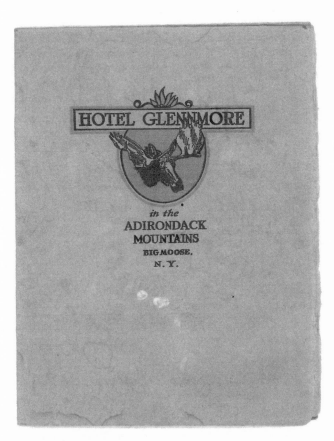

Cover of a Hotel Glennmore brochure, ca. 1920. Courtesy of William S. Scheffler.

at the store or to gas up their boats. They also came to play a round of miniature golf or a game of tennis, to sit down for a haircut, to enjoy a Sunday baseball game, or to dance the night away in the "casino" (as it was known, even though there was never any gambling) above the boathouse.

Built in 1899, the Hotel Glennmore, the fourth hotel at Big Moose Lake, was no doubt named for Sperry's in-laws, William Glenn and Daisy Sperry Glenn, hence the two "n"s. Early photographs and post cards confirm this spelling, but later one "n" was dropped.

Details of the Glennmore's early years are few. Although there were other managers, Philo Wood held the job from 1901 through 1903. An invoice dated July 17, 1902, indicates that the room rates were $2 to $3 per day, and that the hotel featured "long-distance telephone, steam heat, electric bells and gas in every room." By 1906, when Chester Gillette and Grace Brown registered at the hotel, Andrew Morrison was the proprietor, and it was his father who rented the couple the boat that carried them to the ill-fated tryst upon which Theodore Dreiser based his 1925 novel, *An American Tragedy.*

Over the years, the Glennmore grew into a large complex of buildings. At one point, four guest cottages were added to the east along the shore—the White Cottage near the hotel's main building, the Green Cottage a little farther along the sidewalk, then the Taylor Cottage (named for the family that for years vacationed there and later changed to the Davis Cottage), and finally the Hinman Cottage down where the sidewalk gives way to the lake trail with its woods and wild blueberry bushes. Later on, three more cottages were added along the shore on the hotel's opposite side—the Bell, Fitzgerald, and Walker—also named after the families who used them.

On the lakeshore, just to the south of the main building, stood the steamboat landing and the boathouse where Gillette had rented the boat. The boathouse was moved to the east in 1911, and a larger one took its place.

The Hotel Glennmore sign at the Glennmore public dock, ca. 1920s. Courtesy of Wanda K. Martin.

Three cottages southwest of the Hotel Glennmore: the Walker, the Bell, and the Fitzgerald, ca. 1930s. Courtesy of Caroline Seaman.

The new boathouse had four boat slips and, above them on the second floor, the dance hall.

The main hotel building was also surrounded by structures. Across the Glennmore Road stood the store that served the Big Moose Supply Company. An icehouse was connected to the meat coolers at the store, and another stood directly in back of the hotel kitchen. The hotel's woodshed was underneath the second-floor waitress quarters in the alley behind the hotel. Beyond the woodshed were a couple of rooms reserved for the cooks. The tennis court was between the alley and the Glennmore Road, and northwest along the Glennmore Road were the rest of the service buildings—a barn for the horses, garages for automobiles and equipment, and one large outbuilding that accommodated two electrical generators that powered the hotel and the store. At one end of that building sat two huge Fairbanks-Morse single-cylinder gasoline engines, each with two flywheels five or six feet in diameter, which were used to drive the generators. For years, Henry Callahan, the engineer, operated and maintained these behemoths.

At some time around 1912, the ground floor of the main hotel building was changed to house a barroom to augment the dining space on the first floor. An undated brochure from about this time listed the room rate at $5 per day.

THE GLENNMORE'S GOLDEN YEARS

An important shareholder of the Hotel Glennmore Corporation was Harry Kellogg of Glens Falls, New York. Kellogg had come to Big Moose with the Bissell and Yousey Lumber Company around 1914, when they opened their sawmill operation on the lake. His father,

Hotel Glennmore's boathouses, 1911; the two-slip boathouse was moved to make space for the larger one. Courtesy of Frank Carey.

*Harry and Gertrude Kellogg, ca. 1930. Courtesy of
Harry Kellogg, Jr.*

Ashley Tupper Kellogg, was married to Carrie Bissell, sister of the co-owner of the Lumber Company. According to Harry's son Gordon, Ashley Kellogg was quite a wheeler-dealer and had his fingers in a number of enterprises in his hometown. He probably left a significant estate, and Gordon believes that Harry Kellogg bought the hotel with an inheritance from his father. There were other investors, but Gordon also believes that the bulk of the money, besides Harry's inheritance, came from Harry's three sisters. Harry Kellogg assumed the management of the Glennmore shortly after Dwight Sperry relinquished his interest in the property, and so began what many consider to be the hotel's golden years.

Harry was handsome, gregarious, and relaxed. He met his wife, Gertrude Keenan, one summer when she and her family from New York City vacationed at the hotel. Gertrude, a pretty girl with stylishly bobbed hair,

dimples, and a hint of a pug nose, appealed to the nattily dressed, prematurely balding resort manager. Gertrude chose to give up her city life, and they were married in April 1920.

During the years that Harry Kellogg ran the hotel, the building underwent steady changes. Balconies opening off the second floor were added under the main two-story porch. Cement sidewalks replaced slippery wooden walkways. In place of slender posts, tapering stone piers supported the main porch. In the late 1920s or early 1930s, the hotel expanded, adding a large wing to the east end that brought its capacity up to about two hundred guests. Dormer windows in the roof created space for more rooms on the fifth floor. The hotel had its own dock on the waterfront just to the east of the public landing used by the boats of the Transportation Company. There was every facility to make guests comfortable.

Harry's son Gordon had this to say:

Guests frequently arrived around the Fourth of July and stayed most of the summer. The breadwinner would return to the city to take care of his business from time to time and leave the family at the hotel. New York City provided a good portion of the guests and Mr. Kellogg advertised in the papers there. He had no middle name and he devised a method to discern which paper was the most helpful by listing his name in the ad as Harry T. Kellogg, Prop. for the *Tribune,* Harry S. Kellogg, Prop. for the New York *Sun,* etc.

June was not a good time for guests because of the black flies, punkies, mosquitos, and deerflies. September was cool and school was back in session. A few hayfever sufferers showed up as the ragweed was not as prevalent in the mountains. Also a few Catholic retreats

*The renovated and expanded Glennmore Hotel,
with the launch* Big Moose *at the public dock,
ca. 1935. Courtesy Wanda K. Martin.*

were tried in the fall which turned out to be a financial disaster. Thus there remained only July and August to make a living for the whole year. Even then I remember late August being chilly and guests leaving early.

Many good times were had at the hotel by guests and help alike, and the hotel owner's two little boys [Gordon and his brother Harry] were in the thick of it and enjoyed it all!

The water for the hotel came from a spring in a little hollow about 150 yards from the hotel. It was Jim McAllister's job to fill the glass bottles and bring them to the water coolers on the porch. Lynda, Harry Jr.'s wife and granddaughter to Fred Williams, who was then running Lake View Lodge, and I engaged in arguments as to whose spring water was better, Glennmore's or Lake View's.[30]

The hotel also featured a large game room with table tennis and a pool table, as well as a barber shop and restrooms. In the crook of the stairs leading to the lobby floor was a brightly colored Wurlitzer jukebox stocked with all the latest tunes by the Ink Spots, the Mills Brothers, the Andrews Sisters, Benny Goodman, Tommy and Jimmy Dorsey, Glenn Miller, Artie Shaw, and many other popular musicians.

George Byer presided over the hotel's barbershop, which was jokingly referred to as "George's Clip Joint." George was a fascinating man with an unusual and winning personality. Tall and lanky with a head of black curls, he traded off days between the Higby Club and the Glennmore, and each hotel claimed him as its own. Gordon Kellogg tells of an incident involving George, himself, and his best buddy, Lawrence Potter. (The Joel Potter family, employed by the Woodburys on the North Shore, was living at that time in the Transportation House on the Glennmore Road, a house originally built by Sperry to accommodate his Big Moose Transportation Company workers.)

It seems that Gordon and Larry found that George was up a ladder painting his shop and began to tease him. When George had had enough, he descended the ladder with some mischief of his own in mind, and the two youths took flight. Gordon ran up the road but Larry bolted toward the lake with George, armed with his paintbrush, in hot pursuit. At the public landing he cornered Larry and painted his nose. In later years, George moved to Alaska, where he must have been equally well liked, because he was elected mayor of Anchorage.

Outside the game room on the hotel's ground-level

porch, elderly Jim McAllister could often be found in a rocking chair, enjoying his pipe and his semi-retirement, and holding listeners enthralled with tales of the buckboard and carriage days and his role in the Grace Brown–Chester Gillette murder case.

The barroom was at the east end of the porch. During Prohibition, it served as a tearoom and an ice cream parlor. After repeal of Prohibition, it again became a popular nightspot for hotel guests.

Every summer, Kellogg hired a head chef out of New York City and paid him $100 a week, a generous wage in those days. An African American with very dark skin, the chef was a formidable presence in the kitchen, and no one doubted for a moment that he was boss. Because of his culinary expertise, the Glennmore in the remoteness of the forest was able to offer the finest gourmet cuisine to its guests.

Dances were held in the casino over the boathouse, where there was a spacious dance floor, a raised bandstand, and a piano in one corner. The music was provided by Pete Masson, whose father had at one time been stationmaster at Big Moose Station. Pete played the trumpet and wrote the signature theme song for the orchestra that he put together each summer. On the evenings that they played, they would sign off with "There's a Jack for Every Jill," Pete's tender love ballad.

Jean Seavey Humphrey, a longtime summer resident of the lake, recalls in her unpublished memoir the impact that the Glennmore had on her:

The most exciting nights of our lives, when we were 10 or 11, started at the Casino. The big band sound coming over the water, moonlit or rain soaked, was magic.

I went there once with my friend who was a hotel guest. I was entranced watching the dancing couples swirl across the floor. After that, our dear Aunt Jane would take my sister and me through the woods, even in the rain, where we would leave our rubbers under a bush at the beginning of the hotel sidewalk. We hurried on to the Casino, leaving Aunt Jane to write letters in the writing room off the lobby. For a whole hour we sat on the benches around the floor, just watching. She must have been part saint to have done such things for us with always a spirit of pleasure. After that wondrous hour, we tramped through the woods again, back to camp, where there was usually almost as much going on right there.

[Later,] all grown up and ready to dance with boys (if ever one would ask), Aunt Jane was finally relieved of her trip through the woods. We would start out with the girls on the trail, each with a canoe (no life jackets but all good swimmers), paddling our own canoes. Grace Collins stopped for the Seavey girls, then on to pick up Joy Waldau and any visitors in our area. If we did not have feet on the floor when the first note sounded, we were late, a revolting situation, usually blamed on Mid Seavey, who had a "slow-starting" canoe. Eventually, boys did ask us to dance and sometimes one would be allowed to paddle us home. He would take the canoe and return it the next morning. This was a very good arrangement, since it insured seeing the boy at least once more. All this usually involved Aunt Jane's molasses cookies on the porch and great making of plans for the day ahead.

When I see the old building still standing, overlooking the lake, I want to remind it that, like us, it was once young and beautiful with memories to match.[31]

No history of the Glennmore would be complete without mention of the two bachelors who worked for many years at the hotel—Floyd Mitchell and Ray Sanderson. Floyd, nicknamed "Skinny" because he barely cast a shadow, had no special title but was a jack-of-all-trades. Skinny had a penchant for hard liquor, and after the Glennmore closed for good, he went to Utica and disappeared for a while, later returning to the lake for a short time. Ray, among other duties, drove the wood-sided station wagon to the train to pick up hotel guests. Ray married Hazel Glenn, the daughter of William and Daisy Glenn, who had sold the Glennmore site to Hazel's Uncle Dwight Sperry. She had worked at the hotel as head housekeeper. Ray and Hazel eventually retired and lived in Old Forge for their remaining years.

The hotel, Kinne's Boat Line, and Forkey's Big Moose Supply Company, all of them businesses that operated in the Glennmore Hotel area, worked in close harmony. All three attracted people from all over the lake, and it was an ideal situation. But times were changing; that little urban spot beside the beautiful lake thrived at the just the right time—and in just the right place—and will never be seen again.

THE FINAL YEARS

Several factors contributed to the sad ending of this popular resort, and most of them had a similar effect on nearly all of the hotels around the lake and throughout the Adirondacks. The advent of the automobile made an enormous difference. People now found themselves mobile and free to travel and see the world rather than vacationing in just one spot. Also, the general decline of the economy after the crash of 1929 meant that many Americans had less (or no) money to spend on nonessentials such as vacations. Later, World War II, with gasoline rationing and the six-day work week, limited access even for people who were less affected by the Depression.

During this period, the hotel had minimal success and slowly declined in spite of Kellogg's valiant efforts. The Glennmore Corporation had borrowed money from Harry Kellogg's sisters and the Old Forge National Bank. Eventually, it was unable to meet the payments. In 1942, Daisy Kellogg Grogan, one of Harry's sisters, began foreclosure proceedings against the corporation. That summer, neither the store nor the hotel opened for the season. The bank, realizing that the investment was at risk, arranged to have everything removed from the hotel in one day (June 30) and put into storage in Eagle Bay. To protect her interests, Daisy Grogan engaged Laverne Orvis from Albany as her attorney, in an effort to retrieve at least some of the money she had lost.

Gordon Kellogg remembers that, in time, his father's other sisters, who were not getting their due, joined in the lawsuit and foreclosed. "I can't say as I blame them," he said, "but the money trail is vague at this point. [And], as you may imagine, a permanent rift developed between my father and his sisters which existed to almost the end of their time on earth."[32] For his services, Orvis was given the Glennmore's Hinman Cottage, which is still in the Orvis family. Daisy Grogan also deeded to Orvis the parcel of land where the then-defunct Big Moose Lake School had been located. He, in turn, gave it to the State of New York as a trailhead for West Pond and Safford Pond. The area is now labeled "Orvis School House/Trailhead Parking." Although the lake schoolhouse stood on the site, there never was an Orvis Schoolhouse.

With the closing of the Glennmore Hotel, the end of Kinne's Boat Line, and the demise of Forkey's store, the area stood idle for four summers. In 1946, a Mr. Kleinman partly refurbished the hotel and tried to operate it for a couple of years, but with little success. In 1948, the hotel was leased to a Michael Conry, but he did no better. Then, one night in September 1950, fire ravaged the hotel building, taking with it the nearby White Cottage.

Bill Dunn's eyewitness account of the conflagration follows:

Shortly after Labor Day in 1950, I was awakened by very loud explosions [caused by exploding propane tanks]. About the same time, Uncle Charlie Dunn, who was living with us at the time, banged on our bedroom door.

"Boys," he yelled, "let's go, the Glennmore is afire!"

Since we lived only a short distance west of the hotel, we (Uncle Charlie, my brother Nelson and I) ran over and were the first people on the scene. Soon George Deis and Uncle Walt Dunn arrived with the Big Moose fire truck. The building was by this time totally engulfed in flames. Since it sat quite close to the road that led to the lakeshore, the truck drivers paused for a few seconds, pondering whether to drive so close to a fiercely burning building for fear of entrapping and endangering the equipment. But it was the only way to get the fire truck to water, so they drove it down to the public landing adjoining the former Kinne Boat Service. Soon, fire-fighting equipment arrived from Inlet and Old Forge, but it was too late. The fire simply had too much of a head start. Water was pumped all that night, but by daylight the entire structure had been leveled. One piece of fire equipment was left to pump water to put out remaining hot spots. I was the fireman elected to remain for this mopping-up operation.[33]

Wanda Kinne Martin remembers watching the conflagration from the Kinne dock in West Bay, and Grace Vander Veer McDonough could see the flames from the Vander Veer house at the other end of the lake, some three and one-half miles away.

RECOLLECTION OF THE GLENNMORE FIRE | *Bill Lux*

The fire that destroyed the Glennmore happened at night. When we heard the fire siren, I went out in the boat so I could see [Echo] Island, and those flames were twice as high as the tallest trees on the island. We all knew the Glennmore was doomed. Meanwhile, the fireboat had left its berth in the boathouse [in Higby Bay] and gone around to the front dock to pick up Roy Higby. Bill Judson was driving, and Ray Hanlon and Don Lux were the crew. Bill hit the front dock when he picked up Roy, and part way down the lake Ray noticed that the water was getting deep in the boat. They made it about to Lake View, where they abandoned ship and went the rest of the way by road.

Rumors of arson circulated, because the four corners of the building appeared to have caught fire simultaneously. Gordon Kellogg observes, "The next day, the fire insurance was due to lapse, but that is just hearsay."[34] Bud Dunn was briefly a suspect because, according to his sister-in-law Ann Dunn, he had once casually remarked, "They ought to burn the Glennmore down." However, at the time of the fire, he was in Scarsdale, New York. Walt Dunn, Bud's father, testified at the arson hearing. The judge asked, "Did you see all four corners aflame?" Walt replied, "Any damn fool knows you can't see four corners all at once!"

Whatever the speculations were in the aftermath of the fire, no foul play has ever been proved. What we do know is that, true to its character, the Hotel Glennmore went out in a blaze of glory.

Burdick's, Waterman's, and the Big Moose Inn, 1903

BURDICK'S CAMP

In 1903, a fifth hotel appeared on the lake when Burdick's Camp opened for business. The year before, George Burdick had bought seven lots (lots 6–12) from Charles Williams on the south shore of West Bay and contracted with E. J. Martin to build the new hotel.

Compared with the Glennmore and Lake View Lodge, Burdick's Camp was modest. It was just 24 feet by 30 feet in size and constructed of milled lumber. The second floor had no more than eight rooms. The cost of $1,100 was modest indeed. But the building sat on a gentle rise above the lake and had a commanding view of West Bay. Burdick and Martin signed the contract on May 15, 1902, and the work was to be completed within two months, by July 15 of that year.

George Burdick was yet another Lewis County immigrant to Big Moose. A short, stocky, dark-complexioned man, he was considered one of the best Adirondack guides in the area.[35] With the help of his wife, Bertha, and son Theodore, he maintained a very successful enterprise for almost twenty years, in large measure because of his reputation as a guide. Bertha Burdick is remembered as a prim and proper lady. However, although she dressed conservatively when it was called for, she was not above rolling up her sleeves to chop wood or joining the men in their rigorous ice-harvesting efforts.

Burdick's success enabled him to expand the hotel. By

Cover of an early Burdick's Camp brochure. Courtesy of William S. Scheffler.

George Burdick as a guide, clowning around with his axe, ca. 1900. Courtesy of Wanda K. Martin.

1915 he had added a wing to the west side, creating more public space on the lower floor and a greater number of guest rooms upstairs.

George Burdick could be eccentric and unpredictable—some said ornery. Children often kept their distance from him. Indeed, when the first school at Big Moose Lake was built almost across the Big Moose Road from Burdick's Camp, it soon became apparent that the school and the noisy children were an irritant to Burdick. Bill Dunn claims that to his knowledge, the children never harassed Burdick or his property, but their very presence seemed to aggravate him.

One cold winter morning, the school burned to the ground. Rumors immediately started that George Bur-

dick had set it aflame. Some people even claimed that he had been seen carrying a can of kerosene that morning. However, Walter Dunn related this story to his nephew Bill:

> [As an eighth grader,] I was the janitor when the school burned. I would get up early in the morning, walk from Rose Cottage to the school, start the fire in the wood space heater in the middle of the school room, then go home to eat breakfast. When we would get to class, the schoolhouse would be nice and warm. I remember the morning of the fire well. I was running real late getting to school to start the fire and in a hurry to get back to Rose Cottage to eat breakfast. I may have forgotten to set the chimney damper. If I did, the fire in the firebox probably started to burn furiously. It could have overheated the stovepipe and started a fire where the pipe went to the outside.[36]

George Burdick was never charged with arson.

Some time in the early 1920s, Burdick sold the hotel operation to a young couple with a small son, keeping for himself the eastern half of the property. Two years later, the son drowned off the hotel's dock. Grief-stricken, the couple sold the hotel to Leonard Waterman of Syracuse, New York.

When George Burdick sold the hotel, Waterman claimed that Burdick had made a verbal agreement that he would not build another hotel on the section of the land that he had kept. Whether or not Waterman's asser-

Completed Burdick's Camp, ca. 1906.
Courtesy of Frank Carey.

Burdick's Camp with addition, ca. 1915.
Courtesy of Frank Carey.

The New Burdick Camp, ca. 1925.
Courtesy of Frank Carey.

tion was true, Burdick did build another hotel with three cottages, which he named the New Burdick Camp. Waterman was incensed. About 1925, perhaps out of spite, he built a two-story boathouse and dance hall immediately adjacent to Burdick's property. This building effectively blocked the view of much of West Bay from the New Burdick Camp's front and side porches.

Some suspected George Burdick of starting the fire that destroyed the Big Moose Chapel the night before it was to be dedicated on July 20, 1930. However, both Bob McAllister and Bill Dunn have effectively dispelled that rumor, explaining that the cause was very likely spontaneous combustion from oily rags: they had been used that day to seal the wood finish and hastily left in a closet.

The cover of the New Burdick Camp brochure, ca. early 1920s. Courtesy of William S. Scheffler.

Shortly after the chapel fire, George Burdick was found dead in a small shed that adjoined the icehouse and cooler of his New Burdick Camp, an apparent suicide from a gunshot wound. It was a sad and violent end for a colorful and controversial man.

After Burdick's death, his widow and son ran the New Burdick Camp with limited success until 1939, when they sold it to Paul Allen. Bertha and Theodore Burdick retained one of the cottages between the lake and the Big Moose Road, however, winterizing it and living there until 1946. Eventually, Theodore became ill and virtually bedridden, which prompted the Burdicks to move to Boonville, New York, and eventually to Lowville.

Paul Allen soon saw that he was not going to make a success of the New Burdick Camp, so in 1940, he sold the hotel to Walter and Bertha Dunn, who changed the name to Dunn's Lodge. A few years later, they too closed their doors, concentrating instead on the boat service and their other enterprises.

WATERMAN'S CAMP

Under Waterman's ownership, Burdick's original camp, renamed Waterman's Camp, remained a viable business enterprise for several years. Nevertheless, like other resort hotels on the lake, it felt the effects of the Depression, World War II, and the popularization of the automobile at the end of the war. Hotel patronage started to decline, leaving the owners with only the taproom-restaurant and guiding for deer hunters as their main sources of income. At the end of the 1946 summer season, Leonard Waterman sold his camp to Dorothy and William Ebel of Albany, New York. He then left Big Moose and bought a small inn with a restaurant and taproom in Brewerton, New York.

THE BIG MOOSE INN

The Ebels changed the name of their purchase to the Big Moose Inn, but they generally followed the pattern set by the Watermans in their later years, concentrating on the bar and restaurant business and paying minimal attention to the hotel. Sometime in the early 1950s, Ebel tore down the boathouse and dance hall, which by that time had fallen into serious disrepair. With the lumber that was salvaged, he built a dance hall east of the hotel and back from the lake. This did little to improve business, how-

Boathouse built by Leonard Waterman shortly after purchasing the original Burdick's Camp, ca. 1930. Courtesy of Frank Carey.

ever, and about 1955, the Ebels sold the Big Moose Inn to Ralph E. Hutchins.

Hutchins did not operate the bar and restaurant for long. On August 10, 1957, the Big Moose Inn went on Charles Vosburgh's auction block. Concerned that the inn could evolve into an undesirable operation, Frank Newman, owner of Stag's Leap, purchased it.

Newman then talked Betty and Barney Barnum, who were operating Lake View Lodge at the time, into managing the inn. The Barnums first leased it from Newman and later bought the hotel. For eleven years they operated a dining room and a small bar and rented a few rooms. The bar became a hangout for young people on the lake, but the Barnums managed it carefully and never served alcohol to anyone under age.

In 1968, Douglas and Bonnie Bennett bought the Big Moose Inn—now affectionately referred to as the BMI—and have operated it successfully ever since as a restaurant with a bar and sleeping accommodations. The Bennetts operate the BMI year-round, catering not only to summer vacationers but also to hunters and snowmobilers. The dance hall remained in the Barnums' hands until 1989, when the Bennetts bought it in order to put in a new 600-foot well at that location. The Bennetts remember fondly the square dances that were held there when they were dating in the 1960s.

Not much changed in the basic architecture of the original Burdick's Camp over the first sixty years or so, although a fire did destroy the roof on the western end of the building. However, shortly after the Bennetts took over, the collapse of the greater part of the front porch prompted the Bennetts to expand the dining room. In 1985, the Bennetts remodeled the rooms above the living room, and four years later they built the Fireside Room and the office. In 1992, the dining room was remodeled,

and the entire front of the building was rebuilt to accommodate twelve rooms with private baths, eleven of them overlooking the lake.

When asked if they rented rooms in the beginning, Bonnie replied:

> We did rent rooms to hunters in the beginning, giving them room, breakfast, dinner and a bag lunch for $7.00. As we had only one employee (after a fashion) in those days, Doug and I were meeting ourselves coming and going during the hunting season. We even put a cot in the dining room for a nap between closing the bar with hunters around 2:30 and awakening to serve breakfast for them at 4:30. Doug had to knock on doors to awaken them (that was part of the ritual). I was not allowed in the bar during the hunting season—but I was the cook, dishwasher, and late-night sandwich maker for the bag lunches. I was also the breakfast assistant to Doug. I guess we were both servers—can't remember. And in between we got our son Scott off to school.
>
> We did not (enthusiastically) rent rooms in the summer for a couple of years, as we had few employees and couldn't keep up with running the restaurant and bar and being parents at the same time. But we did rent to hunters and snowmobilers. The snowmobile couples would pay $25 for their weekend visit with five meals. They were wonderful, helping me with cleaning the dining room after meals and sometimes even washing dishes. In those days (the days before insulation), the guests would sometimes have ice on the inside of their walls and still be smiling.

Today, the BMI remains a fixture in West Bay, a century after George Burdick hired the Martin brothers to build his modest camp. Indeed, still visible on some of the window casings are the inscribed names of E. J. Martin and his brother Charles.

The Big Moose Inn, 2000. Courtesy of Douglas and Bonnie Bennett.

Cover of a brochure for the Waldheim, ca. 1920.
Courtesy of Wanda K. Martin.

The Waldheim, 1904

Of all the resorts in the Adirondack Park, the Waldheim is one of the oldest and possibly the only one continuously operated by a single family. This enterprise, which preserves many features of the early palisade style of architecture on Big Moose Lake, is the result of the determination and perseverance of one man—the shrewd, irascible, and long-lived Edward Joseph Martin, known to nearly all as "E. J."

Although he died in 1973 at the age of one hundred and one, many people on the lake still remember E. J., a stocky, square-jawed man with penetrating blue eyes surmounted by a tangle of abundant, curly, white hair. As a boss he held his employees to high standards; thus he was feared by the lazy but admired and emulated by the energetic.

E. J. was never known to throw anything away. His grandson-in-law, who now manages the hotel, recalls that the first job he was assigned by E. J. was straightening nails so that they could be reused. After his death, E. J. left behind barns full of mysterious and obsolete machinery and tools, ranging from galvanized-metal water boilers (to be recycled as culverts) to froes for splitting shingles.

In the early 1890s, E. J. and his younger brother Charlie set out to look for employment. The two young men came to Big Moose Lake and found various construction jobs in the area, building camps and working at Dart's Hotel and later at Higby's.

In 1896, E. J. took some time off in the winter and studied at Albany Business College for three months. When he ran out of money and was forced to leave two weeks short of completing the course, the director of the college wrote,

He is a faithful, diligent student, and has won the confidence and respect of associates and teachers.

He is an efficient bookkeeper, accurate and neat in his work. He is capable of keeping any ordinary set of books, and whoever secures his services will have an able and trustworthy assistant.[37]

E. J. returned to the Big Moose area and continued his building activities over the next four years. By 1900, he had a contract to build a hotel for George Burdick on the south side of West Bay. In 1901, when he was only twenty-nine, E. J. was able to buy a large tract of land on the north side of the lake from William Seward Webb. He negotiated a mortgage for $4,000, the equivalent of at least $75,000 in today's currency. The mortgage was held by Arwed Retter, a Utica dentist for whom he had just built a summer home on the point across from the entrance to North Bay. E. J.'s new purchase extended from the east line of the present Traverse property (lot 316, then belonging to John Ellis Roosevelt, a cousin of President Theodore Roosevelt) to just east of the point where the present Waldheim swimming beach is located. After the sale closed, E. J. hastily put up a one-room cabin with a loft.

In January 1902, E. J. married Harriet "Hattie" Eliza Brown, a schoolteacher whom he had met while she was working as head waitress at Higby's. In the depths of that winter he brought her, a brave and energetic soul, to his isolated house. Most likely they traveled by horse-drawn sled from the Big Moose railroad station over a rough road to the lake, and from there across the ice to the cabin.

Between 1902 and 1904, E. J. and Hattie lived in this tiny house while building what is now known as the Main

The Waldheim main camp before a dining room was added, ca. 1905. Courtesy of Wanda K. Martin.

House. This structure, which is still in use today as part of the dining complex, had a living room with a fireplace, a dining room, and a large kitchen on the first floor. On the second floor were five bedrooms ranged along both sides of a corridor. The "modern" bathroom, which was mentioned in the hotel's first brochure and was very unusual for the time, was on the first floor near the kitchen. The bathroom included a claw-footed bathtub and a flush toilet; no doubt the proprietors and their employees used more primitive facilities.

In 1904, with the building complete and ready for occupancy, E. J. and his brother Charlie started in the hotel business together. (The partnership with Charlie lasted only until 1906, however, when E. J. bought out his brother's share.) Their letterhead read, "THE WALDHEIM, Martin Brothers, Proprietors." The name Waldheim— "home in the woods" in German—was a sign of the brothers' Swiss heritage.

The Martin brothers soon attracted paying guests. E. J.'s neighbor, Retter, who naturally wished to see a dependable return on his money, recommended the Waldheim to a lady in Utica who wanted a place "for friends." And so it happened that the very first guests at the Waldheim were the wife of the governor general of Panama, her three grown daughters, a son-in-law, and a Japanese maid. The governor general himself, Major General George W. Davis, joined the group later in the summer. Most of the family stayed all summer,[38] and the income must have given the new enterprise a solid start.

Between the Retter camp on Turtle Point and the Martin property was an extensive piece of land owned by Leslie W. Brown of the Utica cigar-making firm of L.

Warnick Brown Tobacco. In 1900, Brown had purchased, from Webb's Ne-Ha-Sa-Ne Park Association, land that stretched from the east border of the Martin property along the north side of North Bay all the way to the Totten and Crossfield line (lots 262–302). Brown then hired E. J. and his brother Charlie to construct his camp near the entrance to North Bay and facing the main lake,[39] a large log-and-palisade-style structure with porches on three sides. The camp was identical in style to the house west of the Waldheim property (lots 319–21) that they had built for a Dr. Koller (a house later owned for many years by Charles and Alice Martin).

During the first few years after the Waldheim opened, Hattie Martin kept the business going while E. J. worked around the lake, building or helping to build a prodigious number of camps. He hired teams of workmen who built camps under his supervision. Besides the Retter and Brown camps, E. J. built, among others, the twin houses on the North Shore, Edilgra (now owned by the Wertz family), and Brightwood (now owned by the Lux family); five cottages at Lake View Lodge; and the Burtch and Walker camps on the south side of West Bay; as well as two cottages at the Seventh Lake House in Inlet. At the Waldheim, June Cottage (just east of the Main House) was completed in 1905 while Cozy Cottage was finished in 1906; others followed steadily. In 1909, E. J. and Hattie's first son, Everett, was born and a cottage was named after him; a second son, Howard, was born ten years later.

Other activities also demanded E. J.'s attention. He cut firewood for his many fireplaces, and he also had his own crew of men who filled a good share of the icehouses

The Waldheim main house with dining room, after 1909. Courtesy of Wanda K. Martin.

on the lake. In a letter that E. J.'s neighbor, Leslie Warnick Brown, wrote in 1904 to the Martin brothers, he informs E. J. that he has ordered "200 # [yards? pounds?] of barb wire in 50 # spools & 8 # [pounds?] of staples, freight prepaid." He adds, "Am glad to hear that the pasture looks fine and hope my cow will get a crack at it before your cows finish it up."[40] It seems that, not only was E. J. building fences for Brown, but he also kept cows to supply dairy products for himself and his guests. The Waldheim also had a large garden that flourished well after World War II and probably was an even more vital part of the operation in earlier years. E. J. supervised the garden, which included a large raspberry patch, until the 1960s.

At some point in the first decade of the Waldheim's operation, E. J. sold three lots to the west of the house in which he and Hattie lived. The money he accumulated from this and his other activities enabled him to build, in 1909, the large dining room and summer kitchen attached to the Main House. Above the kitchen were five rooms where E. J., Hattie, and some of their employees lived during the summer. E. J. and Hattie slept in separate rooms because their schedules were so different. Hattie rose very early, probably between 3:00 and 4:00 A.M., so that she could use the ovens for the day's baking. Because dinner was served at midday, the chef needed the ovens later in the morning.

In the winter, the heated Main House was available for what was, by 1909, the Martin family of three. When Everett was old enough to attend school, Hattie bought a house in Boonville and spent winters there. She and E. J. visited back and forth on weekends. E. J. would travel by train to Remsen and from there to Boonville, a trip of about two hours. Later, when roads were cut through,

The Waldheim cottage Heart's Content, ca. 1929. Courtesy of Wanda K. Martin.

Family seated in the Waldheim's dining room, 1929. Courtesy of Wanda K. Martin.

The original Waldheim boathouse and office, ca. 1910. Courtesy of Wanda K. Martin.

Hattie drove back and forth, often bringing supplies for the hotel. In some of her letters, Hattie describes her struggles with the primitive roads and early vehicles. In all of his one hundred and one years, E. J. never held a driver's license—which is not to say that he did not drive at all.

The Browns' property was sold in 1920. It passed through various hands, among them those of Charles Williams and Frank and Amelia Naporski, before becoming part of the Waldheim in 1935.

Meanwhile, E. J. and Hattie continued to add to and improve their property. By 1929, they had completed a row of eight cottages along the lakeshore to the east of the Main House. Because each cottage had at least two bedrooms, the hotel's capacity was fairly large. Unlike the custom today, cottages were typically rented to more than one family at a time, and bathrooms were shared. Likewise in the dining room, it was usual to have several couples or families seated at one table. The office, then as now, was attached to the boathouse, because the entire resort was oriented toward the lake, with guests always arriving and departing by boat. But by 1928, the road from Eagle Bay to the Glennmore was in reasonably good shape, and automobiles were beginning to replace the railroad-wagon-boat method of transportation.

As E. J.'s diary attests, ingenuity was never in short supply. In the cold winter of 1929, E. J. persuaded his son Everett, who was home from college, to join him for a short time. They lived in the only insulated building, the Main House, while they lumbered the woods for fuel for the summer and harvested ice from the lake to fill the icehouses. One morning they woke to find a massive invasion of cockroaches in the cellar. Building a fire in a stove in the workshop in a neighboring building, they dragged their mattresses out and closed up the Main House. Within forty-eight hours the house had cooled to the below-zero outside temperature and killed all the pests.

In 1935, the Martins acquired a large tract of land to the east when the small hotel Veery's Nest—located on the property once owned by Leslie Warnick Brown—went out of business. This new acquisition gave the Martins not only a large amount of land but also several buildings that could be converted and added to the Waldheim complex. Although the main house of Veery's Nest had burned in 1929, the Martins converted the woodshed that was nearly lost in the fire into Ivy Cottage, the boathouse that looked out upon North Bay into Whipsaw Cottage, and the playhouse once used by Mr. Brown's daughters into a single-room cottage called Dream Cottage. (This building, never very popular even with honeymooners, was torn down and replaced in 2000 by a new Dream Cottage that faced the open lake.) Two other cot-

The Leslie Brown boathouse on North Bay as it was when the Waldheim acquired it from Veery's Nest, 1935. Courtesy of Wanda K. Martin.

tages, Pointview and Longview, are also legacies from Veery's Nest.

In 1938, E. J. bought from Charles Williams the portion of the Brown parcel not owned by Veery's Nest, extending all the way to the Totten and Crossfield line where New York State land begins (lots 262–93). Much of this land is now owned by Howard Martin's children, Jon, Nancy, and Philip, who have built their own residences on it. The remainder is owned by his grandchildren.

The Waldheim cottage Whipsaw, ca. 1995. Courtesy of Roger Pratt.

The conversions and refurbishings of all the Veery's Nest buildings took time, but with Cedar Lodge and Knoll Cottage (both built in the 1930s) the Waldheim complex was almost complete. Guests continued to find the hotel a welcome retreat, and many stayed for a full month at a time. By the end of the decade, most guests arrived by automobile rather than by train, but the Martin family continued to run the establishment in the traditional way. No alcohol was sold, although guests were free to bring their own. The food was simple and ample, as it is today.

The coming of World War II did not affect the Waldheim business greatly. Gasoline rationing and crowded trains may have made it more difficult for people to get to Big Moose, but somehow they managed. It was, however, extremely difficult to find the cooks, waitresses, and handymen needed to operate the hotel.

Everett Martin, now married, spent the war working as an engineer at General Electric in Schenectady. His younger brother, Howard, attended college for three years and then went into the army, where he saw action in Europe shortly after D-Day. Howard became engaged to Wanda Kinne, who was working at the American Emblem factory in New Hartford after attending business school. When the war was drawing to a close, Howard's mother, Hattie, wrote on April 11, 1945, "We haven't any of us heard a word from Howard since March 4th, his last letters to either Wanda or us. I am so worried. I am so afraid something has happened or that he is started on to Japan with troops."[41] Finally, on May 14 (the war having ended on May 8), Hattie wrote to Everett again: "Wanda just called up from Utica to tell us she had just received a letter from Howard, and he is well and stationed in Germany somewhere. [Wartime regulations forbade soldiers

Wanda and Howard Martin when they managed the Waldheim, 1977. Courtesy of Wanda K. Martin.

E. J. Martin at his desk at the Waldheim, ca. late 1960s. Courtesy of Wanda K. Martin.

from revealing their location.] The letter was written April 30 and mailed May 2nd. He said they didn't get much war news as they didn't have a radio in their barracks, but judging by what they read in a paper they had, the war must be nearly over."[42] Howard was indeed sent home in the fall, and he and Wanda were married in the Big Moose chapel on a snowy Saturday after Thanksgiving in 1945.

Hattie Martin with grandson Jon Martin, 1948. Courtesy of Wanda K. Martin.

With Howard's return, the Waldheim gained welcome help in operating the business. E. J. was then seventy-three years old and Hattie only a few years younger. The transition to Howard's management was gradual. E. J. spent more time in the warmth of the workshop building furniture, one of his favorite activities, while Howard took on the more rugged outdoor responsibilities. The young married couple lived at the Kinne house on the Martin Road because Wanda's mother, the widowed Lillian Kinne, was working in Utica. For the first few years, Wanda was occupied in bringing up their three children, Jon, Nancy, and Philip, who arrived in rapid succession. As soon as the children reached toddlerhood, Wanda hired a babysitter in the summers and took over the office responsibilities. E. J. retained his desk in the office, where he kept an eye on the activities and offered all the advice he deemed necessary. During these years after the war, Howard, aided by E. J., Frank, and Charlie Martin, built a large slab-sided house overlooking the lake beyond Cedar Cottage for his family.

Howard's management ushered in a new era. Such conveniences as tractors, pickup trucks, and backhoes became available after wartime factories reconverted to peacetime production. Just as his father had, Howard took responsibility for all of the mechanical systems that kept the place running. He not only maintained all the cottages, coping with their fireplace, plumbing, and electrical problems, but also oversaw the springs that supplied their water, the access roads, the septic tanks, and all of the other systems necessary to operating a hotel in the country. In addition, Howard was for many years the Waldheim's head chef, running the kitchen with the proverbial iron hand in a velvet glove. Of course, he hired help: the staff grew enormously in the summer, and then, as now, many children of lake residents received their first paychecks from the Waldheim.

During this time, the Waldheim became a favorite place for families with children. Although such guests came for shorter periods than had prewar visitors, they enjoyed having a single cottage to themselves, freedom from television and telephones, and the opportunity for a nearly infinite number of unscheduled outdoor activities. The days of shared bathrooms in the cottages were gone, and the tables in the dining room were limited to groups (families or friends) who were vacationing together. This arrangement was particularly attractive for vacationers who wanted the ambience of the wilderness without the burden of preparing meals.[43]

PROFILE OF HOWARD MARTIN | *Libby Barlow*

I learned to cook from my uncle Howard, who became chef at his own establishment in the 1970s when he got tired of firing cooks and decided to do it himself. I became his apprentice at the age of fifteen. He needed an assistant for the summer, and, because he had a reputation for being unpredictable and sometimes ornery, no one stepped forward to volunteer. I hadn't applied, but Howard picked me anyhow. I met this news with a tiny bit of pride and a great deal of trepidation. He hadn't liked most of his previous assistants, and I had no reason to think I would be different. At that age I was too meek to say no, so I arrived for my first day hoping that he would boot me quickly or, failing that, that I could stay on the other side of the steam table from him at all times.

My first day was a Sunday. Since before time began, the Sunday noon menu had been roast turkey, roast stuffed pork, mashed potatoes, butternut squash, and peas. Howard had just finished the pork gravy. He pointed to the boiling liquid and said, "Stick your finger in it." Pondering the probable effect of the boiling fat on the live flesh of my fingertip, I said, "I'll get a spoon." "No spoons," he said. "Stick your finger in it." So I stuck my finger in it, tasted it, and to my great surprise I lived to type the tale. "Stick your finger in it" was Howard's measure of success for every dish. If you stuck your finger in it and it tasted good, the matter was settled.

I was most distressed to discover that, in the absence of recipes, I would be dependent on Howard for instruction. He owned one cookbook, and it dated from the 1930s. As near as I could tell he used it only as a file folder, sandwiching between its front and back covers the few recipes he kept on paper. These were scraps of paper that listed ingredients only, leaving the reader to identify both the resulting item and the technique for producing it. Worse, there were only a few such recipes. Most of what he made was by sight or by feel. For macaroni and cheese, he would scoop elbows out of a box of bulk macaroni, break "a few" eggs into a bowl, and beat them with milk poured from half-gallon containers until it looked right. Then—often while belting out a phrase or two from "Rock of Ages"—he would grate cheddar cheese

This article was published in slightly different form under the title "Whisky Business" in the *Adirondack Life Annual Guide* for 2000 and is reprinted here with the permission of *Adirondack Life* magazine.

Howard Martin in the kitchen of the Waldheim, 1975. Courtesy of Wanda K. Martin.

until the pile looked to be the right height. He would mix it all together in a large baking pan and top it with bread crumbs, and it always came out perfectly. Howard's method of teaching me how to produce these things often came in the form of chuckles and grunts while he sat in his chair over by the window. He would give the vague instruction of "a few" eggs, then grunt or cough if I was about to put in too many.

Since 1904, when Howard's parents opened the Waldheim, families have come in the summer to stay for up to one month at the Adirondack "camp" in one of the rustic cottages along the shore of Big Moose Lake. The camp is still running, hot water is still generated in many cottages by piping the water through the andirons in the fireplace, a "fire boy" still tiptoes through the cottages to build fires early every morning, and guests still gather three times a day in a central dining room for Adirondack fare. And still, once a week, camp guests are invited to hike together and enjoy a picnic in the tradition of the

Adirondack guides. Upon arrival at the picnic site, the guests are put to work gathering firewood and peeling potatoes. The cook fries a couple of pounds of bacon in a twenty-five-inch skillet and saves the grease for frying the potatoes. After the potatoes are done, steak is grilled for everyone, followed by pancakes with real maple syrup. Camp coffee, made by tying grounds into a piece of cloth and boiling them over the campfire, finishes the meal.

Over time, Howard and I grew to appreciate one another, and he would usually greet my arrival in the kitchen with a mischievous grin and "Libby-Dibby-Doo! How are you?" We began to share ideas and activities from outside the kitchen. I found that the practical approach he took to cooking extended to first aid and medicinal practices as well. Whenever I had an upset stomach, Howard gave me baking soda and water. When I lost a small battle with the meat slicer, Howard healed my finger with judicious applications of bear salve, an ointment he produced from a bear who had met her end after breaking into the kitchen one too many times. When I had a cold, Howard cleared my sinuses by taking me up to the old garden to find some horseradish to grind up and sniff. And when I had the hiccups, Howard would sneak up behind me and bang two heavy aluminum saucepans behind my ears. He didn't have a cure for sleepiness, but when I yawned he would say, "Catching flies?"—a cliché that always gave him a hearty chuckle.

In the lull between meals, Howard would often perch on the stone wall outside the back door to the kitchen, a spot that afforded a view of the lake and the main hub of the camp. Occasionally he would wander down to the office in the boathouse, or even out onto the dock to check the progress of the summer. The trees on the hill behind the southeast corner of the lake are the first to turn, so Howard would keep an eye out starting in early August. In the afternoon before staff dinner, Howard would occasionally take me out on a mystery errand. Often he would toss me in the back of his unregistered, doorless jeep for a jolting ride up to the garden, but once he took me into his workshop out by the old horse stalls and handed me a steel file, apparently long past its prime. Over the course of several days, we converted this file into a buck knife by grinding one end of it into a blade. For a handle, we sawed a piece of deer antler in half and affixed it to the file with copper rivets manufactured from salvaged telephone wire. To keep my hand from slipping off the smooth han-

dle onto the sharp blade, Howard sawed off a quarter-inch piece of brass pipe and flattened it over the file at the top of the handle so that the protruding brass would form an effective—and attractive—barrier. Finally, Howard produced a piece of leather, which he cut to the shape of a sheath. I sewed it closed, and he reinforced it with more copper rivets.

When it came time to prepare dinner for the staff, Howard surveyed the leftovers in the cooler, a thickly insulated room originally cooled by an adjacent icehouse. A compressor keeps this room cool now—a modern innovation but, in a region often without electricity, much less reliable than ice. The walls of the cooler were lined with bins of vegetables, milk cans full of maple syrup, pots of soup stock made from the bones of the week's prime rib or roast turkey, and shelves of meat, cheese, and slow-proofing dough. Howard usually had a concoction or two of his own in the corner—a crock of sauerkraut or corned beef curing, or his own side of beef hanging to age until it turned green on the outside and tender as could be inside.

If we were nearing the end of the season and there were insufficient leftovers for staff, Howard would make an omelet with two dozen eggs in a two-foot frying pan. He turned the omelet over by grasping the handle of the pan with both hands and swinging the pan down toward the floor and up again. Just as he caught the omelet on the other side of the flip he would snicker at me and say, "Ha! Try that at home." Late in the fall when an omelet just didn't suit the turning leaves and cool breeze outside, Howard would make corn fritters. We snatched them from the fryer as soon as they were done and doused them in maple syrup. Howard's corn fritter recipe, written in his inimitable style, is one of the few that reside today on my refrigerator. This is partly a reminder of good food I like to make on occasion and partly a memorial to someone who developed my appreciation of the origins and context of simple cuisine. Howard died when I was twenty-three. Because I was the one who knew her way around his kitchen, I became head cook. I am a master at corn fritters, pancakes, and gravy for roast stuffed pork, and I credit myself with having fingertips of asbestos. I later became executive chef at a Boston restaurant and, although no cooking school would endorse my training, I count what I learned from Howard among my most valuable and marketable skills.[51]

After Howard died in 1985, the rest of the family took over and ran the hotel jointly. However, both Jon and Philip had developed businesses of their own, and in 1993, Nancy Martin Pratt and her husband Roger became the official managers. The Waldheim continues to attract guests who love the peace and quiet of the woods and the lake. The year 2003 marked the Martins' one hundredth year in business operating the Waldheim at Big Moose Lake.

Veery's Nest, 1925
(operated at Camp Veery, 1923–24)

Handsome Frank Naporski was a dapper man who sported a mustache, combed his hair straight back, and habitually wore knickerbockers and colorful socks or riding breeches and high-laced boots.[44] (See illustration on page 243.) Both Frank and his wife, Amelia, spoke with foreign accents, Polish and possibly also French, but this did not seem to slow them down; according to Bill Dunn, the Naporskis "were always jovial and fun to be around."[45]

When it came to running a business, however, Frank Naporski's touch was less successful. During the summers of 1923 and 1924, he ran Minnie Maddern Fiske's Camp Veery on Echo Island as a hotel. Frank borrowed money from his wife to buy dishes, furniture, linens, and other hotel supplies.[46] Amelia knew her husband, and every item was listed in minute detail in a legal contract that ensured that her money would not be lost. At the end of just the second summer, however, Frank and the Fiskes came to a parting of ways.

Cover of brochure for Veery's Nest, ca. 1926. Courtesy of William S. Scheffler.

Undeterred, Frank and Amelia soon borrowed money from E. J. and Hattie Martin[47] and purchased the property between the Waldheim and North Bay that had formerly belonged to Leslie Warnick Brown. On the land stood a complex of buildings that included the large house built in 1900 by E. J. Martin and his brother Charlie. Naporski's plan was to operate the property as a hotel, calling it Veery's Nest. He borrowed the name from the Fiskes' Camp Veery, perhaps in the hope of retaining the clients he had attracted during the two previous summers.

Veery's Nest, ca. 1925. Courtesy of Wanda K. Martin.

For four years, the Naporskis ran Veery's Nest, although we hear little about it. Then, in 1929, disaster struck. That spring, the Naporskis were preparing to open Veery's Nest for the season. On Sunday, April 7, Hattie Martin wrote to her son Everett[48] (who was then an engineering student at Clarkson College):

Thursday noon we had quite a little excitement. I started in cleaning in the Bay window room [in the Main House] Thurs. A.M. Got dinner at noon and during the fore noon I saw Mr. & Mrs. Naporski go past each with a pack basket of provision. They were on their way to Veerys Nest. While I was waiting for Ed and Chas to come to dinner Mr. Naporski came running down [the] walk and said where is your men? I said "down on the road," he said, Oh, my God my main house is all afire. I rushed down stairs and said to him go back up there. I'll call men. He tried to telephone but phone out of order. Howard [Hattie's second son, then nine years old] and I kept up a screaching [sic] of fire till Ed left his work & he and Chas started on run. When near enough I told them. They rushed up there. Kitchen and dining was all afire when they first got there so all that could be done was to wet down the other buildings and try and save them. Howard hurried after them with two more pails and I after them with pails and mop.

Hattie then goes on to describe the difficulties of fighting a major fire in an inaccessible location, with only the most rudimentary equipment, few people, and no way of calling for help.

Ed got on [the] new wood shed building and poured water on [the] roof. I began carrying water from lake with Chas. Howard rushed down and told Alice and

Catherine [Charlie's wife and daughter] and we carried water as fast as we could, but the fire was pretty hot and eating over in main house quite a little. Wind blowing toward bay side, rather uncomfortable carrying water past there, then Roy Higby and 3 men came which helped a lot. Then [the] Dunn boys. Later McEdwards from Station and last when all down [i.e., fire out] fire men from Inlet with one fire extinguisher. Guess they picked it up at Glennmore. Got C[h]emical truck from Inlet as far as Glennmore. Mrs. Naporski collapsed at first then leaned against a tree and squalled a little then came down to our house and shut herself in the bathroom. When I got up there with my pails and mop Naporski was running around in the brush holding his dog [a Saint Bernard] by the collar. It seems they went up there, built a fire in kitchen then one in Franklin fireplace in dining room and then both went up on hill to connect up the water and saw smoke from up there. So you see they were in a pretty bad way for water, and I suppose the pipe or chimney was poor and when it caught in the birch bark [which had been used to paper the walls][49] in the dining room it was like oil. It certainly crackled and roared. It made you feel sick to see and hear it. They could not save a thing from house. All went—bedding, dishes, silver, piano, victrola, bathtubs and beds all a crumpled burned mess. Quite a few of the nearest trees are badly burned and will have to be cut down. When the blaze would lap out from the building and run up the tree the needles flew like chaf[f] being shaved off. My hair was full of burned needles.

Dad's hands and face was so red they were nearly blistered, also some of the other men had pretty red burns from the heat. No other buildings were burned.

Just an hour from the time he called me till it was all down and [no] danger of other buildings catching fire. How is that for swift work . . . I must stop or this will be a book. Love, Mother

Ruins of Veery's Nest after the fire, April 4, 1929.
Courtesy of Wanda K. Martin.

The fire, combined with the Great Depression of the 1930s, dealt a mortal blow to Veery's Nest. Frank Naporski, who by then was calling himself Frank Veery, struggled through the early 1930s and found himself unable to make the mortgage payments to E. J. and Hattie. Finally, in the winter of 1934–35, E. J. foreclosed on the mortgage.[50]

The new property provided a major expansion for the Waldheim but was a sad setback for the Naporskis (now Veerys). Nevertheless, they still had their ambitions and purchased, to operate as another hotel, the house on the road to Big Moose Station now called Irwin Lodge. This enterprise also failed. Finally, the Naporskis left the area but apparently retained fond memories of Big Moose Lake. They returned for a visit some time in the late 1930s, borrowing a boat and rowing up the lake, possibly to look at the site of their hotel. On this visit (or perhaps a later one), they camped for a few days in a tent pitched on the bluff behind what is now the Wayback Inn on the road to Big Moose Station. After this, handsome Frank Naporski and his wife faded from Big Moose history.

Covewood, 1925

The history of Covewood is also the story of a father and a son and their often unhappy relationship.

Earl Covey, born in 1876, was only a youngster when his father, Henry, settled on his Crag Point property. Because his tubercular mother, Emma Chase, had to live in Old Forge in order to get proper nursing, Earl stayed with his mother and spent little time with his father on the lake. When he came of school age, Earl and his mother

Cover of Covewood Lodge brochure, ca. 1925. Courtesy of Mary Covey Williams.

went to live at her home in Lewis County, where she eventually died in 1890.

One and one-half years later, in 1892, his father married Margaret Rose, who had been Emma's nurse. Earl attended school with some of his stepmother's family at Moose River Settlement. Earl also became close friends with Tom Rose, a nephew of his stepmother, and joined him and his family when they moved to Jayville, an upstate mining and iron-smelting town. At about age sixteen, Earl left school and came to Camp Crag to work for his father.

Earl's entry into his father's home could not overcome the effects of those long years of separation. Their relationship was, at best, complex. Some older residents on the lake can recall the tension that existed between the young man and his father, and even Henry's Camp Crag record books are spiced with discord and occasional rancor. While Earl's loyalty to his father was never in doubt, he was never servile. Like his father, Earl was an independent-minded person. A biography of Earl written by his wife, Frances, reveals some sense of this.[51] In her book, Frances recounts a verbal exchange between Earl and his father.

> During Earl's early years at Twitchell, a family at the Station was destitute because the father spent his earnings on liquor . . . Earl learned of the situation and collected donations for the family from some of the local hotel men. When he approached his father for a donation, Henry Covey asked, "Is that the man who drinks?" On being told it was, he refused to contribute. It is doubtful that Henry ever received from anyone a more stinging rebuke than came from his son on that occasion.[52]

A few years later, Earl became interested in a Camp Crag waitress, Addie Butts. In February of 1895, they married and moved to Washington, D.C. But less than a year later, Earl got word from his father asking if he could return to do some work for him. He responded without hesitation, returning with his wife and first-born, William, to spend the summer and fall of 1896 in a cottage not far from the entrance to North Bay. It was most likely a camp belonging to a squatter named Hamlyn. (See illustration on page 183.) When winter arrived, Earl, Addie, and William went back to Washington, but they returned to Big Moose the following summer to help Earl's father with more construction. Henry paid his son only $10 a month (at a time when Earl could earn $3

Earl and Addie Covey with Emma and William, ca. 1898.
Reproduced from Frances Alden Covey's book, The Earl
Covey Story *(New York: Exposition Press, 1964), with the*
permission of Mary Covey Williams.

a day for guiding), plus an additional dollar a day for
board.

Earl remained at Big Moose with his family, which
soon grew to include five children—William, Emma,
Henry, Sumner, and Mildred—supporting them by guiding, trapping, and working at Camp Crag. However, he
was not content to depend on those skills for a livelihood,
and he was just as certain that he did not want to work for
someone else. He also figured that one Covey on Big
Moose Lake was enough. Hence, in the winter of 1899,
he purchased land from Webb at the southwest end of
Twitchell Lake and promptly began construction of the
Twitchell Lake Inn.

After the inn opened for business its success was immediate, and it soon required both a larger dining room
and more sleeping space. To that end, Earl asked his father for a loan to purchase the necessary building supplies. He received a rather enigmatic response: "Get the
money in a way you would know how you came by it."
Earl did get the money from a Herkimer bank without

any additional security, a fact that speaks volumes for his
reputation.

In the years just before and after 1920, Earl suffered a
series of tragedies. In 1918, his eldest son, William, died
from the Spanish influenza while serving in the U.S.
Army in Europe. In September 1920, his wife, Addie,
died of pneumonia. In 1921, his eighteen-year-old son
Henry (no doubt named for his grandfather) died of a
perforated vertebra, an injury sustained while working on
the bridge over Twitchell Creek that was being built in
memory of his brother William.

Earl became depressed and began to lose interest in
the Twitchell Lake Inn. He wanted to leave the tragedies
associated with Twitchell Lake behind him and make a
fresh start. He considered moving to California, but then,
recognizing the frailty of his father, Henry, and the decline of Camp Crag, he instead set his sights on a return to
Big Moose Lake. Earl saw an opportunity to restore
Camp Crag and continue the camp's rich tradition.

Earl talked with his father about buying Camp Crag
and felt that the negotiations went well. Indeed, Henry
tentatively accepted his son's offer. But on October 14,
1922, Henry Covey recorded the following in his Camp
Crag record book: "Temp. 35. Clear. Wind southern,
Earl Did not Call as we Expected Him to Do to arrange
Payment for the Place. Mr. Covey Received a letter from
Mr. Morse Making a very attractive offer for the Camp
Crag Property around [South Bay] to Mr. Kelsey's Prop-
erty [next to the present Chapel manse]."

Four days later, on October 18, Henry wrote, "Mr.
and Mrs Morse . . . Came over from Hermitage this A.M.
and closed Bargin [sic] for the Camp."

Earl had lost the property, and Henry gives no clue as
to why. Perhaps it was because Earl had not contacted his
father as expected on October 14, perhaps because Earl
wanted only Camp Crag and not all of his father's land, or
perhaps because Mr. Morse was simply willing to pay
more. Nonetheless, Earl was devastated. "To lose Camp
Crag with all its exciting possibilities for development,
when he almost had it, was a bitter blow to Earl."[53]

Eventually, however, Earl rallied. In the summer of
1922, he had started to take an interest in a young lady,
Frances Alden, who had been hired for the summer to do
office work at the Twitchell Lake Inn. Frances, a graduate
of Wellesley College, was living in Syracuse, where she
studied voice. Their courtship is delightfully told in *The
Earl Covey Story.*

On the surface, the two did not appear well suited.

Henry Covey Cottage with a later addition to the first floor, 2003; an example of palisade construction. Photograph by Diane Bowes.

Earl's formal education had ended when he was sixteen, and he had spent most of his adult life in the woods. Frances, who was thirteen years his junior, had attended a private preparatory school and then college and had been brought up in urban surroundings. Nonetheless, Earl pursued Frances with remarkable tenacity, and they were married on April 14, 1923.

After their wedding trip, they returned to live in a house that Earl had built at the Big Moose Station. But Earl did not intend to live there long. Just before the wedding, Earl had purchased from his father sixty-six acres of land in the bay east of the Big Moose outlet, where he intended to develop a resort. In the spring of 1924, Earl built a house on this land near Fern Spring Brook, which he named the Henry Covey Cottage. It

would eventually be the first guest accommodation for a new resort, but Earl and Frances were the first occupants. By this time, Earl's father, Henry, had become quite frail; he moved in with the couple, dying shortly thereafter. Earl and Frances remained in the Henry Covey Cottage while Earl undertook the construction of the main lodge.

Earl knew the woods around Big Moose Lake intimately. As Covewood's current owner, Major Bowes, recounts,

> He searched for the posts, beams, slabbing, and other timber needed to build the main house. The graceful arch between the living room and the foyer is a natural one found after months of combing the forest. No steaming or processing was used to shape it. At Covey's mill, then located by the Outlet south of the bridge, trees were cut and proportioned. Stones for the fireplaces, foundations, and road were obtained from the river's outlet.[54]

Earl Covey's fireplaces are famous, and the one in the living room of the Covewood's main lodge is a fine example of the care and attention to detail that Earl gave to their construction. It was made of Adirondack granite, each piece carefully cut to Earl's specifications. The building of the fireplace in the lobby took well over a month to complete and was witnessed by an early guest. Earl had found a large circular stone in the bed of the Outlet that he wanted placed in the center of the chimney above the mantel. At the point when they were ready to put it in place, it was time for lunch. Earl was "so possessed to see how [it] was going to look, he couldn't wait until [the

Covewood Lodge living room with one of Earl Covey's celebrated fireplaces, ca. 1930s. Courtesy of Frank Carey.

Covewood Lodge, 1925. Courtesy of
Wanda K. Martin.

men] got back from lunch. So, he took a pack basket and put it over one of the [ceiling] beams . . . and filled it full of rock to give him some weight to [balance the heavy stone and] put it in himself."[55]

Earl and Frances stayed in the Henry Covey Cottage until the main lodge was completed. The new resort, called Covewood, opened for business in the summer of 1925, and, like the Twitchell Lake Inn, was an immediate success.

Earl continued to build—four more cottages at Covewood and several camps on Big Moose Lake, as well as some on Twitchell and Fourth Lake and even in Canada. He earned an enviable reputation for his fireplaces, not only for their design but also for their efficiency. Those who own camps that Earl Covey built still boast of their Covey fireplaces.

Earl was involved in the community and served as a justice of the peace in the Town of Webb in the early 1900s. He was also a lifelong Republican.

INNOVATIONS

On South Bay, Earl built a replacement for the original Fern Spring camp under the direction of Walter Colpitts, a resident of the North Shore. Colpitts gave the house to the Chapel, and it is now the manse.

The house was a unique construction. Instead of the usual one-inch-thick pine boards nailed to two-by-four studs, it was made of four-by-eight sheets of two-inch thick Cemestos, a kind of wallboard that was fastened with screws rather than nails. The construction seems as solid today as when it was built.

Like most of the year-round residents of Big Moose, Earl Covey had to be self-sufficient and devise solutions

Earl Covey's Polar Grip Tire
demonstration on the lake, 1929.
Courtesy of Mary Covey Williams.

Advertisement for Covey's Polar Grip Tires, 1929. Courtesy of Richard Widdicombe.

used them were convinced that the traction was excellent. However, the tires did not wear well on bare roads. That problem, coupled with the Depression of the 1930s, caused the invention to fail. Nevertheless, its innovation won the tire a spot in the Adirondack Museum at Blue Mountain Lake.

The Big Moose Community Chapel remains Earl Covey's crowning achievement. The architectural plans were entirely his own and remained primarily in his mind. With the same perfectionism he had brought to the construction of Covewood, Earl Covey, with a group of volunteers from around the lake, carefully selected the logs and honed and shaped them by hand. He also handpicked the stone for the chapel from Dart's quarry, which was then chipped and carved by a stone cutter. With great skill and patience, and under Earl's supervision, the volunteers constructed the building that today sits so invitingly on the Big Moose Road. The history of the chapel, from its construction in 1931 to its tragic destruction by fire the night before the dedication and its subsequent rebuilding, is told in Ellie Reed Koppe's book, *The Big Moose Community Chapel: The First Fifty Years.*[56]

While not as renowned as her husband, Earl, Frances Alden Covey was well-known in the Big Moose area. Her daughter, Mary Alden Covey Williams, recently wrote of her,

to the problems that inevitably arrived—and, as demonstrated by his single-handed placement of the stone in Covewood's main fireplace, he was never short on ingenuity.

After seeing how hard it was for cars and trucks to make it up the hill between Covewood and the Big Moose Road in winter, Earl invented a tire with a tread made of crepe rubber, much like the crepe soles on shoes that were popular many decades ago. Firestone Tire and Rubber Company made samples for Earl, and those who

She was definitely a LADY in her woods environment. As she was the first to admit, housekeeping duties were not her favorite activities, but she acted as secretary, bookkeeper, and receptionist and helped with the "help" at Covewood with remarkable poise and grace. Certainly her background and education were helpful to her but

Big Moose Community Chapel, 1931. Courtesy of Elizabeth K. Singleton.

*Frances Alden Covey, 1976. Courtesy of
Mary Covey Williams.*

*Frances and Earl Covey, 1938. Courtesy of
Mary Covey Williams.*

the determination and perseverance displayed were the personal characteristics uniquely her own. She carried on extensive correspondence with legislators, organizations, and even the Governor of New York about events that she considered significant. And she had some very definite opinions including admiration of Eleanor Roosevelt which was in direct contrast with her very Republican husband and the surrounding community.[57]

Frances was also a strong force in the life of the Big Moose Community Chapel, serving for many years as its chairman of the board. Along with Earl, Frances offered the hospitality of Covewood to both year-round and summer residents. Many can recall the memorable square-dance evenings they held in the summer, which are described later in this book.

In the mid-1930s, Earl began to suffer increasingly from arthritis, which hampered his work routine. He tried several remedies, including a stay at a sanitarium, with little success. In the winter of 1938, he and his family spent a month in Florida, with some salutary results. Before leaving Florida, he purchased some land with the idea of spending winters there. By this time, he had also put Covewood up for sale. In that same year, he somewhat reluctantly agreed to lease the resort (with an option to buy) to Walter Reid. To accommodate Reid, Earl quickly built a house for Frances, himself, and their daughter Mary Alden on a piece of property west of the Outlet that he had inherited from his father. This house would be for their use in the summer when they returned

from Florida. After three years, however, Reid chose not to buy the hotel.

Covey then sold Covewood to Gladys Bourner, a former guest. Bourner operated Covewood until 1951, relying heavily on Earl for help and advice. In 1950, she leased it to C. V. ("Major")[58] Bowes, who then bought it that autumn.

Bowes was familiar with the Adirondacks, having spent summers in the area as a youth and as a student at Colgate, from which he graduated in 1941. After a stint in the U.S. Navy during World War II and some study at the Cornell Hotel School, Bowes leased Dart's Lake Hotel from 1948 to 1950 from George Longstaff, who also owned the Moss Lake Camp for Girls. In 1950, Bowes made an offer to buy Dart's Hotel, which Longstaff appeared to accept. However, Longstaff stalled long enough to lumber a large section of the Dart's Lake property, quite unbeknown to Bowes. When Bowes found out, he withdrew his offer, disgusted at what he considered Longstaff's disingenuousness. Bowes promptly saddled a horse and rode to Covewood, having heard that Gladys Bourner wanted to sell.

Upon purchasing Covewood in 1950, Bowes, sensing that the future would be in motels and not in the typical Adirondack resort hotel, went so far as to engage Earl Covey to draw up plans for a ten-room motel near the Outlet. (Such a project probably would be prohibited now, because that area would be classified as wetlands.)

However, Earl Covey was in very poor health by this time, and Major Bowes's scheme was suspended. Earl had had a stroke a few years earlier. With that, a weakened heart, and a resulting lung condition that made breathing difficult, he was severely limited. After arriving at Big Moose Lake for the summer of 1952, Earl's condition quickly deteriorated, and he died on August 22. His contributions are honored in a memorial plaque on a boulder near the Twitchell Lake Inn, which reads, "In memory of Earl W. Covey, 1876–1952, a master builder who lived so much in tune with the life of nature, that he was able to duplicate and enhance its beauty in the creation of beautiful buildings from Adirondack trees and rocks."

Major Bowes operated Covewood for some fifteen years on the "American Plan"—three meals a day. This was the pattern followed by all the original hotels at Big Moose Lake. In 1966, Covewood acquired Buzz Point, across the Outlet, a complex of summer cottages that had belonged to the Milligan family. Discovering that some of those camps had kitchens and noting many guests' interest in housekeeping cottages, Major Bowes began reducing his dining operations and installing kitchens in some of his other cottages. At one point Covewood was serving only three meals a week: a Caribbean dinner, a buffet, and a brunch. Finally, this trend, combined with other changes, prompted Major Bowes and his wife, Diane, to eliminate the restaurant altogether. One factor was the increasing number of health-department regulations; Bowes, a fiercely independent person, took great umbrage at being told what he could and could not do. Another factor was the increasing difficulty in hiring summer

kitchen help. Today, many of the Covewood's eighteen guest cottages not only are equipped with kitchens but also are winterized and available year-round.

Bowes has carried on Earl Covey's tradition of innovation, personifying the adage that necessity is the mother of invention. Noticing how fast his plumbing pipes were corroding from the high lead and copper content in his water system, he devised a channel some twenty feet long and filled it with limestone at the source of his water. This feature dramatically reduced the acid content. Apparently, New York State was sufficiently impressed with this ingenious scheme that they dumped some fifty tons of lime on the ice in North Bay, hoping to reduce the acidity of the lake. This experiment, however, was not successful.

Major Bowes is a great lover of forest animals. He helped the New York State Conservation Department in its efforts to bring Canada geese to the area and worked to return wild turkeys to the woods. He has assisted in the propagation of loons by building nesting platforms to protect the newborn chicks from sudden high water after rains. He has built a photography blind so that Covewood's guests can observe bear, fox, snowshoe hare, and other birds and animals native to the area, and he has a herd of deer that guests can feed.

Not unlike the prohibitions stated by the hotels one hundred years ago, Covewood has established its own rules: jet-skis and snowmobiles are not welcome!

3 *Making a Living at Big Moose Lake*

MUCH OF BIG MOOSE LAKE is hidden from nearby roads. In the early days, it took a knowledgeable woodsman to find it because it lay off the usual paths through the wilderness. Whichever route the guides followed, most first encountered the lake at West Bay. The bay is divided from the larger part of the lake by Echo Island, which leaves a narrow passage on the north and a generous channel on the south. Steep cliffs on the north generate an echo, probably the origin of the name of the island. Surprisingly, there are few records of guides' camps on West Bay itself. Early sportsmen apparently continued onward to the larger part of the lake.

However, when the railroad arrived in 1892, convenience dictated development. The decade of the 1890s was crowded with activities that were to change the lake from an obscure spot in the forest to a place that would draw fishermen and hunters away from smoky cities to fresh air, romantic views, and as many amenities as ingenious hotel keepers could provide. Teamsters, blacksmiths, cooks, and craftsmen who had come to find employment with William Seward Webb liked the spot and stayed to become guides, entrepreneurs, and jacks-of-all-trades. West Bay slowly became a commercial hub for enterprising businessmen.

The location of West Bay as the terminus of the main access road made it a natural site for skilled year-round residents who could supply the services needed by occasional visitors or by the growing number of summer residents. The transportation company that soon sprang up not only brought visitors from the railroad station but also operated a steamship that took passengers to hotels or private camps along the shore. Before the end of the 1890s, West Bay featured two burgeoning hotels, the Glennmore and Lake View Lodge, to add to the two that were already established in other parts of the lake (Camp Crag and Higby Camp). West Bay also boasted a store, a boat line, the homes of most of ten or twelve year-round families, and several private summer camps. It was the beginning of a community within the larger lake that would become the hub of Big Moose Lake.

Early in the decade, William Seward Webb owned all the land around the lake. He foresaw the demand for summer camps and even facilitated the building of at least one hotel, Lake View Lodge. Working through his Ne-Ha-Sa-Ne Corporation, he divided the lake into building lots and began, with the help of various agents, to sell land to individuals. By the end of the decade, he had sold nearly all the land around the lake including several large tracts to Theodore Page, a lumber magnate from Oswego, New York, who reserved Echo Island for his own use.

The story of how the men and women who were full-time residents grew and flourished is a large part of the story of the development of Big Moose Lake.

The Glenns, the Sperrys, and Their Nearby Enterprises

THE BIG MOOSE TRANSPORTATION COMPANY

Soon after the railroad began its operations, Dwight B. "D. B." Sperry cut a crude road from Big Moose Station through some two and one-half miles of forest to the closest point on the lake, West Bay. Dwight Benjamin Sperry, born in 1860, had grown up in Sperryville, a small community in Lewis County named after his grandfather.

A buckboard that operated between the Big Moose Station and the site of the Glennmore Hotel, ca. 1894. The drivers are Ed Dolan and Tom Rose, and the passenger is Aras Williams. Courtesy of the Big Moose Property Owners Association.

Of the four Sperry children, three—Dwight, Francena, and Daisy—were to play important roles in the development of Big Moose Lake.

Dwight's sister Daisy married William Glenn. In 1897 the Glenns bought the two large lots on West Bay that later became the site of the Glennmore Hotel. A younger sister, Francena, became Jim Higby's second wife and a memorable personality on the lake.

In 1899, D. B. Sperry purchased from the Glenns the land at the point where the new road from Big Moose Station met the lake (lots 374 and 375). Later that same year he bought an additional 126.6 acres along the shore of West Bay to the east (lots 366–73). Anticipating the need for certain services, he, with his brothers-in-law William Glenn and James Higby, formed the Big Moose Transportation Company. Besides handling lumber and other freight needed to construct both new hotels and private camps (and to supply the two hotels that already existed), the company was to provide transportation for hotel guests at Camp Crag and Higby Camp as well as for private camp owners. Clearly, Sperry could see the growth that was to take place. The customers and their quantities of gear arrived from the railroad station by horse-drawn buckboard or carriage at the public landing of the Glennmore. Teamsters John Denio of Big Moose Station and Jim McAllister, among others, drove these vehicles over the short, rough road.

Between 1895 and 1897, Sperry also played an important role in building the Eagle Bay Hotel on Fourth Lake, and by 1899 he had built the spacious Hotel Glennmore, whose guests further increased the need for transportation services.

At the dock, the company's steamboat *Zilpha* waited to take guests to the hotels and camps on the lake, all of which were, at the beginning, inaccessible by land. When there were passengers destined for Dart's Hotel, Bill Dart's celebrated bull would be at Dart's Landing to convey them to Dart's Lake.

The *Zilpha* had her beginnings at Beaver River, where she was known as the *X 10 U 8* (possibly short for "Extenuate"). She was brought over to the Fulton Chain, where she was rechristened *Zilpha* in honor of Nat Foster's sister, who had been abducted by Indians. In 1901, the Big Moose Transportation Company sledded the boat from Eagle Bay to Big Moose Lake—not an easy job, because the vessel was thirty-five-feet long and had

Hotel Glennmore with carriages arriving, 1906. Courtesy of the Adirondack Museum.

Steamboat Big Moose, *owned by the Big Moose Transportation Company, ca. 1910. Courtesy of Mark Barlow.*

the capacity to carry seven tons. She was probably launched at Dart's Landing. Dwight Sperry piloted the wood-burning boat, and Frank Crabbe served as engineer. (It was searchers aboard the *Zilpha* who recovered the body of Grace Brown of *American Tragedy* fame in 1906.) The company used the twenty-five-passenger boat for six years, after which she was scrapped.

In 1906 the Big Moose Transportation Company was incorporated, with Sperry holding the vast majority of the stock and a few family members holding the remaining shares. Six hundred shares were issued at $10 each, totaling $6,000.

The *Zilpha*'s replacement was the *SS Big Moose,* which was actually built at Big Moose Lake. This larger, more up-to-date steamboat could carry thirty-five passengers

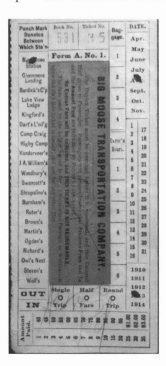

Big Moose Transportation Company ticket, August 1913. Courtesy of Janet S. Holmes.

and crew. She continued the work of her predecessor, delivering mail, passengers, and cargo. The vessel, however, proved too large to fit in any boat slip at the Glennmore. Bob McAllister, Jim's son, remembered a set of rails between the present boathouse and the swimming dock, on which the steamboat was drawn up and stored for the winter. Dave Humphrey and Sam Van Atta, among others, served as helmsman and fireman on board. The boat remained in the service of the Big Moose Transportation Company until 1918. Bob Rowell, a childhood friend of Everett Martin's, remembered the *SS Big Moose* well and believed that it was eventually burned.

Sperry's Big Moose Transportation Company grew into a prosperous enterprise. Besides the steamboat, there were teams of horses, carriages, buckboards, freight wagons, road-maintenance equipment, a house on the Glennmore Road for managers and teamsters (still known today as the "Transportation House"), and a building at the Big Moose Station that served as a boarding house and storage facility at the railroad end of the enterprise. Papers found connected with the company include a punched ticket dated 1913 showing that there were at least twenty-one stops around the lake at that time.

In addition to the transportation company's enterprises, Sperry and his brother-in-law Jim Higby brought the first telephone line to the lake about 1898. According to Roy Higby, "The central office was in Old Forge Village. Heavy galvanized wire was strung to trees through the woods and the phones were the old style wall-type, operated by a large battery filled with acid and water. Each subscriber was identified by one, two or three rings, or perhaps one long and two short rings." [1] Of course it was possible for anyone on the line to listen in. It could also be dangerous if a person was talking on the phone, or was even near it, if a thunderbolt struck the line. Young Roy Higby was twice felled by such an accident.[2]

Sperry had a hand in other enterprises as well. In 1915, he gave up his interests at the Glennmore in order to buy out the other directors of the Eagle Bay Hotel Corporation located on Fourth Lake. To finance this move, he sold his property at Big Moose. According to a bill of sale dated January 3, 1916,[3] Sperry sold the Hotel Glennmore, the Big Moose Supply Company, and his interest in the private telephone line (known as the Big Moose Telephone Company) to the Hotel Glennmore Corporation. Postcards show a distinct similarity between the architecture of the Eagle Bay Hotel and that of the Glennmore, although the former was larger. It burned to the ground in August 1945.

An Article of Agreement between Bramon Bissell et al. and the Hotel Glennmore Corporation, dated October 12, 1916,[4] lists the stockholders at that time: Dana Bissell, Jennette Bissell, Harry Kellogg, Harold Bissell, and Bramon Bissell, with Bramon Bissell holding a large majority of the stock. Bramon, brother of Dana Bissell, who was a partner in the Bissell and Yousey Lumber Company, was killed shortly afterwards when the truck he was driving was hit by a train at Big Moose Station. Upon his death, the stock he held probably passed to other members of his family.

From 1918 (after the Bissell and Yousey Lumber Company left Big Moose Lake) until 1924, the Big Moose Transportation Company was owned and operated by the LaFountains. George "Pop" LaFountain was a giant of a man, tall and heavyset. His wife, Maudie, was as diminutive as he was large. She was possessed of a clever if rather abrasive wit and a sharp outlook on life. Their son Ernie, born in 1899, was trim and fit, and his swarthy complexion showed off a set of even white teeth when he smiled, which he did often. He was an affable combination of his two parents and was well known for his easy homespun humor. Of the Big Moose Road before the Cascade and Kingsford Hill bypasses, he quipped, "It's so crooked a snake could break its back going over it."

Pop LaFountain had operated the first steamboat on Tupper Lake, working for a George Hurd. Later he used his experience with steam engines to become an engineer on Hurd's railroad from Tupper Lake to Ottawa. Railroading became Pop's passion, and he earned the distinction of having moved more pulpwood than any other engineer in the area. During their married life the

Group connected with the Big Moose Transportation Company, 1923; left to right: Lillian S. Kinne, Ernest LaFountain, George "Pop" LaFountain, Glenn Scanlon, and Maude LaFountain. Courtesy of Barbara K. Wheeler.

LaFountains lived in such Adirondack railroad towns as Tupper Lake, Cranberry Lake, and Brandreth. When he came of age Ernie served as his father's fireman.

During the years that the LaFountains operated the transportation company, the era of horse-drawn vehicles passed, and the new owners gradually shifted to trucks, buses, and gasoline-powered launches to transport people and freight from the station to various points around the lake.

The LaFountains continued to own the transportation company, probably also operating the station-to-dock portion. Romaine Kinne worked for them in various capacities during this time. In 1924 the LaFountains left Big Moose and moved to Florida to buy an orange grove. (The investment proved to be unfortunate, and they returned to Big Moose in the early 1930s.)

It is not clear exactly how long Big Moose Transportation continued as a stockholding company. On November 23, 1929, E. J. Martin wrote a check to the Big Moose Transportation Company, and it was so endorsed.[5] In 1936 there is an ambiguous reference in the *Adirondack Arrow* to Ernie LaFountain, whose parents had by then returned to the lake, accepting a job with Kinne for the summer. It was reported that Ernie was employed by the "Hotel Glennmore Transportation Company,"[6] perhaps a garbled reference to the Big Moose Transportation Company or possibly to the Hotel Glennmore Corporation.

With the advent of motor cars and the building of paved roads on which to drive them, hotels around the

The Store at Hotel Glennmore. Big Moose Lake
Adirondack Mountains, N. Y.

Big Moose Supply Company, also known as the Glennmore Store, ca. 1925. Courtesy of Frank Carey.

lake soon were meeting the trains with their own wood-sided station wagons to pick up guests and luggage. The changing times undoubtedly diminished business for the Big Moose Transportation Company. Eventually, its land services faded into oblivion and other businesses grew up.

THE BIG MOOSE SUPPLY COMPANY

The earliest residents of the lake bought their groceries and supplies from the hotels. Both Camp Crag and Waldheim records show running accounts for various camp owners for such staples as milk, meat, butter, eggs, potatoes, apples, and soap, as well as tobacco and cigars. Lena Retter, in her diary for 1900, mentions rowing across the lake to buy milk from Higby's. Waldheim ledgers record food purchased by occupants of many different camps.

D. B. Sperry may have been the first to take advantage of the demand for foodstuffs and other items by establishing a store next to his Glennmore Hotel. The store became part of the Hotel Glennmore Corporation and probably started soon after the hotel opened in 1899. It was located in a building across the road from the hotel, the same building that today is the Glenmore Bar and Grill.

The most detailed information we have about the store comes from Barbara Kinne Wheeler, who remembers Charles Forkey, the manager from about 1919. When Dana Bissell moved his sawmill operation to Big Moose Lake, Forkey was working for him as yard boss and scaler. (The job of scaler is highly skilled; the scaler looks at standing trees and estimates the number of board feet that can be harvested.) Forkey also ran the company store near the mill at Big Moose Lake, perhaps discovering his entrepreneurial skills there.

In 1918, about the time the Bissell and Yousey operation closed, Forkey enlisted in the U.S. Army. When the war was over, he returned to Big Moose and took over the operation of the Big Moose Supply Company.

Forkey was a slender, bespectacled man, not very tall but with an air of dignity. His neat appearance and pleasant smile inspired confidence. He was a kindly, capable

Charles Forkey, manager of the Big Moose Supply Company, ca. 1934. Courtesy of Barbara K. Wheeler.

Big Moose Supply Company interior, ca. 1930.
Courtesy of the Adirondack Museum.

man who managed the company and the general store in an efficient manner and was well liked in the community. Most people thought he was a confirmed bachelor, so it was a surprise to many to learn in 2001 that he had been married to a cousin of Joel Potter, who lived in the Transportation House and worked for the Woodburys on the North Shore.[7] No details about the marriage are known.

Aside from canned goods and packaged staples, fresh vegetables and fruit were available in the store. The store featured a full-fledged meat market with walk-in coolers; a soda fountain; a clothing department selling shirts, jackets, pants, and shoes; and lots of souvenirs. A big glass-fronted candy case stood to the right of the door, the popular destination of the lake's small fry. In those days, a five-cent candy bar could ruin a kid's supper.

Beyond the candy case, a counter ran back to where the cash register was located. The wall behind supported shelves to the ceiling that held canned goods and other staples. Clerks reached articles on the higher shelves with a long-handled pole with metal jaws on the end, which gripped the item and brought it safely down to counter level. The meat market was in a separate room. Meat was cut to order by the amiable butcher, Mr. Dean, who was always in uniform with his white jacket and hat. Perishables such as eggs, fresh fruit, and vegetables were kept in the coolers.

In the front corner to the left was a large marble soda fountain counter with tables and wire-backed chairs near the front door. Aside from being a haven for cola-thirsty and ice cream-hungry customers during the heat of the day, this area also served as an after-dinner meeting place for the lake's young people. Here they would decide how the evening should be spent—partying at Curley's (cur-

rently the Wayback Inn) on the Station Road, enjoying a marshmallow roast and songfest around the embers of the campfire, attending a square dance at Covewood, or whatever. Outside in front of the store were two gas pumps that dispensed Socony Vacuum regular or ethyl gasoline to those who needed it.

The "Pickle Boat," run by Forkey's enterprise, made a daily trip around the lake delivering grocery orders that had been placed the day before.

During the summer season, some ten or twelve people were hired. Among the local people employed were Forkey's nephew Earl and his wife, his niece Dorothy, Raymond Marleau from Big Moose Station, the teacher Ted Manning, Frances Leonard (later Mrs. Barney Lepper), Mrs. Henry Callahan, and Donald and Byron Collins, who ran the Pickle Boat. Those from out of town were housed in rooms on the second floor, where Mrs. Callahan cooked

The "Pickle Boat" at Brown Gables, 1931. Courtesy of
Harrison Bicknell, Jr.

for them. Also in the building was a three-room apartment where Forkey stayed in the summer.

In the fall, before the store closed, the year-round residents would lay in a winter supply of nonperishables from the stock left on his shelves.

Occasionally on a fall evening, if something like an important prizefight was broadcast on the radio, Forkey would make the place available for local folks to gather for an evening of entertainment. He reopened the building briefly in November to seat the election board, and it then remained closed until spring.

Charlie Forkey and Romaine Kinne were good friends. They used to hunt with a group of locals during the deer season, until one day Kinne drew a bead on a buck and pulled the trigger. The bullet ricocheted off a tree and came within a whisker of Forkey's head. Romaine Kinne never hunted after that day, and it is probably safe to assume that Charles Forkey never did either. They both enjoyed a good card game, a much less risky pastime, and during the winter they could be found with others playing pinochle on cold and snowy afternoons.

In 1938, Forkey bought the old Transportation House on the Glennmore Road, renovating and modernizing it and making it his year-round home. The summer after the Glennmore Hotel closed in 1942, he attempted to carry on his business on a much smaller scale, stocking his front porch with some staples, such as bread and milk, to accommodate his old customers.

Charlie Forkey died of a heart attack in 1945. He was found in his car in the driveway, apparently getting ready to drive to the station for his mail.

Businessmen on the Lake

BILLY STEVENS

In 1902, William Stevens, with his wife and six children, came from the Lowville-Greig area seeking to exercise his skills as a carpenter and a guide. He purchased two lots (lots 361 and 362) for $400 and built the very first private home on West Bay, locating it on the north shore of the bay and naming it Winona Lodge. Once his own house was finished and his family was provided with shelter, he worked at Owl's Nest and at other places that were then being built on the shores of the lake. Perhaps his most important early job was to serve as caretaker and guide for Theodore Page at Echo Island.

Billy's wife, Frances ("Fannie Fae"), took in washing

Fanny Fae and William Stevens, ca. 1890. Courtesy of Frances Leonard Lepper.

from the hotels. It is said that the area in front of the house, still almost entirely devoid of trees, was cleared to provide sunny space for clotheslines to dry the sheets. Fannie also worked for the Vander Veer family on the southeast shore of the lake and probably later for Minnie Maddern Fiske.

The Stevens family endured several tragedies. Their youngest son, Robert, when he was three or four years old, seized a cup of dark liquid and drank it down, thinking it was maple syrup. It was in fact lye that his mother was using in her laundry operations. Robert suffered terrible internal damage. Dr. Herbert Williams, a neighbor, did his best to save him, even taking him into his own home, but his efforts failed to save the child. Another son, Harold, died of influenza at an early age.

The Stevens's eldest daughter, Inez, married Moses Leonard in 1914. Moses's father, a blacksmith, had come to work at the Bissell and Yousey Lumber Mill when it opened. Their eldest daughter, Frances, was born at Winona Lodge, helped into the world by Dr. Robert Lindsay, Sr., who came on the train from Old Forge. Frances claims to be the first baby born on West Bay, and perhaps on the lake. Inez, Frances's mother, died after the birth of her eighth child, forcing Mose to place the children in the Masonic Home in Utica until they were old enough to rejoin the family.

Meanwhile, Billy Stevens, Frances's grandfather, had sold Winona Lodge in 1923 to William Autenrith (who renamed it Crestwood) and was living with Mose and Inez in Thendara. Toward the end of his life, Billy became blind and died in the Utica State Hospital.

JIM MCALLISTER

James McAllister, teamster, logger, man of many talents, and founder of a Big Moose family, ran away from his home in Brewer, Maine, at age twelve. Born in 1866, he was part of a family of twelve children that had too many mouths to feed and too little income to fill them. One day, Jim and a brother, while bringing some cows home from the pasture, swam them across a stream. When the cows reached the barn, they were unable to give milk. The boys received harsh punishment. That episode sent Jim on his way to a better life.

He managed to stow away on a ship, hiding from the authorities, and soon became a cabin boy. The captain became his teacher and gave him all the formal education he ever had. Later he lived in Watson, New York, in Lewis County and worked on Webb's railroad line. As part of the railroad crew, he got as far as Big Moose and liked it so much that he decided to stay. He left his railroad job and used his teamster skills to work for D. B. Sperry, who was also from Watson. Jim, then about twenty-one years old, transported goods and passengers for the Big Moose Transportation Company. In the winter, he often worked for Charles Williams at Lake View Lodge and for Bill Dart at Dart's Lake, splitting wood or harvesting ice.

Jim married Gertrude Ludekere on November 30, 1910. She had worked for Bill Dart both in Florida and at Dart's Lake, where she met Jim. They first lived at Big Moose Station, where their son Bob was born. In 1916 they moved to Big Moose Lake to a house near Burdick's called Wigwam (now called Strawberry Hill) (lot 10). Their second son, Willard, was born there.

Jim was tall and lanky and, like many around the lake at that time, a man of many abilities. His son Bob tells the story of his father being hired to remove some stumps on the Glennmore Road. Henry Callahan, who was supervising the operation, felt that Jim was not doing a good job because the stumps were not coming loose fast enough. Jim knew the capacity of the horses and the limits of the equipment and knew how far to push both. After Callahan badgered him enough, Jim decided to unleash the power of the horses. The result was a pile of broken equipment.

As the driver for the Big Moose Transportation Company that operated between the Big Moose railroad station and the lake, Jim had a role in the real *American Tragedy* drama. He drove the principals of the story to the *Hotel Glennmore,* where they registered, and later was a key witness at the trial.

At one time, Jim worked for Clarence Strife, a logger in the area of Big Moose Station. A Linn tractor, a crude forerunner of the World War II half-track, ran over Jim's big toe, crushing it so that it had to be removed and leaving him with a permanent limp.

James McAllister, ca. 1944. Courtesy of Dennis McAllister.

Jim and Gertrude McAllister remained at Big Moose until 1953. By that time Jim's health had deteriorated, and he went to a nursing home where he died in October 1955. Gertrude moved to Old Forge and later to Rochester, New York, where her son Willard lived. She died at the age of ninety years.

Her other son, Bob, and his wife, Evelyn, lived at Big Moose Lake for many years. In 1969, they bought Dunn's Boat Service and ran it as a family corporation. Evie took over the land portion of the mail route, and their son Denny supervised the operation of the marina. Even after they sold the marina to Kenneth Hinkley in the winter of 1996–97, Denny continued to work with Ken Hinkley and to run the mail boat, remaining a familiar figure on the lake. Bob McAllister died in 1999.

ART BURTCH

Nineteen-year-old Arthur Burtch came to Big Moose from Lowville, New York in 1908. He got off the 4:00

A.M. train at the station and registered at Ainsworth's Camp. He immediately made his way to Dart's and ate his noon meal, after which he went into the woods and cut wood. As he put it, "I've been working ever since."

He was a slender man of average height. His clean-shaven features were fine, and it looked as though his narrow nose had been broken at some time. This did not detract from his appearance, however, but rather added a distinctive quality to his countenance.

Art Burtch quickly developed skills as a guide and a carpenter, working for H. H. Covey and Jim Higby, and then building his own business. His scow, filled with lumber and whatever else was needed for a building project, was a familiar sight on the lake as he towed it behind his boat toward a work site. In the summers, Art Burtch was sometimes hired by Glennmore guests to take groups of people up the lake for picnics at the sand beach by the old Bissell and Yousey Lumber Mill, at Andes Creek, or at Russian Lake.

During World War I, Burtch served as a foot soldier in the trenches of France. Later, he was taken from the front lines to attend Officer Candidate School. Upon discharge from the service, he returned to Big Moose, buying a house on the south shore of West Bay that had originally been built for Charles Williams (lots 14 and 15).

In 1925 he married Celia Ballard in Lowville on the same day that Walter Dunn and Albertha Deschenes were married, the couples standing up for each other. But cruel fate stepped in just two months later, when the minister that had presided at the Burtches' wedding officiated at Celia's funeral.

In 1927, Goldie Burke, accompanied by her daughter

Arthur Burtch (left) with George "Joe" Dunn putting ice blocks into an icehouse, ca. 1958. Courtesy of Richard Widdicombe.

Maxine, came to Big Moose to marry Art Burtch. Goldie was a "mail-order bride." No one seems to know which one of them advertised, but it makes little difference. In the 1920s a woman with a child was a lot more secure with a husband for support and protection, and a man in the Adirondacks was much better off with a place to call home and someone to cook for him. Art and Goldie enjoyed a good and lasting marriage, and they were well liked and highly respected by their Big Moose neighbors.

For a number of winters, Goldie and Maxine went to West Virginia, leaving Art to fend for himself. But the Big Moose wives made sure that Art Burtch got a good home-cooked meal at least once a week by taking turns inviting him to dinner. Barbara Kinne always looked forward to the times he came to her house. She remembers once when she was learning to knit and not doing too well. Art Burtch took the tangled nest of wool from her and said, "Well now, here's how my mother taught me to knit when I was a little girl," and proceeded to show her how to do it. Art and Barbara shared the same birth date, March 10, and he always said they were the same age.

In their later years, Art and Goldie Burtch sold their home on Big Moose Lake. Art built a smaller house on the Big Moose Road near Eagle Bay, and they lived there until he died at the age of eighty-eight in 1977. Goldie then moved to Utica, where she died a few years after that. As far as anyone knows, Maxine, who was married during World War II, is living in California.

THE MARTIN FAMILY AND THEIR BUSINESSES

The founders of the Martin family in this country, Jacob and Katherina, came from Switzerland in the 1840s and established a farm on the over-lumbered, swampy, and infertile Tug Hill plateau of upper New York State. They lived in Highmarket, a small town near Turin. Not surprisingly, all four of their sons saw greater opportunities toward the east, where the railroads were beginning to open up new Adirondack territory. All of the children eventually left home, and three of them were to become important members of the Big Moose Lake community.

Arthur Martin. Arthur, the eldest of the four sons and the only one who did not live at Big Moose, taught school at Raquette Lake, where he is remembered for taking his students to school at Long Point by guideboat. He died of diabetes in 1913 at the age of forty-two.

Frank Martin. Frank stayed at home to help run the

family farm, and he was therefore the last to come to Big Moose. In 1917, after the elder Martins died, Frank, perhaps the most colorful of the four, followed his younger brothers to the lake. He worked with them on many of the buildings they constructed over the years. Rowanwood (the Gamble/Quimby/Long) Camp is attributed to him, as are the Bruyn camp on the North Shore and Dunn's Marina.

Frank's hero was the famous Buffalo Bill (William Cody), and he took on the persona of his demigod with his long, flowing white hair and goatee. (As a boy, Bill Dunn recalls seeing Frank remove his Stetson hat and watching in wonder as a long braid cascaded down his back. Bill's mother had to chide him for staring.) Frank earned some renown in Big Moose by playing the role of this hero at the annual horse show at Dart's. Frank never married. He lived many years at Cabellsdale, the small camp on the North Shore that faces on North Bay, while he was still on the lake. In his later years, he became something of a recluse and finally spent his last days at an adult home in Port Leyden.

Edward J. "E. J." Martin. E. J. and his younger brother Charlie entered the Big Moose scene in 1894, working at Higby's, at Dart's, and helping to clear the right-of-way for the Raquette Lake Railway. In the early years they worked at constructing camps and earned reputations as skilled and reliable craftsmen. They built many

Edward "E. J." and Harriet "Hattie" Martin, 1902. Courtesy of Wanda K. Martin.

of the camps on the North Shore, some houses on West Bay, and six of the Lake View Lodge cottages. In addition, they built two nearly identical large camps, one for Leslie Warnick Brown of Utica west of the entrance to North Bay, and the other west of what was to become the Waldheim property on lots 319–21.

E. J. and Charlie opened the Waldheim in 1904, but after two years Charlie decided he preferred to be independent. E. J. went on to become the sole operator of the resort that continues to this day.

E. J. married Harriet Brown from the Boonville area. Their first son, Everett, was born in 1909. When he was attending Clarkson College in Potsdam, New York, Everett spent his vacations working at the Waldheim, where local people remember him as a dapper college boy sporting a raccoon coat and driving an Oakland roadster. He dashed around the lake in his racing boat, *Baby Must* (labeled *Baby Mustn't* on the other side), and later owned a pontoon airplane that he anchored in the shallow water just inside North Bay. After graduation, Everett spent some time at the Waldheim and served as the first president of the new Big Moose Fire Company. His engaging smile attracted the young ladies, and in 1944 he married Vera Bleckwell, a teacher from Syracuse who was a valuable and versatile staff member at the Waldheim. Everett worked as an engineer at General Electric in Schenectady, but he always retained an active interest in the family business. Spending weekends at the Waldheim, he turned his hand to many things, among them nurturing a variety of colorful water lilies near the dock. Everett and Vera had no children. Late in life, both suffered from long illnesses, dying in 1997 and 2000 respectively.

E. J. and Hattie's second son, Howard, was born more than ten years later, in 1920. Like Everett, he graduated from Boonville High School. After attending Duke University for one year, he looked for a more practical course of study and finished his education at the State University of New York at Morrisville. Howard inherited his muscular build and dark curly hair from his father, and

The three Martin brothers, Frank, Charles, and E. J., ca. 1900. Courtesy of Wanda K. Martin.

EXCERPTS FROM E. J. MARTIN'S DIARY FOR 1925

E. J. Martin, known as "E. J.," lived on the lake year-round. These excerpts from his diary for 1925 are primarily a business record of the multitude of activities that occupied him in running his hotel business, but they also give us a vivid glimpse of life on the lake in the early days. Not all the names are identifiable. Nelson is Nelson Dunn, Chas. or Charles is Charles Martin; Frank is Frank Martin, both of the latter brothers of E. J.; Everett and Howard are, of course, E. J.'s sons. Naporski, Kinne, Kingsford, Milne, and others are familiar names on the lake. Sumner Covey was the son of Earl Covey by his first wife. Peter, Garrett, Brian, Ray, and Earnest were presumably employees whose last names are not given.

The record here is a transcript. Although we could not print the entries for every day, or even the entire entry for any single day, the entries that do appear have not been edited. The diary begins on January 5, 1925, when E. J. returned from Boonville after spending the holidays with his wife, Hattie, and his children, who lived on the lake only during the summer months. E. J.'s trip back by train took from 8:12 A.M. until 11:45 A.M., when he arrived at Big Moose Station after a change in Remsen.

Tuesday, January 20, 1925. 16 above zero in the morning, 24 at noon, and 21 at night. Cloudy all day, snowing at times, so that [by] night it had snowed about 5 inches. Nelson, Peter and I went up to Naporski's at l0 o'clock to make [the] road . . . clean out sawdust and get [the] ice house in shape.

Wednesday, January 21, 1925. Frank, Nelson, Chas. Garrett and I worked until ten o'clock filling [the] Naporski ice house, then we all went to putting new sawdust on the ice. We put three loads on it, before we had it properly covered. In the afternoon, we gathered up the tools and went down to open up Chas. ice patch. We plowed eight strips—26 cakes to a strip—and put them all in the ice house. The ice was 13 inches thick.

Saturday, January 24, 1925. We just had a short view of the eclipse of the sun this morning. Papers say this was [the] first total eclipse of sun since 1806, and there will not be another until 2024.

Friday, January 30, 1925. It snowed 24 inches of the beautiful snow last night, and everything was covered 4 feet and 6 inches deep. The worst snow storm we have had in a long time.

Thursday, February 12, 1925. Rigged up [the] plow and started down the road. Got down back of [the] Glenmore and found I had a sick horse—legs all stiff and could not walk, had "black water." Tried to get some [medicine] from Mr. Kinne, but they did not have [any]. Found Frank and Pete in the edge of [the] clearing back of Owl's Nest with [the] horse down, and [they] could not get it up. Worked until dark trying to get it up and building a shelter for it. Got a bale of hay and a tent, packed brush and hay around the horse and under [him] as far as we could, and put the tent over him and blankets on him. Could not get him home or . . . back to [the] Glenmore, so that was the best we could do.

Tuesday, February 24, 1925. I fed the stock in the morning, then went down to Chas. house, and Frank and I went to Nelson Dunn's for breakfast, then from there on out to the station. Picked up Dave Des Jardin and went on down to George Bushy's camp, 3½ miles from Woods Lake Station looking [to buy] . . . a team of horses. We found two teams that looked rather favorable, but one team he wanted $350 for and the other $450, which we decided was too much money for the horses. Walked back to Woods Lake and took the train to [Big Moose] Station and [then] walked home, getting there at 4 o'clock, having walked better than 20 miles.

Monday, March 23, 1925. We gathered the tools together and drew them up to the Retter boat house, and then went to work to jack it up and get rollers under it [and] move it over [onto] the new foundation east of the house. We got it raised and the large rollers cut, and moved it about three feet toward the lake in the forenoon. In the afternoon, we moved it so that about one half of it was out on the ice, then as the ice had become soft, the weight was too much for it and it began to sink . . . so we cut a hole in the ice and put a prop under the end of the boat house.

Tuesday, March 24, 1925. Went up [to] the Retter boat house. We moved it out about 40 feet in the forenoon, then the pin we put in to hold the drum from turning on the shaft sheared off, and we were in trouble right away. Bored two new holes and put in two new pins. In the afternoon the ice became poor, and when we went to raise the front end of the boat house to put under rollers, the ice broke and settled to the bottom under the weight of the boat house, so they decided to hang it up until in the summer when the water is warm. So we picked up the tools and material and came home.

Monday, March 30, 1925. I drove down to the Glenmore in the forenoon and brought up the rest of the oats and three bales of hay. Then went to work on the dresser [furniture for the cottages] at the barn and worked until 6 o'clock.

Saturday, April 4, 1925. I worked on the dressers in the shop over the barn all day. Roughed out two paddles in the forenoon.

Friday, May 8, 1925. Ray and I worked on the dressers in the shop until 10.30, then went at the slabbing of the front of the house. We got the slabs all on the front, except [for] the casing of the front door.

Saturday, May 9, 1925. Ray and I slabbed on the bay window and put sawdust in the partition—taking off the slabs and sheathing, and making a good job of it about 4.30. We [then] went up in to the garden and planted cauliflower and squash seeds. In the evening I planted nasturtium seeds.

Sunday, May 10, 1925. They made a trial run of the Bluenose with the new 220 h.p. motor, and it made the boat fairly skim the water.

Monday, May 11, 1925. Ray and I went down on the road and put the old Bob horse under the sod, and then planted corn and potatoes in the garden.

Thursday, May 14, 1925. Ray set out the strawberry plants we had taken up, and helped plant cabbage and squash. Howard and I set out the gladiolus bulbs and planted cabbage and squash.

Monday, May 18, 1925. Walter Dunn came over and put the new gear wheels on the engine to the [Waldheim] sawmill, but [he] had no more than got the engine nicely started when it stripped the gear all off the new wheels.

Tuesday, May 19, 1925. We cut a road in to the upper end of the sawmill so that Sumner Covey could get in to the . . . mill with his tractor. . . . In the afternoon I worked on the new laundry slabbing, and Ray went over to Mr. Kingsford's and tuned up the car. After he got back we went up in the garden and set out 300 strawberry plants.

Monday, May 25, 1925. It was 37 in the morning, 44 at noon and 42 at night. When we got up in the morning, [we] found the ground covered with snow and the air full of flakes, and it snowed more or less all day. In the forenoon I tinkered at a lot of different things, and Ray put the water on [in] some of the cottages . . . in the afternoon we put up the new rails to Camp Hearts Content and cleaned up the brush near Everett cottage. Then we went to slabbing the new laundry.

Thursday, June 4, 1925. We drew up the hay and put it into the barn, and then we skidded up Mr. Milne's logs from the water and drew a scow load of lumber from the pile down to the lake shore. We worked for him from 3 to 6 o'clock. In the evening I planted some cauliflower seeds.

Saturday, June 27, 1925. I worked in the bath room of the main camp all day. Everett helped me and changed the electric wiring in the cooler and our dining room. The rest of the men had a general clean up day. Worked a little while in the garden. Had eight people arrive today.

Sunday, June 28, 1925. Had quite a number of people come in yesterday, so we were all quite busy all day.

Sunday, August 30, 1925. I gave the mirrors the 2nd coat of varnish and finished up the backs. In [the] afternoon we all went down to the tea house [probably Alice Martin's] and had ice cream.

Friday, September 4, 1925. We got things ready to put the roofing on the barn, and I crimped several sheets of steel in the forenoon. In the afternoon we put on 12 sheets. Everett and I started up the saw mill just before noon, and it was working fine until the pin came out of the flywheel and let it off far enough to cause it to turn on the shaft, breaking the governor fasteners and two cogs out of the large gear wheel.

Friday, September 11, 1925. In the afternoon we went down on the road to work. We drilled a two foot hole in the large rock in the middle of the road just back of Chas. House, and got it done at noon. In the afternoon put four sticks of dynamite in it and set it off, and the rock was in small pieces. Also blew up two stumps that were close to the road. About 4 o'clock, Everett and I went over to put the new parts in the engine at the saw mill. We got them in all right but they did not send any new key for the flywheel, and it came off again and we had to stop the engine.

Thursday, October 1, 1925. We finished [digging] the ditch on the upper side of the road above the ledge, and blew out a large birch stump that was near the ledge, then [spent] nearly all forenoon filling up the hole. In the afternoon we dug potatoes, and in the evening we went up in North Bay for a picnic supper.

Friday, October 9, 1925. Earnest and I got the rest of the steel ready for the roof to the sawmill, and in the afternoon we went down [in the] cellar and began digging out the earth so as to enlarge the cellar. Everett came home at noon and helped us some. Towards night [at] about 5.30 it began to snow, and it snowed quite a little before dark, the first of the season.

Wednesday, October 14, 1925. Ray, Earnest and I cut wood all day up next to the lot line. We got up about six cords, then we moved down near the potato field.

Wednesday, November 11, 1925. We hunted in the burnt ground [from the 1903 forest fire], and then went south of the south branch and hunted along the stream. Did not put up a buck today at all. Got back to camp about 5 o'clock. The two city hunters would make very good threshing machines.

Saturday, November 14, 1925. 30 in the morning, 32 at noon, and 30 at night. Rained all night until morning, then commenced to snow all forenoon, then rained all afternoon and evening. A right nasty day.

We hunted down along the trail and outlet to the sister lakes until around 3 o'clock, then built a rousing fire along beside the trail and got warm. While there, Earl Covey and his outfit came along—eight of them—and they had seven deer. We hung up another one today—four prongs on one horn and the other a broken horn.

Friday, November 20, 1925. We dressed off the four hogs in the forenoon, and in the afternoon Ray and I went up in the woods and cut wood.

Sunday, November 22, 1925. The lake froze over last night with about ½ inch of ice, and when the wind began to blow about 10 o'clock in the forenoon, the ice began to move up the lake and it did quite a lot of cutting on the boards along the front of the dock.

Sunday, December 13, 1925. 24 in morning, 26 at noon, 22 at night. A clear morning but soon clouded over and began to snow . . . it snowed all day right down hard, and in the afternoon it blew a regular blizzard. I started for Big Moose about 10 o'clock and I made Moose River by 2.30 and stopped there to feed the horse and got some dinner . . . started from there around 3.30 and arrived at Thendara around 6.15 stopped at Van Aukens Tavern, and I shall say it was some day. It must have snowed about 8 or 10 inches, and part of the time I thought my two-wheeled gig was going to collapse. Walked part of the time where the road was the roughest. Could not make any time until I got on the road from McKeever to Thendara.

Monday, December 14, 1925. 6 in morning, 16 at noon and 20 at night. A cloudy day with quite a wind. I stayed over night in Thendara at Van Aukens Tavern, and this morning I started with my road cart for Big Moose. Got started about 8.30, found lots of snow—some places around 15 inches. Arrived at home around two o'clock. There were very few on the road today. Cost me $2.50 for supper, lodging, and breakfast, and $.50 for horse.

Wednesday, December 16, 1925. Charley Nower and I put the bob sleighs together in [the] morning and made or ironed off a new whiffle tree . . . then we helped Frank and Chas. push the docks out from shore. In [the] afternoon we all got [a] harness fitted to [the] new horse[s] and hitched them up and drew Frank's sawing machine up in the woods back of the upper garden, where we were cutting wood.

Tuesday, December 29, 1925. I came in to the woods today—arrived at the station and got a ride down to the Glenmore corner with Earl Covey's team. Arrived here about 1.30, got some dinner and then Chas. came up and we went up in the electric house and started a fire with charcoal to thaw out the batteries, which had become chilled . . . got them pretty well thawed out, and about 9 o'clock started the machine. Got pretty well used up for want of fresh air. Had the house all shut up and the fires burned up all the oxygen out of the air, had blind staggers and a fierce headache.

Wednesday, December 30, 1925. I started the electric machine in the morning, and got the batteries working. . . , then Chas. came along and made a road from the shore out on the ice plot, and I went to work on the sleigh runner. After dinner, we took the outfit down to Chas. shop, and I worked at it there and Chas. made [a] road to his ice plot, and he finished about 3 o'clock, and then came and helped me on the runner. Fred Brack lined out a road across the lake from Lakeview, to haul their wood over from the Brown lot, and marked it with brush.

E. J. Martin and pilot in front of the Seagull (barely visible here), the first airplane to land on Big Moose Lake, 1926. Courtesy of Wanda K. Martin.

An entry from E. J.'s diary for the next year, 1926, is of particular interest:

Saturday, July 31, 1926. A seaplane came over from Fourth Lake in the forenoon and landed on the water about 10:30. First plane that has ever landed on Big Moose. In the afternoon Everett, Howard and I went over to Higby Camp and Howard and I went up in it. Saw quite a number of lakes and had a fine view of the country. Was up about ten minutes.

Further information comes from the Martin family papers and from recollections. It seems that later, in August, young Franklin Joseph, a longtime guest at Lake View Lodge and a neighbor of the Ottos in Garden City, took a trip in the same plane. That ride was the inspiration for his life's work as an aeronautical engineer. Franklin was a friend of young Carl Otto, Everett Martin, and Richard Carey (brother of Frank Carey, Sr., who summered at Fern Spring Camp), all of whom joined in youthful adventures around the lake.

In 1929, a Sikorsky seaplane landed on the lake and caught a wave with its wingtip. It was pulled to shallow water near Retter's beach. The accident caused enough damage so that it had to be disassembled and trucked out. In 1931, another Sikorsky was forced to land on the lake, and it too was taken to Retter's beach to await repairs.

Franklin Joseph is a longtime member of the Long Island Early Fliers, an organization that has had a hand in the impressive Cradle of Aviation Museum, which opened in May 2002. Franklin (who was ninety years old in 2002) verified the Sikorsky planes in the old photographs.

The airplane incidents that summer also influenced Everett Martin, who later became the proud owner of a 1937 Aeronca Cub. He moored his plane in North Bay until he moved it to Schenectady during the war when he worked at General Electric.

his outgoing personality and sense of humor from his mother. While Howard was a student at Morrisville, he returned to Big Moose on weekends, transporting on his way his neighbor Wanda Kinne, who was attending business school in Utica. The two became engaged before Howard left to join the army during the war. After serving in France and Germany following the D-Day invasion, he returned home to marry Wanda later that year. As E. J. gradually retired, Howard and Wanda took over the management of the Waldheim, operating the hotel for close to forty years. Their successors are their daughter Nancy Martin Pratt and her husband, Roger Pratt, although the other two Martin children, Jon and Philip, also participate in the family partnership.

Charles Martin, ca. 1900.
Courtesy of Wanda K.
Martin.

Charles Martin. When E. J. and Charlie Martin built the large camp west of the Waldheim, they did not suspect that it would become Charlie's home for more than fifty years. It began life in 1902 as a summer home for Carl and Laura Koller of New York City, who sold it in 1907 to a man named Warren Richards who operated it (or possibly only planned to operate it) as a small resort. Richards published a brochure, calling the establishment Idle Wild. Unfortunately for us, the brochure carried only standard pictures of deer and shoreline, but not one of the building itself, which, however, was almost identical to the L. W. Brown house.

The house, which backs up against a steep cliff, has seven bedrooms, two baths, and a sleeping porch upstairs, as well as a large living room, dining room, and kitchen on the lower floor. Across the front runs a wide porch looking out over the lake.

By the winter of 1910, Richards may have had new problems on his mind. He neglected to have his roof shoveled, and one wall of the house collapsed from the weight of the snow. Taxes went unpaid. Richards was also divorcing his wife. (The Martin family has papers recording the settlement.) The judge ruled that Warren Richards would be legally able to remarry. His wife, in accordance with the laws of the time, would not be permitted to marry again until her former husband had died.

Richards sold the house in 1911 to Charles Martin, who was able to buy the property at a bargain price because of its condition and repair it. In the same year Charles married Alice Foote, who had worked summers at Lake View Lodge. The house was so substantial that they could live there all year. The many bedrooms were often rented out to guests who preferred staying with Charlie and Alice but who took their meals at the Waldheim. Additional living quarters for guests were available over the boathouse.

Their daughter and only child, Katherine, was born in 1916 and, despite Charles's early disappointment at not having a son, grew up to be her father's delight. While Charles continued with guiding, carpentry, and maintenance, Alice took care of her roomers. She also ran a teahouse, sometimes located in a separate screened and canvas-sided building to the east of the house and sometimes on the porch. Alice became an expert on wildflowers and plants, spending time in the woods and in a garden behind their home. She found she had much in common with Lena Retter Otto and her sister Janet Retter Bruyn, who were also interested in wildflower gardens. Alice served as treasurer of the Big Moose Community Chapel in 1931 and later during 1938–1945. When she died at a relatively early age in 1945, the church

The Charles Martin boathouse, ca. 1960.
Courtesy of Wanda K. Martin.

Alice Martin's teahouse, on the porch of her house, ca. 1920. Courtesy of Wanda K. Martin.

dedicated to her a set of stone steps leading from the Chapel down to the lake and the Chapel dock.

In 1949–50, Charles, E. J., and Frank came together again for their last joint project. They built a home for Howard and his wife, Wanda, in the center of the Waldheim lake frontage.

Charles was a contractor and caretaker who was much in demand. His launch, the *Princess* (first owned by Clarence Kelsey, then by Nelson Dunn, and perhaps later by Art Burtch), which he used to tow his long gray scow to work sites on the lake, was a familiar sight. With his signature curved pipe, he was a pleasant man with a soft voice and an amused twinkle in his eye. Charles also was a skilled guide, much in demand, and an early member of the Brown's Tract Guides Association. He died in 1964 at age eighty-five, and at his funeral this poem by Arthur Guiterman was read:

Alice Martin, ca. 1938. Courtesy of Wanda K. Martin.

A WOODMAN'S REQUIEM

The pack is too hard on the shoulders
The feet are too slow on the trail,
The log that was blazing but smoulders
And gone is the zest from the tale.
Then why should we wistfully tarry
Old comrades, grown feeble and few?
Come, rest on the shore of the carry
And wait for the silver canoe.

The silver canoe—and who guesses
What paddle is plied at the stern?
It comes in the silence that blesses
Through forests of cedar and fern;
It comes, when the twilight is fading,
Through shadow to moonlight, and then
It goes with its earth-weary lading
From moonlight to shadow again.

It glides to a lake of the mountains,
As blue as the skies that are fair,
And fed by the purest of fountains
A lake of the woodlands—and there,
Oh, pathfinder, cragsman, frontiersman,
Your cabin is waiting for you;
For peace is the goal of the steersman,
The bourn of the silver canoe.

When Charles and Alice's daughter Katherine grew up, she became a lieutenant in the WAVES and married a naval officer, Robert Vollenweider. Because they were unable to spend much time at Big Moose, Katherine finally sold the house to Thomas Witmer in 1981. Bob Vollenweider died in 1987 and Katherine in September of 1997.

KINNE'S BOAT LINE

Romaine Kinne, like others, had come to the Adirondacks on his doctor's advice, giving up a promising career as a draftsman to do so. He was a victim of the Spanish flu that ravaged the United States after World War I. The disease left his lungs weak and susceptible to many kinds of respiratory infections. He was tall, lean, and handsome, and when he wore his captain's hat and piloted the boats, he cut an imposing figure. Henry Bruyn, recalling his annual trips to Big Moose when he was a small boy, wrote of his childhood impression of Kinne as "a god-like figure who commanded the great ship that carried us on the last leg of our journey from the busy, crowded and heavily structured 'civilization' to the wonderful world of my grandmother's Big Moose."

When Romaine and Lillian Kinne arrived at Big Moose Station in the spring of 1920 with their young son, Gordon, they pitched a tent for their living quarters. Lillian worked for Carrie Jarvis at the Deerhead Inn at Big Moose Station, while Romaine recuperated from his illness in the fresh mountain air. That winter they stayed with the Jarvises, and in March 1921 purchased a lot and camp on the north shore of West Bay from Frank Day. Romaine worked for the LaFountains until they left Big Moose, when he bought the marine end of the Big Moose Transportation Company from them.

Kinne's Boat Line, a spinoff from the steamboat service run by the Big Moose Transportation Company and forerunner of today's marina, was a busy place. The departure and return of the mail boat on weekdays, the comings and goings of the launches loaded with sightseeing passengers, and the arrival of boats from around the lake coming in on some errand, created lively traffic

Romaine Kinne, ca. 1940. Courtesy of Richard Widdicombe.

throughout the day. The workshop was centered in the Glennmore boathouse, where the Boat Line leased slips for its boats as well as office and work space. The Boat Line also handled the dealership for Chris-Crafts, selling several that are still on the lake. It serviced and repaired marine motors, sold marine paints, motor oils, spark plugs, flotation devices, canoe paddles, and other boating needs from its workshop at the Glennmore dock. The big seller, the lowly shearpin, saved many a propeller when the irregular floor of the lake rose almost to the surface and took the uninformed boater by surprise.

The core of the business was its fleet of boats. The gasoline-powered *Glennmore,* the *Spray,* and the little eight-passenger *Duchess* had all belonged to the Big Moose Transportation Company. Kinne renovated and

Romaine and Lillian Kinne with unknown companion (left) in front of their tent at the Big Moose Station, 1920. Courtesy of Wanda K. Martin.

The launch White Lady *at the Kinne family dock, ca. 1930. Courtesy of Wanda K. Martin.*

The launch Big Moose *at the Chapel dock, ca. early 1930s. Courtesy of Barbara K. Wheeler.*

modernized the *Glennmore,* changing the seating from benches along the sides to forward-facing benches. He also moved the steering wheel from the port side amidships (where it was located on the *Big Moose* launch) to the bow, and added a windshield and side windows there. He renamed the boat the *White Lady.* The smaller *Duchess* was sold in the early 1930s to Fred Ellmers on Twitchell Lake, where it had a long tour of duty.

Kinne also purchased a larger launch, built in 1909, from Fourth Lake that he named the *Big Moose* (not to be confused with the earlier steamboat *SS Big Moose*). This vessel could carry thirty passengers, who sat in comfortable wicker chairs under a roof. The boat had space for luggage and for the barrels of food that camp owners would have shipped in on the railroad. On its regular twice-daily trips around the lake, it also carried mail. Canvas curtains at the sides protected passengers and cargo from rain.

A new Chris-Craft, the *Skippy,* bought from Jack Dunn on Fourth Lake, completed the Boat Line's fleet.

The *Skippy* came from the factory with a Chrysler engine that Kinne replaced with a larger and quieter Grey marine engine. It planed the water's surface easily, making it at one time the fastest boat on the lake, able to outrun the Greenwoods' *Natty Bumppo* and others. For three dollars, or fifty cents a person, Kinne would offer "thrill rides" to his customers.

Kinne also ran moonlight excursions when the moon and the weather cooperated—a very popular offering. Harry Whitmore, who played the banjo and guitar at the Glennmore bar, accompanied the passengers as they harmonized to such appropriate songs as "Moonlight Bay" or "In the Evening by the Moonlight." Listening to them as they cruised by was almost as much fun as being on board.

Romaine Kinne's son Gordon had been born in 1915; as he grew older, he was able to help his father in the painting and maintenance work as well as in running the mail boat and taking passengers around the lake. However, at the outset of World War II, Gordon was in the

Kinne's Boat Service sign, ca. 1940. Courtesy of Richard Widdicombe.

first contingent from Herkimer County to be drafted in the spring of 1941. The Kinne daughters, Wanda and Barbara, helped their father and took over Gordon's duties. At age nineteen, Wanda earned a New York State pilot's license for inland waters, the first woman to do so. Both girls received publicity in central New York for helping to carry on while local men served in the armed forces.

In the autumn of 1942, Romaine elected to return to Rome, New York, and take up his old position to help in the war effort. Sadly, he contracted lobar pneumonia in January of 1943 and died in the hospital after a two-week battle with the illness.

It was a difficult return to Big Moose that spring. Barbara Kinne Wheeler recollects:

All Dad's machinery had been left in the Glennmore boathouse and the boats in their slips suspended over the water. Walt Dunn had floated the *White Lady* to get

Wanda Kinne (Martin) and Barbara Kinne (Wheeler) operating the mail boat, 1942. Unattributed newspaper photograph from Muriel Groves, Reminiscences of West Bay, *following p. 52.*

the mail delivered around the lake. The *White Lady* was at the landing at the Glennmore making ready to leave on the mail run when Walt asked if I would like to go along and crew for him.

It was good to be on board again and swapping the mailbags at the docks. Walt, however, had an ulterior motive. He told me he had learned that the next year's rent on the boathouse was due by the end of the month and that the lawyer for the Glennmore was expected to be here this weekend *two days off*. If we could get everything out of the boathouse before then, he could have no opportunity to lay claim to any of Dad's equipment or to charge Mother further rent. Walt suggested that I get her permission for the community to empty out the premises.

Mother had assumed a job at the Waldheim, and I informed her about this turn of events.

Word went out, and the next morning, bright and early, people began showing up, ready to work. The hotels brought their pick-up trucks and summer people with empty boat slips available had been contacted by phone for temporary storage of our boats.

As I worked alongside these good neighbors, I caught a glimpse of dignified Mrs. Callahan, white locks escaping from her head scarf and a dirt smudge across her face, busily coiling up a piece of cable. I wouldn't forget that image. To me it represented all of them there, giving up time from their hectic spring schedules to help us. There was a lump in my throat.

At the end of that momentous day, there was not a scrap of evidence that anyone was occupying the premises. Everything, even the electrical outlets, had been removed. All the boats had been towed away or moved to boathouses around the lake. All Dad's machinery had been moved to our garage and other temporary refuges, and the place was empty.

Walt Dunn, who had bought the *White Lady* (or perhaps rented her), used the boat to deliver mail around the lake. In early August 1943, the *White Lady*, the flagship of the Kinne fleet, came to a sad end. By this time, Wanda Kinne was working in Utica and had come back for the weekend. She was unpacking at the Waldheim, where she was staying with her friend Vera Bleckwell (soon to marry Everett Martin, E. J.'s older son). Vera wrote to Everett on August 6, 1943:

We were all going for a boat ride around the lake. Wanda [and I] were calmly talking when we both heard an explosion . . . I stepped out and couldn't see anything so I told Wanda I was going down to see if the kids

GROWING UP AT
BIG MOOSE LAKE | *Barbara Kinne Wheeler*

Much has been written about the lake in summer and the influx of loyal families to their summer homes. A great feeling of community and friendship has developed among them, the love of the lake being their common bond. Less has been recorded, however, about the lives of those year-round residents, who, for one reason or another, chose to make Big Moose Lake their permanent home.

In 1927, the year I was born, "Silent Cal" Coolidge was in the White House, Lindbergh flew solo across the Atlantic in his *Spirit of St. Louis,* and the "Roarin' Twenties" were winding down to their ignominious end. The crash of '29 left the country in a deep depression, the grip of which reached even remote Big Moose—already considered a depressed area. The resourceful residents, who were already accustomed to frugal living, went on with their lives much the same as before, the women canning their food and baking their bread, the men getting in the wood and harvesting the ice for the icehouses. Although people had less than before, their lifestyles were not drastically changed. In the winters of the thirties, some seventeen or eighteen families hunkered down around the shore of the frozen lake like frogs around a pond. Hunting was less a sport than a means of providing meat for the table. There were, of course, the ice jobs, and those men who had caretaker obligations kept a watchful eye on their charges, taking care of repairs, restocking woodsheds, and keeping roofs shoveled. Otherwise, there was little to do to add to the family coffers. No one twiddled his thumbs, though. An industrious lot, the winter residents filled their time with worthwhile projects. My Dad, for example made furniture. Much of the furniture we had, Dad built during the off-season. Handsome, sturdy, and functional, it is still in use today.

Like all the women in this pioneer setting, Mother worked ceaselessly. Because of Dad's chronic lung weakness, she was the first to arise on the frigid winter mornings to stoke the fires and warm things up. On Monday the wash tubs were set up in the kitchen, wash water in one, rinse water in the other, with the hand-operated wringer in between. Mother removed stubborn dirt spots on a wooden scrub board and used bleach to remove stains. White shirts were boiled in a copper boiler on the stove. Clothes were hung on the clothesline outside. I was impressed by woolen long johns hanging on the line, seeming to take on a life of their own when frozen stiff.

Tuesday was the start of endless ironing, using old flatirons heated on the stove. The newer ones had detachable handles, a big improvement over the hot iron handles that had to be held with a potholder. Now, when the iron in use cooled, the handle could simply be removed and attached to a new iron hot from the stove.

Without the convenience of a handy grocery store, much had to be made from scratch in the winter. One of my chores was to assist Mother when she made mayonnaise. Oil had to be added to the seasoned egg yolk and vinegar mixture, and I had to pour the oil ever so slowly while Mother manned the eggbeater. Margarine came with an enclosed color packet, which had to be mixed in to make the white margarine more appealing for table use. This also was a chore for my sister Wanda or me.

Mother was skilled at running the wood-fired cook stove, controlling the fire to produce the proper oven temperature for the breads or pies or casseroles. Dad enjoyed old-fashioned oatmeal, and with the fire banked for the night, Mother would set the double boiler at the back of the stove; by breakfast time, the cereal would be just right.

In lieu of new-fangled vacuum cleaners, brooms, dust cloths, and dust mops did the day-to-day cleaning, while soap made from lye and applied with elbow grease did the scrubbing. Households had to keep lye on hand for soap making, which presented a real danger, as we shall see. When my sister Wanda was a toddler, she got into the lye container under the kitchen sink. Fortunately, she was discovered before she got too far, but she still bears the scars on her abdomen, her thigh, and her tongue. She was one lucky child! The worst consequence in later life was her inability to whistle because of her scarred tongue. (Not so blessed was Billy Stevens's boy, Robert.)

Spring cleaning was a season unto itself and the whole family was conscripted for this task. Windows and doors were opened and the house was aired out. Rugs were hung on the clotheslines and the winter dirt was beaten out of them. The O'Cedar oil mop and cloths captured the dust on the furniture and wood floors. Windows were washed with "Glass Wax" (I don't ever remember streaks), and, oh yes, what was left of the winter supply of potatoes was brought from the cellar, and Wanda and I had the job of removing the sprouts to keep them from softening further.

Any structured social life centered mostly on the church. Services were held on Sunday afternoon by the minister from Old Forge. Commandingly tall, the Reverend Frank Reed was a figure inspiring trust and confidence as he brought the message of the Gospel to our little flock. The Willing Workers met regularly to stitch and sew and create items to sell at the summer bazaar—and to enjoy each other's company. I remember elderly Francena Higby, Jim Higby's widow, using her severed forearm as a darning egg while sewing. The men gathered to play cards, to socialize, and to discuss and plan for the care and maintenance of the church building. A big winter event was the Christmas candlelight service. Lake and Station people took part. The children from both schools performed and received gifts, fruit, candy, and a box of animal crackers. Those were happy evenings to remember!

One vivid flashback over some seventy-odd years is my recollection of sitting alone on my parents' bed, looking out an upstairs window at the dark night and a blazing fire across the bay. It was the church burning. The gravity of the situation probably meant little to me, for at the time I was only three years old. Undoubtedly it was the stress of the adults and the disquiet of the household that etched that moment so indelibly on my mind.

The one-room school provided social as well as educational experiences for the children in a place where "next door" could be as much as one-half mile away. My best friend, Mary Alden Covey, lived way over on South Bay near the Outlet, and our parents had to go out of their way to see that we got together on a regular basis at her home or mine. Because of these distances, there was little casual visiting from home to home, so to break the winter monotony, the families sometimes arranged gatherings at the different houses. The hosts would put on a meal for all, and after dinner was cleared away, the adults would spend the evening playing cards, the children would play games together, and the little ones would be tucked away upstairs to sleep, safe and snug. It was always fun to get together with the neighbors!

As a child, I hadn't the slightest inkling that we were really "poor." Everybody was in about the same boat. There was always food on the table, warm clothes to wear, and the great woods outside our door for a playground. Looking back, I'm sure that our house was not as warm as our city cousins' homes. I remember before bedtime Mother warming the flannel sheets over the coal-burning space heater in the living room for my sister and me, and

the race up the stairs to our icy bedroom to settle between them before they cooled down. But we were a healthy lot. Except for the usual childhood diseases brought home from school and an occasional cold, we all seemed to stay hale and hardy.

We did very little traveling. We never did so in the summer because of the boat business, and we seldom went any farther than Utica or Clinton to touch base with family. A trip to the "outside" (as anything beyond the "blue line" was called) was a full day's undertaking in our 1929 Chevy over the old roads. I have a vague recollection of stopping to buy popcorn from a vendor at Bagg's Square on the way out of Utica and stopping at a place in Alder Creek for refreshments and a break in the trip on the way back home at night.

One of the highlights of our young lives was a trip to Lake Placid in 1932 to attend a day at the Winter Olympics. Dad was interested in seeing the bobsled races. I remember starting out in the middle of the night in the '29 Chevy with heated bricks at our feet and an old bearskin coat spread across our laps. It was bitter cold, and what left the greatest impression on little almost-five-year-old me were the giant bonfires burning at various spots on Mount Van Hoevenberg and how I managed to stay near one to keep warm. My brother Gordon, then well into his teens, went up to where the teams were preparing to start their runs (no security in those guileless days!) and was politely told "Nein" by a German contestant—not to touch the runners of their sled. In 1980, when our daughter and son-in-law accompanied my husband, Jerry, and me to Lake Placid, I wondered if I had entered an exclusive club consisting of those who had attended both of the Lake Placid Winter Games.

At home, evenings were spent around the radio listening to Jack Benny, Fred Allen, Lux Radio Studio, and other programs. I remember in particular listening to Admiral Byrd reporting from the South Pole. That seemed like a miracle! And the Lindbergh trial—a cause of much discussion among the adults. Mother was amazed by the report of the birth of the Dionne quintuplets and saved pictures and news clippings about them. Before supper there were the special children's programs: Buck Rogers in the 25th Century (sci-fi, thirties-style), Jack Armstrong, the All-American Boy, and Little Orphan Annie. Oh, the Ovaltine we drank so we could send for those decoder pins! Listening to the radio, the only picture you saw was the one you conjured up in your mind.

Friday night at our house was popcorn night. There was no school the next day so we could stay up a little later. Grandpa Kinne grew popcorn in his garden in Clinton, the purpley-red kind that popped into tender, big white morsels, and he always kept us well supplied. Dad would get the coals just right in the cook stove. Then he'd remove the stove lids and pop the corn in a handled screen basket, styled just for this purpose, shaking and agitating it so the kernels wouldn't burn. Finally, he would fill the big dishpan full, flavoring the popcorn with butter and salt. What a treat!

The best fun, we all agreed, was when the ice was right on the lake and the West Bay coterie—Bud (Walt Jr.) and Joe (George) Dunn, Bill and Junior (Nelse) Dunn, Bill (Willard) McAllister, Wanda, and I—all got together to skate. Mostly we would skate on the weekends, but when the skating was really good we would go out after supper when it was dark or there was a moon to light the scene. Sometimes the northern lights made exciting displays in the night sky, and the stars would look so close you felt you could reach up and pick them. One open winter of note, when the unusual cold produced deep black ice and it was too cold to snow, we would be awakened at night by the booming of the ice expanding as the temperature plummeted. The lake became a four-mile-long, mile-wide skating rink, and we skated before school in the early mornings, after school as late as we were allowed, and all weekends. Allison and Pat Higby from the main lake and Mary Covey from South Bay joined us, too. Mary and I skated to each other's houses and up the lake and all over. The old-timers said they couldn't remember a winter like it. All the kids and some of the grown-ups (Dad, a good skater, included) had a great time. Everett Martin and Gordon did a lot of wind-sail skating, which looked like fun.

One of my favorite people was Art Burtch. He used to come over to our house once in a while to have dinner when Goldie and Maxine were south. When I was married in November of 1949, Art attended the reception, and it was he, of course, who made certain there were tin cans tied to the car as Jerry and I drove away.

I also have clear memories of Mr. Forkey, the storekeeper. He was a thoughtful man. One Christmas there was a package under the tree from him for me. It was a book from the store's book section entitled *The School Favorite*, and the young heroine's name was Barbara.

The old telephones were oblong wooden boxes that hung on the wall, eighteen inches high by eight inches wide by five and one-half inches deep and made of furniture-finished oak. If you were a little kid, you had to climb on a chair to use them. The metal mouthpiece was on the lower front, and two round metal orbs at the top produced the sound of the ringing. Kids today might be reminded of the facial features of the *Star Wars* robot R2D2. Instead of ears, though, the box had a hook on the left side that held the receiver, which was connected to the inner works by a cord. On the right side was a crank that, when rotated, caused the bells to ring on all the telephones on your party line.

The telephone number for our phone was 8F6. That meant that when it rang six short rings, we would answer by taking the receiver off the hook and speaking into the mouthpiece. When the phone started to ring, all activities stopped in the households on the line while people counted the rings. The Waldheim's number was 8F5. If the number stopped at five rings, it indicated that the call was for them. If the ringing stopped before that, the Kinnes and the Waldheim didn't have to listen any further. Six was the maximum number of short rings. When Dad had a telephone installed at the Boat House office, the number was 8F21. This didn't mean twenty-one rings, but two long and one short.

To make a call, you removed the receiver from the hook and listened. If you heard the dial tone, you could go ahead and make your call. If you heard voices talking, someone was already using the phone, and you would have to hang up and wait a while to make your call. If your call was urgent or time-dependent, though, you could break in, explain your plight, and simply ask the parties if they would please relinquish the line.

Roy Higby related how his mother and her sister, his Aunt Daisy Glenn who lived in Old Forge, would gossip over the phone by the hour, probably with half the neighbors' wives listening in. The women were carrying on a long-winded conversation when a subscriber wished to use the phone. The latter chimed in and said, "Mrs. Higby, I smell your pie burning." As his mother really did have a pie in the oven, the phone was made available in a hurry. "The pie did not burn," Roy assured us, "but my mother was pretty peeved." [51]

To make a long-distance call, you used one short ring to get the operator. She—it was almost always a "she"—would say crisply, "Number, plee-uz." You would give her the number you wanted to reach and wait to be connected. It may have taken a little more ingenuity to operate the old phones, but they were owned by the telephone company, and if anything went wrong with them, they were repaired by the company. At the end of the month you got a bill to pay, usually one page and one amount, quite unlike the several bills you receive today, which require a Philadelphia lawyer to figure out.

I must say a brief word here about daylight savings time, introduced toward the end of World War I. Feelings were strong on the subject. Some viewed this meddling with the long-established measure of time as a sort of sacrilege: they clung to standard time as "God's time." Daylight savings time was not adopted by the railroads for their time schedules, so standard time was also referred to as "railroad time"—almost as sacrosanct as "God's time." Many members of this conservative bastion doubted the sanity of the administration in Washington and speculated on what other cockamamie plans the government there would dream up. Gradually, though—and in spite of the twice-yearly risk of being either an hour early or an hour late—the luxury of the longer summer evenings and lingering sultry twilights won over even the most ardent critic.

These evenings were perfect for enjoying the beauty of the lake. We had beauty everywhere we looked. Each season had its own. The gaudy autumn colors of the deciduous trees—brilliant reds, oranges, and yellows—mingled with the dark green of the evergreens to create glorious vistas around the deep blue of the lake. The uniform skyline was randomly broken by the venerable white pines piercing the sky, head and shoulders above the rest, while along the shoreline, the fir trees appeared to be neatly manicured by the level browse line of the hungry white-tailed deer.

In winter, bitter cold created its own beauty: the stillness of the morning, the sun rising in magnificent color over the eastern end of the lake—the view as breathtaking as the cold air that hit the lungs—the daylight dazzle of sunlight strewing myriad diamonds over the pure white snow, and in the evenings, the colorful light show of the dancing aurora borealis in the northern quadrant of a star-spattered sky.

In the spring, as the sun warmed the air, the grip of winter slowly lifted as the cold left us reluctantly. The melting snow created a new kind of beauty as it sent torrents of water in sparkling, noisy cataracts over the escarpment along the north shore of West Bay. New leaves

shone pale green against the damp, black earth, and wild azaleas blossomed in pink profusion around the lakeshore, perfuming the breeze with their exquisite fragrance. And the Lord must have decided that that was just a little bit too good, so He sent black flies.

Yes, we grew up without the cultural advantages of city life. No, we could not avail ourselves of the many resources the large schools could offer, and no, we could not count ourselves as worldly wise or street-smart. But we had other advantages, gifts our city counterparts could only dream of: a close-knit community and the great outdoors.

Our community really cared about how we behaved. Just because your parents weren't there didn't mean you weren't observed, and you might have to account for yourself. Our school bus driver was Walt Dunn. He never raised a hand—he didn't have to—but he could silence the naughtiest of us with a glance in the rearview mirror. As for our playground, it was the safest in the world: the great outdoors, where no unsavory characters ever lurked.

One incident illustrating the character and heart of the Big Moose people is deeply implanted in my mind.

In 1919, Dad had contracted the Spanish influenza. His health was badly affected by this, and a subsequent life-threatening bout with pneumonia prompted his doctor to order him to the Adirondacks. Although his health improved, any sickness with respiratory complications usually sent him to bed. Thus it was that one fall Dad was in bed under doctor's orders, and our winter wood supply was not in. Vital wood.

It grew in abundance all around us. The side of the mountain behind our house was an adequate and productive woodlot, but the trees had to chopped down with an ax—no power saws in those days—skidded down the slopes, sawed into usable lengths (with a certain amount split for kindling), and stored in a woodshed handy to the house. Although coal was our main fuel for heat and cooking, wood was necessary for starting the fires. Once the wood fire produced a good bed of hot embers, coal could be added.

Word got around that Kinne was "laid up," and the men of the community got together and gathered, cut, and split our wood, piling it handy in our woodshed. Big Moose folks took care of their own, and in return Mom and Dad never shied away from helping a neighbor in trouble any way they could.

[Waldheim employees] were ready to go for the boat ride. . . . I was just stepping into [the station wagon] when I heard the fire siren. Your dad [E. J. Martin], Otis and Van Hazel, Vincent and I drove off. Got to the fire station and found it [the explosion] was at the Glennmore. It was the *White Lady* up in flames.

Georgie [Joe, Walt's son] Dunn got quite badly burned about the face and hands, and Walt [Dunn] a scratch on his face from flying glass. There's nothing left of the *White Lady* but her hull. When Wanda saw it she went all to pieces and cried and cried. Poor Kinnes. Poor Walt. He certainly was floored and nearly collapsed from shock when we got him back to his house. Little Georgie is all red faced—puffed. His eyes were burned too and [Dr.] Lindsay wants to see him tomorrow to see if his eyes are okay." [8]

The explosion was probably caused by inadequate ventilation of the bilges. It was a difficult beginning for Walt Dunn, who was soon to start a boat business and marina on his own property, but he was thankful that his son had not been more seriously injured.

As more private boats appeared on the lake after the war, roads were built, and gasoline for private cars was removed from the ration list, there was less need for large boats. The *Big Moose* was left without a slip big enough to hold it. At last, Howard Martin and Gordon Kinne undertook to scuttle the boat in West Bay. They filled the vessel with stones, chopped holes in it, and watched it sink to the bottom of the lake.

THE DUNN FAMILY AND THEIR BUSINESSES

By about 1920, after the deaths of Charles and Catherine Rose, grandparents of Nelson, Charles, Walter, and Edward Dunn, and when Nelson was twenty-three or twenty-four, the boys decided to build a house of their own. They bought a lot from Charles Williams that was located between Lake View Lodge and the New Burdick's Camps (lot 13). "Aunty" (Margaret Rose), their mother's sister who had played an important role in bringing them up, was to keep house for them. With this house as a base, three of the boys started their businesses. Of the four, only the youngest, Eddie, left Big Moose to work "outside."

Nelson A. Dunn. The eldest of the four boys, Nelson, left school after completing eighth grade because neither his grandparents nor Aunty could afford to send him

The four Dunn brothers: Charles, Walter, Nelson, and Edward, with Walter behind Nelson, ca. 1929. Courtesy of William S. Dunn.

away for further education; thus he turned to his uncle, Alex Rose, who taught him carpentry. He also became a registered Adirondack guide, learning the skill from both H. H. Covey and George Burdick. Nelson eventually became a master carpenter and started his own contracting and camp-caretaking business. He built camps, did maintenance work, cut wood, put in ice, shoveled roofs—all the various and sundry tasks and responsibilities that went with the summer resort business. It is clear from some of the later entries in the Camp Crag record book that H. H. Covey greatly trusted Nelson Dunn and appreciated the quality of his work.

When the small contracting business was slack, Nelson would take on logging jobs—hard work but good money. He was considered to be one of the area's hardest-working ice handlers during the ice-harvesting season.

In 1921, H. H. Covey hired a young lady with secretarial training, Ada Jones, to do the office work at Camp Crag for the summer. Nelson met her that first summer, and when she returned the following year he began to court her seriously, much to Covey's approval. The next year Nelson bought one of Covey's West Bay lots and an option to buy a second (lots 1 and 377, adjacent to each other).

Nelson built a substantial house on his newly acquired

property. He left the house where he had been living with Aunty and his brothers, and he and Ada were married in March 1923. She did all the accounts for his contracting and caretaking business and took on the housekeeping responsibilities when Nelson's work crews were housed and boarded in the house or the apartment over the garage on the road. They raised two sons, William, now retired and living in North Carolina, and Nelson, Jr., currently living in Florida.

In 1925, having exercised his option to buy the adjoining lot to the east, he also bought Will Woodard's adjacent undeveloped land still farther to the east (lots 2 and 3). (Woodard had left his job as caretaker at Tojenka and returned to the Mohawk Valley.) In 1928, Nelson sold the lot on the east, which was to be used for building the Big Moose Community Chapel.

Nelson was a highly respected year-round resident of Big Moose Lake, and he could count many well-known summer residents among his clients and friends. He frequently worked with E. J. Martin at the Waldheim in the construction of camps. His activities were not limited to Big Moose, however. In the mid-1930s, he contracted with the Hollywood Hills Hotel on First Lake to supply the logs for that construction. In 1937 he built a log cabin camp on Brandreth Lake for John Quincy Adams VI, a descendant of the early presidents.

In the early 1930s, Charles O. Nichols, a supplier of longleaf pine pilings for the New York harbor, engaged Nelson to build a log cabin camp on May's Lake. As with many of Nelson Dunn's customers, a warm and friendly relationship developed. (One Christmas, for example, Nichols sent an electric train to Nelson's son, Bill.)

In June 1943, Nelson went to May's Lake to get the camp ready for the Nichols family. It was a job of several days, and he was to return home on Friday. When he did not return as expected, his wife Ada sent Nelson, Jr., to investigate. Nelson found his father lying at the bottom of the lake near the dock, a victim of a heart attack. He was just one month short of his forty-sixth birthday. Although Nichols came to May's Lake that summer, he soon sold the camp and never returned. "It is just not the same any more without Nelse around," he told Ada. The kind of respect and trust that many of the summer residents had for Nelson was an example of the quality of the relationships many of the year-round residents had earned.

Nelson had been able to leave Ada only a small legacy, and for a few years she found work either at Big Moose or

Nelson Dunn at Mays Pond, ca. 1940. Courtesy of William S. Dunn.

in Herkimer, where she had relatives. For a few summers she operated a small gift shop in the garage by the Eagle Bay Road. In 1953, when Ruth Marleau retired as the Big Moose postmistress, Ada applied for and received the appointment, serving until she retired in 1966. She remained in Big Moose in her main house or, when it was rented in the summer, in the apartment above the garage until the fall of 1980, when she entered Herkimer Hospital. She died on New Year's Day, 1981.

Charles G. Dunn. Charles, the second of the Dunn boys, had the least physical stamina of the brothers. There was always speculation that he had had tuberculosis as a youngster, but because H. H. Covey, their uncle-in-law and sometime employer, had a strict policy against consumptives, any word of Charles's illness was kept under tight wraps. When he graduated from the eighth grade at the Big Moose Station school, his family realized that he would not be able to do the hard manual labor his brothers could do. Somehow his grandparents and Aunt Margaret were able to scrape together enough money to send him outside for a business course, although not for a full high school diploma.

MY BIG MOOSE BOYHOOD | *William S. Dunn*

I was born in June 1924, while my mother stayed with relatives in Herkimer awaiting my arrival. I was brought to Big Moose six weeks later. My earliest remembrance is of a walk by trail to the waterfalls on the West Pond outlet. My mother took me to the falls because my father was laying a water pipeline to supply our home. I can still remember my father putting my brother Nelse and me in a pack basket and climbing the steep trail alongside the falls and seeing the view from the top.

When I was a real small boy, I had an all-breed dog named Scout. Scout used to watch me like a hawk, and if I wandered off (which, according to my mother, I had a propensity to do), he would warn Mother by continuous barking. But Scout had one serious fault: he liked to chase horses and nip at their legs. One day John Denio was driving by our camp with a team pulling a carriage full of summer guests. Scout went out after the horses. John got the team tamed down and yelled out to my dad, "Nelse, you either shoot that dog right now or I'll be right back down here with my gun." I can still remember my father taking Scout down the West Pond trail with his gun. I was bawling my heart out, but Scout just had to go. My mother also took it pretty hard. She would never have another dog after that until I was grown and gone from Big Moose. So we had to settle for cats as pets.

Big Moose did not have the amenities that city children had, but this did not mean a lack of activity. The lake boys at that time were Willard "Bill" McAllister, Gordon Kellogg, Larry Potter, my brother Nelson, and myself. We became adept and ingenious in finding our own activities.

In summertime, swimming was our favorite fun, first at Samson's small sandy beach and later at the Glennmore swimming dock. One time, as a very young boy before I could swim, I tried to imitate the swimmers on the Glennmore diving raft by diving off the front of our dock—much to the horror of my mother, who jumped in, clothes and all, to save me. We avoided Mother's "no swimming until after lunch" rule by "accidentally" falling off the dock almost every morning. Then there was fishing. Fishing for trout and bullhead kept us busy many, many evenings.

With the warm weather also came the black fly scourge, which kept us occupied in June trying to keep them off with Dad's fly dope concoction of pine tar, beeswax, and citronella.

Trail hiking became a favorite Big Moose sport early in my youth. I liked the trail to West Pond the best. Once when very young, I hiked up there to pick blueberries and was scared out of my wits by the crazy call of a loon I had not noticed on the pond. I ran all the way home, of course spilling my blueberries—my very first encounter with a loon.

When we got bigger we loved to build our own trails to various locations. One summer in the mid-1930s, Gordon Kellogg and I decided we wanted to improve the trail to Squash Pond. Selecting a point on the Martin Road, we built a new trail, joining the original trail near the Squash Pond dam. Then we built a trail from this one along the ridge to Billy's Bald Spot. Sometimes we recruited my brother Nelse and Willard McAllister to help, but they were not as enthusiastic as we were about the project. The trail along the ridge that Gordon and I blazed as kids was still in use in the 1970s.

And then of course there were the motorboat trips on the lake, some for fun, some to show our relatives or our summer guests the lake, some for chores our father assigned. Two of my favorites were up the Marsh and to the Sisters Lakes' landing and also around to South Bay and Punky Bay. If we had camp guests or relatives, we always pointed out the spot in South Bay where the *American Tragedy* murder actually took place.

As we grew older, my father pressed my brother and me into service on fishing, hunting, and trapping trips. His favorite spots in the 1930s and early '40s were Upper Sisters, Mays Lake, Cascade Lake, and, to a lesser degree, Queer Lake. But to Dad, who had once been a professional guide, fishing, hunting, and trapping were a business, not a sport. He went all out in all three endeavors. Most of his customers, being city people, were not too good in the woods, so Dad would spot them on watch points and tell them to sit in one spot while my brother Nelse and I drove the deer to them. We would be put at the beginning of the drive, and after a designated length of time, when Father had walked the watchers to their watch points, we would start the drive. We would beat sticks against tree trunks as we went along to spook the deer to the watchers, which meant, of course, that we hardly ever saw a deer. This was hard work, and after doing it for many years I kind of lost my taste for hunting, which I've never regained.

My father always trapped beaver during the trapping season. On weekends my brother and I were obligated (whether we liked it or not) to help run his traplines. One trapline trip I remember all too well. Early one morning we started from Higby's, hiked up Constable Creek and Mays Lake outlet to Mays Lake, bushwhacked to Chub Pond, went down Chub Pond outlet to Constable Pond and around Constable Pond to Pigeon Lake, bushwhacked to Haymarsh Creek and then down South Branch Creek to the Inlet of Big Moose Lake, went along the Inlet and the Marsh to Big Moose Lake, and finally got back to Higby's. It was far, far too long a trapline for a single day. Being loaded down with traps, poplar branches for beaver bait, axes, and other trapping paraphernalia, we carried only a light lunch of a couple of sandwiches. All went well until we reached South Branch Creek, where Father's leg started to give out. This slowed us considerably. As dusk approached, Dad told my brother and me to snowshoe on ahead to the George Stone camp on the main lake (North Shore), open the camp (the key was hidden), and try to find something to eat. Because we had had only a light lunch we were ravenously hungry. At the camp we found only a box of frozen raisins about three-fourths full. We devoured them. When father arrived we snowshoed across the lake back to Higby's. For the rest of the beaver season this trapline was broken into two days! Dad told George Stone about the incident and the raisins. George Stone always jokingly asked me when I was going to replace his raisin supply. In the spring of 1942 we helped Dad catch over $600 worth of beaver pelts. Another spring activity was our maple syrup and sugar production—yum yum!

The winter activities of our youth included ice harvests, sledding, snowshoeing, skiing, skating, roof shoveling (especially during the winter of 1935), wood cutting, and thawing water pipelines. After supper, evenings were occupied with games of Pitch or listening to the radio—Tom Mix was my favorite. And for me there was always schoolwork.

Uncle Walt Dunn started his ice harvests during Christmas vacation to gain the advantage of free help from the lake boys. Our job was to push the cakes from the open ice to the loading chutes. I can still remember one windy day, with Jim McAllister yelling out, "Don't let those cakes blow out into the open hole." If they did he would spud off an ice raft and make us paddle out to retrieve them. Hard work, but we loved every minute. Skating was always possible while Uncle Walt kept the ice fields cleared for harvest. Occasionally conditions were such that there was no snow on top of black ice, and we could skate anywhere on the lake.

Sledding was our fun sport. When conditions were right we would slide down the long steep Higby Road hill. Uncle Walt Dunn and George Deis always accompanied us. One would stand guard at the bottom of the hill to watch for motorists (never many) and the other would pull our sleighs back up the hill with a pickup truck. With my big Flexible Flyer sleigh, I always won the distance contest at the bottom.

Skiing became more fun after Alice Martin enticed the Town of Webb to bulldoze a ski hill behind where the firehall is now, on a hill Fred Williams donated. We also always enjoyed skiing or snowshoeing up the lake when snow conditions permitted. On one such trip I went through the ice at the entrance to North Bay and filled both boots. I had a very cold trip home on a very cold day.

Snowshoeing was another favorite for Nelse, Bill McAllister, and me. We each had our own pair. West Pond and Squash Pond were our best short-trip destinations. Once there, we would build a bonfire from the dead wood in the pond swamps to toast marshmallows.

In the mid-1930s I had a route selling magazines and Cloverdale Salve, which was like Vicks Vaporub. To cover the route, I would walk, snowshoe, ski, and occasionally skate, all without seeing a soul on the lake. The last Christmas I visited my mother, I walked out to Echo Island and was startled by the noise of several snowmobiles. Progress?

When he returned to Big Moose, he went to work in the office of the Bissell and Yousey Lumber Company, but after it ceased operation in 1918 he learned the carpentry trade. At the same time his health began to improve and he grew stronger. However, he never started his own business, always working for others—his brother Nelson, the Martin brothers, Frank Day, and Art Burtch.

Charles never married, and his Aunt Margaret Rose kept house for him until she died in 1937. After that time he boarded at various places. At other times he lived in the apartment over the garage next to the Dunn house.

During World War II he went outside to work at different defense jobs, returning to Big Moose after the war. As some of the older established contractors began to look toward retirement and cut down on their businesses, a need developed for a small-time contractor in and around Big Moose. Charlie responded, keeping busy for a number of years. However, his health started to fail, and he gave up the business in the mid-1950s. Toward the end of his life he went to live with his brother and sister-in-law, Walt and Bert. Charles died in 1958.

Walter A. Dunn. Walt Dunn's various jobs between the end of World War I and the 1930s are somewhat obscure. Like most Big Moose residents, Walt had many skills and used them when they were needed. According to his nephew, Bill Dunn, he may have worked for the Bissell and Yousey Lumber Company and for the International Lumber Company at Woods Lake until those operations closed. He also worked during the summers at Higby's and at the Glennmore. Occasionally, after automobiles began to come to the lake, he chauffeured for some of the summer residents.

In November of 1925, Walt married Alberta Deschenes, the daughter of August Deschenes, a successful lumbering contractor. Walt was the second to leave the house where he had lived with Aunty and his brothers. He had built a house near the Big Moose-Eagle Bay Road up the hill from the lakefront house but on the same property the boys had purchased from Charles Williams.

Walt's wife, Bert (as she was always called), was born Marie Eugenia Alberta Deschenes on September 18, 1904, at the Benson Mines in Newton Falls, New York, where her father happened to be working. She started school in Tupper Lake and then moved to Lowville. When she was sixteen and the family was living at Carter Station, her mother died and she took on responsibility for six younger brothers and a younger sister. Her father eventually placed the four youngest children in a Catholic convent in Ogdensburg while the older ones went to work. Bert worked for three or four years at one of the Utica Knitting Mills and then came to the Summit Hotel at Big Moose Station. It was there that Bert met Walter Dunn.

After their marriage, when her father visited his daughter at Big Moose, he always beseeched her to speak French. Unfortunately, she had lost her childhood language and refused to try to regain it. Although Walt was handy with the hammer and saw like his older brothers, he was more interested in automobiles and motors. In 1930, the Town of Webb School Board initiated a school bus route from Big Moose to Eagle Bay, along with a second route from Inlet to Eagle Bay and on to Old Forge.

Big Moose students now had much easier access to the Town of Webb high school. Walt successfully bid on the Big Moose route. His first school bus was a large Packard limousine that he purchased from P. J. Crowley, president of the New York Central Railroad and a summer guest at Lake View Lodge. In a few years the Big Moose high school population outgrew the Packard, and Walt purchased a large Reo school bus (see illustration on page 235).

At about the same time as the school bus routes were established, the U.S. Post Office opened a mail delivery route from the post office at Big Moose Station to the lake. They also initiated a mail boat route on the lake, because many camps were not served by road. Walt received the contract for the auto route and engaged Romaine Kinne, of Kinne's Boat Line, to deliver the mail around the lake. When Kinne died in 1943, Walt assumed the delivery responsibilities. Later, the Postal Service gave up the rail mail service and switched to trucks that took the mail from Old Forge to Inlet and from Eagle Bay to Old Forge. Walt then ended up with all three mail routes as well as the school bus contract. He was assured of this employment through patronage, although little was said of that.

Bert Dunn had grown up in a man's world. She had six brothers, married a man with three brothers who were usually living nearby, and reared two sons, Walter Edward "Bud" and George Henry "Joe." All of these men were

Walter and Alberta "Bert" Dunn, ca. early 1940s. Courtesy of Ann Dunn Hall.

hunters, so she was familiar with guns and rifles. One day a bunch of the men went out to hunt deer while she stayed at home keeping house. Later that day Bertha chanced to look out her kitchen window and saw a good-sized buck in the side yard. She took down a rifle from the wall, aimed it, and in one shot brought the buck down. At the end of the day the men returned empty-handed. They complained that they had tracked all day and had not even seen a deer. Bert nonchalantly nodded toward the side yard where her prize lay.

In 1941, Walt and Bert purchased the New Burdick Camp from Paul Allen of Albany, who had bought the property from Mrs. George Burdick and her son, Theodore. After George Burdick's death, his widow had tried unsuccessfully to make the camps a paying operation. Walt and Bert renamed the hotel Dunn's Lodge. The Lodge, which included three cottages, functioned for a few years in the 1940s but was only mildly successful.

They soon realized that the property had potential as a good location for a much-needed marina in the absence of Kinne's Boat Line and the services it had provided. Walt engaged Frank Martin to build the large boathouse, dock, and boat ramp, all of which still exist. They called the thriving business Dunn's Boat Service, and it gave Walt scope for his love of motors and mechanical things. Bert continued the hotel operation and also started a small grocery store with some basic foodstuffs, including meat, that Walt delivered (on orders given the day before) along with the mail.

The hotel operation gradually became secondary to the marina and faded away. Walt and Bert eventually sold the enterprise to their son George ("Joe"), who expanded the marina but did not continue the hotel.

Walt continued to be a jack-of-all-trades. When the Big Moose Station Post Office (zip code 13307) closed December 30, 1972, Walt received the contract for the mail service from Eagle Bay. In addition, he harvested ice for various camps that had yet to convert to electric refrigeration. Using his mechanical talents, he built himself a circular saw for cutting ice, and he was the last person on the lake to undertake this endeavor commercially. He built a small icehouse and sold ice as well as fireplace and stove wood.

Walt retired in the late 1960s, although he continued many of his old activities. He died in 1972. At the Chapel's annual memorial service that year, the Reverend Dean McCombe chose to speak about the life of Walter Dunn as someone who lived the parable that Jesus taught.

In a sermon entitled "The Good Samaritan," he said, "Walt did not frequent churches incessantly. In fact, . . .Bert told me that since 1925 Walt had been in church something like four times . . . I believe however that Walt was a profoundly religious man. It's quite true that he invoked the name of our Lord more times than most clergy do. He found upon many occasions an opportunity to express what in other circumstances just might be called a pietistic vocabulary." Many year-round and summer residents can recall with deep affection the care and concern that Walt manifested when anyone needed help.

Bert stayed in her house until health problems set in, then moved to the senior complex in Old Forge. She spent her last years at the Eastern Star home in Oriskany, dying in December 1996 at the age of ninety-two with her mind nearly as clear as it had been her youth and her sense of humor very much intact.

Edward H. Dunn. Eddie, the youngest of the four Dunn brothers, never had a business at Big Moose. A note on his life is included here in order to complete the story of the Dunn family.

When Eddie finished eighth grade, his brother Nelson supported him while he attended Lowville Free Academy, taking a postgraduate course there in business and commercial subjects. He had a successful career, spent largely with the Ford Motor Company in and near Detroit. After his first wife, Doris Dearing, died, he married Margaret Boersma. There were no children from either marriage.

Eddie never lost his love for Big Moose. In 1956 he purchased Deerlands, the historic camp at the entrance to the Inlet, but was able to spend little time there. Eddie had the gift of rhyme and wrote many verses that touchingly express his love of his camp and of the woods. (See page 176.) Eventually he and Margaret retired to Florida, where Eddie died in 1985 and Margaret in 1997.

PHIL ELLSWORTH
AND HIS AIRPLANES

Before the term was invented, Phil Ellsworth knew what was meant by "extreme sports." Having become interested in boats at age ten, he was an outboard-motorboat racer when he was a college student. As a sophomore at Bucknell University, he won the Lipton Trophy and $6,000 for driving his outboard motorboat faster than anyone else in the United States. He went on to compete in international trials in Italy in the early 1930s.

Philip Ellsworth's Adirondack Air Service hangar, ca. 1941. Courtesy of Richard Widdicombe.

Later he was to organize a mosquito-boat regatta at Big Moose.

More important, Ellsworth learned to fly in the days when flying was an adventure, turning it into a career. Phil became a licensed instructor and was among the first to teach instrument flying to American Airlines pilots. For many years he ran the Tri Cities airport, which served Binghamton, Endicott, and Johnson City.

Phil's parents, Guy P. and Nancy Ellsworth, had long been summer residents of Big Moose and had built a house, Philson Lodge, on the Big Moose Road not far from the lake. Guy Ellsworth, from Vestal, New York, had interests in lumbering activities and owned a great deal of land along the road to Big Moose Station and in the vicinity of Twitchell Lake.

In 1941, Phil purchased an undeveloped lot (lot 369) on the north side of West Bay. There he built a hangar large enough for two small pontoon planes and started the Adirondack Air Service. His business operation at Big Moose was part-time, almost recreation. He taught flying, flew vacationing fishermen to inaccessible ponds, and took passengers to their homes after weekends spent at the lake. He also occasionally took hunters to the Canadian wilderness to hunt moose and took his friends on similar trips.

Phil made one such trip in the fall of 1979 with two Big Moose friends, Art Harvey and Barney Barnum. Barnum, an avid fisherman and hunter, Harvey, a South Bay resident, and Ellsworth owned a hunting camp in Canada about 160 miles north of Ottawa. The three friends had planned a moose-hunting trip at the cabin. Barnum was licensed to fly and often flew copilot with Bud Windhausen, whose business in Inlet took him into the woods and around a wide area of New York, New England, and Canada.

At first, Barney decided to stay home, but at the last minute he threw his gear into a pack basket and told his wife, Betty, "I *gotta* go on that trip. I just have that feeling." He rushed to Phil's hangar at the lake and barely arrived before the plane took off. The plane was a Grumman Widgeon, a small twin-engine flying boat with wingtip floats as well as alternative conventional landing gear.

The hunting was enjoyable, but the moose eluded the party. Then the sky began to look nasty, making Phil, who hated flying in bad weather, very uneasy. The three men decided they had better get out while they could, and they hastily closed camp.

Phil piloted the plane, Barney sat in the copilot's seat on the right, and Art crammed himself, along with all the gear, in the tiny low space remaining in the back. There was some debate about whether to stop in nearby St. Anne's or whether to go all the way to Ottawa for refueling. They decided to go by way of Ottawa, but, once in the air, they found that they had to keep the plane low to stay under the cloud ceiling. The low altitude forced them to wind around mountains, and Phil began to worry about whether their fuel would run out.

Phil, in the pilot's seat, was studying a map when Barney noticed that he was not moving. "Hey, Phil," Barney said, "this is no time for a nap." Phil did not answer. Barney looked at him and realized that he was not sleeping. He was dead. He had never made a sound. Art and Barney looked at each other. What to do? Barney, in the copilot's seat, had rudder controls on his side. The plane had a "throw over" steering wheel that could be moved to the right side. But there were no brakes and no other controls. In order to land the plane, Barney had to be on the left in the pilot's seat. The plane's cabin was cramped, and between the two seats was a fixed armrest. "Okay,"

Barney said to Art, "we've got to get Phil out of there, and the only way to do that is to take out the armrest." Luckily, Barney never travels without a tiny tool called vise-grip pliers. Art found the pliers and got to work trying to detach the armrest. It was not an easy job. While Barney was giving directions and helping move Phil with his left hand, he was also steering the plane around the hills and trying to keep an eye on the Gatineau River below in case they had to make an emergency landing. At last they wrestled Phil's body out of the pilot's seat and Barney was able to take control.

He immediately radioed the airport at Ottawa and explained the situation. The airport authorities gave clearance for an emergency landing. Meanwhile, the fuel gauge was dropping and the anxiety level in the cabin was rising. Finally, Barney brought the plane in. He looked out the window and saw that the plane was surrounded by all kinds of emergency equipment and a ring of police. The plane, which consumes twenty gallons of fuel an hour, landed with five gallons in its tanks.

Safely on the ground and the sad situation explained, Barney called his wife, Betty, in Big Moose, to tell her what had happened and to ask that she carry the dreadful news to Phil's wife, Hazel. Slowly, Betty drove to Hazel's. Awakened from a sound sleep and distraught, Betty began to wonder, "Did Barney really call me and tell me what I am to tell her, or was I just dreaming? What a terrible thing it would be if I delivered this awful message and it has only been a dream."

Phil had never had any notion that he had a medical problem. Later examination showed that his heart had literally exploded.

Ice Harvesting:
A Community Enterprise | *William S. Dunn*

When I was a boy at Big Moose in the late 1920s and 1930s, cutting and harvesting ice was an important and necessary activity. These were the days before electric power and the refrigerators we depend on today, and all of the hotels on the lake had large icehouses with adjoining walk-in coolers for preserving food. Ice was also used in the kitchens, to fill the iceboxes located in the hotels' cottages, and to supply the guests with chipped ice for drinks. Most private camps had icehouses to supply their kitchen iceboxes. Camps that did not have icehouses would get their ice from the Big Moose Supply Company, which would deliver blocks of ice on their "pickle boat" route.

During the winter, ice holes were opened at each hotel and at some camps, such as Camp Veery on Echo Island and Deerlands at the east end of the lake. Icehouses at most private camps were filled from ice fields opened near one of the hotels. The icehouses at Big Moose Station were generally supplied from the Glennmore ice hole. Contrary to some stories, there was never a commercial operation at Big Moose that shipped ice out of the area.

Opening an ice field was an art that took a good deal of planning and hard work. First of all, the area had to be located over deep water to avoid bits of vegetation from being frozen into the ice. Also, snow had to be kept off the field in order to allow thick, clear ice to form. A path to the shore had to be scraped clear so that the horse-drawn bobsled or truck on which the ice would be loaded could be brought nearby. Clearing away the snow was done first by hand, using large hand-pushed scrapers. When the ice became thick enough, horse-drawn scrapers and, later, trucks with front-end plows were used.

Once the ice on the lake was at least twelve inches

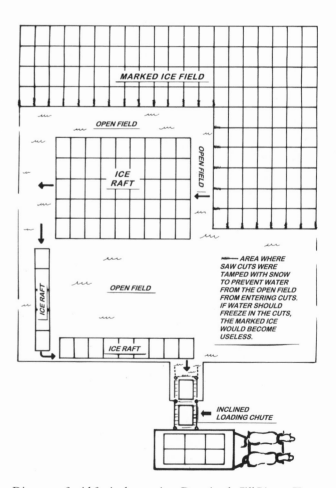

Diagram of grid for ice harvesting. Drawing by Jill Binyon Kurtz.

Horse-drawn ice saw in collection of the Town of Webb Historical Association. Photograph by Jane Barlow, 2000.

side of the saw as needed. When the field was marked in one direction, the same procedure was followed in the other direction, producing a grid of blocks that were usually twenty-four inches by eighteen inches.

After the field had been laid out in this way, the men opened a hole in one corner and used hand-operated ice saws to finish the cut. These saws were more than six feet long and had a cylindrical wooden handle at one end. The handle was attached at its center and placed at a ninety-degree angle to the blade. This made it possible for the operator to grasp the saw with both hands and, with considerable effort, pull it up and down. The work was very tiring and demanded enormous strength.

The ice job supervisor (for many years my Uncle Walt Dunn) had to be sure that the saw cuts in a marked field had been properly tamped with snow dams. In an open field, the water would rise nearly to the top of the ice. Unless the ends of the cuts nearest the water were blocked, the water would run into the saw channels. If the water froze in the cuts, the unharvested ice would become a useless solid mass.

I remember that Jim McAllister, a tall, lanky teamster, was considered an expert at working an open ice field. With a hand ice saw, he would free a large ice raft of about sixty cakes, which would then be floated to the side of the ice hole with long-handled ice picks. Then, Jim would break off a single strip of about ten or twelve cakes with a special tool called an ice spud. Using ice picks with medium-

thick, a string was set up tight in a line to guide the saw that would cut the ice into blocks. The first cut had to be made very carefully. It had to be absolutely straight because ice cakes had to be uniform in size so they would fit easily into the icehouses. Horse-drawn ice-cutting saws were used to mark off the cakes of ice. The saws were specialized blades six to eight feet long, and made of heavy-gauge steel with large teeth. The blade was mounted in a thick hardwood frame that held a steel rod above it. Smaller steel rods with flat guide plates attached perpendicularly to the end, projected out to one side. The guide plates enabled the teamster, who drove his single horse from behind the saw with the help of a special rigging, to use handles at the end of the saw frame to keep the blade straight on the marked course. These guide plates fit into the crevices made by the first mark on the ice, and once the first accurate cut was made, the teamster could use the guides to mark out a series of parallel lines. The entire guide mechanism could also be swung to the opposite

Horse pulling an ice-cutting saw. Drawing by Jill Kurtz.

Hand ice-cutting saw. Courtesy of C. V. Bowes. Photograph by Jane Barlow, 2000.

Hand-sawing ice into blocks, winter 1930–31. Courtesy of Wanda K. Martin.

Poling blocks of ice to the horse-drawn sled, winter 1930–31. Courtesy of Wanda K. Martin.

Ice blocks on sled, winter 1930–31. Courtesy of Wanda K. Martin.

Fred Brack and Joe Dunn sliding blocks of ice into icehouse, 1958. Courtesy of Ann Dunn Hall.

length handles, the youngsters (often my brother Nelson and I, Willard McAllister, Gordon Kellogg, Larry Potter, and later Bud and Joe Dunn) pulled the strips through the open water to near the loading chute.

One end of the chute was in the water, the other on a bobsled or truck bed, and the cakes had to be hauled up. This was backbreaking work because the cakes could weigh up to one hundred pounds. Two men stood on either side of the chute to slide the cakes along while another stacked the cakes on the wagon with ice tongs. The work was easier in below-zero weather because the ice would dry quickly, which prevented the cakes from sticking together.

Once the blocks of ice arrived at the icehouses, they were off-loaded onto chutes so they could be put inside and stacked in place. Some icehouses were easy to fill, especially those at private camps. They were not too big and were usually located for easy access. The icehouse at the New Burdick Camps (now Dunn's Boat Service) was relatively easy to fill because of its location on the slope behind the hotel. Although the icehouse was big, the vehicles carrying the ice cakes could move farther up the hill so that the angle of the chutes would always be gradual. However, other icehouses were very difficult to fill, such as those at Camp Veery, the Glennmore Hotel, and the Big Moose Supply Company, all of which had either long, difficult approaches or steep inclines into the icehouse. When some of the really steep icehouses were close to full, a horse attached to a rope and pulley had to be used to pull up the cakes. At the Glennmore, as the icehouse filled up, the cakes had to be manhandled up the chute. Later, Charlie Forkey used a pulley system rigged to his car to lift the ice. At Lake View Lodge, the icehouse was filled from a ledge above the building. Because it was a steep incline down, special speed-reducers were built into the chutes to make it safer for the workers inside. Once an icehouse was filled, the mass of ice inside was surrounded with sawdust to help preserve it during the summer months.

The entire operation called for enormous energy and stamina. The men often fortified themselves with hard liquor, usually either gin mixed with grapefruit juice or just straight gin. The bottles would be stuck in a snow bank. Somehow, the hard work must have eaten up the liquor, because there were never any serious accidents.

The women got together and produced huge meals to fuel the workers. There would be mounds of mashed potatoes, platters of pork chops, and either canned vegeta-

bles bought at Sperry's store before it closed for the winter or vegetables that had been put up at home during the summer. Home-canned venison, beef, or chicken swimming in gravy might be part of the meal, along with peaches, pears, or dried fruit. Cakes of all varieties might appear on the table along with pies made from home-canned berries or apples that had been stored in a root cellar.

After electric power came into the Big Moose area, ice cutting and harvesting started on a slow decline. The Big Moose Supply Company and Higby's Hotel were probably the first businesses to convert to electric refrigeration, along with many of the private camps. However, the Hotel Glennmore, Lake View Lodge, Camp Waldheim, the Nelson Dunn camp, and the Greenwood camp were some of the last. As ice harvesting declined, my Uncle Walt Dunn (on a self-appointed basis) took over supervising the ice operation. For a number of years, Uncle Walt consolidated the lake's ice harvesting operations at the Hotel Glennmore's ice field because this field had easy road access with only a small, short incline. Ice cakes were then drawn by truck from the Glennmore to other hotels, stores, and camps that had not converted to electric refrigeration. Usually, Camp Waldheim opened its own ice hole, but sometimes ice was drawn from the Glennmore field.

At some time in the late 1930s or early 1940s, Uncle Walt purchased a gasoline-powered ice saw to mark off the ice cakes in the field. This did away with the horse-drawn saws, but keeping the marking lines parallel so the cakes would be square still required a great deal of care. One

Ann Dunn Hall showing the remains of Walt Dunn's handmade gasoline-driven ice-cutting saw, 2000. Photograph by Jane Barlow.

winter, Camp Waldheim was late opening its field. A winter thaw developed and water formed on top of the ice, and the motorized cutting saw kicked up water instead of ice spray. We were wet from head to foot all day long.

It was not unusual for someone to slip and fall into an ice hole. It happened to me one year and once to Harry Kellogg. Jim McAllister liked to tell the story of D. B. Sperry falling in. D. B. became real perturbed when he thought Jim reacted too slowly to run around the ice hole to help pull him out. Jim told him (not his exact words but a reasonable facsimile), "If I had been the Good Lord Almighty, I could have come right across the water and been here a lot quicker." [Bill Marleau tells another version of this story in which Jim pushes D. B. under the cold water in order to gather momentum to pull him out. D. B. promptly fired him.][9]

When my brother and I were youngsters, we loved to work on these ice jobs, but of course we were in school and were not often available. But Uncle Walt Dunn had a way of making sure we could provide some free labor when our Christmas vacation started. Earlier in the winter, just as soon as the ice was thick enough to hold him, he would take his hand-pushed scraper and keep the ice field free of snow. When the ice got thicker, he used his pickup truck and plow. By Christmas vacation, he would have the ice thick enough for harvesting. My brother and I worked hard, but we loved every moment of it. (I can remember two times when Uncle Walt lost his truck through the ice while plowing, but he was able to retrieve it each time.)

After World War II, there was very little ice harvesting on Big Moose Lake, but Uncle Walt still opened a small ice field near his house and filled a small icehouse he built at his marina, Dunn's Boat Service. From here he would sell ice to summer residents and sometimes make deliveries to camps on the lake during his mail boat runs. My mother, Ada Dunn, was a customer of his until about 1947 or 1948, when she finally bought an electric refrigerator. The Waldheim maintained iceboxes on the porches of its cottages as late as the 1950s. Many of the guests insisted that their predinner drinks tasted better when made with Big Moose ice.

AN ICE STORY | *Jack Judson* [10]

I once participated in the cutting of ice in front of Dunn's marina. Men, machines, and trucks were all over the place. Somehow Walt Dunn fell in the ice hole. He was quickly retrieved and brought up to the kitchen. The oven door was opened wide, the fire stoked, and that—plus a glass of 86 proof—got him back on the job a half hour later.

A TRUCK UNDER ICE | *Henry Bruyn* [11]

One of the men working at the project brought his one-and-a-half-ton Ford truck a little too close to the edge of [the open water]. The ice gave way, dropping the truck to the bottom of the lake. The absence of waves and wind made the truck quite visible. And, as I remember it, the roof of the truck was three to four feet below the surface of the water.

The five or six men involved in the project included, among others, our good friend Walter Dunn. A large variety of suggestions were thrown out for methods to retrieve the truck. Walter suggested that we send for Charlie Martin, who was about two miles up the lake at his camp, spending the winter as he always did, reading paperback cowboy stories. Somebody took off and carried the word to Charlie who, after several hours, appeared on the scene. He stared at the truck for some time, smoking his pipe and saying nothing. Finally, he started giving directions.

He wanted two saw cuts through the ice, separated by a space about four feet wider than the truck. These two cuts were to run toward the shore and were to be in length $1\frac{1}{2}$ times the depth of the water at the spot where the truck rested. He then directed that a cable be placed on the front end of the truck and run over the edge of the ice to two trucks on the shore, which would provide traction. His theory was that the pressure of the cable on the edge of the ice would press down the large piece of ice separated by the two cuts. This would form a ramp from the bottom of the lake up to the surface of the ice, which would, he hoped, break to form a hinge at the end of the two saw cuts. Amazingly enough, the idea worked perfectly, and the truck slowly rolled up the ramp out of the water onto the surface of the ice and eventually onto the shore. The next summer, it was notable that the two cushions on the seats of the truck cab still squeezed water when one sat on them.

HOWARD MARTIN'S ICE ACCIDENT[12]

It was a Christmas vacation in the early 1970s, and Howard's son Phil was home from college. Howard had taken his jeep and was clearing the ice about 150 feet from shore in front of the Waldheim beach, preparing it for later cutting. The jeep was an old one from which the doors had long since fallen off. Howard came across a snowbank that had been piled up in a previous plowing and decided to push it back a bit. Headed toward the middle of the lake, he moved the jeep a few feet and discovered that the snowbank had kept the ice underneath from freezing solid, leaving a soft spot. The front wheels of the jeep sank slowly into the spongy ice, and Howard was unable, even with the four-wheel drive, to back it out.

Phil ran to attach a long chain to the rear of the jeep and fasten it to a big green truck he had backed onto the ice. He started the truck and began pulling slowly. Instead of the jeep coming back up onto solid ice, the rear wheels began to disappear. Phil felt his truck being drawn backwards and realized that the truck was skidding backward over the ice. There was nothing he could do to stop it.

The truck, which fortunately had a long chain, stopped within about eight feet of the open water. But the jeep, with Howard in it, disappeared beneath the dark water. Phil jumped out of the truck and grabbed a shovel with a long handle. For a long moment he stood at the edge of the hole wondering whether he could do any good by jumping in after his father. The air temperature was five below zero, and both men were wearing heavy clothing and thick boots. Phil saw the oil can pop to the surface. Then the gasoline tank emerged. Both containers spilled their contents, turning the water murky.

At last, after what seemed an age but was probably forty-five to sixty seconds, Howard's head appeared. Phil shouted to him to grab the shovel. Howard swore at him and yelled, "Let me get my breath, will you!" Phil manipulated the shovel, trying not to get so close to the edge of the hole that the ice would break and land him in the water. After a great deal of effort, he managed to help his heavily water-soaked, oil-covered father onto the ice.

The next problem was to get Howard home as fast as possible. It was getting dark and the temperature was going down. If they detached the chain from the green truck to use it for transportation, it would be impossible to pull the jeep out of the water the next day. But by a stroke of pure luck, Phil's snowmobile was close by. He bundled Howard into it and headed for their house, nearly a quarter mile away. They arrived only to find that Howard's wife, Wanda, had just finished several loads of laundry and had used all the hot water. Howard peeled off his wet clothes and headed for the bathtub. Wanda scurried to put every pot she had on the stove to heat water. Howard finally thawed out and was none the worse for his close call.

They all knew the jeep would be safe under the water because, without air, it would not rust. However, they could not let the water freeze over, or rescue would be impossible. So the next day, Howard and Phil started to figure out how to pull the jeep out of the water. The project took about three days. They made a flat frame of six-by-six-foot beams that surrounded the hole in the ice. Above it, they built a frame that supported another beam that held a pulley, over which they could run the chain that ran between the jeep and the truck. The jeep turned out to be in eighteen feet of water. Careful maneuvering of the truck finally brought it to the surface, and they towed it to the heated garage under the Martins' house. After only about three hours, they had it running again.

MORE ICE STORIES[13] | *Charlie Adams*

I worked on two different ice jobs at Big Moose with the Dunns, probably about 1949 or 1950. Both were harvesting jobs done out in front of the marina or what was then Dunn's Hotel and store.

Walt Dunn had built a motorized saw with a circular blade. It rested on runners and was steered by a double handle, like a plow. After a hole had been drilled in order to measure the depth of the ice, the blade was set so that it cut about three inches above the bottom of the ice. The ice could not break apart, and the saw could be run to mark the field into squares. At the end of the first row—the "spud row" that was hacked out to free the field so the other cakes could be moved—stood the ramp to a truck parked near the shore. The ramp was made of wood, and the men slid the cakes up and into the back of the truck. The first cakes were sometimes slid aside because they were not completely square or had broken as they were taken out. But once the first course of ice cakes was out of the way, it was just a matter of walking down and spudding off the others into the open water. It was cold, hard, back-breaking work, and dangerous as well. Thumbs or legs caught between one-hundred-pound cakes of ice made for very painful injuries.

We had a little contest to relieve the monotony and agony of the job. After about four rows of cakes had been spudded off the solid portion of the ice, we would move those cakes along with pike poles and line them up to be taken out of the field. Our fun was attaching creepers to our boots and betting on who could run across the field on the floating cakes without falling in. I only tried it once and made it without a dunking. I watched a couple of other people, like Dick Rivet, get an unwelcome cold bath in Big Moose Lake in January or February.

Walt Dunn was famous for his extensive "religious" vocabulary. One day we heard the entire repertoire after we had forgotten to hook the netting that kept the ice from sliding off the rear of the truck. When I started up the hill with the load, half the ice slid back onto the ground. We had to haul the cakes back down to the ice, back into the water, up the ramp and then go through the whole process again. As you might guess, Walt had things to say about that.

When Bill Dunn and I were both at Syracuse University, I owned a 1931 Model Ford (which I ultimately sold to Bill) that we used to travel to Big Moose on weekends. Because of the high wheelbase, we could go through virtually any kind of snow, and with heavy chains on the tires it worked almost anywhere. We used to pull the throttle and spark down on that old machine and go wide open up the road toward the Adirondacks at the alarming speed of probably fifty or fifty-five miles per hour. In the rumble seat we often carried gallon jugs of cider, which once we arrived at Walt and Bert Dunn's home (in the summer, also the marina), we put into the snow bank to freeze. When cider freezes, a transparent liquid forms in the center of the ice that makes for a very interesting drink. You set the gallon jug in the snow, and when it freezes the ice expands and breaks the jug. You then take the ice "ball," drill a hole into the center and pour out a beautiful clear

liquid that looks like water but is 100-proof alcohol. We mixed it with Coca-Cola and Three Feathers rye whiskey to give it a little flavor.

After the ice job, we liked to slide down the hill behind the marina on the Dunns' big four-man sleds. We would put them in the truck, haul them to the top of the hill and ride down out onto the lake over a jump, sometimes as much as a hundred yards. One night we forgot to tell Dick Rivet, who had not been working that day, where the ice job was. When he got to the top of the hill, away he went and wound up, of course, in the ice field and got soaked. Fortunately, he held on to the sled, so both he and the sled escaped without harm.

We also made a jump at the bottom of the Higby hill. The snow plow came from Eagle Bay, turned up the Higby road and, when it came back, turned toward the Outlet, leaving a rough triangle of unplowed snow. We built up the snow and made a launching platform. We would come shooting down the Higby hill, and if the fellow we had posted there to check the traffic gave us the okay, we hit the jump. We actually got to the point where we could jump almost completely across Big Moose Road into what is now the parking area there. On more than one occasion we were going fast enough at the bottom of the hill to turn the corner, assuming the sled did not tip over, and ride all the way over the bridge across the Outlet and up into Dart's Road.

The ice jobs were awfully hard work, but we didn't know any better, didn't worry about it, and we enjoyed it. We ate well, drank well, and at night always had some fun before we got ready for the next day's work, which started when you got up at dawn.

4 Ventures from Outside the Lake

SEVERAL ENTERPRISES were started by organizations or individuals who came to Big Moose Lake from "outside," usually on the initiative or with the encouragement of those who were already there. One was the Boy Scout Pioneer Camp sponsored by the Fort Orange Council of the Boy Scouts of America in Albany, New York. It flourished during the 1930s and continued for a few years after World War II.

Other undertakings that affected the lake were lumbering operations. The earliest was run by Theodore Page, who had built the house on Echo Island shortly before he bought land to be logged. His enterprise evolved into that of Bissell and Yousey, owners of the sawmill that stood at the east end of the lake. With the versatility that is part of the Adirondack tradition, some local residents also logged the woods, sometimes using the wood for their own operations and sometimes selling it for profit. The activities yielded stories that became a part of Big Moose Lake history.

The Boy Scout Pioneer Camp

Hikers in the woods at the end of East Bay still find pieces of bed springs and other relics of the Boy Scout camp that was located here during the 1930s and 1940s. The camp, known as the Big Moose Pioneer Camp, was run by the Fort Orange Boy Scout Council of Albany, New York, but it was the brainchild of Dr. Edgar Vander Veer, a physician from Albany who was a strong supporter of the Boy Scouts.

Dr. Albert Vander Veer, Edgar's father, was among the earliest summer residents of the lake and owned a large amount of property along the south shore at the east end of the lake, as well as a large camp that had been completed in 1908 (lots 152–62). In 1930, James Vander Veer, Edgar's brother, wrote a letter to Nelson Dunn, Sr., who acted for many years as caretaker of the Vander Veer property.[1] He notified Nelson that the family had given permission to the Fort Orange Council to use land at the far end of their property for a camp. "The camp will be of the tent type, will have one of the forest rangers in charge together with a Scout Master; will have about fifteen boys there, and under the supervision of the ranger, arrangements have been made to clear out a number of trails that Mr. Howard [the ranger] is planning out for the Big Moose Section."[2]

The camp had its first season in 1930, and for the first two years was located on Vander Veer property. The site was near the Caslers' camp, significantly west of the camp's later location at the far end of East Bay. The camp opened on or about July 15 and was in session until September 1. That first year, there were only fifteen boys. To be eligible to attend, boys had to be at least fourteen years old and First Class Scouts. In later years there were six patrols of eight Scouts each, a total of forty-eight boys.

In 1932 the Fort Orange Boy Scout Council in Albany bought several lots at the very end of East Bay (lots 190–97) and in 1933 moved the camp farther up the lake. It is likely that Edgar Vander Veer gave money to the Boy Scout Council so it could buy the land from Robert G. Harry of Schenectady, who had earlier purchased the area, and much other land, from the Edward P. Morse estate.

RECOLLECTIONS OF CAMP LIFE

Arnold Drooz of Cary, North Carolina, a longtime guest at the Waldheim, attended the Boy Scout camp during 1936–38, and his brother, Herbert, was there during 1933–35. Howard Menand, Jr., now a resident of the North Shore, also attended as a counselor during the 1930s.

According to their recollections, most Scouts came for two-week sessions, although some stayed for the full six weeks. The campers slept in two-man, open-sided Baker tents that had wooden platforms and open sides, which invited bugs and required the boys to use large amounts of the classic insect repellant, citronella. The tents stood in two rows facing the lake, one row behind the other. There were also a few tents along the trail leading up the hill. For warmth during cool summer nights, the early campers were allotted three World War I army blankets and one-half of a World War I pup tent to throw over the blankets. After World War II, campers were given army sleeping bags filled with down.

Access to the camp was by water only, and boys had to earn their canoe merit badge before they could leave camp. The director of the camp was George Sparkes, who, according to Drooz, also "saw that we did lots of work—trail clearing, hiking," and the like. Sparkes also maintained a cordial relationship with the Big Moose Property Owners Association, seeking its suggestions for projects and making sure that the boys' work met with its approval. His picture appears in the 1934 group photograph of those attending the annual meeting of the BMPOA (see chapter 8, page 243). The campers contributed valuable services, working on the trails to Russ-

ian Lake, Gulls, Andes Creek, and Billy's Bald Spot. The minutes of the Big Moose Property Owners Association acknowledge their help several times.

At the end of each group's stay, the boys were treated to a special excursion. In the 1930s, the traditional routine for first-year campers was to hike up West Mountain and sleep under the fire tower. The second year they climbed Mount Marcy. The third year's highlight was a three-day, one hundred-mile canoe trip.

Drooz recalls that the cook, Art La Belle, was the most important fellow in camp. He was loaned by the New York Central Railroad, where he worked as an executive chef. (Perhaps the president of the New York Central, P. J. Crowley, a regular resident of a cottage at Lake View Lodge, may have had something to do with this.) Art La Belle presided over a kitchen located in an enclosed area at one end of the dining pavilion, the only permanent building at the camp. This good-sized structure was constructed by Charles and Nelson Dunn. The cook used a wood stove, and his refrigerator was a large hole in the ground chilled by ice that probably came from Higby's. The meals he produced, Drooz recalls, were excellent, and he always made sure there was plenty of food for the long camping or hiking trips.

Every night the campers gathered around a campfire built upon a mound of dirt and surrounded by a circle of boulders. The roaring fire was ringed with logs on which the boys sat while they sang Scout and cowboy songs. One of the campers accompanied them on his guitar. The chef, Art La Belle, joined in with French Canadian tunes. It was a wonderful way to end the day.

During the early days of the camp, the boys paddled canoes to Higby's on Saturday evenings, where they

Tents at the Boy Scout Pioneer Camp, ca. 1933. Courtesy of Wanda K. Martin.

Art LaBelle, cook at the Boy Scout Pioneer Camp, ca. 1933. Courtesy of Wanda K. Martin.

could buy candy and watch a movie in the boathouse. This fragment of a song, recalled by Drooz, reflects their happy relationship with Francena Higby, widow of James Higby:

> Come with me to Higby's
> Up on Big Moose Lake
> Mother Higby's waiting
> In her arms to take
> All her friends the campers
> From the Boy Scout Camp
> Come with me to Higby's
> When the day is done.

What the verse lacks in literary quality is made up by its warm sentiment. Many residents remember the Scouts singing as they paddled on the water in the dusk.

The counselors were also known to pursue some of the young ladies on the lake. A whimsical perspective appears in the minutes of the Property Owners Association for 1940. Mr. Colpitts, a resident of the North Shore, warned families with attractive daughters to be careful of the Boy Scout Camp if they did not want to lose their daughters. Colpitts's daughter, Lucy, married Howard Menand after a romance that started when Howard worked at the camp. The story is that the Colpitts's daughter heard that there was a Princeton man on the lake who was a counselor for the Scouts. Lucy was determined to find him and discovered him at a dance at the Higby boathouse where he was enjoying a blind date with Letha Higby. The incident had a happy ending for Lucy and Howard, but Letha's response is unknown.

William C. Gordon and David E. Norton, two former residents of the Albany area, also have recollections of the Boy Scout Camp as it was in 1948. At this time there were about thirty-six campers, most of whom stayed for two weeks. As before, they were all First Class Scouts, aged fourteen or fifteen, working for merit badges related to swimming, lifesaving, canoeing, rowing, and rugged camping. There were six to eight staff members, including a director and instructors in water activities, crafts, and other programs. Most campers arrived with a group from their home area. Bill Gordon remembers hiking into the woods, probably to Russian Lake, sleeping in a tent or lean-to, and hiking back.

The food at the camp was apparently not up to the gourmet standards of the 1930s. Powdered milk and other reminders of World War II were on the menu. Campers peeled potatoes and otherwise helped with preparation. They also set tables and helped in the dining room.

The waterfront had two long docks that extended out into the water and were about fifty feet apart. There may have also been a small raft. Speedboats, probably from Dunn's Marina, delivered mail, food, and any necessary equipment every day. The drivers of the boats loved to dash into the narrow channel, cutting the engines sharply just before they curved into the side of one of the docks. "More than one canoe," Gordon recalls, "tipped over in their wake. Some Scouts liked to time their boating to the arrival of the power boats and get the waves or the dunking. I know the camp authorities did not like this unsafe high speed arrival and spoke to the boat drivers and eventually to their bosses."

THE WATERFRONT, BIG MOOSE PIONEER CAMP, B.S.A., BIG MOOSE, N. Y.

Waterfront at the Boy Scout Pioneer Camp, ca. 1933. Courtesy of Wanda K. Martin.

Bill Gordon recalls the ritual of induction into the Order of the Arrow, an honor that he received as a camper in 1948:

The whole camp stood in a circle around a campfire one night. A counselor with a lighted torch would run around outside the circle and "tap" (a polite word for a very heavy blow) the three or four selected candidates on the shoulder or upper back. We who were tapped had to follow the tapper through the woods to begin the twenty-four-hour initiation.

First we were blindfolded. All was very quiet, and there were few or no words spoken. We were each put in a rowboat and after twenty or thirty minutes were landed on a rocky shore. I was led off the boat and told to keep the blindfold on for five minutes so that I would not know who dropped me off. A canoe was left with me but no paddle, and I was to stay for the night. I used the canoe as shelter, collected leaves and boughs in the dark as best I could for softer sleeping, and went to sleep with all the sounds of the deep Adirondack woods. The canoe was my protection from bears, at least that was my comforting thought. I was glad that I had previously camped with my family in the Adirondacks and was familiar with the sounds of the night and the bird calls that I heard in the morning.

The next day I was picked up by boat and taken back to camp. Breakfast, lunch and dinner that day were each a big glass of water and two pieces of bread. Hard labor, chopping logs for a trail, digging and moving stones to make better paths was our project. We had to work all day in complete silence. It was hot and sticky, but I loved the heat rather than the cold. I was quiet all day except once when a newly cut log started rolling down hill toward another initiate. I yelled, "Look out!" and

received a penalty for this transgression, probably a few pushups. About eight or nine o'clock we had a good meal in the dining hall and received congratulations on becoming a member of the Order of the Arrow.

THE CAMP'S END

The Scout Camp continued into the late 1940s, when it finally closed. Any records in the Albany office related to the camp are now lost. The Fort Orange Council soon expanded to include a broader area and eventually merged into the Governor Clinton Council, which is still operating.

Ennis and Edith Pilcher purchased the land in 1967 and 1968 and cleared away the debris surrounding the camp's only permanent building, the kitchen-dining room. The weakened structure collapsed under the heavy snows of the winter of 1971–72. Nelson Dunn, Jr., whose father had helped to construct the original building, helped to clear away the remains.

Lumbering at Big Moose Lake

THE CLIMATE AT THE TURN OF THE CENTURY

Within New York State, political controversies raged over Adirondack lumbering. Land boundaries were imprecise, drawn on maps but not marked upon the ground. Timber theft from state-owned lands was pervasive. Corruption was rampant, and many of those involved in the lumbering business or in its regulation, including state officials, were out to make a fast buck. Within this climate, William

Seward Webb and Theodore Page each made a dramatic impact on Big Moose Lake. Both were entrepreneurs, Webb as a landowner with clear ideas about how his land was to be used and Page as a lumbering magnate willing to stay within the letter of the law but willing also to push the limits of neighborly good will. With the state's "forever wild" clause as background, the deed restrictions of Webb and the business interests of Page (and of his successors, Bissell and Yousey) epitomize how competing interests in Adirondack lands and timber played out.

Because of its isolation, the Big Moose region escaped the early destruction of Adirondack forests that started in the late 1700s and continued through the nineteenth century. Loggers, miners, charcoal burners, and tanners all exploited both public and private lands in New York State for their own profit. In the 1870s, clear-cutting became common because the burgeoning paper industry, led by the growing need for newsprint, demanded pulpwood. By 1900, two-thirds of our northern forests had been stripped of pine, hemlock, spruce, and other softwoods.[3] As time went on, new papermaking technology made it possible to use hardwoods, such as birch, beech, and maple, so that it became profitable to cut all the trees.[4]

Clear-cutting left bare slopes that were vulnerable to erosion. In its natural state, the Adirondack forest had functioned like a vast sponge, soaking up water and releasing it at a steady rate. However, its capacity to hold water decreased as timber was clear-cut. The result was flooding in the lowlands during wet weather and droughts during dry periods. Mills and power plants were unable to function during water shortages. Canals and rivers that depended on feeder streams became too shallow for commercial shipping. Merchants and upstate farmers found it difficult or impossible to send their products and produce to big cities such as New York or Buffalo. Water shortages also affected delivery of trade goods from cities on the Great Lakes and farther west, which had to be brought via the Erie Canal.

FOREST PRESERVATION VERSUS SCIENTIFIC FORESTRY

Members of the New York City Board of Trade, among other businessmen, seeing their economic interests threatened by the unpredictable supply of products from upstate and beyond, became leaders of an enlightened effort to save the forests. Other concerned groups soon joined them—conservationists, sportsmen, a growing number of summer vacationers, and many artists and art lovers who valued the streams, waterfalls, and forests for aesthetic reasons.

Arrayed against these interests were lumbermen, both inside and outside the state bureaucracy, who saw trees as a resource to be used either for filling state coffers or for their own personal gain. The subject was still highly controversial in 1885, when both the Adirondack and the Catskill Forest Preserves were created in an unsuccessful effort to halt lumbering on state lands. The state appointed a Forestry Commission to oversee both preserves.

However, lumbermen were appointed as the new commissioners, the equivalent of assigning foxes to guard the henhouse. They continued to sell state-owned tracts of land or the "cutting rights" on lands within the Forest Preserve. Even after the Adirondack Park was established in 1892, the commissioners permitted land sales, timber cutting, road building, and leases for private camps.

Finally, in 1894, a group of businessmen and embattled citizens insisted on more effective measures to save the forests. They prevailed upon delegates at the state constitutional convention to adopt the famous "forever wild" clause, which affords protection to Adirondack (and Catskill) forests that is more stringent, even today, than any other land protection scheme in the world: "The lands of the State . . . constituting the forest preserve . . . shall be forever kept as wild forest lands. They shall not be leased, sold or exchanged, or be taken by any corporation, public or private, nor shall the timber thereon be sold, removed or destroyed."[5]

Nevertheless, the "forever wild" clause was controversial. In fact, some state officials who were directly responsible for enforcing it actively opposed it and sought to undermine it. The superintendent of forests himself, Colonel William Fox, and others on the State Forestry Commission, along with Gifford Pinchot (earlier engaged by Seward Webb and then of the U.S. Forest Service), believed that for their long-term health, the state forests should be *managed* not *preserved*. This meant that lumberers should be able selectively to harvest trees that had a commercial use. Thus, scientific forestry was much in vogue, and many private Adirondack preserves had developed what initially appeared to be successful lumber-management plans.

However, many difficulties arose. Barbara McMartin, in her book *The Great Forest of the Adirondacks*, offers a revealing account of the problems of forest management, not only on private estates such as Webb's Ne-Ha-Sa-Ne, Whitney Park, and the Adirondack League Club (all run by forward-looking, conservation-minded owners), but also on lands owned by large corporations such as the Gould Paper Company and the International Paper Company.[6]

The state, too, was discovering that scientific management was easier in theory than in practice. For example, the state was chiefly interested in spruce, by far the most important merchantable lumber at that time (partly because it would float and could be easily transported out of the wilderness in the era before railroads).[7] A major problem in maintaining a supply of spruce, scientific foresters eventually discovered, was that young spruce trees (especially desirable for paper because of their long, tough fibers) needed shade and cool temperatures in order to regenerate so that a second or third cut could be made at twenty-year intervals. Heavy cutting that left sunny, warm areas encouraged the growth of hardwoods, but the supply of valuable spruce declined steadily.

Proponents of scientific forestry dominated the State Forestry Commission for many years and worked actively to oppose the new "forever wild" protections in the state constitution. They began publishing plans for lumbering the heart of the central Adirondack area on what they considered to be scientific principles. Their first Forest Working Plan was published in 1900 in *The New York State Report of the Forest, Fish and Game Commission*. It concerned Township 40 around Raquette Lake and recommended "that the Constitution be so amended as to provide for the practice of conservative forestry on State Lands . . . and the sale of dead, dying or mature timber under proper safeguards."[8]

Many feared that the State Forestry Commission was simply lobbying for permission to sell land or cutting rights.

A Forest Working Plan for Township 41, which included the east end of Big Moose Lake, was part of a report of the New York State Forest, Fish and Game Commission in 1902–03. Like the earlier report, it was developed by federal foresters, believers in scientific forestry, on loan to New York State's Forestry Commission.

Commissioners duly noted restrictions by William Seward Webb in deeds of sale (see Appendix B) but then went on to discuss ways in which logs might be removed after cutting. The commissioners considered whether timber from Big Moose Lake should be floated down the Inlet from Lower Sister Pond, with a flood dam erected at its outlet. In the end, the plan advocated, instead, hauling logs to the lake in winter, dumping them on the ice, and enclosing them with booms until spring freshets could move them downstream.[9] "There is . . . a large amount of mature timber on this compartment [the northern half of Township 41] which should be removed . . . There would undoubtedly be considerable opposition to timber being driven down through Big Moose Lake and the stream below . . . [but] this is the natural and most advisable way to remove the timber."[10]

Publication of the Forest Working Plans aroused defenders of the Forest Preserve, and the battle both outside and within the Conservation Commission raged for years between "forever wilders" and "scientific foresters." ("Scientific forestry" was widely believed to be a euphemism for indiscriminate cutting.) Although "forever wilders" were ultimately successful, the Forest Working Plan for Township 41 did influence later lumbering around Big Moose Lake. In addition, the commissioners were absolutely correct when they predicted that there would be opposition to timber being floated down the lake. Incidentally, as Barbara McMartin notes, "Implicit in the design of the study was the desire to show the timber potential of the tract and thus bolster arguments for changing the State constitution."[11]

Meanwhile, a conscientious but frustrated German immigrant, John B. Koetteritz, whom the state had hired as a lowly agent for the comptroller,[12] was doing his best to protect state lands from rampant illegal lumbering. A small, wiry man, Koetteritz wrote numerous letters to state officials expressing his bewilderment at the state's lack of interest in enforcing its own laws, its reluctance to pay his expenses, and the injustices he was suffering. In one instance, he wrote, "The [state] agents . . . are threatened and molested, every accommodation, like boarding, putting of horse in barn, etc, refused. During this winter my wife received five threatening letters from different quarters, telling her that I never would return alive if I dared to come in the woods again and offering for my transfer to another world a variety of routes viz: by hanging, shooting and by putting me in a hollow tree."[13]

Perhaps because of his honest efforts to enforce the laws and in spite of his complaints, Koetteritz was hired by a new Forest Commission in 1885 as a state forester and surveyor.[14]

CONFUSING BOUNDARY LINES

In 1890, the Forest Commission gave Koetteritz the nearly impossible job of compiling a large map of the Adirondacks that would reconcile all previous maps. He was to show correctly all patents, tracts, and townships; lakes and streams; roads, railroads, and settlements; and be the first to indicate which lands were state owned. (Previous maps had inexplicably omitted many primary features.)

At Big Moose Lake the Koetteritz Line, drawn on maps and marked on trees, was used in 1897 as a basis for settlement of a lawsuit and large land sale to the state by Webb, and thus it designates the borders between state and private lands. It is blazed by yellow paint on trees, renewed periodically, and is still visible about two hundred yards east of the end of East Bay, where it crosses a small stream that is the outlet of Russian Lake. Running north and south, it also crosses the Inlet, serving as the boundary between state land and Dunn family property on the shore.

These state-owned lands in Hamilton County that lie east of the yellow line are part of the area that state foresters were hoping to lumber. At the time of the Webb sale, the Koetteritz Line was generally believed to coincide with part of the boundary between Herkimer and Hamilton counties.

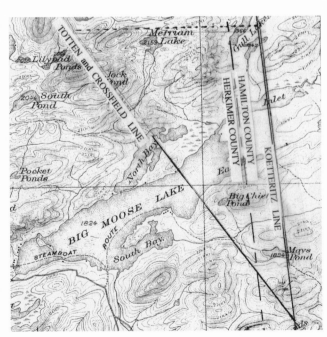

Boundary lines affecting Big Moose Lake as shown on a 1903 U.S. Geological Survey map, Big Moose Quadrangle.

In addition to the Koetteritz Line, which separates state from privately owned lands, two other major boundary lines cross Big Moose Lake and concern lumbering and land-ownership questions.

The Totten and Crossfield Line separates the pre-Revolutionary Totten and Crossfield Purchase from the Macomb Purchase of 1793. These are the two major land tracts in the Adirondacks, from which all subdivisions flow. (See more details in chapter 1.)

The third line is the boundary between Hamilton and Herkimer counties, which was not marked upon the ground until 1900. This line had been in dispute for many years and was believed, some years earlier, to coincide with the Koetteritz Line in the vicinity of Big Moose Lake. The State Surveyor's Office located its crossing about four-tenths of a mile west of the Koetteritz Line, creating a gore of disputed territory between the old and new county lines. This discrepancy figured prominently in legal disputes and lumbering operations in later years.

The most important facts to grasp are, first, that Big Moose Lake includes land in both Herkimer and Hamilton counties, and, second, that Township 41 (a subdivision of the Totten and Crossfield Purchase) crosses the county line and, like the lake, includes both state-owned and private land in both counties.

1897: WEBB'S LUMBERING RESTRICTIONS

In the course of buying land both for his Mohawk and Malone Railroad and for his private use, William Seward Webb had acquired vast tracts of the northern forest. Included were 75,000 acres of nearly virgin territory near the Beaver River north of Big Moose Lake and all of Township 41, which overlaps the east end of Big Moose Lake. Webb's plans for lumbering these remote lands were damaged when New York State built a dam on the Beaver River near Stillwater in 1887 and in 1893 raised it to a higher level. Webb instituted a lawsuit against New York State, alleging that the dam not only caused flooding on 275 acres, killing valuable timber, but also barred access for further lumbering to another 66,000 acres.

In settlement of the lawsuit, Webb sold 75,000 acres to the state in 1897. It was a very profitable deal for Webb, who received $600,000 for the tract, a price that was far in excess of the going rate for comparable lands.[15] In addition, Webb included restrictions in his deed of sale to the state and in all his private sales that are today in the deed of every landowner on Big Moose Lake. These unique restrictions, known as the Webb Covenant (Appendix B), are evidence of Webb's conservation concerns, and they must reflect his low opinion of typical state forestry practices.

FIRST LUMBERING CONTRACT AT BIG MOOSE LAKE

After his sale of lands to the state, Webb still retained title to all the land at Big Moose west of the Koetteritz Line. In 1897, he arranged the original lumbering contract with two experienced lumbermen from Russia, New York: Firman Ouderkirk and Daniel Strobel.

William J. Thistlethwaite of Old Forge, one of Webb's agents, handled all details of the arrangement. The agreement was not a sale of land but of lumbering rights, and the lumbermen were required to complete their operations by May 1, 1906. They were given the right to cut softwoods on a tract of land west of the Koetteritz Line that constituted the part of Township 41 not sold to the state.

Restrictions in the contract included the latest scientific forestry practices, making it more restrictive than the covenant with private property owners (see Webb Covenant, Appendix B). The contract with Ouderkirk and Strobel, which went beyond the covenant with private owners,[16] stipulated that:

• Lakeshore lots were protected and were to be used exclusively for hotels, camps, cottages, or forestry purposes; all commercial, agricultural, and manufacturing uses were banned.

• Lake and pond shores were protected; there was to be no lumber cutting within 330 feet of any shore; no sawdust, bark, or other debris was to be dumped into any lake, pond, or stream. Most cuttings were to be restricted to softwoods only.

• No sawmills were to be located within 500 feet of any body of water.

• Only mature trees were to be harvested; no clear-cutting was allowed.

• All existing trails and waterways were to remain free for public usage.

• Any lumber roads that were built were to be unobtrusive near bodies of water and not run in a straight line toward the water's edge. (Webb wanted lumbering roads to curve before reaching the shore so that unsightly roads would not be visible from the lake.)

• Timber could be floated out across lakes (largely in spring freshets), but lake levels were not to be raised above the natural high-water mark.

In short, Webb intended to ensure that Big Moose Lake would remain desirable for future residents and vacationers. New York State agreed to these regulations,[17] but, under pressure from businessmen who wanted to profit from less-restrictive rules, the state gradually lost interest in enforcing them. In later years, Webb's heirs disclaimed any interest in forcing the state to contest violations of the Webb Covenant.[18]

The land to be lumbered was a triangular tract at the east end of the lake between the Totten and Crossfield Line and the Koetteritz Line. Roughly, it was bounded on the north by Merriam Lake, extending across Mount Tom to Upper Gull Lake and south across Constable Creek (following the Koetteritz Line) to the apex of the triangle south of May's Pond. The northwest line of the boundary (the Totten and Crossfield Line) crossed the summit of Sugarloaf Mountain west of Big Chief Pond, crossed East Bay, bisected North Bay, and ended west of Merriam Lake.

Although all timber cutting was to be completed by 1906, there were delays in starting the project. First, surveyor M. O. Wood, supervised by Thistlethwaite, who was acting for Webb, blazed the trees that marked the limits of the tract, completing his task in 1903. Second, another Big Moose landowner entered the picture.

1902: THEODORE PAGE AND THE HERKIMER LUMBER COMPANY

Theodore Alanson Page had purchased Echo Island in 1900 and in 1901 built the elaborate summer home he called Camp Veery. Page was experienced in supervising lumbering operations and regularly imported timber from Canada to use in the shade cloth factory that he owned in Minetto, New York, just outside his hometown of Oswego. He became associated with the Herkimer Lumber Company, and in 1902 he bought all of the lands designated in the lumber-cutting contract between Thistlethwaite, and Ouderkirk and Strobel. The latter two men then also became affiliated with the Herkimer Lumber Company, which had previously logged large amounts of land around Beaver River, Carter, Rondaxe, and McKeever.

Page took charge of lumbering operations in 1903. In addition to the generous reserves specified by Webb, an additional 500 acres at the head of the lake were exempted from logging. This area included the north shore of East Bay and two points of land between the entrance to the Inlet and East Bay. On one peninsula stood a small fishing camp, later the site of the Deerlands camp, and on the other the property occupied by Irvin "Headlight" Williams, then called Old Pine Point. (In 1904, Williams was forced to sue Page for possession of his property, for which he held an option under the original Ouderkirk and Strobel contract.)[19]

Within the 2,500 acres to be logged, Page's three field supervisors were George Harvey, Solomon Carnahan, and George Raymond, all well-known local lumberjacks. Each set up a separate camp within the cutting area.[20] They cut only softwoods, primarily red spruce. The logs were floated down the lake and through the Outlet. No objections from lake residents were recorded during this period.

A photograph from Henry Covey's album, taken about 1905, shows logs (probably Page's) covered with snow in the lake (see illustration below). From the lake, the logs were driven down the North Branch of the Moose River, ending at the Herkimer Lumber Company's mill at Moulin (*moulin* is French for "mill"), a station between Thendara and Carter on Webb's Mohawk and Malone Railroad.

While this was going on, the county line had been moved. In 1900 the State Engineer's Office, apparently without consulting the Forestry Commission, directed surveyor Edward A. Bond to relocate the Herkimer-Hamilton county line and mark it *on the ground*.

Theodore Page's logs frozen in ice, ca. 1905. Courtesy of Robert and Elizabeth Smith.

This was not as easy a task as it might seem. The line had never been defined in undeveloped parts of the Adirondacks. Hamilton County had been subdivided from Montgomery County, and the early lines when Montgomery County was marked out used magnetic north rather than true north. Magnetic lines follow the curvature of the earth, whereas true north lines are straight. In adjusting the line, Bond consulted records from 1797, tracing original boundaries from the Macomb Purchase to determine the proper starting point. Then he established the correct line running true north and marked it with surveyors' monuments at intervals. The new county line (now in use) is sometimes called "the Bond Line."

When he finally calculated the current line, running true north like other lines in New York State, the correction resulted in a gore between the old county line (the Koetteritz Line) and the new county line.[21] The distance between the two, where the line crosses East Bay of Big Moose Lake, is, as noted above, only 1,930 feet, or less than one-half mile. The area tapers slightly, wider at the northern end and narrower at the southern end, because of the curve of the magnetic line.

Theodore Page's lumbering operations had been proceeding smoothly for two years when the Forest Commission suddenly concluded that Page was lumbering on state lands. On September 29, 1905, Page received a telegram ordering him to cease operations immediately. The state's attorney general accused Page of stealing timber. Page questioned the injunction on grounds that he was acting within the guidelines of his original contract. New York State withdrew the injunction, and later in 1905 Page resumed his lumbering. His operations continued until May 1, 1906, the date when the original contract expired.

A court suit followed.[22] New York State accused Page and his contractors of lumbering illegally on state lands. Briefly, the state alleged that Page's operations in the gore between the Bond Line (the new county line) and the Koetteritz Line (the old county line) were illegal. Under the terms of the contract that Ouderkirk and Strobel had signed in 1897 and that Page had taken over in 1902, Page was operating legally. New York State had not made clear where the boundaries lay. The lawsuit dragged on for three years, between 1906 and 1909. Eventually, Page was exonerated. He had proved his point and maintained his honor.

In the course of the proceedings, the honest and persistent Koetteritz, always something of a thorn in the side of the state, testified that early maps gave Big Moose Lake the wrong shape and were therefore inaccurate. In effect, Koetteritz, although called as a witness by the state prosecutor, testified in Page's favor. Therefore, an incidental result of the case was confirmation of the new Herkimer Hamilton county line.

Beginning in 1912, Page sold two tracts of land to Dana Bissell, one in 1912 and one in 1914.[23] In 1916, the year Page died, his widow sold the remainder of his timber landholdings to Dana Bissell,[24] thereby marking the beginning of the second commercial logging operation on the lake.

1912–1914: BISSELL AND YOUSEY COME TO BIG MOOSE LAKE

In 1912, Dana Bissell of Glens Falls and his partner, Peter Yousey of Carthage, New York, began planning to lumber again on the so-called Page tract. They intended to mount a much more intensive lumbering operation than Page had conducted.

Rather than the selective cutting that Page had done, Bissell and Yousey planned to clear-cut both soft and hardwood trees. They also intended, in flagrant violation of the agreement with Webb, to erect a complex of buildings on the lakeshore just west of the entrance to the Inlet. They planned to build a sawmill, a lumberyard, and a huge banking ground with a long and very high dock on property adjacent to the mouth of the Inlet. In addition, they anticipated building another large dock in West Bay where lumber could be unloaded and transported to Big Moose Station for shipment by rail to points south. All of these plans were in direct violation of Webb's original contract, and many items seemed to be based upon the Forest Working Plan for Township 41.

When property owners along the North Shore and elsewhere on the lake heard about this, they rose up in alarm. Lake residents were much more numerous than they had been when Page's operations took place, and they were extremely concerned about pollution of the lake and the noise and disturbance to the lake community.

Dr. Arwed Retter, Edward S. Woodbury, and Dr. Albert Vander Veer led the fight. The battle was financially supported by contributions from at least eight property owners, including Retter himself, Leslie Warnick Brown, Henry Covey, Clarence Kelsey, Thomas Kingsford, and Mrs. W. Bradley Ogden, as well as Vander Veer and Woodbury.

The group hired a Utica lawyer, Theodore L. Cross, to persuade the newly created State Conservation Commission, a combination of the Forestry, Fish, and Game Commissions formed in 1911, to purchase the land and add it to the Forest Preserve. They pointed out that the proposed lumbering plans violated the Webb Covenant, which the state had agreed to uphold. Cross wrote to the Conservation Commission: "Here is the most beautiful lake in the Adirondacks which has been kept better preserved . . . than possibly any lake other than Raquette Lake. . . . [T]he State of New York . . . through inadvertency . . . left this little triangle between Township 8 and Township 41 in such form that a claim can be made that they are bound by no restrictive covenants."[25]

The Conservation Commission, however, seemed indifferent and took no action.

The fight moved to a new level later in February 1913, when George Burdick of Burdick's Camp on West Bay wrote to Retter in Utica that Bissell had told him that Bissell and Yousey also planned to lumber on New York State lands. At the time, Bissell was renting a cottage next to Burdick's, and, Burdick wrote, Bissell came "over to the house the other evening, so I had a good chance to find out their plans."[26] Burdick further wrote

> Mr. Bissel [sic] tells me that the State has offered him if he would go on and cut timber on the State Lands that they would commence action against him and make a test case of it, and that they would pay him all expenses and a good commission besides, just to find out if it cannot be done, as they want to dispose of a lot of their soft timber. If this be so I don't see where we would stand a bit of a show in any way with them. But you know they are a lot of grafters, and a party outside of their clock does not stand much show.[27]

In other words, Burdick reported skulduggery. He was afraid, with some justification because of previous underhanded deals within the state, that Bissell would agree to allow the state to sue him for illegal lumbering. The commission, nearly twenty years after the "forever wild" clause was inserted into the state constitution, was still testing whether the courts would permit lumbering on the Forest Preserve. To induce Bissell to be the guinea pig in this proposed case, the commission apparently was willing to pay Bissell's expenses plus extra money as a "commission." (Bill Marleau mentions hearing of this proposal but says, "I don't know if Bissell and New York State ever had such a deal."[28])

In a handwritten note to Cross in February 1913, Retter stated that Bissell's agreement with the commission that his cutting operations would be a "test case" was nothing less than a "case of graft."[29]

Theodore Cross, the Utica lawyer, sought support for Big Moose residents from many sources. He contacted the Association for the Protection of the Adirondacks (with offices in New York City) as well as other conservation organizations. He persuaded at least one officer, Edward H. Hall, secretary of the association, to visit Albany and meet with the chairman of the new Conservation Commission, which had replaced the Forestry Commission. Unfortunately, the chairman of the Conservation Commission asserted that the state could not afford to buy the land and thus bring it under the Webb Covenant. Hall ended his report, "I got no encouragement."[30]

Taking another tack, Cross protested to Bissell that he had no right to pursue his elaborate plans. Cross tried to persuade him to sell the lands to the state before logging or at least to refrain from cutting hardwoods (i.e., not clear-cutting) and from building a sawmill.[31]

Unfortunately, at this time the state, in its eagerness to acquire land at less expense, was still allowing lumbermen to reserve timbering rights on land they sold to New York State. Cross, therefore, was not on firm ground when he tried to persuade Dana Bissell to sell the land to the state without cutting. Bissell could have sold and still been permitted to strip the land of trees.

Meanwhile, Cross assured Retter that the property owners' claim was valid and that he was confident that they had a strong case: "Examination of all deeds in the chain of title shows these convenants [the Webb Covenant] were meant to apply to the whole Big Moose Lake allotment, including the shore of the entire lake as plotted and mapped for sale as residence lots."[32]

However, Cross must have become somewhat discouraged. He began to look for compromises. Lake residents objected especially to a whining sawmill, with its mill whistles and the noisy steamer that was to operate day and night to carry the lumber down the lake.[33] Officials from the Conservation Commission, representatives of the property owners, and Bissell and Yousey conferred. At one point, Bissell and Yousey agreed to locate the sawmill and boardinghouse on North Bay, to cut only mature timber, and to take the lumber to the railroad station by roads that would be built around the back of North Bay. However, in return for these allowances property owners would have had to agree to pay the enormous costs of building roads and transporting the lumber over land, an exchange that Bissell probably knew would be rejected.[34]

Cross took up the matter with the state's attorney general, Thomas Carmondy, and persuaded him to order the Conservation Commission to institute a legal action against Bissell and Yousey in June of 1913.[35] (Whether this was the test case, the "deal" that Burdick and Retter suspected, we do not know.) In any case, Cross advised the Conservation Commission that "our [Big Moose] people would give no bond to induce the state to do its plain duty in this matter and to protect its own interests."[36] Because the group of property owners who had

Bissell and Yousey's sawmill, ca. 1915.
Courtesy of Janet S. Holmes.

The boardinghouse at Bissell and Yousey's sawmill, ca. 1915. Courtesy of Janet S. Holmes.

fought so hard refused to spend more money to force the state to do what they felt was morally and legally right, Bissell prevailed in the end. Big Moose Lake residents steeled themselves against the disturbances that were to come.

BISSELL AND YOUSEY'S ACTIVITIES AT BIG MOOSE LAKE

Bissell and Yousey's lumbering operations, which differed dramatically from most operations of the time, extended from 1914 to 1918. Theodore Page had followed the conventional method. After his teamsters had hauled the timber out of the woods, the logs, cut into standard lengths, were floated down the Outlet to a distant sawmill for further processing. Bissell used the lake and the Inlet to store floatable softwood logs, but the new sawmill cut all its timber, both softwood and hardwood, into dimensional lumber.

Tom Hartz, owner of a camp once part of the Bissell complex of buildings, has investigated the site and also researched the operation of mills of this type.[37] The sawmill itself measured thirty feet by eighty feet, as shown by the remains of the supporting piers. It housed an enormous circular band saw that whirled around two vertically positioned cylinders. The saw, discovered by Tom Hartz abandoned in the woods and now in the Adirondack Museum, was thirty-six feet in diameter. Its nine-inch width was edged by sharp, coarse teeth. The logs, clamped into position, traveled on a platform while the saw cut them into slices. The slices were then milled again to produce two-inch by six-foot boards or whatever size was required. Steam pistons powered the blade. Enormous quantities of sawdust flew into the air and piled up into huge heaps. The earsplitting whine of the saw dominated the area of the lumber camp and could be heard all around the lake.

The steam boiler could not consume all the sawdust, bark, and trimmings used for fuel. An incinerator was necessary to dispose of leftovers. The photograph of the sawmill shows two large smokestacks. The one on the larger building was for the fire that drove the pistons in the main mill. The stack in the foreground emerges from the smaller building, itself at least twenty feet by thirty feet in size, which housed the incinerator. This stack appears to have a spark guard at the top.[38]

As a concession to the lake residents, Bissell placed the loggers' boardinghouse, a large building twenty feet by sixty feet, back from the shore where trees screened it from the lake. It was a two-story structure with its gable end toward the water. Near it stood the essential icehouse and, closer to the lake, a warehouse for the store. Farther into the woods at the base of Mount Tom stood a scatter-

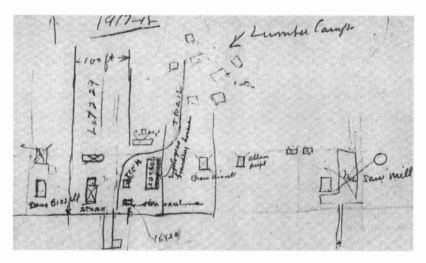

Sketch of the layout of Bissell and Yousey's lumbering operation, drawn by George Stone, ca. 1919. Courtesy of Janet S. Holmes.

The store at Bissell and Yousey's sawmill, ca. 1919. Note the ladder leading to the second floor. Courtesy of Janet S. Holmes.

The house of lumber mill owner Dana Bissell, renovated and now owned by Thomas and Doris Hartz, ca. 1981. Courtesy of Thomas Hartz.

ing of buildings that housed the lumberjacks. Small houses for staff, including Dana Bissell's brother Bramon (killed when his truck was struck by a train at Big Moose Station in 1915), stood between the boardinghouse and the mill. These residences were destroyed when the ever-present danger of fire became a reality and the sawmill burned in 1918. A roughly sketched map from about 1919 shows the location of the various buildings.

Farther west on the shore was the camp store, which Charlie Forkey ran. (After Bissell closed down, Forkey took over the operation of the Glennmore store.) The Bissell store, sometimes used by lake residents, was basically a one-room structure with a small addition at the back that served as an office. Stairs on the outside of the

building led up to the second floor. Now, much renovated, it is the summer camp of Janet and William Holmes.

The adjacent house, one lot to the west, was then occupied by Dana Bissell and currently belongs to Doris and Tom Hartz.

Bissell lumbered the whole side of Mount Tom toward the lake. He piled the logs on skidways in the woods and constructed corduroy roads to transport the logs to the sawmill, where the timber was cut into lengths for various uses. Softwood logs for paper pulp were four feet long; hardwood logs destined for building construction were eight or sometimes twelve feet.

Some of Bissell's lumbering practices were similar to those proposed in the Forest Working Plan for Township 41 printed in the Forestry Commission Report for 1902–03. He did use Big Moose Lake and its Inlet for storing softwood logs as suggested. However, he failed to honor the Webb restrictions on cutting lakeshore trees, he violated the shoreline by locating his sawmill directly on edge of the lake, and he ignored the lumbering reserve on summits and hillsides facing the lake. His cutting on Mount Tom and hillsides east of it was a major desecration, although the area today has filled in with maples and other trees that now glory in splendor every autumn.

Once the logs were brought out of the woods, the softwood, which would float, was stored in the lake, confined by booms at the mouth of the Inlet until it could be cut in the mill. Hardwood was stacked on the shore. Bissell owned a steamboat, the noisy and dirty *Merrimac*, which he used to tow the trimmed lumber on barges to West Bay.

BISSELL AND YOUSEY'S STORE

The lumberjacks were not the only customers for Bissell and Yousey's store. Lake residents often found it convenient for buying some of their supplies. Fran Leonard Lepper remembers an occasion when she and Letha Higby were taken to the store as children. While their parents were busy conducting their business, Fran and Letha amused themselves by playing with the open containers of beans that sat near the counter. They mixed the coffee beans with the baking beans. The result was a "lickin' " that Fran says she will never forget.

Dimensional lumber from Bissell and Yousey's sawmill being towed to the West Bay transshipment dock by the steamboat Merrimac, ca. 1915. Courtesy of Janet S. Holmes.

On property near the Glennmore (lot 376, now owned by George and Barbara Schunck), Bissell built a large dock with a crane. Here the boards were loaded onto trucks and taken to the Big Moose Station to await shipment by train.

After the sawmill burned in 1918, Bissell and Yousey's operations came to an end. Later in 1918, New York State bought part of the tract between the Totten and Crossfield Line and the county line, and in 1924 the state added six hundred more acres to the east, between the Koetteritz Line and the county line. However, the southern part of the original triangle, including most of Mays Pond and the south shore of East Bay, remained in private hands, as it is today, with the Koetteritz Line still the boundary between state and private lands.

Curiously, we have very few recorded reactions of lake residents to the logging operation. Admittedly, few people are left who might remember. A transcript of recollections by Grace Vander Veer McDonough tells us that "the

sawmill would start about seven o'clock in the morning. Everybody had a fit on the lake because it made such a racket."[39] In contrast, Roy Higby remembered the jingle of the brake chains with nostalgia. He says in his book, "I have often arisen before daylight and watched lanterns of the road monkeys [men who poured sand on the icy roads to slow the loaded sleighs] and teamsters going up and down the mountain."[40] Those who are old enough now to remember stories about logging are likely to forget the complaints and instead recall the romantic aspects of such an operation.

When the sawmill burned, the two tall smokestacks fell out into the water. They helped to hold the natural sand in the area and enlarge the beach. Children on the North Shore and indeed from all around the lake enjoyed the area for years. When World War II came along, the stacks were donated to the government as scrap metal to be used for the war effort.

The large dock that had been part of the mill made a convenient landing place for the *Daydream,* the Lake View Lodge launch that took guests to the mouth of the Inlet. They could then paddle their canoes or row their guideboats upstream to various picnic spots. Many lake residents also found the dock a convenient landing place, and the beach nearby became a favorite location for Sunday School picnics.

Local Loggers and Lumbering Stories

The Page and the Bissell and Yousey operations were not the only lumbering that took place around the lake. The other jobs were on a much smaller scale, and their primary purpose was only incidentally commercial.

Dimensional lumber being unloaded at the West Bay dock for transfer to the railroad, ca. 1915. Note the crane. Courtesy of Richard Widdicombe.

In the winter of 1919–20, Charles Williams, who ran Lake View Lodge, lumbered the area behind North Bay that had belonged to Leslie Warnick Brown and now belongs to the Waldheim. Williams bought the land and took out softwood pulp, which he hauled to Big Moose Station, where Earl Covey ran a small sawmill that cut the logs into four-foot lengths.[41] John Denio and Fred Brack also helped as tractor driver and "whistle punk" respectively. It was Williams who built the small bark-covered lumber camp, now vandalized and decrepit, that stands on Waldheim property. The building is on the private road that extends from the Waldheim garages east into the woods along North Bay. Williams used part of his timber for heating, for fireplaces in his hotel and cottages, and he sold the rest.

Roy Higby also conducted a small lumbering operation on his own land on Sugarloaf Mountain behind where the Judson Road now runs. As far as we know, the timber was largely for use at his hotel. Later, after World War II, Higby lumbered other land he owned around South Bay.

Several other Big Moose residents, including J. Munson Gamble, Fred Williams, Thomas Kingsford, Florence Martin, Walter Dunn, and Mrs. D. W. Rutherford, hired various contractors, among them Clarence J. Strife, to cut timber on their private lands.[42] Most of these operations were to procure lumber for personal use, but a few sold part of the wood for profit.

The process of cutting timber and moving it from the woods to the market required not only great strength but also great skill. It was also extremely dangerous. The operations at Big Moose took place after the axe and the

Remains of Charles Williams's lumber camp, now on Waldheim property, 2001. Photograph by Jane Barlow.

bucksaw were the primary tools used to cut trees. The two-man crosscut saw, introduced to the Adirondacks in 1891 and still dependent on muscle power, was used at Big Moose along with the trusty axe.[43] The chain saw did not appear until about 1940.[44] Horses, guided and controlled by skilled teamsters, hauled the logs out of the woods to a point where they could be moved by water or by rail to a central sawmill that prepared them for market.

Page floated his logs down the Outlet to Moulin, where they were milled and delivered to the railroad station there. When a river drive took place, a whole new team took over. River men sometimes included Mohawk Indians, whose cultural traditions put a high value on hazardous work.

Bissell barged his dimensional lumber, already milled, down the lake and took advantage of the Big Moose Station rail terminal, but his operation lasted only four years and probably was not available to local loggers. Roy Higby, who not only did some lumbering himself but also witnessed both the Page and Bissell operations, gives a detailed description of the lumbering process with all its risks.[45]

The operation began in the fall, clearing roads through the woods in order to remove the cut logs. The roads required a downhill slant, continuous but not so steep that the teamsters could not control their horses and keep them from being overrun by the heavy loads. When the weather became cold, the roads had to be prepared by smoothing and icing so that the sleighs could move down them without hitting rocks, logs, or other obstructions. Some of the old logging roads still exist on Mount Tom, and occasionally a rusting chain or a piece of a horse harness can be found along the overgrown trails. During the Bissell years, Charlie Williams of Lake View Lodge, Henry Covey of Camp Crag, and perhaps D. B. Sperry of the Hotel Glennmore, all skilled teamsters, worked on the project. According to Bill Marleau, "John Denio drove team, Charlie Forkey was scaler and clerk, Harry Kellogg drove one of the hard rubber tired, chain driven lumber trucks . . . Spafford Ainsworth ran the steam boat that hauled the lumber barges."[46] Other local men, including Art Burtch, Fred Brack, and Nelson Dunn, were also glad to find employment in the lumber business.

In general, most of the lumberjacks were transients. They came from many ethnic groups—French Canadian, Russian, Finnish, Polish, Irish, and Scotch. If a fight broke out, it was usually between men from different ethnic groups, and of course their fellows often joined in either to support their friends or to restrain them.

Peter Bruyn remembers his grandmother, Janet Retter Bruyn, telling about the lumberjacks passing by the Retter camp on Turtle Point at the entrance to North Bay. They would walk by with their horses, most likely wading in the lake in some areas, heading toward Big Moose Station for an evening of drinking and merriment. Janny's parents would dash out and bring their two daughters off the porch so they would not be exposed to such individuals. However, the girls were fascinated. Late at night, Janny would hear them return. In the stillness of the night, the lumberjacks could be heard for a considerable distance because the logging chains and equipment hanging on the horses would clank and rattle as the horses walked. It was also not unusual to see a drunk lumberjack draped over a horse, the beast walking back to camp on its own.[47]

Bissell and Yousey drove anchor logs vertically into the bottom of the lake in order to hold the booms that confined the cut softwoods. When the lumbering operations had ended, some of the anchor logs remained in place. Many at Big Moose believe that one tragic result was the accident that took the life of Dan Ainsworth, a well-known, popular guide.

After months in the woods, the lumberjacks would emerge at the time of the spring thaw. The men, having just been paid, would head straight for the towns and the bars. Bill Dunn remembers that the children always liked to see them coming, because they never failed to spend some of their money on candy for the kids who flocked around. The jacks were always respectful of women, and there is more than one tale of residents leaving their wives at Big Moose Station to catch a late train—even when drunken lumberjacks were there—without any worries that they would be accosted or bothered in any way.

Bill Marleau gives a vivid description of the jacks' appearance:

> The old time lumberjacks had their own uniforms: stagged pants above or just below boot tops. Their boots were Croghan brand or Chippewa, with or without caulks. The pants were dirty and baggy, held up by yellow suspenders. The jacks carried kitchen matches in their pockets or in the hat band of their battered felt hats. . . . To strike a match, they hooked a thumb back of the buckle on the suspenders, pulled it out and struck the match on it or else raised one cheek of their fannys and struck the match on the seat of their pants. . . .
>
> Most of them wore long underwear or union suits, one hundred percent wool in winter and cotton in the summer. In their pipes they smoked Prince Albert, Velvet . . . Warnick-Brown [from the Utica company whose president had a camp at Big Moose Lake]. . . . lots of chewing tobacco. . . . They rolled their own cigarettes, usually a cloth bag of Bull Durham or Duke's mixture and cigarette papers in their pocket. . . .
>
> Their favorite medicine for sore muscles was Sloan's Liniment and most lumberjacks reeked of it when they came to town. The only fly dope available then was pine tar and citronella that, with the Sloan's Liniment, let you know when the lumberjacks came to town.[48]

After World War II, lumbering changed drastically. The chain saw came into use, at first in the form of heavy two-man saws. Charlie Adams, who helped on a logging job while he was on vacation from college in the late 1940s, recalls the work:

> one night going back to Dunns' after we had worked a logging job down on the Big Moose-Eagle Road near what today is called the "Old Big Moose Road" . . . We had one of the "new fangled" chainsaws that was old, heavy and with terrible vibration built in, and when we got back to Dunns' that night for dinner, I remember my arms shook so much it was hard to hold the fork and eat because of hanging on to that saw for a good part of the day. I have often wondered if the foolishness we went through contributed to my hearing problems today, since we never saw anything like earmuffs when we used those things.[49]

Jack Judson recollects an occasion in the 1940s when the International Paper Company was logging between Big Moose Station and Beaver River: "These were times when the lumberjacks would come into Big Moose Station, usually on a Saturday night, and there would be a state trooper on the scene to oversee matters. I went to a logging camp in that area with Bud Dunn for early breakfast. The lumberjack by my side had four pork chops on his plate among eggs, pancakes and ham. When he finished the plate was clean. Gone were the pork bones."[50]

The Reverend Frank Reed, Pastor of the Niccolls Memorial Church in Old Forge for many years and also associated with the Big Moose Chapel for nearly one-half century, was an important figure in the lives of many of the lumberjacks. Traveling to the most remote camps in the Adirondacks, Reed became a friend to all he met and a spiritual guide to most. Although he never drank any-

Philip Martin and Peter Bruyn at the Waldheim sawmill, ca. 1960. Courtesy of Wanda K. Martin.

thing stronger than ginger ale, he participated in celebrations as well as work throughout the area. Always ready to help a man who got into trouble, he was greatly admired. When he retired from the church in 1964, he started an organization called "Northeastern Loggers," which in the 1970s had national scope.[51] In the course of his career he published several volumes with North Country Books, including *Lumberjack Sky Pilot, Rails in the North Woods, The Hills Beyond the Hills,* and *The Eternal Hills.* He also made home movies that illustrated the hardships and dangers of lumbering. A compilation of his films appeared recently on certain National Public Television stations,

opening the eyes of many to the hard life and, sometimes, the gruesome deaths of lumberjacks.

Lumberjacks and lumber camps disappeared more than one-half century ago. Today, loggers usually work alone with the help of chain saws that are much lighter and quieter than the old ones. They have tractors and huge trucks equipped with cranes to pile the logs on board. The trucks not only take the logs to market but also take the loggers home at night. One man can do the work of twenty. The lumber camps and their colorful histories are gone. All that remains is the occasional privately operated sawmill.

5 *Private Homes and Camps Before World War II*

IN 1942, there were sixty-two private camps on the lake. We will mention in this section only those early camps about which we have been able to gather information. In some cases we have diaries, memoirs, and scrapbooks that the descendants of the original owners have generously lent to us. In other cases, written history is lean and information has been gleaned largely from interviews and public records. Most purchase and sale dates have been checked at the Herkimer County Courthouse, but we have omitted the endnotes that gave the volume and page of each deed book. (Those interested can easily check for themselves with the assistance of the helpful staff at the courthouse.) Camps located in Hamilton County are recorded in the courthouse in Lake Pleasant. In many cases, we have information from owners' deeds and direct verbal or written confirmation from the owners themselves. In other cases, we have little or no information.

For purposes of this section, an early camp is defined as one that came into existence before World War II, or by about 1940. The war provides a convenient dividing line. After the Great Depression of the 1930s and the end of the war in 1945, growth accelerated, modes of transportation changed, and lake residents used their camps in different ways. In telling the story of each camp, we have taken the history forward to the current residents, even though this means continuing up to the present. Details on the families of the current occupants are in Appendix A: Big Moose Lake at the Beginning of the Twenty-First Century, arranged either by Webb survey lot numbers or Town of Webb tax numbers.

The first private camps appeared in many different areas of the lake, but to discuss them chronologically would be confusing. Instead we have divided the lake into

major segments. Indeed, in the early days, each area tended to form its own small community. The residents referred to themselves as living on, for instance, the Glennmore Trail or the North Shore Trail. Trail parties were, and sometimes still are, a long tradition.

The earliest camp of which we have a full account is Fern Spring, the 1880s predecessor of the Chapel manse, which later took over both the site and the name. Frank Carey's account is a vivid example of the ways that many of the first families to vacation at the lake changed their routine over time. In the beginning, the men alone came to fish or hunt. As transportation became easier and as guides metamorphosed into skilled carpenters, plumbers, and stone workers, visitors found local residents who could build camps and provide other services that made the woods more inviting to their wives and children.

The amount of information available on the early camps varies greatly. An unusual amount comes from the North Shore, particularly the occupants of camps on the west end near the entrance to North Bay. Those residents were among the first on the lake, and the descendants of many of them still own the original property. Although more space is given to these families, many of their recorded experiences were typical of others who were at the lake at about the same time.

Most families depended heavily on local residents not only to build their camps but also to maintain them. The work included opening the camp in the spring, cleaning kitchens and other rooms, retrieving blankets and rugs from storage, and preparing the building for occupancy. It also meant readying boats for use, putting out docks, seeing that wood supplies were on hand, checking plumbing and lighting arrangements, and all the other myriad chores that were necessary. The summer residents, on their part, more often than not brought with them or hired locally a cook and a handyman who could help with the routines of daily living that today are taken care of by modern devices and appliances.

Most families also typically planned and ordered barrels of non-perishable food, often from Macy's in New York City, to supplement the fresh meat, fruit, and vegetables that were available in limited quantities locally. Sometimes the fathers would send or bring from the cities special treats. We hear of Dr. Retter, for instance, sending peaches and apples from Utica in 1900.

Dependency on local workers continued during the entire year. Closing the buildings demanded work to see that camps and their contents were protected from animals, large and small, and the threats brought by heavy snows and freezing weather. Winter also was the time when supplies of wood were renewed and icehouses filled.

Travel in the early days was by train. Indeed, it was the only practical way to get to the lake with a family. Once vacationers arrived at Big Moose Station, the Big Moose Transportation Company provided transport for baggage and passengers to the Glennmore landing, where the steamboat or launch would take the entire entourage to their summer retreat. For many years, most camps could be reached only by water and most families stayed for the entire summer.

Interrelationships between year-round and summer residents were complex, and we once again urge the reader to use the index for further stories about people and places.

Early Camps on West Bay

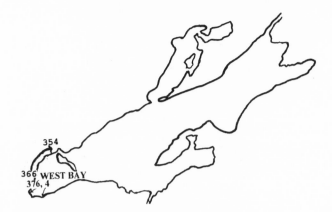

BIG MOOSE LODGE, WILDWOOD, AND WINONA LODGE

BIG MOOSE LODGE (LOTS 364E–65)

Before Dwight Sperry purchased the land for the Glennmore Hotel, one private camp probably stood on West Bay. Located on the northern side, painted white (as was traditional then), and called Big Moose Lodge, it may have existed even before Webb bought the land. Information about the early history of the lodge is obscure and comes to the current owners, Roy Waldau and Joy Waldau Hostage, by word of mouth. A Mr. Fitch, a squatter who moved in without benefit of legal registration, had first tented on the land and then built the camp and a boathouse. When Webb took ownership of the land, Fitch apparently chose not to buy. In 1899, Webb sold the land, which could be reached only by boat from the

Big Moose Lodge, ca. 1905. Courtesy of Wanda K. Martin.

Glennmore dock, to DeWitt Wells and William B. Davis, both from New York City.

Augusta Waldau, mother of Roy Waldau and Joy Waldau Hostage, was told that Davis and Wells soon had a falling out and agreed to go their separate ways. They split the ownership of lot 365. Davis kept Big Moose Lodge and in 1901 purchased the adjoining lot 364 to the east, then owned by Theodore Page. Wells built a camp on the western half of the original lot.

From the beginning of his ownership of Big Moose Lodge, William Davis kept a log. The initial entry, dated July 7, 1901, records the names of William B. Davis of New York City and J. T. Davis of Middleville, New York (near Newport), probably father and son. The log continues, but until 1908 it records only names, addresses, and dates. Groups of visitors apparently came and signed together, because several names appear in the same hand. The groups were usually from the New York City area or from Middleville. Only occasionally do they include Davises.

Big Moose Lodge evidently operated under a cooperative arrangement similar to that of Club Camp and perhaps that of Frank Williams's camp at the mouth of the Inlet. Visitors brought their own food and bedding, did their own cooking and cleaning, and contributed to the expense of upkeep. Four bedrooms upstairs and one downstairs accommodated a sizeable number of guests. A living room and dining room on the first floor shared a fireplace that opened into both rooms. (The wall between was later removed.) A porch at the front, the boathouse, a kitchen in a shed at the rear, an icehouse, and an outhouse completed the arrangements.

Later entries in the log report catches of fish, often in May when snow was not unusual. There are also indications that the camp was used for hunting in the fall as well as for more conventional summer vacations. In 1910, a regatta at Higby's is mentioned. The Davis name appears every year but by no means throughout the season. William B. Davis's name shows up for the last time in 1909.

The log contains the name of at least one guest who remained for years at the lake. William T. Autenrith, from Middleville, New York, later became part owner and, still later, owner (at different times) of two camps to the east.

In 1920, John T. Davis sold Big Moose Lodge to Augusta S. Waldau. The Waldau family, Maximilian, Augusta, and their children Roy and Joy, settled in and spent many years there. They added a proper kitchen and a bathroom (eventually two). Augusta spent summers with the children while Max commuted from Scarsdale, New York, on weekends and for whatever vacation time he could manage.

Augusta recalled the drowning accident in the early 1920s, when the young son of the proprietors of Burdick's Camp (now Big Moose Inn), just across the lake, lost his life. The anguish of the mother's cry echoed across the bay and remained in Augusta's memory. That incident inspired Augusta, a swimmer when few women had that skill, to give swimming lessons to all the children along the trail, a practice she continued well into the 1930s.

WILDWOOD (LOT 363)

One summer evening in 1902, three friends from Middleville, New York, John T. Molineux (banker), William E. Autenrith (mayor, livery owner, and funeral director), and one Dr. W. Edsell (physician), were sitting around the dining room table at Big Moose Lodge gazing out the window through the woods toward the east and contemplating the idea of buying land and building a camp. In 1906, they bought the lot adjacent to the lodge and erected a camp next door.

The new camp was called Wildwood and was jointly owned by the three friends. However, Edsell soon terminated his ownership because of the death of his son. Molineux's daughter Mildred was engaged to be married to a young man who contracted tuberculosis and died at an early age. Autenrith gave up his ownership in 1918 when his first grandchild (now Jean Seavey Humphrey), daughter of Emma A. Seavey, was born. He did not want to risk exposing her to the tuberculosis baccillus in a house once frequented by a consumptive.

Autenrith's departure left John Molineux as sole owner. After his death, his daughter Mildred Molineux continued to vacation at Wildwood for several summers. In 1943 she sold the camp to Carroll Sporer and Ella Bellinger, a niece of Frank Day.

This pair built a small camp on the Martin Road, which they used while they rented Wildwood to others. Eventually a niece, Helen Franz of Clinton, New York, inherited both houses. She sold the two camps in 1990 to John Carney, of Lake George, New York, a nephew of Bernard Carney who is Mildred Seavey Carney's husband. (Mildred is a granddaughter of William Autenrith.)

When the land was surveyed for the sale of the property to John Carney, it was found that the little house on the road had accidentally been built on lot 364, land that belonged to Roy Waldau and Joy Hostage. In the process of moving it, John Carney had it remodeled and enlarged.

WINONA LODGE (LOT 361)

When Billy Stevens, businessman, carpenter, and guide, built this house in 1902, he called it Winona Lodge. In 1923, his widow sold it to William Autenrith, one of the trio of men who, as renters, had gazed from the window of Big Moose Lodge and dreamed about owning land to the east. Autenrith moved from being a renter to being a joint owner of the newly built Camp Wildwood. Later he became sole owner of the Stevens camp, which he renamed Crestwood. He and his wife Mary had a daughter, Emma, and two sons, William and Stanley.

Emma married Charles L. Seavey, and their children were Jean, Mildred, and Joe. A strong musical gene apparently ran through the family. Emma was an accomplished pianist and gave lessons, and her daughter Mildred taught Suzuki violin lessons to very young children. Jean occasionally sang with Pete Masson's band at the Glennmore pavilion. Joe's talents were sublimated into baseball (he played regularly in the hotel baseball league), but the musical gene showed up in his son Tom, who is a violinist.

James, the elder son of William, Jr., and grandson of the original William Autenrith, grew up to be a professor at SUNY Potsdam's Crane School of Music. As a young man, James was organist for the Big Moose Community Chapel and has given concerts there periodically. His most recent performance there was a concert in the fall of 2002.

Jane Clark, an Autenrith cousin, presided over the

Winona (later Crestwood), home built by William and Fanny Fae Stevens, ca. 1910. Courtesy of Frances Leonard Lepper.

camp for many years. Much beloved and known to the young people up and down the trail as Aunt Jane, she watched over all the children who stayed at Crestwood. Reed straight and slim, with white hair parted in the middle and pulled neatly back, she was always ready with her gift of gab.

In 1979, Jean Seavey Humphrey and her sister Mildred Seavey Carney sold the camp to their neighbors to the east, Charles and Olga Adams, but retained half the land, lot 362, for their use in the future.

CAMPS BETWEEN BIG MOOSE LODGE AND THE GLENNMORE

On the opposite side of Big Moose Lodge, away from the two houses that flank it on the east, are two groups of camps along the shore. The first group stretches between Big Moose Lodge and the beginning of today's Glenmore Subdivision, and the second (in the next section) extends from beyond the subdivision around the end of West Bay to just beyond the Chapel. The first camp to the west of Big Moose Lodge is nearly as old as the lodge itself.

GIFFARGET (LOT 365W)

DeWitt Wells built a camp on the western half of the lot he and William Davis had jointly owned when they bought Big Moose Lodge in 1901. Wells died in 1913 at age seventy-six from injuries he had sustained in the Civil War. His widow sold the camp in 1916 to two sisters, Mary Gifford and Minnie Argetsinger of Yonkers, New York. They named the camp Giffarget, a combination of their last names.

Mary Gifford was an enthusiastic hiker, walking daily the three miles to Big Moose Station to fetch the mail. Minnie had been a missionary in China and used to invite neighbors from along the trail to see her collection of articles from China. She spoke with great affection about the Chinese people and enthusiastically answered questions. Although Minnie died in 1947, her sister Mary kept the camp until 1967, selling it to Robert and Ann Young from Pittsburgh, Pennsylvania. Jean Thoburn of Solon, Ohio, has been the owner since 1979.

SHAWONDASEE (LOT 366)

This easternmost lot purchased by D. B. Sperry from Webb's Ne-Ha-Sa-Ne Corporation in 1899 changed hands several times over the years. In 1901, Sperry sold the lot to Wilson F. and Ollie H. Wallace of Springfield, Massachusetts. The Wallaces built the camp they named The Maples. Their daughter, Inez, is known for having witnessed Chester Gillette and Grace Brown leaving on the ill-fated boat trip that culminated in Gillette being charged for Brown's murder, a case that became the basis for the plot of Theodore Dreiser's novel *An American Tragedy*. Inez had come to the Glennmore to pick up the mail just as the two were setting out on the lake.

John L. Clark bought the camp in 1907 and in 1917 sold it to Florence Martin, an unmarried schoolteacher.

The Martin-Jouffriou family consisted of Flo, her two older stepsisters, Helen and Eugenia Jouffriou, and their mother, Jane Martin. As an infant, Eugenia had had an injury that resulted in a severely hunched back. The family renamed the camp Shawondasee after an Indian god in Longfellow's poem "The Four Winds": "Shawondasee, fat and lazy,/ . . . In the never-ending summer."

This camp is where Florence Martin taught school for a short time after the first lake schoolhouse burned. However, she contracted pneumonia and also broke her elbow, thus ending her teaching in Big Moose. Joy Waldau Hostage, whose camp was close by on the lakeshore trail, knew the family well over the years. She reports:

> Aunt Flo had nature walks for children. She considered it important for us to be aware of our environment and

Some of those who lived along the trail to the east of the Glennmore Hotel, 1928. Seated: Augusta Waldau, Eugenia Jouffriou, Roy Waldau, Jane Clark, and Ann Kanzy; standing: Florence Martin, Jennie Martin, Max Waldau, Joy Waldau Hostage (in pack basket), Lena Anderson, Jean Seavey Humphrey, and Jennie DeLong. Courtesy of Joy Waldau Hostage.

taught us how to identify the various evergreen and deciduous trees. Princess pine, staghorn and Indian pipes were treasures of the woods. Wild berries and wild flowers had their places in our lessons, as well.

> As I grew older Aunt Flo's camp continued to be an inviting place to visit. Under her stairs was a collection of good books to read. A welcoming bear rug lay before the fireplace and on cold or rainy days there was a crackling fire. Activities I remember included scavenger hunts and treasure hunts with hikes up mountains or to neighboring lakes.

The Reverend Arthur Merrihen Adams from Rochester, New York, bought the camp from Florence Martin in 1955. He sometimes preached on Sundays at the Big Moose Community Chapel when a substitute was needed. He died in 1979 and his daughter, Janet Fearon of Lawrenceville, New Jersey, inherited the property. She and her family spent time at the lake regularly but in 2001 sold to Gregory and Patricia Mohr of Camillus, New York.

BROOKSIDE (LOT 367)

Still closer to the site of the old Glennmore Hotel is this prewar camp that was built in 1928. The lot on which it stands was included in the property that Sperry had purchased in 1899. Henry and Mary Callahan, who were associated with the Glennmore for many years, bought the land in 1926. They later conveyed it to their son John and his wife Frances. While the senior Callahans remained at Spruce Lodge across the road from the Transportation House near the Glennmore, the younger Callahans built a camp beside the Squash Pond outlet and named it Brookside.

In 1967, the Callahans sold the property to Edward and Virginia Sitzer of East Herkimer, New York. Paul and Ingrid VanSlyke bought the lot in 1997 and replaced the camp with a year-round home.

CAMPS WEST OF THE GLENNMORE

As one moves counterclockwise around West Bay beyond the Glennmore, there are several more prewar camps. The first group belongs to one extended family. At about the turn of the century, Theodore Page purchased from the Ne-Ha-Sa-Ne Corporation all of the 12.4 acres of lot 376 at the west end of the lake. Early in the first decade of the 1900s, he sold five acres to Dwight Sperry, upon which Sperry built the Big Moose Supply Company building,

MEMORIES OF
BIG MOOSE LODGE | *Joy Waldau Hostage*

When I was a little girl in the 1930s, I ran and played on the trail in West Bay. Nine camps along the trail were all privately owned and made up my summer world. It was a world of women and children. Sometimes a father was on vacation for a week or so, but mothers stayed all summer with their children. Schoolteachers on their summer break were an important and integral part of this close-knit community. The atmosphere was quiet and peaceful, and we children felt safe and secure.

Wildlife

Wildlife seems more abundant today. I remember no prowling black bears or yipping coyotes or chortling loons. There were plenty of raccoons pilfering the garbage pails, and red foxes were sometimes seen. Deer were occasional and awesome sights.

My father, Max Waldau, had been to Big Moose Lodge several times but had never seen a deer. "I don't believe there *are* any deer in these mountains!" he said. At dusk one evening a schoolteacher from Camp Shawondasee came running breathlessly to the back door. "Max, Max, hurry, hurry! There is a deer out behind our camp!" Daddy ran over the trail as quickly and quietly as possible. Yes, there was the deer watching and moving its head around very alertly. Daddy stole silently closer. "It's a very brave deer," he thought. "Why doesn't it run away? It surely sees me coming." Suddenly two schoolteachers jumped up from behind the tree trunk on which they held a stuffed and mounted deer head from the wall in Camp Shawondasee. Everyone had a good laugh, and in the years following my father did see many a live deer in these mountains.

Fishing

Big Moose Lake used to have many more fish than it does today. Trout and bullheads were caught in abundance by hooks with worms on strings right off the docks. Sunfish were readily caught but were always thrown back. Joe Seavey and my older brother Roy were about the same age, and when Joe was in camp with his family at Camp Crestwood, he and Roy fished off the Crestwood dock.

At dusk, they caught trout and bullheads, which were kept in buckets of water to keep them fresh.

I always wanted to be part of the action. "OK, Joy, you may come on the dock, but don't make any noise," Roy said. Joe said, "She can put the worms on the hooks." So I did, pleased to be included in the fishing party. I had to pay attention not to skewer a finger on the hook there in the gloaming. The worms were often very wiggly and could emit black goo from their insides as the hook went through.

Once or twice I was invited to help dig the worms. A good place to find them was where garbage was buried out in the woods away from a camp. When we looked for worms, it was important to know those burial grounds.

Swimming lessons

My mother was the self-appointed volunteer swim instructor and lifeguard for the trail community. I cannot recall any other adult, besides my father, who could swim. Where Mother learned to swim I do not know.

Jean Seavey was Mother's first pupil. She came from Camp Crestwood, which was owned by the Autenrith family at that time. Lessons took place at the Shawondasee dock because the bottom was all sand there and a small child could walk twenty-five yards into the water before being shoulder deep. Today Jean reports that no one was allowed at the Shawondasee waterfront until 10:30 A.M., when Mother found time to give swim lessons.

Jean Seavey was an apt pupil. At age five she was entered in a twenty-five-yard race for five—to seven-year-olds. Jean swam the fastest with her breaststroke. "I won an Indian doll," she bragged, "and your mother was proud of me." Charles Adams was Mother's last pupil. Between the two were Grace Collins, Mildred Seavey, Wanda and Barbara Kinne, and, of course, my brother Roy and me. There were many others, too. Any children of families renting camps along the trail were welcome, as were visitors.

Amusements at Aunt Flo's

Florence Martin's camp, Shawandosee, was pleasant to visit. She lived with her two older half-sisters and their much older mother. Aunt Helen was a physical therapist. Aunt Jean had a hunched back. "Dropped as a baby, you know," was the report. Their mother was just plain old and nice. This was the Martin-Jouffriou family.

Camp Shawandosee was one over from our camp, and my mother could watch as I safely reached Aunt Flo's back door on my daily visit, hoping for chewing gum or cookies. She always greeted me pleasantly and immediately called out, "Jean, Joy is here for a visit. I'll send her up to see you." I knew their camp as well as my own and had no difficulty climbing the stair and finding my way through a bedroom to a large screened porch that wrapped halfway around the camp.

The portion of porch on the west side was arranged with a row of beds, dormitory style, while the south side overlooking the lake had comfortable brown wicker and rocking chairs. I always found Aunt Jean resting on a wicker chaise. Conversation with her was never long because she tired quickly. Then she said those magic, awaited words, "Flo, perhaps Joy would enjoy a piece of chewing gum." Sometimes it was a ginger cookie still warm from the oven, or a sugar cookie with one raisin carefully placed in the exact center. Besides the treats I received much attention, which greatly reinforced my self-confidence.

Aunt Flo planned many parties. Sometimes there was one for my early-August birthday. Energy and time were spent designing and crafting table decorations and party favors. These were made from materials found in the woods, such as silver birch bark, ferns, staghorn, or wild berries. Guests were always welcomed in the planning and then the celebration. Elaborate organizing occurred concerning the menu and entertainment. What kind of cake and what flavor and color frosting were big decisions. Many substitutions had to be made because provisions in the local store could be limited. Entertainment was always our own. Solo and group singing, rounds, recita-

tions, storytelling, and round and square dancing were all eagerly enjoyed. For music there was a wind-up Victrola with a small selection of flat, black records.

No telephones or motorboats and rarely a car intruded on our tranquility. Nor did radios blare, but the trail along the lake and in front of the camps was well worn.

Aunt Flo was our trail newspaper. It was her habit to visit all the camps daily and carry news and gossip. She never walked but scurried, and she was a bit bow-legged. "Hotdog roast this evening at the lean-to," always caused excitement.

This Adirondack lean-to was a shed made of logs with the bark still on. Across the open front was a flattened log on which to sit or work. A few steps away was a fireplace for warming people and cooking food. The lean-to was next to Aunt Flo's camp. At the appointed hour, the little trail community gathered around that fireplace to roast the hotdogs on sticks and toast marshmallows. As the fire burned down and darkness fell, we sang the songs that everybody knew, and usually there were stories and sometimes a spooky ghost story.

In back of Aunt Flo's camp was a shed where she went to be alone to study and write. One of her hobbies was astrology. She also dabbled in numerology. She wrote up horoscopes for all of her family and all her friends as well. Writing horoscopes for our entire family, she calculated each of my four sons' astrological profiles within their first month of life, based on the exact minutes of their births.

It was difficult to do anything for Aunt Flo. She was always busy doing kind and thoughtful deeds for others. Finally, I was able to do a favor for Aunt Flo. According to her express wish, her cremated ashes were returned to Big Moose.

the Glennmore boathouse, and three guest cottages: Bell, Fitzgerald, and Walker. After the Glennmore Hotel fire in 1950 and the subsequent auction, the cottages were sold.

HAMELINE CAMPS (LOT 376)

By the early 1970s all three original Glennmore cottages came into the possession of the extended family of William and Anne Hameline.

BURRSTONE LODGE/BALSAM REST (LOT 376)

In 1914, the Bissell and Yousey Lumber Company (see chapter 4, pages 111, 120–24) leased the remainder of lot 376 from Theodore Page as a site for the transshipment of lumber headed for the railroad at Big Moose Station. When the lumber company ceased operation in 1918, the lease on this land with the long dock and the maintenance

Burrstone Lodge, ca. late 1930s. The large cement block in the center foreground is part of Bissell and Yousey's transshipment dock. Note the large erratic at the foot of the tree. Courtesy of William S. Dunn.

shack was assumed by a group of sportsmen from Utica, who in 1909 had established themselves at Big Moose Station and called themselves the Summit Club. They seized the opportunity to move closer to the lake.

Membership of the club included brothers Frank[1] and Fred Hameline (who operated Hameline's Dairy) and Peter Samson, an associate in the dairy. Through this club the Hamelines and the Samsons became acquainted with Big Moose Lake. However, the Summit Club moved back to Big Moose Station in 1921, when Kate McCal-

lum Page (Theodore's widow) died and the lease presumably expired. Fred Hameline and Peter Samson purchased this seven-acre lot from Kate Page's heirs, Julia McCallum Dayton and Adelaide McCallum Gordon, and built a house on the Eagle Bay road called Balsam Rest. Later, Hameline sold his share of the property to Samson.

On the same lot but close to the shore, Pete Samson built a winterized house that commanded a spectacular view of the lake. He and his wife, Marjorie, came to live at the lake year-round. Marjorie was a pleasant, rather heavyset woman who, because of a degree of deafness, was inclined to speak loudly. They called the house Burrstone Lodge after the street in Utica on which they had lived. Pete removed the maintenance shack and revived the Pages' garden along the road for a vegetable garden that he maintained for several years.

John and Florence Ditmas of Pompano Beach, Florida, were the next occupants of the house. As a boy, John had summered at Burdick's Camp. In the early 1930s he and his wife had purchased the second camp east of what is now Dunn's Boat Service. When they bought Burrstone Lodge from the Samsons in about 1951, they renamed it Balsam Rest. Nelson Dunn, Jr., blasted away the large rock, a glacial erratic, that had been near the front of the house, a feature that shows up in many early pictures.

John Ditmas was a pillar of the Big Moose Community Chapel. He took care of countless details—counting the collection and delivering it to the treasurer each Sun-

THE OUTDOOR GIRLS | *Grace Collins McCullough*

When I was a little child, my family had a summer home at Big Moose Lake. We left New Jersey on the day school closed in June and returned on the day before school opened in September. And, for two and a half months, I had an idyllic time at the lake with four other little girls as lucky as I was to spend whole summers there. They were Mildred Seavey Carney, Joy Waldau Hostage, Wanda Kinne Martin, Barbara Kinne Wheeler, and myself. We formed a rather special group, calling ourselves "The Outdoor Girls' Club," and I suspect that because we met at *my* boathouse, I made myself president. I do not recall that we served any purpose or championed any cause. I do recall that we listened to records on my old Victrola, talked

about movie stars and boys, and giggled a lot. We had meetings when I felt like it (and when the boathouse was available), and I even collected dues (two cents per girl per meeting) but for what purpose I cannot remember.

Well, just recently I was invited to spend a few days at Big Moose with one of these childhood friends and, you'll never believe it, we had a meeting of the Outdoor Girls' Club with all five of us present! That's sixty-five years later, mind you, and all of us walking, talking, and able to take nourishment. We still giggled a lot (and there were some questions asked about what I did with those dues), but I feel privileged—no, blessed—to have had this experience. Imagine the joy of bonding again with my childhood friends and doing it at what must be one of the prettiest places on earth!

day, serving frequently as an usher, and performing innumerable duties that kept the church running smoothly. For more than twenty years his wife, Florence, was the organist. During the many years the Ditmases were at Balsam Rest, Mary Miller, Florence's sister, lived with them.

The Ditmases owned a Chris-Craft speedboat with a straight windshield named the *Flo-Jo*, which had once belonged to Walt Dunn (who had called it the *Renée*, pronounced "Reeny"). It is said that when the Ditmases bought Balsam Rest, Walt Dunn swapped the Chris-Craft for their former camp.

In 1985, George and Barbara Schunck from Jamesville, New York, bought the house that the Ditmases had occupied.

NELSON DUNN'S PROPERTY
(LOT 377-LOT 3)

Henry Covey sold lot 377 and the neighboring lot 1 to Nelson Dunn in 1923. In the same year, Nelson and Ada Dunn built a house by the lake and a garage with an apartment above it on the road. Shortly thereafter, Nelson bought lot 2 from Will Woodard. In 1928, Nelson sold lot 2 to the Big Moose Community Chapel. The property was later split on a line parallel to the lakeshore. The apartment and garage on the road, which Ada lived in after Nelson's death, is now owned by Scott and Roberta Bennett. Scott, a year-round resident, is the son of Douglas and Bonnie Bennett, who own the Big Moose Inn. The camp near the lake is owned by Rocco and Mary Maggiore of New Hartford, New York.

BIG MOOSE COMMUNITY CHAPEL
(LOTS 2 AND 3W)

The Chapel was built on lot 2; lot 3w was added in 1961. For more on the Chapel, see chapter 8, pages 239–41.

ROCKEFELLER/WALKER CAMP
(LOTS 3–4)

E. J. Martin constructed this camp in 1902 on the property immediately east of where the Chapel now stands. It was built for John P. Rockefeller of Utica (no known relation to the oil baron John D. Rockefeller). Rockefeller had purchased the land from Charles Williams of Lake View Lodge for three hundred dollars. An early picture shows that the house was rather distant from the lake and

close to the rough road that led to Eagle Bay. Rockefeller held the property for only a year before selling it to H. H. Covey in 1903.

Five years later Covey sold it to a longtime Camp Crag guest, William H. Staake, who held it for only three years and sold it back to Covey. It was a decade before Covey found another buyer, but in 1921, Dr. Charles Walker of Rye, New York, bought it for three thousand dollars.

Walker, a physician who had his own hospital (possible in those early years), was married to Mary Elizabeth Gauthier. The couple had one daughter, Mary Wheeler. When the family first came to Big Moose, they stayed across the lake at the Waldheim. Becoming enamored of the lake, they bought the property and had the cottage moved much closer to the shore. Charlie Martin, E. J.'s brother, worked on the camp, building much of the furniture it contained, and Walker considered him a close friend.

The Walkers were the owners of two boats that were unlike any others on the lake. One boat belonged to Dr. Walker, the other to his wife.[2] The boats were made by the same company and were very similar but not identical.

Dr. Walker's boat was made in 1929 by the Disappearing Propeller Boat Company, in Lindsay, Ontario.[3] The deck was made of alternating thin strips of carefully finished laminated oak and mahogany. The lapstrake sides

The John P. Rockefeller Camp, set back from the lake before it was moved closer to the shore, ca. 1902. Courtesy of Robert and Elizabeth Smith.

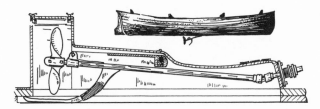

Diagram of Dispro boat from The Greatest Little Motor Boat Afloat *by Dodington, et al., 97. Drawing by Jill Binyon Kurtz reproduced with permission.*

A Dispro (disappearing propeller boat), one of the two originally owned by Charles Walker, with Walker's great-grandson, Andrew Getty, Jr., in the Getty boathouse, 1999. Photograph by Jane Barlow.

tapered to a point at either end (a "double-ender"), and it had three cockpits. The gasoline motor sat just in front of the center cockpit under doors that could be left open to prevent fumes from accumulating. To start the single-cylinder engine, the operator had to pull straight back on a starter rope that terminated in a spade handle. A ratchet device on the control board behind the forward seat had to be delicately adjusted to advance or retard the spark.

In the center of the floor was the feature that gave the boat its name, a cylindrical metal recess under which was the propeller. If the boat hit an obstacle such as a submerged log or sand, a slanted, projecting skeg pushed the propeller into its housing, at the same time throttling down the engine. A small oval window, an "aqua-scope," at the top of the housing enabled the pilot to see the propeller and, after stopping the motor, to open the window and reach in to clear the propeller of debris or weeds if necessary.

Many Big Moose residents remember Dr. Walker pulling time after time to try to start the temperamental motor. Instead of a steering wheel, the boat had a rope that ran under the gunwales. The pilot pulled on the rope to control the rudder, and of course he could steer from any position in the boat. Once the boat was under way it ran very quietly, proceeding at a slow, dignified pace of somewhere between two and four miles per hour.

The Dispro boats, as they were called, were among the first boats to be motorized. Each was built by hand, and by about 1940 they became too expensive to manufacture to be practical. Although new gasoline and electric outboard motors provided too much competition, the Dispros, or Dippies as they came to be called, developed a loyal following. As recently as 1985 (and perhaps to this day) there was a Disappearing Propeller Owners' Association that met semiannually in Canada. Owners had mixed reactions to their boats. At the meetings, members told anecdotes about their vessels:

> One old codger . . . had had one particularly happy experience concerning the boat that he wanted to relate.
>
> "The very best thing I ever did with my Dippy happened the day I bought my new bulldozer," he recalled. "I pulled that boat up on the shore and ran the bulldozer back and forth over it dozens of times until there was absolutely nothing left of it. I don't think I've ever enjoyed anything quite as much as getting back at that cursed Dispro for all the dirty tricks it pulled on me!"[4]

Another member had a different story.

> Around 1950 I spent a portion of a summer in Muskoka with my rather frail and elderly aunt. As an impressionable young boy I soon gained great respect for her prowess in handling her "putter" . . . which by that time had seen many summers and was in much the same condition as she.
>
> In those days Dippy owners took it as a matter of proper seamanship always to pass on the wrong side of every buoy, and my aunt was no exception. On a trip to Port Carling one sunny day, we were heading over a very shallow sandy area in the Indian River, on the wrong side of the markers as usual, when the large 750-ton passenger steamer *Sagamo* passed by. For a brief moment, the ship drew all the water out from beneath our little Dippy, and there we were, sitting high and dry on the sand, with the propeller thrashing about up in its

The second Dispro boat originally owned by Charles Walker, with later owners Dr. and Mrs. T. B. Steinhausen, on the water with Howard Martin as passenger, ca. 1984. Courtesy of Wanda K. Martin.

housing. In a silent panic, I glanced at my aunt to see what she would do in this terrible predicament. A second or two later, when the wash returned, we were gently floated off the sand and my aunt, with an air of utter nonchalance, shoved the device handle firmly back down again with her foot. . . . I doubt that I [could] have been any more impressed.[5]

Mrs. Walker, a fishing enthusiast, used her boat for trolling. Bill Dunn tells of her bringing in a bass that was so big she had to drag it from the Glennmore dock all the way to the Sperry store so that it could be weighed. Dr. Walker used his boat for cruising around the lake and for the family's daily trip to the Waldheim for dinner at noon. The two German shepherds that were family pets and guard dogs sat in the boat and the Walkers' daughter rode in the bow.

After Mrs. Walker died, her daughter, Mary Wheeler Walker Getty, sold her mother's boat to Seward Spoor with the request that it remain on Big Moose Lake. However, when the Spoor camp was sold, the new owners took the boat to Skaneateles Lake some time later. The Walker's grandson, Andrew W. Getty, who summers on Crag Point, owns the other boat and plans to renovate it.

In 1951, the Walkers sold their camp to James Jackson. Ten years later, Jackson sold it to the trustees of the neighboring Big Moose Community Chapel. The Chapel, wanting more land for protection on its east side, retained the western half of the lot and sold the remaining property to David Ames of Clinton, New York.

THE FRANK DAY AREA (LOTS 360–56)

Across West Bay on its north shore to the east of Crestwood stand five lots that were all once owned by Frank and Cora Day of Mohawk, New York. Frank was a carpenter who, when the couple first came to the lake (at least by 1911 when Frank was on E. J. Martin's payroll),

Cora and Frank Day, 1934. Courtesy of Wanda K. Martin.

worked for the Martin Brothers building camps for vacationers.

Cora Day worked hard during the spring, cleaning their camps and getting them ready for renters. She was a little elf of a woman, perpetually busy. She adored cats and would always bring one with them when they came. She also loved to fish and would spend much of her limited spare time on the dock thus engrossed. Occasionally she provided her neighbors, artist David Milne and his wife Patsy, with fish. In her memoirs Patsy Milne noted, "Mrs. Day fished practically the whole day for trout, in or out of season."[6] Patsy further reported that "Mrs. Day chummed the water with bait, shamelessly and illegally, to increase her chances of success."[7] Cora was prone to enlarging on the truth, and more than once Frank was heard to say, "Now, Corie! Tell it as it 'twas!"

Frank had a heart condition and Cora worried and stewed the minute Frank or "Frisky," as she called him, was overdue. Ironically, Frank outlived her.

THE KINNE/ADAMS HOUSE
(LOTS 359–60)

In 1918, the Days bought two lots from Kate McCallum Page, widow of Theodore Page. On lot 360, the western-most lot, Frank built a small house where the Days lived in the summer. Three years later, in 1921, he sold it to Romaine and Lillian Kinne, who had come to the woods in 1920 because of Romaine's health.

George Stone, who in 1919 had purchased the building that had been a store for the Bissell and Yousey Lumber Company, had recommended Big Moose Lake when

he and Kinne were both working at the Hooker Electro-Chemical Company in Niagara Falls, New York. The year after they arrived at Big Moose, the Kinnes bought the small lakefront house that Frank Day had built. With their young son Gordon (born in 1915), they lived in the house in the winter and rented it in the summer. When the house was rented, they pitched a tent near the dirt road along the old stone boat trail on the upper level of the lot. For two summers, 1922 and 1923, they rented the house to the artist David Milne and his wife Patsy.

In 1924, the same year that Romaine bought the marine end of the Big Moose Transportation Company, the Kinnes purchased the adjoining undeveloped area (lot 359) to the east. When the Martin Road was put through in 1925, they built a house and garage on the road, later modernizing the house so the family could live in it year-round. The Kinne family grew with the arrival of daughters Wanda in 1923 and Barbara in 1927. Needing more space, they constructed a large addition to the lakefront house, although they continued to rent it in the summer.

When Romaine died in January 1943, Lillian sold most of the lakefront property to Karl and Charlotte Adams, who with their son Charles had been renting the camp since 1932.

Karl Adams, who ran his own insurance agency in Auburn, New York, first came to the Adirondacks in the 1920s, when he spent time in Old Forge and the Fulton Chain and visited Big Moose on two or three occasions. In 1932 the Adamses were looking for a summer place to rent to find relief for their young son, Charles, who was bothered seasonally by asthma.

Charles picks up the story here:

House built by Frank Day in 1918 and purchased by Romaine and Lillian Kinne in 1921. Photograph 1923, courtesy of Barbara K. Wheeler.

It ended with my mother and father driving up for an overnight stay in Old Forge, and then traveling to Big Moose Lake for a look at the Kinne camp. Interestingly enough, when they arrived no one from the Kinne family was around but had left a note for them to take a look at the camp, which they did, and when they left, my father pinned a $10.00 bill and a note on the screen door saying "we will take it" and we will be back on so and so date.

When they returned with me for the first visit, Mrs. Kinne had a nice apple pie on the kitchen table, which became a most pleasant occurrence every year when we came back to Big Moose.

We rented the camp summers from Kinnes until 1945 when Mrs. Kinne offered my father first refusal as she intended to sell it. He bought it and we have been there ever since.[8]

Charles's father, Karl, was an outgoing man, just a tad on the portly side, with a winning personality. He enjoyed the relaxation of fishing, and he was instrumental in the establishment of the Big Moose Fish and Game Club. Charlotte, his wife, a dedicated registered nurse, was generous with her skills when neighbors needed help. Many were the shots she administered in the lake community to those who required them. They made several additions and improvements to the house, adding a boathouse, a screened porch, and a flagstone terrace.

After Karl Adams died in 1971 and Charlotte in 1978, Charles inherited the camp. When Charles and his wife, Olga, renovated the house, they found notations written on parts of the structure that indicated that Frank Day

House built between 1922 and 1927 by David Milne.
Photograph by Jane Barlow, 1999.

had worked there in 1926 and again in 1928, when Kinne was building the large two-story addition. A rehabilitated wood-burning stove in the kitchen is a reminder of earlier days.

Lillian Kinne retained the house and garage on the road and twenty-five feet of shoreline for herself. She lived in the house until she died in 1986. Her son Gordon married Patricia Steinhorst of Utica; he died of heart disease in 1970. Wanda married Howard Martin, whose family runs the Waldheim, and Barbara married Jerry Wheeler from Old Forge. Lillian's daughter Barbara Kinne Wheeler purchased the property shortly before her mother died and has summered there since her retirement in 1989.

THE DAVID MILNE CAMP (LOT 358)

In 1919, the Days had invested in the three lots adjoining to the east (lots 356, 357, and 358). When Frank Day sold lot 358 to Canadian artist David Milne, who had previously rented from the Kinnes, he did not suspect that the new owner was not only already well known but would become one of Big Moose Lake's most famous celebrities. Milne spent five unhappy years (when he wanted to be painting) building a beautifully crafted camp, and in November 1928 he sold it to Byron Collins of Leonia, New Jersey.

Collins and his wife, Elfriede, had two sons, Byron, Jr., and Donald, and a daughter, Grace. The family spent twenty summers at the camp. Byron, Sr., was a devotee not only of golf but also of baseball, and he often umpired games between the hotels in the area. His two sons played on the Glennmore's team and worked on the Big Moose Supply Company's pickle boat, which delivered supplies around the lake. Grace Collins and her friend Mildred Seavey worked at the soda fountain at the Big Moose Supply Company. In 1929 the Collinses commissioned Art Burtch to build a boathouse in front of the house.

In November 1949, Floyd and Muriel Groves of North Syracuse, New York, bought the camp from the Collinses. Muriel Groves published a book, *Reminiscences of West Bay on Big Moose Lake in the Adirondack Mountains,* which expressed her affection for the lake.[9] The Groveses' daughter Janice worked at Covewood.

John and Lou Lester of Hamburg, New York, purchased the property in 1966. In 1991, the Richard Lester family of Orchard Park, New York, bought the camp for their own use.

DAVID MILNE: CANADA'S CELEBRATED PAINTER

For several summers in the 1920s, West Bay on Big Moose Lake was the home of a struggling, reclusive artist who later became one of Canada's most famous painters. Such was David Milne's talent that five of his paintings were included in New York's revolutionary Armory Show of 1913, where he shared space with Picasso, Gaugin, Matisse, and Cézanne. He worked in a variety of media throughout his career (watercolor, color drypoint, and oil), and today he is regarded as a luminary in Canadian art. His pictures hang in galleries in Toronto, Ottawa, Hamilton, Montreal, New York (the Museum of Modern Art), and in many other places, as well as in private collections. But wide recognition came only toward the end of his life. He was not an outgoing person and concentrated more on executing his work than on promoting it. Nevertheless, some of the work that contributed most significantly to his lasting fame were the paintings that captured the mood of the woods and lakes around Big Moose.

Born in 1882 on a farm near Paisley, Ontario, David Milne was the son of Scottish immigrants. After graduating from school in 1899, then scraping together a living for three years as a rural schoolteacher in Canada, he attended the Arts Students League in New York City. He married Patsy Hegarty in 1912, lived briefly in New York, and then moved to the quiet New York State town of Boston Corners in the Hudson Valley. During World War I he joined the Canadian army as an enlisted man and war artist, arriving in France just after the Armistice. He remarked that he found the experience "thrilling . . . [but] I could never quite decide whether I was the last soldier or the first tourist."[51] Shortly after leaving the army, Milne spent the summer of 1921 at Dart's Lake, where he had a half-time job as a handyman at Dart's Hotel and where his wife worked in the office. Between 1921 and 1928, the couple spent long summers at Big Moose Lake, often arriving early in April and sometimes staying as late as November.

During all but one of these years, the Milnes operated a teahouse. (The first summer they were fully occupied at Dart's Hotel.) The next year, they ran a tearoom on the ground floor of the Glennmore Hotel,[52] probably in the space that later became the bar. The following two summers, in 1922 and 1923, the teahouse was in the house the Milnes rented from Romaine and Lillian Kinne, now owned by Charles and Olga Adams.

The teahouse operated by Patsy Milne in the dining room of the Kinne house, 1923. The painting on the wall next to the staircase is probably "Rocks in Spring," an oil painted by David Milne in 1922 and now in the Winnipeg Art Gallery, Winnipeg, Manitoba, Canada. Courtesy of Wanda K. Martin.

Such teahouses were popular as destinations for afternoon walks or guideboat excursions. Most served tea, light refreshments, and ice cream. In addition, Patsy cooked hams and chickens, and baked cakes and cookies. David painted walls and window boxes, built furniture, and helped generally. Altogether, it was a time-consuming enterprise, and profits were much lower than the Milnes had anticipated.

Minnie Maddern Fiske, the actress who owned Echo Island, was a frequent visitor. Milne's watercolor "Black Porch (Verandah at Night IV)" shows the teahouse when it was located at the Kinne house and captures the quiet mood of the lake. In one exhibition catalogue, the picture is accompanied by commentary taken from one of his letters to a friend:

Waiting for business like spiders in a web. When we hear a rattle at the dock, which is the outermost thread of our

David Milne (Canadian, 1882–1953), "Black Porch, Verandah at Night IV," 1923 watercolor on paper, Art Gallery of Hamilton, Gift from the Douglas M. Duncan Collection, 1970. Hamilton, Ontario, Canada.

web, we run out to pull in the victim. We have been thorough about setting our trap. A searchlight that lights the dock, two Japanese lanterns on the walk to the landing and two on the porch, lights in the house. Painted tables about which people enquire—two new ones added this year to the Roman striped one of last. One of the new ones portrays a running deer which someone, not learned in natural history, mistook for a kicking mule. The other is taken from the pattern on the "Blue Dragon" china which the teahouse uses. The dragon itself was at once dubbed "an Adirondack Chicken."[S3]

Clearly, residents of the lake walked along the trails to the teahouse during the day and came by boat at night, lured by the Milnes' wiles and, to judge by excerpts from his letters, David's wit and warmth. Another watercolor, "Lanterns and Snowshoes," painted about a month later in the summer of 1923, shows the interior of the teahouse in the rented Kinne house.[S4] The viewer looks through a window or door to see two tables with chairs drawn up to them in a room with a set of open shelves (used to display crafts and candy) and a stairway in the background. Groups of Japanese lanterns hang inside and out, and a pair of snowshoes hangs on the rear wall.

Milne's Big Moose paintings also feature other familiar local scenes, including a picture entitled "Glennmore from under the Porch" (1923)[S5] and "Black House No. 1, 1925,"[S6] which shows the J. Munson Gamble house (a house now owned by Brett and Beth Long). He also executed several versions (in watercolor, color drypoint, and

oil) of a view of the buildings at Dart's Lake, entitled "Across the Lake."[S7]

In the summer of 2000, two hitherto unknown dry brush watercolors, painted in 1923, were discovered at Big Moose Lake. They show exterior and interior views of the Colpitts camp on the North Shore. The paintings are now in the Adirondack Museum at Blue Mountain Lake and are scheduled to be exhibited there in 2004.

Unfortunately, Milne's years at Big Moose were not happy for him. The need to earn money interfered with his painting, to which he yearned to devote all his time. His output declined drastically, although he produced several paintings that are considered masterpieces, among them "Painting Place,"[S8] a view of the lake from high on the hill behind the Gamble property.

In 1924, Milne undertook to build a cottage just east of the Kinne house, and the teahouse operated from there between 1925 and 1928.[S9] (The Milnes ran their business at the Glennmore the year that the construction of the cottage began.) The building project was financed by his close friend and patron, James A. Clarke, who initiated the idea as a way for Milne to bolster his income. The profits from the sale of the house were to be split equally between Milne and Clarke.[S10] The house, exceptionally well designed and constructed, still stands just east of the Adams house (lot 358, currently owned by Richard and Barbara Lester).

In the spring of 1929, Milne returned to Ontario, "anxious to get away from his building project and his

David Milne at his easel at Six Mile Lake in Canada, June 1938. Photograph by Douglas M. Duncan. Courtesy of David Milne, Jr.

wife,"[S11] with whom relations were becoming strained. Patsy was lively and personable, but she was not intellectual and had no particular interest in discussing art or her husband's painting. They drifted further apart and finally separated officially in 1933,[S12] much to Patsy's distress. While the Milnes were at Big Moose, Patsy formed a friendship with Florence Martin, a schoolteacher from Yonkers, whose camp, Shawondasee, was a few doors away. Florence Martin was interested in numerology and astrology, and tried to comfort Patsy after the separation with statements that Milne was "under the influence of erratic planets."[S13] During the mid-1930s, many of Milne's effects, including paintings, were stored in the Shawondasee boathouse.[S14] At a point in the late 1930s, Florence visited Patsy in Canada and helped her financially to establish herself in a tiny house near Dorset, Ontario.[S15]

David Milne was truly obsessed with painting, and anything that interfered with his spending full time on it disturbed and angered him. He moved from one place to another, living at the very edge of his finances in isolated towns. At last he found some support from patrons and attracted the attention of well-known Canadian critics. A photograph of him taken in 1938 shows a light-haired, balding man wearing glasses sitting in a cabin, a painting beside him, gazing pensively at something or someone out of range of the camera.

In that same year he met Kathleen Pavey, twenty-eight, a nurse half his age, with whom he could share his interest in art. He moved to Toronto with her. Their son, David Milne Jr., was born in 1941 when his father was fifty-nine. Although Milne continued to live mostly in country towns, his work finally began to gain recognition. As one of his admirers remarked, "Milne became a respected name in Canadian art, and was considered the dean of Canadian painters in watercolour."[S16] In 1952, Milne suffered a stroke and, after another the following year, died on December 26, 1953.

Celebrities of Milne's stature are rare at Big Moose and often more obscure than they deserve. The author of one of the books about his life and work notes that

> Since Milne's death nearly forty years ago, his work has steadily gained in stature, value, and price. Yet Milne—in life always somewhat apart as an artist, whether by choice, or by character or by default—has remained relatively unknown to the general public. What he has been, unquestionably, is the quintessential painters' painter . . . [L]ike Vincent van Gogh, with whom he felt a strong empathy, Milne did not care much if anyone owned his work, but cared very much if his work could touch someone profoundly.[S17]

An indication of his growing reputation is an exhibition scheduled to open in 2005 at the British Museum in London and travel to the Metropolitan Museum in New York and to the Art Gallery of Ontario in Toronto.

UPPER AND LOWER CAMPS ON ONE LOT (LOT 357)

In the early 1920s, on the next lot to the east, Frank Day constructed a one-story building on the road containing a small apartment and a one-stall garage. On the shore of the same lot, he built a boathouse with sizeable living quarters above. In the summer the Days lived in the garage apartment on the road and rented the boathouse with living quarters located on the shore.

The two houses that the Days had built on this lot proved to be attractive to several owners. When the Days decided to retire in 1948, they sold the property to Charles and Dorothy Coon from the Syracuse area. The Coons became year-round residents. Charlie, with his skills as a carpenter, a plumber, and an electrician, was in much demand. He scooted around the lake in his boat attending to maintenance jobs but returned home for a noon meal that always included homemade pie. In the early days, Dotty worked part-time as a physical therapist at the Veterans' Hospital in Ray Brook. Later she devoted herself to community activities and became the first president of the Jolly Moosers. In the early 1970s the Coons retired to Florida.

Faith Wertz Eastwood, daughter of Robert and Olive Wertz of the North Shore, owned the property for two years and then sold it to Henry "Andy" and Barbara Pope, year-round residents. Andy worked at Higby's while Barbara taught school at Raquette Lake. The Popes sold the houses to Arthur and Elizabeth Singleton from Richmond, Virginia, in 1989.

Libby Singleton, the daughter of David and Abigail Kreitler, is a granddaughter of the Reverend Percy Wightman. The Singletons made many improvements to both houses, including converting the boathouse attic into a master bedroom suite and adding steps down the steep hill. During the course of renovations to the lakeside house, they uncovered a cut of rough lumber on which was scrawled in the broad lead point of a carpenter's pencil, "No snow Dec. 4, 1921. Pleas. [pleasant] and cold. FFDay."

THE EASTERNMOST OF FRANK DAY'S CAMPS (LOT 356)

The Days alternately rented and personally used the last camp that he built on his easternmost lot until they sold it

in 1941 to Audley and Adelaide Dutton of South Otselic, New York. The first year or two that they came to Big Moose, the Dutton family rented the boathouse Frank had built next door. Audley, a man in his thirties, had been stricken with poliomyelitis (generally considered a child's malady at the time) and was confined to an iron lung, paralyzed, and unable to breathe on his own.

The iron lung was an enormous, heavy device ninety-two inches long with a twenty-one-inch headrest. It stood nearly five feet high, and the metal cylinder within which the patient lay measured twenty-nine inches in diameter. It worked by pumping air into the long tube and thus forcing air out of the patient's lungs. Only the patient's head protruded, enabling him to eat, speak, and fill his lungs with fresh air.

At first, the most convenient way for Audley to reach the camp on the lake in his life-sustaining mechanism was to be taken from the public dock at the Glennmore by Kinne's Boat Line on its substantial launch the *Big Moose*. In subsequent years, Audley began to regain some ability to breathe on his own and could remain outside the lung for short periods. At that point, Audley's father purchased a large station wagon, which, with some renovations, was able to accommodate the cumbersome iron lung. He could then transport his son in a motor vehicle. Hence, in 1941, they bought the neighboring camp, which was accessible from the road.

In a feature article in the *Adirondack Arrow*, Dutton is described as an ardent smoker of cigars. "He has an ash tray lying on his right shoulder where he flicks the ashes without having someone remove the cigar from his mouth."[10]

The iron lung operated on electricity, and electrical power can be questionable in the woods, with outages fairly common and often of great length. One night when the power went off, Dutton's nurse was away. Adelaide Dutton, his wife, ran to seek the help of her neighbor, Charlotte Adams, a trained nurse. By the time Adelaide and Charlotte had returned to the Dutton camp, there were a number of local residents already at the house manually operating the pump. No one had called them. It was simply standard procedure for neighbors and friends to go promptly to the Duttons when there was a power outage.

Each summer brought improvement, and by 1939, Audley was able to sustain himself for most of the day outside the iron lung. The *Adirondack Arrow* commented that "Marvels of modern science, indomitable courage and the healthful air of the Central Adirondacks can bring amazing results."[11]

In 1950, after Audley's death, the Duttons sold the property to Trajan and Ann Shipley of North Syracuse. Trajan, nicknamed Ship, had two sons from a first marriage, Jan and Mike. After Ship died, Ann continued coming to the lake until 1987, when she sold the camp to Jim and Lisa Strasenberg from Rochester, New York. They came for eight years, then sold it in 1995 to Thomas and Mary Moore of Clinton, New York.

THE LAST SQUATTER ON BIG MOOSE LAKE: THE HERBERT WILLIAMS CAMP (LOTS 354–55)

Webb's purchase of Big Moose Lake apparently did not put an end to illegal occupants such as Higby, Covey, and the West Bay builder of Big Moose Lodge. As late as 1916, a family was tenting on the eastern end of the northern shore of West Bay as it gives way to the main lake. Dr. Herbert H. Williams from Mohawk, New York, first camped at Big Moose in 1918.[12] However, the abstract of his deed reveals that it was not until 1925 that he bought the land from Kate McCallum Page's heirs. He then built a camp that he called Just-a-Mere.

In a letter to Barbara Wheeler dated July 4, 1999, C. Robert McCoy, a grandnephew of Dr. Williams, addresses this discrepancy in dates:

> One of the old pictures shows an old white tent and a nice string of trout. I realized that the trees in the background, although much smaller then, are some of the same trees that are still standing on my property now and that the tent was on the spot the old camp now rests. I spoke to my mother about this and she recalls Nina Williams (Mrs. H. H. Williams) talking about tenting at Big Moose after WW I. Apparently they rowed a flat bottom boat put in at the Glenmore landing.

Dr. Williams responded quickly when Robert Stevens, the young son of Billy and Fannie Stevens, swallowed lye (see chapter 3, page 80). The Williamses even took the youngster to their home in a vain attempt to save him. Herbert Williams died in 1933 at the age of fifty. His wife, Nina, kept the camp until she died, passing it along to her nephew, C. Robert McCoy. McCoy's son (also named Robert) is the present owner and has built a new house on the property for his family.

Three Linked Camps at the West End of the Main Lake

The owners of three camps clustered near Echo Island were closely connected by social strands in the early years of the twentieth century. Camp Veery on the island itself, Owl's Nest on the mainland to the north, and Tojenka on the opposite shore to the southeast were all built between 1901 and 1906. Camp Veery and Tojenka have passed through the hands of various owners, but Owl's Nest has remained in one family for more than one hundred years. Each camp has its own history and accompanying stories. For an explanation of the network of personal relationships that originally held them together, see "The Ties That Bound," page 146.

CAMP VEERY (LOT 378)

Echo Island, the "S" of land that divides West Bay from the main body of Big Moose Lake, was the site of the lake's first permanent building: Billy Dutton's one-story camp, (see chapter 1, page 9). After Billy left the lake in about 1890, the island lay uninhabited for several years. During this time William Seward Webb had acquired all the land around the lake.

In 1900, Theodore Page of Oswego, New York, the owner of a large window shade manufacturing business in nearby Minetto, New York, bought the island from Webb's Ne-Ha-Sa-Ne Park Association. Page owned ships that brought lumber from Canada through the Great Lakes to his factory. He was also involved in lumbering operations in northern New York as well as around Big Moose Lake (see chapter 4, pages 118–20) and had a large house, Argyll, near Richmond, Virginia.

At Big Moose Lake, he built a luxurious house, as well as various outbuildings, slightly north of the Dutton

THE TIES THAT BOUND

Three early camps on Big Moose Lake are notable for their shared history and close ties: Camp Veery on Echo Island, originally owned by Theodore Alanson Page; Owl's Nest, originally owned by Thomas Fox Jeffress; and Tojenka, originally owned by Thomas Pettibone Kingsford. Although each camp stands alone, their close connections, rooted in the geographical proximity of their owners' year-round homes and cemented by firm friendships and family ties, require them to be considered as a group.

Theodore Page and Thomas "T. P." Kingsford both came from Oswego, New York. They also belonged to the same clubs and undoubtedly were friends. In addition to his Oswego house, Page had an estate, Argyll, and a tobacco plantation near Richmond, Virginia. Thomas Fox Jeffress, connected with the American Tobacco Company and a member of its board of directors, likewise had a large house and estate there, Meadowbrook Farm, which adjoined Page's Virginia property. Page and Jeffress must have been acquaintances.

The connections among the families grew stronger through marriages in the next generation. Thomas Fox Jeffress had only one child, Robert. When Jeffress's sister, Alberta, and her husband, E. L. Haskins, both died at an early age, they left two young daughters, Minerva Waller Haskins and Virginia Louisa Haskins. Thomas F. Jeffress took his two nieces into his own family as his wards and raised them along with his own son. When the Haskins girls (Jeffress's nieces) grew up, each married into another Big Moose family. Minerva married Thomson Kingsford, the son of Thomas Kingsford, and the couple continued to occupy Tojenka after Thomas Kingsford's death. Virginia married Alanson S. Page, Theodore Page's nephew, but did not remain at the lake. Theodore Page's Camp Veery on Echo Island eventually was sold to the famous actress Minnie Maddern Fiske.

Thomas Fox Jeffress, the original owner of Owl's Nest, had another sister, Lena, who married Hunter Woodis Finch. The current owner of Owl's Nest, also named Hunter Woodis Finch, is the grandson of this union and is therefore part of the Jeffress family. Robert Jeffress, the son of Thomas Fox Jeffress, married but had no children. When Hunter W. Finch's parents died in 1950, they left not only Hunter but also his sister, Virginia, who was only seventeen. Robert Jeffress became Virginia's guardian, and the close family relationship continued. When Robert Jeffress died in 1967, Hunter inherited Owl's Nest.

camp on the south part of the island. The main house, finished in 1901 and still standing today, is located so that residents have clear views of both West Bay and the lake. The living areas are situated around a large stone fireplace that sits like an island between the living and dining rooms; a stone hearth faces each room. Upstairs are five bedrooms and a bath.

On the southern point of the island, the property features one of the few natural sand beaches on the lake. On the east side of the island, facing the main lake, Page built a commodious boathouse with slips for large boats, storage space for guideboats and canoes, and a second story that encompassed a full residence with kitchen and bath. In the Adirondack tradition, boardwalks connected the buildings. Page's wife, Kate McCallum Page, named the house Camp Veery, after the migratory bird whose northern pass was considered the start of the camp season and whose southern pass signaled the time to close. (The destruction of the veery's habitat in the tropics has led to the decline of this bird, and few are seen today.)

Page owned more land on the lake than any subsequent resident, having bought from Webb's Ne-Ha-Sa-Ne Corporation most if not all of the land that Webb had not conveyed to others. His wife sold lakeside lots at the east end of the lake, in West Bay, and along the southeastern shore. He also built an open hunting camp on Chub Pond and an elaborate hunting camp called The Hermitage near Queer Lake.

In 1916, Theodore Page died, and Echo Island passed by will to his wife. Kate Page held on to the property until February 5, 1921, when she sold it (along with the lots 351, 352, and 353 on the mainland) for twenty thousand dollars to Minnie Maddern Fiske, the most famous actress of her time.

While Mrs. Fiske was in her declining years, her husband allowed the island to fall into disrepair. In 1929 the island had gone into receivership, and it was held by a bank for a few years during the Depression.[13] Fiske redeemed it in 1934 and later sold the property to T. Clifton Jenkins, a lawyer, who owned it from 1937 to

Camp Veery, Echo Island, 1998.
Photograph by Paul Littman.

1941. Whether Jenkins ever used it is unclear. After he died, his wife apparently did not wish to keep it.

Charles Williams, owner of Lake View Lodge, bought Echo Island from Jenkins's widow on September 27, 1941, in order to control the water rights.[14] The water on the island was brought from a spring near Pancake Point (on the northern shore not far west of the Waldheim) by a pipeline running under the lake. The spring was located on a small piece of land that Fiske had owned and Williams bought. Williams built a large cistern on the island[15] with a second underwater pipeline to his hotel, Lake View Lodge, on the south shore of West Bay. However, within less than a month, he sold the property again, although he maintained the water rights. His son, Fred, had convinced his father that it was a bad investment.

Once again Camp Veery lay unoccupied, but not for long. When Echo Island became available in 1941, Clarence Ray Harvey, the owner of the Ford automobile dealership in Boonville, New York, bought it, along with all its various outbuildings, for $2,700.[16]

In the early 1930s, C. Ray Harvey had commissioned Earl Covey to build a camp for him on South Bay (lots 74–76, currently owned by the Hadden family). But during the Depression, the Ford Motor Company required its dealers to buy all the cars in their own inventory, whether they sold them or not. Fearing that he would not be able to pay for the cars he had in stock, Harvey sold the camp. In the end, however, he did sell his cars, and he regretted the loss of the camp.

C. Ray Harvey loved the woods, but he was unable to take part in some of the activities other people enjoyed. As a child, he had had a bone disease that left one leg

Camp Veery boathouse, 1998.
Photograph by Paul Littman.

MINNIE MADDERN FISKE COMES
TO OLD FORGE

On June 30, 1998, Lynn Schrichte, a Washington,
D.C., actress and writer, performed a one-woman
play, *Mrs. Fiske: Against the Wind,* at the Fine Arts
Center in Old Forge. Schrichte wrote the play after
researching the life of Minnie Fiske in the Fiske Collection of the Library of Congress and in the few
publications available.

shorter than the other, and he wore on one foot a shoe
that had a lift about eight inches high, forcing him to use
crutches.

C. Ray had a family of seven children, six girls and one
boy, and it was they who used the original Dutton camp
as a playhouse until it became unsafe and had to be torn
down.

The electricity on the island was supplied by two
Delco generators, one preferred by Mr. Harvey and one
by Mrs. Harvey. They were always known as "Dad's" and
"Mom's." These generators supplied all the electricity for
the island's buildings until 1953, when C. Ray Harvey
brought public electric lines to the island. In order to do
this, he bought a narrow parcel of land on the mainland
from Robert Jeffress. However, when the power company put in the poles they ran over the boundary, and
Harvey had to buy a little more land.

Echo Island has also been touched by tragedy. In the
late 1960s, August "Buster" Schweinsberg, the husband
of C. Ray's daughter Barbara, drowned while taking a
boatload of luggage from Dunn's to the island. With him
was a friend, Donald Satterly of Boonville, who also
drowned. The two men, having arrived with their wives
and children, started out from Dunn's dock with a heavy
load about 10:00 P.M. Buster urged his oldest daughter to
come with them, but she demurred, saying that the boat
was already too full.

The two men started from shore, and somehow the
boat tipped its contents, along with the men, into the
water. Buster had tried to learn to swim, but never succeeded. He always said, "If I go into the drink, I'm a
goner." His friend, Donald, was a good swimmer. However, the night was very dark (Joe Dunn said it was absolutely starless and moonless), and Donald probably
became disoriented and swam in the wrong direction. Joe

Dunn immediately went out in another boat, but his efforts to rescue the two men were fruitless.

Barbara had gone to take the family car to the upper
Dunn parking lot when the accident happened, but the
four children had remained on the dock. Another child, a
daughter, had stayed in Boonville because of a piano
recital. There were five Schweinsberg children, ranging
in age from three to sixteen, who lost their father that
night. Barbara eventually remarried, becoming Barbara
Reggetts.

During this period in the island's history, the Harveys
often rented the boathouse to tenants. For several years in
the 1970s, one of the occupants was the Reverend
Richard "Dick" Morris, his wife, Margery, and their five
children, of Lakewood, Ohio. One of Dick Morris's hobbies was making rugs of abstract design out of pieces cut
from carpet samples. He left several rugs in the boathouse
for the Harveys.

Five generations of the Harvey family used the camp
until it finally became too difficult and too expensive to
manage. They sold it in early 1998.

The current owners are Paul and Louetta R. R.
"Rainy" Littman of Rexford, New York. Paul's parents
have occupied a Higby cottage for many years, so he has
been familiar with Big Moose Lake for some time. The
Littmans are working with loving care to restore the historic complex.

OWL'S NEST (LOTS 345–49)

Owl's Nest sits on a small point of land just to the east of
the Narrows and very close to Echo Island. The camp
probably started its life as housing for the guides who
worked at Theodore Page's large house on the island.
Until the Martin Road was built behind the camp, the
only access to the Owl's Nest was by boat.

Its original owner, Thomas Fox Jeffress (1859–
1938), was a businessman who lived in Richmond, Virginia. His enterprises included tobacco, a company that
manufactured paper products, and real estate ventures.

A family story recounts how Thomas Jeffress and
Theodore Page met while traveling on a train, perhaps
between Richmond and New York City. In the course of
the conversation, Jeffress mentioned that he was interested in finding a summer retreat to escape the Virginia
heat. Page sang the praises of the cool Adirondacks—in
contrast to the muggy weather of Richmond, which had
to be endured before the days of air conditioning—and

MINNIE MADDERN FISKE: AMERICA'S FAVORITE ACTRESS

The most famous American actress in the decades before and after 1900 bought Echo Island in 1921. She was the beautiful and talented Minnie Maddern Fiske. Her fame has faded except in theatrical circles because, in contrast to her contemporaries and actors of today, she shunned publicity and even refused to grant interviews. Whatever time she could spare from her profession was devoted to animal rights, and it was only by devious persistence that Alexander Woolcott succeeded in cornering her for a series of luncheon conversations that he later fashioned into a book outlining her views on the theater.[51] Archie Binns's biography, published in 1955 (twenty-three years after her death), records the course of her life.[52] However, a picture of the time she spent at Big Moose and her relationships with those who lived there can be gleaned from local records and recollections of residents who knew her.

Mrs. Fiske purchased Echo Island from Kate McCallum Page, widow of Theodore Page.[53] The new owner of the island was easily the most famous inhabitant of Big Moose Lake during the entire century. Minnie Maddern Fiske was, according to her biographer, "the acknowledged leader of the American stage for a generation, a skilled and successful playwright, an actress who was rated with [Eleonora] Duse and [Sarah] Bernhardt, a producer who was probably the best outside Europe, the triumphal champion of Ibsen in America [and] the discoverer of some of the best American playwrights of the early twentieth century."[54] Born in New Orleans in 1865 to a stage family, Mrs. Fiske became a celebrity overnight after she played the lead role of Nora in *A Doll's House* in February of 1894 in New York. Her natural performance in contrast to the current tradition of overacting led to worldwide recognition. She went on to star in other Ibsen plays as well as in such productions as *Tess of the D'Urbervilles, Becky Sharp, The Merry Wives of Windsor,* and *Much Ado About Nothing.* There were also numerous comedies, most of which are now forgotten. Mrs. Fiske was also an author, and eight of her fourteen plays were produced. For a time she had her own company of actors with whom she toured the country. She was known for her sense of humor, her self-deprecation, and especially for her beauty. Her biographer mentions her "glorious red hair [and] deep blue eyes shining out of a delicate, wistful face."[55]

Although she was an accomplished actor, Minnie lacked domestic talents. After a brief marriage failed and she was divorced in 1888, she married Harrison Grey Fiske in 1890 when she was twenty-three and he was twenty-five. Harrison Fiske came from a well-to-do family. As the drama critic of the *Dramatic Mirror,* of which he was also owner and editor, he gave her rave reviews. However, she decided to retire from the stage after the wedding and become a traditional wife. Her resolve lasted a mere four years. Her backstage upbringing had not prepared her for household management. Although she ordered a large set of books on the subject from Brentano's when they were living in New York, she was dismayed to find that she was expected to know more about laundry than the laundress who awaited instruction.[56] "While she concentrated on planning a meal, that mealtime passed and it was time to serve the next."[57] The result was that her husband took over managing the house and also, when she decided to return to the stage, managing her career.

For some twelve years between 1897 and 1909, Minnie and her husband fought the Theatrical Trust, a syndi-

Poster by Ernest Haskell of Minnie Maddern Fiske, 1903. Courtesy of Wanda K. Martin.

Lakeside Cottage, Camp Crag, ca. 1912, where the Fiskes spent summer vacations before purchasing Camp Veery. Courtesy of Mark Barlow.

cate of prominent businessmen who sought to control the productions that appeared in leading theaters all over the country. In 1909 a proposal for a national theater was backed by such names as Astor, Belmont, Gould, Huntington, Vanderbilt, and Whitney, but it too eventually faded away. Minnie was adamantly opposed to the idea of repertory theatre companies, insisting that each play deserved to be carefully cast with actors chosen specifically for the roles they were to play.[S8]

Mrs. Fiske was also well known for her sympathy for animals. She was particularly concerned about the horses that drew carriages and carts in the cities that, because of their harnesses, were unable to lower their heads enough to drink from the ground. She gave numerous drinking fountains for horses to cities in which she appeared. She was also adamantly opposed to killing animals for their fur. She exclaimed vehemently in a talk with Alexander Woolcott, who had asked her what she would do with five million dollars, "I could easily spend . . . two million on the effort to make women see that one of the most dreadful, shocking, disheartening sights in the world is just the sight of a woman wearing furs."[S9]

The Fiskes first came to the Adirondacks in 1901 after buying property at Lake Pleasant in Hamilton County.[S10] It is unclear how much vacation time they were able to spend there. In 1910 the Fiskes sold the land and purchased Pine Point, a plot of fifty acres on the far side of Sacandaga Lake; they sold this piece of property in 1917 to Emily Stevens, Minnie's talented and famous actress cousin.[S11] In 1907 there is an entry in Henry Covey's journal at Camp Crag noting the arrival of "Mrs. Fiske— Lakeside Cottage."[S12] The records are incomplete, so, al-

though we know she was there several different years, we do not know exactly how many summers the Fiskes came to Camp Crag. There were certainly times when she was away on tour, but a rumor persists that the cottage, the last on the South Bay side of the Camp Crag property, was built for her. There is little doubt that Minnie loved the peace and quiet of Big Moose Lake.

In the winter of 1921, when Minnie was fifty-six or fifty-seven, a major event occurred. In the late spring of that year, Harry entered their New York apartment to greet his wife after she had been on tour and heard the cry of a baby. Minnie had brought home a nine-month-old baby boy whom she had found abandoned in a hotel room in Boulder, Colorado, and whom she had kept backstage with her since February. Minnie had expected Harry to be delighted, but he was not. He declared, "You will do as you please, but if you keep this infant it will be against my wishes and advice. I will have no part in adopting him; and he is not to bear my name."[S13] In fact, the orphan child had no name at all when he first joined the Fiske establishment. Minnie had called him by a variety of playful names. The one that finally stuck was Boulder or Bouldy,[S14] soon shortened to Bolie. His formal name was Danville Maddern Davey. Davey was the name of Minnie's father, and Maddern the maiden name of her mother. In New York, Minnie made the adoption official and thereby started a trend. Marie Dressler, Al Jolson, and other well-known actors and actresses also adopted babies, gaining publicity that enhanced their careers.

In 1921, the Fiskes bought Echo Island and spent the summer there, along with the child. Harry made arrangements for necessary repairs and also purchased large

Minnie Maddern Fiske seated in her favorite chair, ca. 1912, in a photograph autographed "With much love to Mr. and Mrs. Covey." Courtesy of Doris Lederer.

quantities of household furnishings, kitchenware, and food. He hired a cook, housekeeper, handyman, and laundress. Nelson Dunn was the handyman, as we know from his son, Bill Dunn. Lillian Kinne also worked for Mrs. Fiske as a maid and had the fondest recollections of her kindness and thoughtfulness.[S15] Bill Dunn's great aunts, Margaret Rose (Aunty) and Elizabeth MacEdward (Aunt Lizzie), cooked for the Fiskes at different times.[S16] The laundress may well have been Mrs. William Stevens, who lived in the Crestwood Camp in West Bay and who took in washing from customers around the lake.

While both of the Fiskes generously extended invitations to houseguests, it was Harry who acted as host and took charge of entertaining. Minnie, on the other hand, welcomed her solitude. Muriel Groves tells the story of Minnie's walks along the lakeside trail. Her personal maid preceded her, and Minnie, wearing a large round hat with a veil, would throw the veil over her face whenever she met anyone. When asked why, she explained that when she was on stage, she was compelled to wear makeup. It was a relief to her to leave her skin exposed "to give her face a rest."[S17]

Some of her walks took her to Patsy Milne's teahouse on the shore of West Bay, where she is said to have been a mainstay. She struck up a friendship with Patsy's husband, the painter David Milne, but it was not a close relationship. Occasionally she invited the Milnes to Camp Veery for dinner,[S18] and "she coaxed Milne into taking them both [Minnie and Bolie] hiking and camping for a night a not wholly successful venture . . . Mrs. Fiske wanted many pillows and a cuisine suitable to her station and reputation, which imposed additional and distracting responsibilities on Milne; but after dinner she paid for these services by entertaining the Milnes and Bouldy, seated around the campfire, by declaiming Lady Macbeth's soliliquies."[S19]

Her visits to the teahouse may have involved entertaining some guests. A descendant of Charles Cook, who owned a cottage on the Lake View Lodge property, tells us that one of her guests was Diamond Jim Brady. A maid is said to have confided that Minnie was hurrying back from a stage engagement in order to play poker at the Milne teahouse with Diamond Jim Brady. Letters from Brady to Mrs. Fiske are preserved in the Library of Congress in Washington, D.C. Rainy Littman, who with her husband now owns Camp Veery, is engaged in extensive research on Fiske and plans eventually to publish information that has hitherto been unavailable.

Mrs. Max Waldau, whose camp, Big Moose Lodge, was close to the island on the north shore of West Bay, recalled that Mrs. Fiske seldom talked to any lake residents except children and animals.[S20]

A favorite short walk, according to Bill Dunn's parents, was on the trail that led from the south end of Echo Island along the west side to a gazebo situated on a large rock. Mrs. Fiske would often carry a lunch to the spot, which offered a fine view of West Bay. When she had guests, she frequently entertained them with this brief but delightful trail trip. As her biographer, Binns, relates,

Minnie loved to row on the lake, believing that the exercise would benefit her arms which by this time had grown somewhat heavy, Minnie would work on a humane speech or article. . . . The boat also served as a study and

Gazebo at Camp Veery on Echo Island, ca. 1930. Courtesy of Wanda K. Martin.

practice stage, where Minnie would take up the typescript of a play and practice reading her lines, sometimes sounding off in a voice which filled a quarter of a mile radius of lake and lonely wood.

Binns also notes that "with her habitual casualness, Minnie quartered guests in the boathouse, and left them to their own devices. Lunch was one of the few certainties of the establishment. About noon, famished guests would struggle out of the woods near where Mrs. Fiske was drifting in her boat, hail her and persuade her to return to camp so that all might eat."[S21]

By 1923 times were changing. The theater was not as popular as it had been and, with Minnie growing older, offers of theatrical roles were no longer easy to obtain. In addition, the house was expensive to run. Minnie, or perhaps Harry as her financial manager, reluctantly decided that it would be necessary for her to spend at least the next two years playing in summer-stock theaters. They leased Camp Veery to Frank and Amelia Naporski, a childless couple whom Minnie had met in New York.

Naporski had come at first as a handyman who wanted to spend time in the Adirondacks for his health. He and his wife, Amelia, ran Camp Veery as a hotel during the summers of 1923 and 1924, but relations with the Fiskes were not entirely smooth.

After two seasons, the Fiskes found the arrangement unsatisfactory and refused to renew.[S22] A copy of a letter from Nelson Dunn, who had continued to act as caretaker, to Harrison Fiske hints at why the lease was terminated.[S23] Nelson had been asked to make an inventory of the contents of the camp after the Naporskis had left to buy the former L. Warnick Brown property (now part of the Waldheim). Nelson lists on three single-spaced typewritten sheets the contents of the camp, ranging from basins in the kitchen to a piano. Among other items, a birchbark canoe was missing. Fiske, in his reply, assures Nelson that he will speak to Naporski about that himself. The letter conveys a feeling of cordial relations between Nelson Dunn and Fiske and an unwillingness to put Nelson in a potentially awkward situation. We do not learn from the correspondence the fate of the canoe.

The Fiskes also rented to others, one of whom was John "Johnny" R. Hopkins of Irvington, New York, the dashing young heir to the Listerine fortune, who occupied Camp Veery for perhaps two summers. When Hopkins needed transportation across the water to the island dock, he would pull his large Packard convertible down on the public landing at the Glennmore and blow his horn until a boat came out of the Narrows behind the island. This was immensely annoying to Harry Kellogg, then manager of the Glennmore Hotel, and to Charlie Forkey of the Glennmore Store, who feared the noise would disturb their clients. However, Hopkins was such a good customer that they dared not say a word.[S24] Hopkins dealt with Nelson Dunn only through a lawyer in New York, who in turn communicated with Hopkins's guardian, probably an agent responsible for a trust fund, in St. Louis, Missouri,[S25] where Warner-Lambert, the makers of Listerine, had its headquarters. This kind of long-distance operation was difficult for people on the lake, who often found it a hardship to wait for payment for their services.

During this time, the Fiskes continued to come to Camp Veery when they could. Wanda Kinne Martin remembers playing with Minnie's adopted son, Bolie, at the Crestwood camp. There was a hammock on the porch, and Wanda, who was then four or five years old, somehow fell to the floor and cut her chin. Although she remembers being comforted by the doctor (probably Dr. Herbert Williams, whose house was nearby), she has no clear recollection of Bolie's appearance or personality. Her only souvenir of this encounter is the small scar she carries to this day.

Bill Dunn, who also remembers Bolie only slightly, recalls that when Minnie Fiske came to the Glennmore store to do her shopping, she always left her boat at the large dock in front of the Nelson Dunn house near the Chapel. Bill and his brother, Nelson Jr., were sent with her to the store to carry her groceries, a trip that "was always worth a generous twenty-five cents worth of candy."

During the 1920s, the Fiskes' fortunes continued to decline. Minnie was less in demand in the theater, and her health was beginning to fail. Her heart was weak and she probably also had cancer.[526] Her last performance in New York was in 1929, and, although she appeared in plays in Cleveland and Chicago until November 1931, she was thin and frail. On February 15, 1932, at the age of sixty-seven, she died at the home she and Harry had bought in Hollis, Long Island.

Her obituary in the *New York Times*[527] was an impressive three columns and included a photograph. Described as occupying the top rank of her profession, she lacked the "egotism so frequently found in theatrical stars. . . . Opportunity and encouragement were given the young members of the companies as freely as advice and instruction." In the sub-headline, the *Times* noted that she "lived virtually as a recluse." At her request, her body was cremated. Although she had asked that her ashes be sprinkled over Echo Island, this was never done. The whereabouts of her ashes are unknown today. In the obituary there is no mention of Big Moose.

Minnie's longtime secretary, Mae Cox, raised the adopted Bolie. He received a good education, joined the armed services in World War II, and eventually married.[528] Efforts to trace him or his descendants have so far failed.

Harry found it financially impossible to maintain Camp Veery, although he hung onto it. Although he visited it occasionally, it was usually either rented or simply unoccupied. Possibly he was unable to find a buyer during the Depression. The deed of the present owner, Paul Littman, shows that the island went into receivership in 1929 and that Fiske redeemed it in 1934. On September 27, 1941, a new owner sold the island to Charles Williams, proprietor of Lake View Lodge, who retained it for only a month before selling to C. Ray Harvey of Boonville.

With these changes of ownership, it is hard to understand the situation when Harrison Fiske returned to Big Moose in 1941, just before the United States entered World War II. Perhaps he had left in the house furniture that belonged to him, but he apparently no longer owned the property. Wanda Kinne, who, with her sister, was piloting the mail boat after her brother entered the army, remembers Fiske as a distinguished-looking man with neatly trimmed, shoulder-length, gray hair and a bald pate. Bill Dunn writes:

Finally, in June of 1941, Mr. Fiske threw in the towel. He hired a moving van out of New York City and took out the antiques and artifacts he wanted to keep. My father, brother, and I scowed these items from the Island to the van in our yard. Dad charged Mr. Fiske nothing for that day's work. It was a poignant, heartrending scene as the van pulled out of our yard. Mr. Fiske shook my Dad's hand and with big tears running down each cheek said, "Goodbye, Nelson. I shall probably never see you again." It was an emotionally packed scene that has been indelibly imprinted in my mind for lo these 56 years.[529]

Harrison Fiske died in 1942.

Harrison Fiske with Nelson Dunn, 1941. Courtesy of William S. Dunn.

Owl's Nest, ca. 1904. Courtesy of Hunter W. Finch.

mentioned that he had property on Big Moose Lake. The conversation had made an impression, and in 1904, Page sold the Jeffresses the camp called Owl's Nest.

The original Owl's Nest, built a year or two before the Jeffresses purchased it, had a large porch on the side facing the lake and on the west. Below the roof of the front porch the words "Owl's Nest" are spelled out in twig work. Camp records show that George Davidson, who also built the Glennmore Hotel and Tojenka, constructed a boathouse in 1906 to house guideboats and canoes. Later the west porch was enclosed in order to enlarge the house. At the same time, a small sleeping porch, railed in twig work, was built on the second floor.

In 1926 the family added to the boathouse a second story with more living quarters, including a living room with a fireplace. Later, Charlie and E. J. Martin built a back bedroom.

Thomas Fox Jeffress's only son, Robert, and his wife, Elizabeth Gwathmey Jeffress, had no children. They occupied the camp regularly for many summers. Robert and Elizabeth would come from Richmond on the train, stopping at the Plaza Hotel in New York on the way and continuing on to Big Moose Station. In the earliest days, they brought servants who occupied the large room over the garage and who cooked and did general chores. Later they hired a British couple, a cook and a chauffeur, who lived upstairs in the main house while the Jeffresses stayed in the suite of rooms over the boathouse.

At some time in the early 1930s, Robert Jeffress owned an electric boat, mainly for the use of his wife. The boat, certainly the first and perhaps the only electric boat on Big Moose, was made by the Electri-Craft Company in Syracuse, New York. It was fifteen feet long and traveled at three different speeds ($1\frac{1}{2}$, $4\frac{1}{2}$, and $7\frac{1}{2}$ miles per hour) either forward or backward. A full charge provided up to ten hours of virtually silent operation. The four six-volt batteries installed under the after deck could be

Owl's Nest and boathouse, ca. 1926. Courtesy of Hunter W. Finch.

recharged overnight by simply inserting two plugs into a battery charger located in the boathouse.[17]

In 1934, the family acquired an elegant twenty-one-foot, gasoline-powered mahogany Chris-Craft named *The Seguin,* which is now restored and is in use today.

Upon Robert Jeffress' death in 1967, the camp passed into the ownership of Hunter W. Finch, who had married Frances Kennedy. Hunter's sister Virginia, a zoologist, has lived most of her life in Africa and Australia but is still a frequent visitor to the camp.

TOJENKA (LOTS 34–58)

The Tojenka camp, facing the main lake near the entrance to South Bay, was rated in 1998 one of the largest and most valuable properties in Herkimer County.[18] Owned by Spartacus DeLia, a retired businessman, it is among the oldest camps on the lake and the only one that might aspire to the title of Big Moose's "Great Camp."

The house was built for Thomas Pettibone "T. P." Kingsford, of Oswego, New York. Kingsford was the owner of the Oswego Starch Company, which manufactured Kingsford's Cornstarch and for many years was the leading starch company in America, turning out more than ten million pounds per year.[19] The plant was sold in 1902 to the Corn Products Refining Company, which later moved the business out of Oswego and closer to the corn crops of the Midwest. Kingsford, knowledgeable in building machinery for all purposes, subsequently converted his factory to the Kingsford Foundry and Machine Works, which made boilers and pumps for locomotives during World War I.[20]

Kingsford was a member of Club Camp and probably came to Big Moose during the decade of the 1890s to hunt and fish. A photograph taken about 1900 shows him outside the camp standing in snowshoes and holding a gun. By 1902, Kingsford had begun to bring his family to the lake for occasional visits. He bought the land in December 1902.[21] Club Camp was destroyed by fire at some time after this.

Although a 1998 article in the Utica *Observer Dispatch* describes the main Tojenka camp as located on seven acres with twenty-two acres of surrounding forest, the original property was much larger. The Kingsford holdings extended from close to Lake View Lodge all the way to the top of Dart's Hill on both sides of the road to Eagle Bay. The initial purchase may have encompassed hundreds of acres.

Kingsford engaged George Davidson, who had helped to build the Glennmore Hotel, to erect a new camp for him and his family. Tojenka was finished in 1906 and looked in outline very much as it looks today. The two-story building is spacious, with an enormous central living room encompassing two fireplaces. A wide porch, now partially glass-enclosed, runs around the sides of the building that face the lake. The name of the camp comes from the names of T. P.'s family—*To* (for Thomson, T. P.'s son), *jen* (for T. P.'s wife, Jennie), and *ka* (for Katharine, T. P.'s daughter).[22]

The first additional building Kingsford erected was a large two-story boathouse in the palisade style surrounded by a porch on each level. The first floor encompassed a large room for storing guideboats and canoes and, behind it, a bedroom and bath for the caretaker. Upstairs was another large room used for recreation, plus two bedrooms and another bath. The boathouse was located on the south side of the property, where Robert Hubbell's camp now stands. (When Hubbell acquired this land, the building was found to be infested with woodworms. Because it was not restorable, it was torn down.)

Tojenka became a nearly self-sufficient complex. The family kept one and sometimes two full-time caretakers. In the days before a good road to Eagle Bay existed, the horses and carriages or sleighs were housed in a building near the top of the hill, which later became a garage. Be-

Thomas Pettibone Kingsford, ca. 1920. Courtesy of Spartacus DeLia.

Tojenka main house in the winter, ca. 1970. Courtesy of Bonnie Hubbell.

Tojenka boathouse, which was built before main house, ca. 1910. Courtesy of Roger Pratt.

hind and below the garage stood a barn for a cow or two to provide fresh milk, which was difficult to obtain. Chickens were kept for eggs and meat, and pigs were also raised and slaughtered. Across the road and still visible today was a large garden (fenced to keep out the deer) that provided food for the family and the caretakers. The complex also included a large caretaker's house, a woodshed with a workshop, a complete blacksmith shop, a plumbing shop, an icehouse, a Delco generating plant, the large boathouse, and a tennis court.

To the east of all these buildings, in a low spot that is still swampy, a small brook was dammed to form a pond that Kingsford stocked with fish. On the north edge of the pond, Kingsford erected a one-room building that was called the "card house" and served as a retreat. The

little bark-covered house had a large stone fireplace at one end and a porch at the other overlooking the pond. (The family named the house Tominka, a word formed from the first letters of the names of Thomson Kingsford, T. P.'s son, his wife Minerva, and their daughter Katherine.) Unfortunately, the fish failed to thrive in the pond. About 1935, the gate in the long concrete dam was opened and the pond drained. George Davidson's name is inscribed in the cement and is still visible near the gate.

Another feature of Tojenka in its early days was the bridge spanning the entrance to a small cove in South Bay. It is said to have been part of the trail system that once ran along the shores of the lake. The bridge may have been built soon after the camp was put up, judging from the style of an early postcard that shows it. A later card, postmarked 1914, indicates that it had been embellished and strengthened. How long it withstood the Big Moose winter ice is unknown.

In 1922, Kingsford sold to Henry C. Milligan of Canton, Ohio, the first of six lots on which Milligan built his Buzz Point camp (now part of Covewood). The remaining Kingsford property still encompassed more than seven hundred feet of lake frontage.

Bill Dunn remembers several of the caretakers who followed George Davidson. Mr. and Mrs. Louis LeClair were good friends of Bill's grandparents. Will Woodard was their successor. Charlie Etheridge, an older man who was childless himself, loved to have children around him. Bill Dunn recalls:

If we happened to be at Tojenka at milking time, he would always ask my brother and me to come on over to the barn. It was always intriguing to us, as young children, to watch him milk the cow. (Kingsfords only kept one in those days.) While we were intently watching, Charlie was very adept at turning the cow's teat in his closed hand and giving us a good squirt of fresh milk right in the face. We always took it for what it was—a good joke.[23]

When T. P. Kingsford died in January 1932, the property passed to his widow, Jennie, his son, Thomson Kingsford, and his daughter, Katharine K. Hall, all of Oswego. In 1935, Thomson Kingsford, his wife, Minerva (née Haskins), and their children Thomas and Katherine enjoyed picnics and water activities with the Jeffresses and others on the lake. The family owned a launch, the *Tojenka*, as well as other boats including guide boats, canoes, and sailboats. During the time he owned the camp, Kingsford sold to Albert C. Ayer of Scarsdale, New York, the property on which Ayer built the Stag's Leap camp. In 1956, shortly before Kingsford died in 1958, he sold Tojenka to Orville W. Hubbell, a businessman of Washington Mills, New York.

The Hubbells and their three children, Janet, Celia, and Robert, spent summers at the camp for sixteen years. After Orville Hubbell's death in 1969, his widow, Celia,

Kingsford's bridge, ca. 1908. Courtesy of Wanda K. Martin.

Kingsford's launch Tojenka, *ca. 1910–20. Occupants tentatively identified as (left to right) T. P. Kingsford in the bow, Tojenka caretaker Will Woodard driving, Robert Jeffress, Minerva Haskins Kingsford, Jennie Kingsford, and three unidentified women. Courtesy of Hunter W. Finch.*

not wanting to be responsible for such a large operation, sold Tojenka to Spartacus DeLia. Members of the Hubbell family retained land on the South Bay side of the property. Celia Hubbell built a camp on the southernmost part of the lakefront, which after her death went to her daughter, Janet Hubbell Knapp. A second daughter, Celia Susan Hubbell O'Donnell, owned the land just north of it, which was purchased in 2000 by Richard Zogby of Syracuse, New York. Robert O. Hubbell and his wife, Bonnie, of Washington Mills hold the land next to the main Tojenka property. The Hubbells retained a substantial amount of the furniture and other accoutrements from Tojenka, including a model that George Davidson had built of the original Club Camp.

Spartacus DeLia took possession of Tojenka in September 1971. His holdings still include large amounts of land on both sides of the road to Eagle Bay as well as a long stretch of lakefront property (lots 37–49). DeLia, who also came from Utica, owned not only a large company that built highways and bridges but also quarries in Boonville and Litchfield that produced aggregates for concrete production. In 1972, DeLia sold his businesses to the Allied Chemical Company and retired. Spot, as he is known, and his wife, Marie, now live in Freeport in the Bahamas but still manage to spend substantial amounts of time at Tojenka, where their five children and their families visit them.

Fred and Myrna Brack, caretakers at Tojenka, could claim much of the credit for the upkeep of the estate under the Kingsfords, the Hubbells, and for nearly ten years under the DeLias. Fred, who died in 1981 at the age of eighty-eight, evoked strong opinions from others. Some found him stern and hard to get along with. Others had nothing but admiration for his humor and his skills.

Bill Dunn recollects, "Myrna was a very gentle, kind woman and always treated my brother and me to home-baked cookies and fresh milk when we went to Tojenka. Fred was a different type—never as friendly as Myrna."[24]

On the Tojenka land was the trail to Windfall Pond and Queer Lake, which started from the Big Moose Road at the bottom of the hill where there is now a small parking lot. This was a New York State trail and was to be open for public use at all times. Bill Dunn comments, "For years [in the 1930s] Fred Brack tried to stop persons from parking at this trailhead, but was, to my knowledge, never successful. And one time he almost got himself into a peck of trouble with the law for letting the air out of all the tires on about four hunters' cars."[25]

Bonnie Hubbell, wife of Orville's son Robert, remembers Fred Brack with great affection. She writes,

Fred Brack laid a fire like no one I have known before or since. Every morning at Tojenka the family would rise to find either, in cold weather, a roaring fire in the fireplace or, on warmer days, the fireplaces laid ready for the touch of a match if a sudden chill should occur.

Fred's opinions on the proper method of fire building were, like all of his opinions, strict and unchanging. The wadded up balls of newspaper commonly used to ignite kindling were forbidden under Fred's rule. His system was far more elegant and at the same time simple. Fred would cut a small piece of firewood into kindling size pieces with a small hatchet. He then used his ancient and razor-sharp Barlow knife to shave little curlicues of wood which he left hanging from the kindling. Larger kindling and three logs were precisely arranged on top. One had only to light a match to a few of those curlicues and wait a few minutes for a perfect fire to fill the grate.[26]

Another story from Bonnie Hubbell about Fred Brack shows a different side of his character:

One afternoon Fred appeared in the kitchen at Tojenka as the family was finishing lunch. The sly expression on his face caused Mr. Hubbell to ask Fred what he had just been doing. Well, Fred explained, he had just come back from visiting Claude [Major Bowes]. The Major's summer staff of college girls had recently arrived and, on their break, were sunning themselves on the Covewood

Fred Brack, the caretaker of Tojenka in later years, ca. 1960s. Courtesy of Bonnie Hubbell.

dock. "There they were," Fred said, "wearing them skimpy little swimming suits. And stacked up along that dock like cordwood. It was quite a pretty sight!"[27]

Fred was a master of the many tasks necessary for the maintenance of the large complex of buildings. He was a blacksmith, a plumber, an electrician, a carpenter, and was famous for his vegetable garden, which lay on the opposite side of the road to Eagle Bay. He was also instrumental in the construction of the Big Moose Community Chapel in the early 1930s. In addition, for several years he was the weather observer for the Black River Regulating District in the Big Moose area.[28]

Myrna Brack died in the late 1950s or early 1960s. Fred lived for many more years and was given the use of the Tojenka caretaker's house until close to the end of his life. He spent more than fifty years at Tojenka and finally, during the DeLia tenure, died at the Presbyterian Home in Utica.

Into South Bay and Around to East Bay

Before World War II, the Kingsford family of Tojenka sold some lakefront property that lay south of the main house to two different families. The first sale was to the Milligans from Ohio and was of land that is now part of Covewood. The later sale of property went to the Ayers, a family from the New York City area. Between Tojenka and Covewood other camps stand today, but before the war these were the only two.

Beyond the Outlet and Covewood stood Fern Spring, one of the oldest camps on the lake, to be replaced in 1938 by the Chapel manse, which took over its name. The camps beyond that belonged to the Kelsey and Bicknell families. The Hadden and Swain camps, built in the 1930s, were on the edge of or inside South Bay, where only a few houses stood on the shore. An elaborate boat-

house near the entrance to Punky Bay, which became a residence, The Ledges, commanded a view to the west along South Bay.

Lucy Craske wrote the section on her family's camp, Stag's Leap. Frank Carey, assisted by his father, is the author of the Fern Spring memoir. Christine Lozner, an architectural historian, has researched and written the piece on Brown Gables.

STAG'S LEAP (LOTS 49E–55)

Stag's Leap camp, located west of Covewood on the widest part of the lake, was built on property purchased from the Kingsford family by Albert C. and Hattie W. Ayer. The Ayers hired professional architects, but the buildings were really the grand design of Albert Ayers, an artistic and creative man. Architecture was a serious hobby, and he had also designed their large home in Scarsdale, New York. He owned a steel-products factory in New Jersey that manufactured items such as tole trays, lamps, and other accessories. He also owned and managed real estate.

To construct Stag's Leap, he hired Earl Covey, whose handiwork is evident in the careful workmanship and especially in the beautiful stone fireplaces. Work on the camp began in 1934 and was complete in 1936. The house, built of gray stained milled lumber, stretches along the shore so that most rooms have views of the lake. The finishing details were done by Albert Ayer, and these consumed every summer until he became ill in 1947. The first building to be finished was a fully equipped workshop where he fabricated all the door handles and hinges, light fixtures, hand-carved moldings, and the like.

Albert and Hattie Ayer came first to Twitchell Lake with Hattie's mother, Lucy Webber Jordan. Her husband, the Reverend Dr. Jordan, had vacationed at the Twitchell Lake Inn before marrying Lucy. The Ayers built a camp directly east of the Lone Pine Camp on Twitchell, along with a cottage for Lucy after Dr. Jordan died. Dr. Jordan was one of the first clergymen to conduct church services both at Twitchell and at Big Moose.

The Ayers had four children. One died at birth, one at age three, and Robert, the eldest, died of an ulcerated sports injury when he was in his early twenties. The Ayers had become devout Christian Scientists after their second child died, and, therefore, did not call medical help when Robert became ill. Their youngest child was a daughter, Elizabeth, who married Frank Newman, a banker and investor. They lived in Scarsdale, where Elizabeth's mother, Hattie Ayer, had grown up. Elizabeth inherited her father's talent for craftsmanship and, working with her father, contributed enormously to the interior decoration of the camp. Together they made many pieces of furniture, mirrors, candle sconces, and other items. Upon Hattie Ayer's death in 1953, Elizabeth inherited the camp. She and her husband made many improvements over the years.

The Newmans had two daughters. Alice, the younger, died in an accident when she was only twenty-five years old, leaving two children, Elizabeth and Robert Youngs. Lucy Ayer Newman, the older daughter, married Robert B. Craske, a dentist. They became the owners of the camp in 1997.

BUZZ POINT CAMP (LOTS 53–58)

Buzz Point, a picturesque group of palisade-style buildings, is now part of Covewood. In 1922, Henry and Edith Milligan of Canton, Ohio, bought property (lot 58) from T. P. Kingsford and put the first buildings on the land. In 1932 they expanded their holdings by buying five more lots from Kingsford's son, Thomson (lots 53–57). A small gazebo, built on the point on the north side of the Outlet, soon became a landmark on the lake.

In the days when driving long distances was an adventure, the Milligans would arrive in their chauffeur-driven Rolls Royce, to the delight of the small boys around the lake. The chauffeur, George Eckleberry, doubled as a handyman. Bill Dunn and his brother Nelson remember Eckleberry letting them sit in the car and use the speaking tube that ran between the front and rear seats, which were separated by a glass partition.

Henry Milligan was president and treasurer of the Republic Stamping and Enameling Company, which made high-grade enameled cookware. Edith Milligan was active in various charities at home. As chairman of the March of Dimes campaign for eastern Ohio, she was influential in Franklin Roosevelt's favorite charity, which was devoted to eradicating polio.

At some point in the mid-1930s, Edith Milligan helped to restore Ruth Marleau of Big Moose Station to her job as postmistress after an unfortunate contretemps with Roy Higby. Roy, an active Republican, somehow got into a shouting match with Ruth Marleau and managed to displace her. Ruth had six small children at home and a husband who was handicapped by war injuries. Edith Milligan, through her influence with the Democratic Party, was soon able to see that Mrs. Marleau regained her job and could resume her contributions to the support of her family.

Both the Milligans were short in stature, and Henry Milligan was rather frail. Bill Marleau tells the story of his sleeping on six mattresses. "One day the old man [then in his seventies] . . . claimed there was a broken spring in the bed. Ernie [LaFountain] and I [Marleau] got a good laugh out of that one but finally the old man insisted we look. So, one by one we removed the six mattresses, and there, right where he said it was, was a broken spring."[29]

The Milligans owned a gasoline launch called *Buzz Point*, which they used for visiting friends around the lake. Nelson Dunn was their primary caretaker, and they enjoyed exceptionally cordial relations with him. After

Buzz Point, the summer home of Henry and Edith Milligan, ca. 1930. Courtesy of Wanda K. Martin.

Henry and Edith Milligan in their launch, ca. 1930. Courtesy of William S. Dunn.

Henry died, Edith Milligan continued to come to the camp by herself. She sold the property in 1966 to C. V. Bowes, and it became part of Covewood.

FERN SPRING CAMP (LOTS 69–70W)

Fern Spring Camp, the camp that gave its name to the Chapel manse, was built on the south shore of South Bay by F. C. Moore of New York City, president of the Continental Insurance Company. Moore built before official property records were kept, but one of the first owners, Edward O. Stanley, described it as having existed in 1888. It may even have been built a little earlier. The complex originally consisted of three buildings plus an icehouse and a woodshed. The main building was located just south of where the present manse is located. As was common practice up until the time Webb bought the land in 1890, Moore was a squatter and did not own the land upon which his camp was built.

Edward O. Stanley of East Orange, New Jersey, was an avid outdoorsman who began visiting the Adirondack Mountains in 1890 or 1891 with three of his close friends. They were Clarence Kelsey and two physicians from the New York area. Kelsey and Stanley were president and vice president respectively of the Title Guarantee and Trust Company of New York City.

Before the railroad was built to Big Moose Station, Stanley and his friends traveled by train from New York to Utica and onward by train to Boonville. They then continued by buckboard to Old Forge, where they met their guides. They went by guideboat up the Fulton Chain of Lakes to Third Lake, carried to Rondaxe Lake, and then continued via Dart's Lake to Big Moose, where they stayed at Club Camp on the site of the present DeLia camp.

At some point in the 1890s, Stanley and his partners noticed that the Moore Camp was no longer in use. The four men were able to purchase the buildings in 1898, and in 1899, through Webb's agent, bought the three 100-foot lots (lots 70, 71, and 72) on which the buildings stood. These lots extended back a little beyond the present Higby Road. This transaction gave them clear title to the land upon which their camp was built. The two physicians dropped out of the partnership, and between 1902 and 1905 the property was divided between Kelsey and Stanley. Stanley retained the west end of the property, on which most of the camp buildings stood, while Kelsey received the eastern end. Shortly after the property was divided, Stanley had Bill Dart build a boathouse for him at the western end of his property, and Kelsey built a camp at the eastern end.

Stanley's main camp was initially of half-log construction (later shingled) and contained a living room, a dining room, a kitchen, a bathroom, and three bedrooms, one

Edward O. Stanley, ca. 1910. Courtesy of Frank Carey.

Fern Spring Camp, ca. 1905. Courtesy of Frank Carey.

downstairs and two upstairs. The dining room had a bay window on the west side of the house. A covered porch extended the width of the house facing the lake. This building was located just south of the location of the present manse. About fifty feet to the east stood a second building, which contained two bedrooms and a bathroom. The boathouse was built across a small stream and had a large single door and plank ramp for boats that led down to the water. Above the boathouse was a large sleeping loft.

Fern Spring Camp was named for a spring 75 to 100 feet from the lake's edge that emanated from a group of large rocks and ferns. The spring was the source of the small stream that flowed under the boathouse. Water for the camp came not from Fern Spring, however, but from a different spring located farther up the hill. The second spring was enclosed within a springhouse and supplied water to both the Stanley and Kelsey camps.

Bedroom at Fern Spring Camp, ca. 1910. Courtesy of Frank Carey.

The entire Stanley family first came to the lake in 1903. Edward O. Stanley brought his wife, Caroline, his daughter Marjorie (who documented the visit with her new box camera), and his son Edward O. Stanley, Jr., to Big Moose for a two-week visit from July 11 to July 25. Within a few years the family was spending the summer months at Fern Spring Camp. During the summer of 1906, Marjorie and her brother Edward, Jr., witnessed events related to the Gillette-Brown murder and subsequently testified at Gillette's trial. (See *"An American Tragedy* and Big Moose Lake" in chapter 6.) Later in 1906, Marjorie married Paul C. Carey, an engineer from East Orange, New Jersey. Her two sons, Francis and Richard, were born in 1907 and 1908 respectively. The Carey family followed the tradition of the Stanleys and spent every summer at Fern Spring Camp at Big Moose Lake.

Francis E. Carey, Sr., Marjorie's son, recalls a family story about the early days when only the men used the camp:

The first ladies at Fern Spring Camp were the wives of the four original men who had bought the place. Obviously male housekeeping left much to be desired, and the mess accumulated over the years. . . . The ladies decided to clean house. Upon opening some cupboard doors in the living room they found dishes. Out they came, were washed, the cupboard cleaned and the dishes replaced. Advancing into the dining room, voilà, another cupboard with dishes. Out they came, and when they were about half-washed, came the realization that they were the same dishes from the same cabinet which opened either in the living room or dining room.[30]

In the early years when E. O. Stanley, his wife, and his adult children spent the summer, they always came by train from Grand Central Station in New York City. Like others who arrived at Big Moose Station, they traveled to the Glennmore landing by buckboard and later by bus. The steamboat dropped them off at Camp Crag because the water was not deep enough in front of Fern Spring Camp. They were then taken across to Fern Spring Camp in a rowboat. After steamboat service ceased, the family could take a motor launch from the Glennmore landing to neighboring Kelsey's dock, where the water was deep enough for the launches.

About 1924 the family began coming by car. By that time the roads from New Jersey were much improved, although long detours were still common. Driving beside the Hudson River on Route 9, the family reached Schenectady by the end of the first day and spent the night there. On the second day they followed the Mohawk River west to Little Falls and drove from there through Poland to Remsen. When they met what is now Route 28, they traveled north and took the rough Big Moose Road from Eagle Bay to the lake.

Stanley often had a man working for him who accompanied the family to the camp and helped with the many chores, such as getting the water turned on and closing the camp at the end of the summer. When it was time to close camp, wires were stretched across the rooms and all fabric items were hung over the wires so that they would be inaccessible to mice. Over the wires went mattresses, blankets, sheets, towels, rugs, and curtains. One year a mattress hung too close to a wall, and the mice found it a fine place for nests. That incident prompted construction of the "tin closet," a small closet fully lined with sheet metal so that no animal could get in. The closet was barely large enough and would be packed from floor to ceiling. When the closet was opened in July, the children loved to plunge their arms in between the layers of blankets to feel the cold that was still there from the winter.

Local residents supplied firewood and ice. Firewood was delivered as slabs, and the handyman then cut the slabs into chunks suitable for use in the kitchen woodstove. When the Carey sons became teenagers they took over this chore.

Like many other camp owners at that time, Marjorie Carey ordered nonperishable food supplies for the whole summer from R. H. Macy's in New York City. These supplies included items such as flour, sugar, pickles, catsup, crackers, cereals, canned vegetables and fruits, spices, condiments, and the like. The order was packed in large wooden crates or barrels and shipped to the Glennmore landing to be there when the family arrived. Perishables came from several sources. A salesman from Bremer's, a company in Utica, periodically visited camps on the lake, taking orders for fresh meat, fruits, and vegetables. The family order would be delivered within a few days and stored in the icehouse. Also, old records at the Waldheim describe the sale of various items to the Stanley family. In 1906, Stanley regularly purchased milk, cream, and maple syrup from the Martin family at the Waldheim. The record included one gallon of maple syrup for $1.50, two quarts of milk for twenty cents, one pint of cream for twenty cents, and one cake of soap for six cents.[31] Later, a wide variety of foods was available at Forkey's store at the Glennmore.

Marjorie Carey's declining health prevented her from engaging in many domestic activities, and the family typically employed a cook for the summer through an agency in Utica. A cook would work every day for the whole summer and never have a day off. This schedule apparently was typical at the time. Most of these women were middle-aged, and on one occasion the family's cook brought her daughter for the summer and the two of them ran the kitchen together. The cooks used one of the upstairs bedrooms in the main camp.

Kerosene lamps provided the basic lighting for the camp. Paul Carey, Marjorie's husband, installed some low-voltage battery-operated lights in the cottage, but these were of limited usefulness. The bulbs, about the size of flashlight bulbs, served mostly to enable one to find and light the kerosene lamps or to light the way if it became necessary to get up in the night.

Water from the spring flowed by gravity to the camp bathrooms and kitchen, and of course there was no running hot water. The kitchen woodstove had a "waterback," a chamber at the back of the stove that could be filled with water, which was then heated by the stove fire. A faucet on the waterback made it convenient to obtain hot water.

Telephone service was virtually nonexistent during the Stanley-Carey years. The only telephone in the area was at the railroad station. Francis Carey, Marjorie's son, recalls an occasion when his brother Richard needed to telephone a friend at Saranac Lake. He went to the station and was able to reach a telephone operator. The operator contacted another operator who was in communication with the Saranac friend, but, for reasons that nobody ever understood, could not connect the two parties. So Richard told the operator what he wanted to say to the friend. The operator conveyed this to the other operator who then relayed it to the friend. And so went the conversation. Telegraph service at the station was more reliable. Paul Carey was a partner in the engineering firm of Runyon and Carey of Newark, New Jersey, and on a few occasions he would send business-related telegrams to his office or to clients from the Big Moose station, a routine business procedure in those days.

Garbage disposal practices varied over the years. In the early years, food garbage was given away as pig feed. "Grandpa and Grandma" Rose lived up at the end of what is now the Covewood Road and they kept pigs. Their grandsons, Eddie and Walter Dunn, would come to Fern Spring Camp by boat to get the food garbage for their pigs. Later, the Stanleys buried household garbage in a sandy area near the west end of the property until Covewood was built. The family then began burying garbage much farther up the hill. However, the soil was difficult to dig because of roots and rocks. So, rather than burying garbage, they saved it in a large garbage can; when full, the can was dumped on the ground way up the hill. They then poured chloride of lime over the garbage. It never smelled and was never disturbed by animals; it simply rotted away.

By the late 1920s, the Carey sons were college students and stayed at Fern Spring Camp for the summer. They became acquainted with others their age staying at the various hotels, often for the whole summer. This social group of hotel guests and camp family members did many things together. Francis Carey recalled such activities as campfires at Pancake Hall, overnight stays at The Hermitage on the Queer Lake trail, and a treasure hunt organized by Lake View guest Caroline Crowley, daughter of Pat Crowley, president of the New York Central Railroad. Francis also remembered paper chases: "Did you ever take a girl and a barn lantern and follow a thin trail of sort of homemade confetti and hope to win the prize? You could go half way up to Billy's Bald Spot only to find that you had to go back to [the lean-to at] Pancake Hall for the supper."[32]

Marjorie Carey's health continued to deteriorate and she died in 1931. The family returned the following year, but fewer family members came and those who did took their meals at the Higby Club. Interest in Fern Spring Camp began to decline. E. O. Stanley's son, Edward, Jr., had married Mary Taylor from Keene Valley and was spending his vacations there. The Carey sons were now adults with jobs and unable to spend summers at the camp. Their father, Paul Carey, remarried. His second wife was a widow with a summer home in New Jersey, and they never returned to Fern Spring Camp. Francis was employed by the General Electric Company in Schenectady as a student engineer during the Depression and would occasionally come to the camp for weekend stays with some of his fellow employees. These visits ended when he moved to New Jersey in 1935. Family members describe the camp buildings as being in poor condition by that time. In 1938 the camp was sold to Walter Colpitts, who retained his own camp on the North Shore.

Under Colpitts's ownership, the old camp buildings were all razed and a new building erected. The new camp, constructed as an experiment using the synthetic material Cemestos made by the Celotex Corporation, is now the Chapel manse.

Marjorie's sons, Francis and Richard, vacationed occasionally at Big Moose in the 1950s and 1960s with their families. In the 1970s, several of the Careys began vacationing at the Waldheim regularly. In 1981, Francis Carey, Sr., who with his brother Richard had ushered at the first Big Moose Community Chapel service in 1931, participated in the fiftieth-anniversary service of the Chapel by ushering Frances Covey, widow of designer and builder Earl Covey, to her seat of honor. The Careys continue to come to Big Moose, often arranging to be there together. The largest such gathering a few years ago brought Careys from South Carolina, New Jersey, Michigan, and Illinois.

Francis "Frank" Carey, Jr. (well known for his collection of Big Moose postcards), and his wife, Grace, recently purchased a camp at Twitchell Lake.

BROWN GABLES (LOTS 70–72W)

In April 1899, when William Seward Webb's Ne-Ha-Sa-Ne Park Association sold a large parcel (155.5 acres) to Henry Covey, including all of the south shore along South Bay, three 100-foot lots were exempted from the sale. The site of Fern Spring Camp, on lots 69, 70, and 71, had been singled out for purchase the previous month by the City Real Estate Company of New York City.

City Real Estate represented a consortium of the four friends and outdoorsmen who began traveling to the

Adirondacks in the early 1890s, staying first at Club Camp and then at Fern Spring. In 1910, after two of the partners had withdrawn, the three lots were divided equally between Clarence Hill Kelsey (1856–1930) and his business partner, Edward O. Stanley, who retained the earlier Fern Spring Camp. After moving two structures that apparently were part of the Fern Spring compound and that still stand today, Kelsey built his camp, Brown Gables, which survives today largely unaltered from its original appearance.

Eugene and Christine Lozner are the current owners. Chris, an architectural historian, has done extensive research on the history of the camp and is responsible for the following information.

Clarence Kelsey was president of the Title Guarantee and Trust Company in New York City and a pioneer in organizing the title insurance business when he built the camp. Sophisticated and generous, Kelsey had been valedictorian of the Yale class of 1878, where the salutatorian, William Howard Taft, was his roommate. Kelsey became a lifelong friend of Taft, later president of the United States and chief justice of the U.S. Supreme Court. Kelsey served on the boards of several banks and insurance businesses as well as in many charitable organizations. Among his affiliations, along with Taft, was as an active board member and fund-raiser for both the Hampton and Tuskegee Institutes.

At Big Moose, Kelsey chaired the volunteer committee that played an active role in planning the community's religious life. A liberal contributor to the Old Forge and Inlet churches, he made the first pledge for construction of the Big Moose Community Chapel. In 1932, after the deaths of both Clarence and his wife, Elizabeth Baldwin Tomlinson Kelsey, their three sons contributed the Chapel pews in memory of their parents.

A family history, published shortly after Kelsey's death in 1930, notes that, "except for an occasional trip abroad [the Kelseys'] summers for thirty years or more were spent at their camp . . . where Mr. Kelsey derived much enjoyment from tramping, rowing, swimming and taking life easy . . . It was here that he laid aside all care, and really played, leaving the camp each year with regret, and counting the time until he could return to it."[33]

Brown Gables, built in 1910, is itself of great architectural interest. It was designed by Max Westhoff of the Saranac Lake firm of Coulter and Westhoff, the first architects to practice in the Adirondacks. The house was built by George Goodsell, a contractor and guide from Old Forge who also completed many camps at the Adirondack League Club.[34] (Goodsell's house is now the home of the Town of Webb Historical Association.) Located very close to the lake, the camp is essentially a balloon-frame, shingle-style building. Its complex, bracketed roof incorporates six clipped gables that expand the second floor and extend to offer shelter to the full-width front porch. Viewed from the outside, the house would be at home in many seaside resorts, where the shingle style was popular in the early 1900s. However, the careful rustic detailing of the compact yet commodious interior, reminiscent (on a small scale) of some of the great camps, is evidence of its Adirondack roots.

Besides the main camp, the Brown Gables property includes three other buildings. According to the Stanley-Carey family, the vertical log toolshed, sometimes called

Brown Gables, designed by Max Westhoff of the firm Coulter and Westhoff in Saranac Lake and built in 1910 for Clarence Kelsey, ca. late 1930s. Courtesy of Christine Lozner.

the "playhouse," was probably part of the Fern Spring compound and was moved to allow construction of the camp. The woodshed was also moved and originally may have been a canvas-sided storage building, most likely for storing boats. The boathouse, with its roofline complementing the camp roof, was built by Kelsey, and although the doors have been replaced, the structure remains essentially unchanged. The stones piled against the shoreline on either side of the boathouse were cleared in about 1933 to provide a more comfortable swimming spot.

Because of the lake's shallow depth in South Bay, Brown Gables was not a stop for the steamboat. When he traveled to Big Moose, Kelsey was accompanied by his chauffeur, Billy Powell, who acted as his guide and boatman. To reach his camp, Kelsey purchased a launch (ca. 1905), which he named the *Princess.* After Kelsey's death, Nelson Dunn, who had been Kelsey's caretaker, bought this boat, and it served him for many years as a working vessel.[35] Charlie Martin and possibly Art Burtch later owned the same boat at different times. Kelsey also owned a guideboat, the *Susie,* which he enjoyed rowing.

In August 1930, after Clarence Kelsey's death in April, his family sold the property to Harrison Bicknell, Sr., for many years associated with the military academy in Manlius, New York. The Bicknell family enjoyed the camp for twenty-five years, adding particularly to its boating history. In 1931, Bicknell acquired a high-speed outboard called the *Gee Whiz* and later purchased from Kinne's Boat Line a 1933 Chris-Craft with a cockpit fore and aft. The Chris-Craft was called the *Brudbick,* a combination of Harriet Bicknell's college nickname and Harrison's last name.

During the wartime summers of about 1943 through 1945, Brown Gables was home to an Austrian refugee, Count Coudenhove-Kalergi, his wife, the actress Ida Roland, and their daughter. The count was a principal proponent of the Pan-European movement and was widely known among Europe's prewar and wartime leaders including Winston Churchill. Churchill wrote the preface to one of the count's books, which refers to the joy of summers at Big Moose as "one of our happiest recollections" of wartime life in America.[36] In August 1945, the count learned of the end of the war via his camp radio and announced the news to others on South Bay who did not yet have electricity.

Brown Gables changed hands again in 1955, when it was purchased by Thurston and Josephine Keese from Fayetteville, New York, who had vacationed with their family at the Higby Club beginning in 1942. They renamed the camp High Fox and spent many summers there with their children. Dr. Keese died in 1986, and his family retained the camp until 2000.

In that year, the children sold the property to Eugene and Christine Lozner of Manlius, New York, who restored the original name.

THE ARTHUR HARVEY CAMP (LOTS 72E–73W)

Harrison Bicknell, Sr., of Manlius, New York, who owned Brown Gables during the 1930s, had a sister, Gertrude, whose husband, Arthur J. Harvey, was a victim of tuberculosis. To provide a place for him to recover, Bicknell commissioned Earl Covey to construct a building next door. Covey built the camp during one month in the summer of 1933 on the eastern half of lot 72. His efforts proved to be worthwhile, and Harvey recovered to live until 2001.

The original cottage consisted of a living room, kitchen, bathroom, one bedroom, and a porch; all except the porch was contained within a twenty-four-foot square. By the second year of use, Alex McEdwards, Earl Covey's son-in-law, added another bedroom on the east side. The fifty-foot portion of lot 72 was eventually deeded to Gertrude B. Harvey in 1946, and in about 1949 another thirty-five feet of the same lot was deeded by Bicknell to his sister. In the mid-1930s, the Harveys bought lot 73, retaining only the western half. The cottage, which looks today much as it did when it was built, is surrounded by spruce trees, most of which have succumbed to spruce blight.

Arthur Harvey accompanied Phil Ellsworth and Barney Barnum on the flight to Canada in 1979 during which Ellsworth died. Harvey himself died in 2001, leaving the camp jointly to his nephew Harrison Bicknell, Jr., of Lexington, Virginia, and his stepson, Vincent Mabert. Harrison and Jane Bicknell are now the owners of the camp.

HADDEN CAMP (LOTS 73E–76)

C. Ray Harvey of Boonville, New York (later an owner of Echo Island), built this camp in the early 1930s. Located not far from Covewood, it was constructed by Earl Covey. In 1938, Harvey (no relation to Arthur Harvey) sold it to Alexander Hadden and his wife, Katharine W.

Hadden, a daughter of Percy B. Wightman. Now that both Hadden parents have died, the camp is owned and occupied by their sons, Robert and Alexander Hadden, their daughter, Edith H. Matthew, and their families.

SWAIN CAMP (LOT 78)

Earl Covey built this camp in 1936 for Ralph and Beulah Swain of Mayfield Heights, Ohio. Beulah was a widow when she died in the summer of 2002. The camp has passed to her two sons, Richard and John of Mentor, Ohio.

THE LEDGES (LOTS 100–106)

In 1928, Earl Covey began to build a large camp in South Bay at the entrance to Punky Bay. This new camp was for D. W. Salisbury, an executive with the Sun Oil and Gas Company in New Jersey. Covey built the boathouse and laid the stone foundations for a house behind it. However, when Salisbury became ill, he decided not to complete the house. More rooms were then added to the boathouse to make it livable, and it became the family camp. In 1937, long before the road to the end of Crag Point was built, the Salisburys negotiated an easement with the Higby Club so they could put in their own road and have access by land.

The Salisburys had three sons, Francis, Richard, and Donald. Donald was a madcap friend of Henry Bruyn. He attended Dartmouth in the early 1940s, but his parents cut short his academic career when they read in the newspapers of a nearly fatal exploit. Unbeknownst to his parents, Donald had been taking flying lessons. According to Henry Bruyn,

> He completed these lessons and went down to Boston to take his license examination . . . High over Boston Harbor, the inspector asked Don to put the plane in a spin and bring it out. Don chose the wrong direction [for the spin] and did not bring it out until close to the surface of the water . . . Happily, [he] made a spectacular landing on a tiny island. The newspapers picked up this event and gave it wide publicity. . . . Don was taken from college immediately and enlisted in the Army Air Corps.[37]

The Salisburys sold the camp to a couple from Cleveland, Ohio—William Donaldson "Don" Watkins and his wife, Alice. They originally came to Big Moose because their daughter, Donna, was attending the Moss Lake Camp for Girls. At first, they rented at Little Moose Lake, then at Dart's Lake, then at the Higby Club, and finally at the Ledges. After renting the Salisbury camp for one year in 1955, they decided to buy it. Donna, now Donna Zorge, and her brother Frederick Watkins are joint owners.

POLARIS LODGE (LOTS 132–36E)

On the north side of Crag Point stood another camp built in the 1930s. Its owners, a childless couple from Utica, New York, loved privacy and found a spot on a small cove that was accessible only by boat.

In 1931, E. Winslow and Katherine Kane, then of Ossining, New York, bought from R. Guy Harry two lots on the north side of Crag Point. In the years that followed, they added more lots, giving them nearly nine hundred feet of shoreline on the main lake, with additional water access on the south to Punky Bay. Kane recounts in his short memoir, *Early History of Polaris Lodge*,[38] that he not only bought the land but also the logs for the building. However, the logs were not taken from his land. "I did not want to cut the trees from my property. Nelson A. Dunn, Sr., did the logging, peeled and hand draw-shaved the logs."

Nelson Dunn built a genuine log cabin with notched logs as much as twelve inches in diameter. The logs were chinked with oakum covered by peeled saplings. (The interior is now chinked with cement.) A deep porch with a view across the lake extends across the front of the cabin. Above the mantel of the large fireplace in the living room hung an enormous moose head. The original building was three rooms: a living room, bedroom, and kitchen.

The camp was completed in February 1932, and Win Kane wrote, "I immediately snow-shoed in from Higby's with a cot and blankets on my pack basket and lived in the kitchen. It was 44 below zero that night! A cool welcome."

In addition to the main camp, Kane built a boathouse in 1934 as well as wings on the main house that accommodated a bath and dining room/kitchen. In 1938 he put up a very small one-room building, about nine-by-fourteen feet, that he called the Igloo, which could be heated by a chunk stove and used in the winter. The Igloo was planned as a guest house but was later converted into a workshop. An even smaller log house was used for guests, a garage was added in 1951, and across the cove an Adirondack open camp completed the complex.

Win Kane was active in lake affairs, serving as president of the Big Moose Property Owners Association from 1957 through 1962. During that time he was instrumental in developing a zoning ordinance for the lake.

In 1966, the Kanes, who were eligible for one of the limited houses in the Brandreth preserve, sold the property and moved to Brandreth Lake.

John "Jack" and Jeanne Taylor of Yorktown Heights, New York, were the next owners of the property. They occupied the camp with their son Jay for twenty-five years. During that time they enlarged the kitchen and made various other interior improvements. When Jack became ill, they sold the complex, retaining two lots to the west for a new camp.

Robert and Elizabeth Scher of Chagrin Falls, Ohio, bought the Polaris property in 1991.

MOOSE LODGE/GREYROCKS (LOTS 151–55.1)

A very early camp stands on the eastern shore of the lake well beyond the property owners' dock. The green-shingled two-story camp was built by the Higby family in about 1902–05. It was used as one of the Higby buildings for several years, inhabited primarily by James Higby during that time. It is the house where the Higby family lived during the few years in the early 1900s when the Higby Camp hotel was in other hands. The camp itself is hardly visible from the lake, but its distinctive, green two-story boathouse, built some ten years later, is prominent. (This boathouse was one of the ones used for Chapel services in the early days.) The lots on which the camp stands extend back across the Judson Road and Constable Creek to state land.

The second owner of this camp was James C. Griffin of Erie, Pennsylvania, who purchased the land and buildings in 1921 and named the camp Moose Lodge. He used it often and maintained a caretaker, Bernie Shriner, during some of the years of his ownership. Camp records indicate that he loved fishing and hunting, but these enthusiasms were apparently not shared by members of his family, who visited only infrequently. After his death the property was sold.

Dorothea and Kenneth Rutherford of Monticello, New York, became the third owners in 1934, changing the name to Greyrocks. Kenneth Rutherford learned about the lake when he was a scoutmaster and brought boys to the Pioneer Boy Scout Camp in its early days.[39]

The Rutherfords began visiting Big Moose Lake some five years before they bought, often renting Brookside Camp in West Bay for summer vacations. From the time of their purchase until 1958, Dorothea summered there from the last week in June until Labor Day weekend. Kenneth came for weekends and a few one-week stays scattered through each summer. In World War II, when gasoline was rationed, he came by train to Big Moose Station. During all this time the camp was accessible only by boat or by foot from the property owners' dock.

In the 1930s, a series of steps and platforms descended to the lake from the front porch of the camp, terminating in a steamboat pier extending well out into the lake. Cribbing for that pier can still be clearly seen from a boat on a calm day. The camp had a gravity-fed water system, kerosene lights, and wood heat. Parking was at the property owners' dock. The camp was very popular and was full all summer long. Sometimes an overflow of guests was accommodated in the lean-to or second story of the boathouse. Both Rutherfords were active in the Big Moose Community Chapel and were staunch supporters of the Boy Scout Camp at the east end of the lake. The camp gained electricity and was somewhat modernized after World War II. A road that started near the property owners' dock was built in the mid-1950s and shared with neighboring camps. After Kenneth's death in 1961, Dorothea continued to use the camp until her health failed in 1981. Various comforts and improvements were added during that period.

After his mother died in 1991, ownership passed to Lawson Rutherford of Penn Yann, New York. Lawson and his family use the camp often on spring and fall weekends, as well as during the summer. He and his wife, Jerry, are active in Chapel affairs and the Big Moose Property Owners Association.

ALKMAAR (LOTS 155.2–62)

Shortly after 1892, when Jim Higby bought the large tract of land for the Higby Camp, he purchased some additional lots along the southeastern shore. Higby started selling the lots in 1905. His first buyer was Albert Vander Veer, a sixty-eight-year-old retired surgeon from Albany, New York, who bought land just to the east of the house that Higby built.

A small house was already on the property, but plans for a large family camp were soon under way. An Albany architect designed a large main building, on which con-

Alkmaar, the Vander Veer camp, ca. 1915.
Courtesy of Elizabeth Vander Veer Casscells.

struction began in 1906, as well as an adjacent cottage and a grand two-story cedar-shingled boathouse. The cribbing and deck for the boathouse were built first so that lumber for the house could be brought in. The doctor named the new camp Alkmaar after the Dutch village from which Vander Veer forebears had emigrated. The existing building remained and became a caretaker's house.

Dr. Vander Veer's family spent two summers at the Glennmore Hotel while the construction was in progress. The group included his three sons, Albert, Jr., James, and Edgar (all also physicians), Edgar's wife, and Edgar's children, Grace, Albert, and Edgar, Jr. Dr. Vander Veer purchased a large launch, also called the *Alkmaar,* that he used to travel from the Glennmore to the camp in order to supervise construction.

In a memoir of their early days, recorded in 1984, Grace recalled train trips during her childhood from Albany to Big Moose Station, where they transferred to a horse-drawn carriage driven by James McAllister.[40] The children sang "Onward Christian Soldiers" to, according to Grace, "spur the horses to greater effort."

In this memoir she describes the main camp—a large, shingled structure with a wide porch on the front side that faced the lake. Inside were a spacious living room with a stone fireplace, her grandfather's study, a dining room, a large kitchen and pantry, as well as a maid's dining room and laundry. There was also a storage room for groceries, an icebox, an icehouse, and a "cooling room"—all on the main floor. Upstairs were four bedrooms with two baths, as well as three bedrooms and a bath for servants.

The boathouse housed the *Alkmaar* launch as well as assorted canoes and guideboats. Above the boathouse was a recreation room with a piano and Victrola and a small study. The second story provided space on occasion for early worship services and Sunday School.

About 1908, after the main camp had been com-

The Vander Veer boathouse, ca. 1906.
Courtesy of Wanda K. Martin.

pleted, a "cottage" was built on lots 158–62, well to the east of the main camp. Its original purpose was to house Edgar, Sr., and his wife and their three children. According to the recollections of his daughter Grace,

> it consisted of a large living room with fireplace, two bedrooms and a bath downstairs, four bedrooms and a bath upstairs and a large attic . . . it was built for my parents and their three children with the understanding that we would eat our meals at the Main Camp with my grandparents and my mother would do the housekeeping, such as planning the meals and ordering the groceries, etc.

In a letter written in 1989, Grace McDonough tells us that "In the early years George and Mary Casler were the caretaker and cook respectively and they lived in the small house that was originally on the property. In later years Will Woodard, Mrs. Casler's brother, was our caretaker.[41]

In the same letter she describes the disastrous fire that consumed the family camp in 1922:

> In April of 1922, my grandfather and his niece, Katherine Vander Veer, and a friend were in camp. One morning the Dr. built a huge fire in his bedroom fireplace and then went downstairs for breakfast. When they had finished, they heard a crackling noise upstairs. It seemed to come from the attic. Upon opening that door, they discovered the whole attic on fire! There must have been a flaw in the chimney of the upstairs fireplace. An alert was sounded, but there was no fire equipment on the lake then. A bucket brigade was formed but to no avail, and

Ruins of Alkmaar after the fire, 1922. Courtesy of Wanda K. Martin.

the whole place burned down within two hours. Grandfather lost a valuable medical library and *two* letters from Abraham Lincoln! The Dr. was a Civil War veteran.[42]

After the fire, Dr. Vander Veer and his wife moved into the cottage and employed Earl Covey to add a dining room, kitchen, two more bedrooms, a bath, laundry, and woodshed so that the whole family could be accommodated.

During the 1920s and 1930s, the family held house parties in the winter. The building was very well insulated and had a wood furnace and enormous radiators that made it snug.[43] Friends would be invited for snowshoeing, tobogganing, sledding, skiing, and even skating if the weather cooperated.[44] Elizabeth "Betsy" Casscells of West Winfield, New York, granddaughter of Edgar, Sr., is custodian of the photograph album that bears witness to these glorious winter activities.

Dr. Albert, Sr., died in 1929, leaving the two camps (the caretaker's house and the Cottage) and the property to all three sons. The complex was heavily used during the 1930s, while a new generation of children was growing up, but it was used less during World War II. Both Edgar, Sr., Dr. Albert's son, and Clarence McDonough, Jr., his son-in-law, died in 1953.

When these deaths occurred, the property was divided. Edgar, Jr., inherited the caretaker's house, which, over time, had been enlarged to accommodate his growing family. The property later passed to his three children—John, Edgar III, and Betsy Casscells—some of whom have deeded their shares to their own children. After John's retirement, he and his late wife, Diane, lived there for an entire year before building a winter home off the Big Moose Road near Covewood with full road access in all seasons. John has since deeded his interest in the family camp to his daughters, Patricia and her husband, Frank Zamperlin, and Barbara and her husband, Jeffrey Walter. Edgar III and his late wife, Marie, had one child, Valerie (now also a part owner of the camp), married to Robert Baldes. Betsy also retains a part interest in the camp, although she and her husband now have their own camp on the southeast shore (lots 167–68).

When the property was split in 1953, Grace and her brother Albert became joint owners of the Cottage. Grace bought her brother's share in 1957 to become its sole owner. Thereafter, she modified it to suit her small family and also built a separate boathouse. In 1987, Grace deeded her camp to her only son, Clarence McDonough, and his wife, Marianne, of Williamstown, Massachusetts, who are the current owners.

WITCH-HOPPLE LODGE (LOT 174)

Harry Swancott and Edith Swancott of Utica, New York, were the first owners of this camp. Harry was the son of Harry Swancott, Sr., one of the original owners of the camp on the North Shore that later belonged to the Colpitts/Menand family. The younger Swancotts built their camp in the early 1920s and appropriated the name Witch-Hopple Lodge, the name of Harry's parents' camp across the lake. Harry worked for the Utica Transit Company and was a good friend of Fordyce Lux, who in 1928 purchased property on the North Shore from Hobe Casler. The Swancotts had one son, who died young. Thereafter they sold the camp so that it could be used and enjoyed by a young family.

The new owners are William and Marlene Humphrey of Liverpool, New York, who bought the camp in 1967.

THE CASLER CAMP (LOT 175)

This lot originally had been part of the Vander Veer family tract and was conveyed by Albert, Sr. to his former caretaker, George Casler, in 1921. George transferred it to his brother Hobart in 1922.

Hobe Casler built a small hunting camp set back 200 feet from the lakeshore. The original camp consisted of a living room and kitchen on the first floor with a loft above. The porch may have been added later. A few years afterward Hobe acquired a camp on the North Shore, the one he later sold to Fordyce Lux in 1928 and which is now owned by Donald Lux.

The Casler brothers were noted fishermen, hunters, and guides. Don Lux recalls that, until Hobe left the lake in the mid-1930s, he often guided for Don's father, Fordyce Lux.

In 1974 the camp was bought by "Dutch" Ray and his wife, Dorothy. After Dutch's death in 1984, Dorothy married Donald Murphy and they retained the camp for another ten years. Many Big Moosers will remember the Irish flag that used to fly at the waterfront when the Murphys were in camp.

Liz and John Jaenike bought the property in 1994 but were at the lake only a few years before a job change forced a move to Tucson, Arizona.

In December 1999, Gary and Norrine Thibault of Skaneateles, New York, purchased the camp.

THE RASBACH CAMP (LOTS 188–91)

In 1932, Daniel Ford Rasbach and his wife, Alice, became the first landowners in East Bay when they purchased two lots (lots 188–89) from Robert G. Harry. Four additional lots (lots 186–87 and 190–91) were added in 1950. Ford Rasbach died in 1965 and Alice in 1984. The tract is now owned by their daughter Jean and her husband, Richard L. Scholet, of Richmondville, New York.

Jean recalls attending many informal parties and campfires at the neighboring Boy Scout Camp throughout her girlhood, and she fondly remembers the construction of her own family camp:

George and Hobart Casler, guides and caretakers, ca. 1930. Courtesy of Donald Lux.

A one-room camp with loft was built around 1936, during the Depression, by my Dad and his friend, Rube Tuttle from Mohawk. Trees on the property were felled with a two-man saw around 1934, the logs peeled and then wired together, two by two, and then towed to [Earl] Covey's saw mill. I was a little girl then, and I remember riding in the boat. It took almost all day to get the logs positioned and towed . . . by a small rowboat rented from Higby's, using my Dad's 2½ horsepower motor, which we still have. After they were sawed into lumber, the boards had to be towed back and were stacked to season.

The original camp was only twelve by sixteen feet. Windows and doors were scavenged from a Remington Arms plant in Ilion. My Dad, who was learning carpentry as he built, had no power tools.

Just before World War II, he added an open porch and purchased the lumber and windows to enclose it. However, he was unable to do this until after the war ended, as he was not able to get to Big Moose due to gas rationing.

By 1956, Dick and I had been married ten years and had three children. Quarters in the camp were very tight for seven people, so Dad added the kitchen (1955 and 1956). This almost doubled the size of the camp! Furnishings, including our big stove (combined wood and gas) were brought to camp in Frank Siegenthaler's scow, *Slowpoke*.

We came to camp by boat, until 1968 when we tied into the Judson Road; we installed electricity at that time. Our camp is pretty much the same now as it was in early days—still one of the very few camps on the lake without running water! We did bring lake water to our tool house in 1992, and installed a hot water heater and a large outdoor shower. We also put in a large floating dock in 1992.

Two Early Camps at the Eastern Head of the Lake

Two of the earliest camps at Big Moose stand at the eastern head of the lake, each perched on a scenic peninsula. The camps are Old Pine Point (adjacent to East Bay) and

Deerlands (adjacent to the Inlet) and were both built in the 1880s, before William Seward Webb owned the land. The occupants were squatters, without legal ownership of the land on which their houses stood. Later, when Webb bought the property, the occupants each arranged short-term leases.

In 1902 lumberman Theodore Page of Echo Island purchased from Webb a large tract of land, most of which was to be used for logging. However, the peninsulas (which were a part of the tract) were exempted from Page's logging contracts.[45]

OLD PINE POINT (LOTS 213–17)

Irvin A. Williams (unrelated to his neighbor Frank Williams on the peninsula to the north) was the builder of the house on the neighboring peninsula close to East Bay. Williams had gained prominence as the inventor of a locomotive headlight. (See page 15.) When Webb bought the land in the 1890s, Irvin Williams secured an option (negotiated through Thistlethwaite, Webb's agent, and the contract between Ouderkirk and Strobel) to purchase the point.

However, when Page became the owner in 1902, he refused to honor the option to buy that Webb had previously given. Although Page did renew a short-term lease,[46] in 1904, Irvin Williams was forced to institute a lawsuit to compel Page to sell him the land upon which Williams had already built a house and made other improvements. The case between the two men, each of whom had plenty of money to spend on it, went through many innings in the courts, lasted at least two years, and was finally resolved in Williams's favor.[47]

For many years, "Headlight" Williams kept a light on his dock, inspiring local residents to dub the land Headlight Point. The Woodbury family at Camp Edilgra on the North Shore later acquired the lamp and used it on their dock for many years.

When Irvin Williams died in 1912, his youngest son, Aras J. Williams, inherited not only his father's share of the business but also the elaborate building that his father had constructed with lumber from pine trees on the site. In 1917, Aras Williams purchased the entire peninsula (lots 213–17) from Mrs. Page and renamed the area Old Pine Point. Aras became a prominent member of the Big Moose Property Owners Association and was particularly active during the late 1920s.

Camp at Old Pine Point, 1903. Courtesy of the Big Moose Property Owners Association.

In 1938, Aras Williams's widow sold Old Pine Point to Mr. and Mrs. Benjamin E. Tilton. Formerly members of the Adirondack League Club, they had rented a camp at Little Moose Lake, where motor boats were banned and which they deemed too quiet. They preferred the less restricted boating at Big Moose and purchased from Kinne's Boat Line a mahogany Chris-Craft named *Caroline*, which their descendants still use.

Irvin Williams's original cabin, consisting of a single room, still exists and was used for many years as a back-

Locomotive headlight similar to that invented by Irvin Williams. Note hinged glass, hollow metal wick, outlet for smoke and concave reflective back surface. Courtesy of Jane Barlow.

kitchen; it was recently remodeled into a game room. The boathouse was built in 1922, and its second floor was winterized in 1971 by Joe Dunn.

In their early summers, the Tiltons brought a full staff with them for cooking, cleaning, and maintenance, and they encouraged their children and grandchildren to spend whole summers at the Point in order to avoid exposure to polio.

When Mrs. Tilton died in 1969, daughter Mary and her husband, Harold T. Clark, became the owners of Old Pine Point. By 1966, the elder Clarks had moved into the small guest cottage and deeded the main camp to their four children. The children subdivided it into plots around 1970, and Ben was the first to build a new camp, facing Rocky Bay on lot 216.

H. Thomas Clark, Jr., of Fayetteville, New York, became sole owner of the main camp at Old Pine Point in 1971. In 1985, after his brother Ben moved south, he purchased Ben's home for use as a guesthouse and now owns lots 215 and 216.

Lucy Clark Popkess, Tom's sister, and her husband, Alfred, occupy the neighboring camp (built by Joe Dunn in 1981 and still on the original Clark property), on lot 214 on East Bay. Lucy's second lot, lot 217, faces the bay between the two peninsulas known as Rocky Bay.

DEERLANDS (LOT 219)

The camp Lakeview that the guides Jack Sheppard and Richard Crego had built for Frank Williams stood just south of the main inlet to Big Moose Lake. Bill Marleau

Deerlands, view from west, 1938. Courtesy of Ann Dunn Hall.

indicates that Lakeview was later renamed Deerlands.[48] The old Lakeview fishing diary found in the Deerlands camp by a later owner indicates that it was in use at least as early as 1882.[49] However, in the absence of land records it is impossible to be sure.

This camp was built in a palisade style. It had two sto-ries, a porch facing the lake, and various outbuildings and sheds. A large cement dock and a commodious boat-house, later additions that are still in use today, faced the main lake. Old-timers at Big Moose remember the camp as a very comfortable and attractive log cabin.

When Theodore Page died in 1916, his wife, Kate McCallum Page, inherited the property. After her death in 1921, she left the peninsula jointly to her two nieces, sisters Katherine Dayton and Ruth Dayton Greenwood, who gave the camp the name Deerlands.

Ruth and her husband, Joseph, were one of the first families on the lake to own a Chris-Craft motorboat, which they named the *Natty Bumppo* after the hero of James Fennimore Cooper's *The Leatherstocking Tales*. Joseph was active in the Property Owners Association and served as president until his death in March 1934 cut short his term. Ruth knew the residents of the lake well and was beloved for her thoughtfulness. Her letter to Katherine Martin Vollenweider, daughter of Charles and Alice Martin, about the steps at the Chapel built in Alice's memory, conveys her affection for her friends and neighbors.

Ruth's sister, Katherine Dayton, was a writer of some repute and built a small studio on the shore of Rocky Bay around 1940.

View from the north of Deerlands, built in 1880. Date of photograph unknown. Courtesy of Ann Dunn Hall.

LETTER TO KATHERINE MARTIN VOLLENWEIDER FROM RUTH GREENWOOD

October 16, 1949

Dear Katherine,

I don't know whether you have heard about the steps which were built this summer as a memorial to your mother, so tho't I'd send a line to tell you about them.

You know, of course, we've wanted to do this for a long time, but have had one setback after another. I am trying to get a picture of these steps to send you and I will soon. Charlie Dunn and his boys have done a fine job, I think. He has been very interested in the work and now wants to cut the inscription on the upper step himself as his personal contribution.

The steps run from the dock all the way up the hill. We have hung over them from the first of August not always sure in our own minds what they should look like and finding our way as the work went along. Sometime I'll have to give you the details—there were bad moments and good; many emergencies due to low water which would take the men away to dip wells, etc. Oh, I thought we'd never get them done in time for the dedication August 14th. We didn't, but enough were ready so people could imagine what was to come. The stone came from up near the [Canadian] border and there were some three trips for it, I think. It is a lovely color, pinkish and greenish in places with a little of the native stone at the water end. On the top slab which is on the lawn at the side of the Chapel the inscription will be cut—"In memory of Alice L. Martin." Your father thought this sufficient.

Those who contributed to the memorial are Mr. and Mrs. Jeffress, Mrs. Gamble, Miss Young, and myself. We did not ask anyone—these people all wanted to do this. I'm sure others will feel they were left out—it just hap-pened this way and little was said of it all till it was finished. It is not known who the contributors are—I am just telling. Even your father doesn't know.

Some pulpit chairs were given by Mrs. Calloway for her husband and these steps for your mother by some of her friends among the summer people. I think I have a copy of what Dr. Holloway [the Chapel minister] said [at the dedication]:

"Mrs. Charles Martin who made her home on Big Moose, was a rare person. She was a good neighbor in the highest sense and all who knew her loved her for her bright spirit and her sense of humor and her kindness and her real desire for service. She gave much to this Chapel in the years of its creation and after, serving as treasurer until her death in July of 1945. She was gifted in inspiring interest and zeal for work for the Chapel and her passing has left a great void in our midst.

"Her knowledge of the local flowers and ferns and moss and birds and all growing things bro't joy to many of the summer residents and it is with very real affection that today they make this gift in her memory. This path leads down the hill to the dock where her boat so often landed to bring her to this place of worship."

I hope so much you will like what we have done. All of us feel so much affection for your mother we are happy to have these steps as a token of that feeling. We want now to do a little planting, but that must wait until spring, I think.

We have missed you and Bob this summer. I hope all goes well and that it won't be too long till you get North again.

I think we must leave by Thursday and *I don't want to*.

Please give all my best wishes to Bob and special love to you, my dear, from

Ruth Greenwood

In 1956, Edward Dunn (youngest brother of Walter, Charles, and Nelson Dunn) and his wife, Margaret, bought the Deerlands property after Ruth Greenwood's death. The following year Ed composed a poem entitled "Deerlands," which touchingly expressed his love for the place; the sixth verse also stated his conviction that at least part of the camp dated from the 1880s.

The main camp was destroyed by fire in the spring of 1964, at a time of year when it was completely inaccessible. The ice was still in, but not strong enough to support weight and not thin enough to allow boats to cross. Residents across the lake watched helplessly as the house burned. The fire was later attributed to trappers who had been in the Inlet some days earlier and were thought to have camped in or near the main camp. Remnants of their campfire probably smoldered in the duff for several days after they thought it had been extinguished. The guest camp that had been Katharine Dayton's studio and boathouse were not damaged, except for the power lines and water system. The little power house that

"DEERLANDS" [S1] | *Composed by Edward Dunn, Martin, Michigan, January 15, 1967 (selected verses)*

1.
I'll take my Dear to Deerlands
In those mountains far away
That cool, delightful haven
Through summers we will stay.

3.
We love it up at Deerlands
By the Inlet and East Bay
Where the beauty of the evening
Caps the breezes of the day.

5.
The shoreline oh so lovely
The pines so straight and high
The air so crisp and bracing
Where memories never die.

6.
The main camp dates to '80
Many stories it could tell
Of those who came distracted
Went home all gay and well.

housed the bank of batteries and a generator still stands today.

In 1986, Ann and Joe Dunn bought the property from Ed Dunn's widow Margaret and renovated the studio house. Several years after Joe died in 1988, Ann married Robert Hall, and they now occupy the property.

The Northern Side of the Main Lake

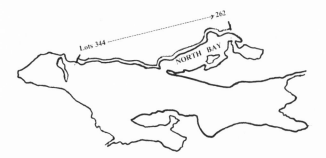

The following early camps are all located on the north side of Big Moose Lake. The listing starts with Rowan-

wood, the first camp beyond Owl's Nest, and continues eastward to the Inlet. Because this section moves clockwise around the lake, unlike the listings in the previous section, the lot numbers run backwards. They are given so that it will be easy to find information on the current residents of the camp in Appendix A.

CAMP ROWANWOOD (LOTS 326W–44)

One camp on the northern shore dating from the early 1920s was built because of the lumbering interests of its owner, J. Munson Gamble. Mr. Gamble owned a paper mill in Brownville, New York, and lived in nearby Watertown with his wife, Blanche, and their six children. Mr. Gamble also owned woodlots near Big Moose Lake, managed by Clarence Strife. When Mr. Gamble visited the woodlots, he liked the area so much that, beginning in 1917, he began bringing the Gamble family to the lake for vacations at Lake View Lodge. In 1922, Mr. Gamble purchased from Theodore Page's heirs an extensive parcel of land across the lake from the hotel. He designed the spacious building himself and had an architect draw up formal plans. Frank Martin built the structure, along with a boathouse, an icehouse, a building for the Delco generating plant, a coal shed, and a woodshed.

The house was situated in a small cove that faced southeast on the western end of the property. Gamble named the camp Rowanwood, another name for the mountain ash tree that is common around the lake. The artist David Milne depicted the house in several paintings while he was a summer resident (see chapter 5, pages 141–43). Especially notable is "Black House No. 1, 1925." [50] Milne also created "Painting Place," a work often considered his masterpiece and certainly one of his most famous works, on the Gamble property from a vantage high on the hill overlooking the lake. [51] Gracie Quimby Flock, Mr. Gamble's granddaughter, writes, "[My mother], the youngest daughter said there wasn't a lot of social life, as a young man would have to paddle over from Lake View to ask her out, return to Lake View, then paddle over again [to take her out] and finally paddle across a third time to take her home. She was very relieved when the road was put through."

Not so her father! In 1931, E. J. Martin of the Waldheim had written to Munson Gamble about buying a right-of-way across the property so that his guests could have access by road. In answer to his request, Mr. Gamble wrote,

KATHARINE DAYTON

Katharine Dayton, a New York City journalist who often visited her sister Ruth Dayton Greenwood at Deerlands, collaborated with the well-known playwright George S. Kaufman on a comedy that was a hit of the 1935–36 Broadway season. Kaufman had written many popular plays and musicals and would in 1937 receive a Pulitzer Prize for *You Can't Take It with You*, which opened in 1936. *The Man Who Came to Dinner* was still three years in the future. Kaufman's and Dayton's three-act comedy was called *First Lady*, a satirical look at the rivalry between the wives of two government officials who each wants her husband to be president so that she can become first lady. The play opened at the Music Box theater and starred Jane Cowl and Lily Cahill.

In an article in the *New York Times* headlined "It Must be Such Fun to Work with Kaufman,"[51] Dayton comments, "It is not, in a word, fun to work with George Kaufman—but it is work being funny with him." She continues:

What a girl needs to collaborate with George Kaufman is not so much a play or an idea as it is a lot of patience and at least two pairs of old, comfortable shoes . . . I used three sets of new heels and toes. This, mind you, was only a light comedy. They tell me, too that there is no real cure for dramatist's foot. The theory, I believe, is that you get it walking around on bared souls . . . The truth is that George Kaufman does his best writing walking around . . . For five hours we walked and we walked and we walked around my small apartment, setting *objects d'art*

shivering and jingling, sending the canary . . . into frenzied roulades.

Then George said, "Well, I'm going to Palm Springs to write 'Merrily We Roll Along' with Moss Hart, but I'll be back next May. Good-bye." He thereby disclosed his second maddening trait.

. . . There is nothing George Kaufman loves so much as doing the thing he isn't doing at the moment, no matter what it is.

Furthermore, she wrote, "[A year later, George said] 'I'm going to Hollywood to do a Marx brothers picture. Good-bye.' There followed a long dry Summer in which the wind soughed through the Adirondack pines 'itmustbesuchfuntoworkwithgeorgekaufman' and telegraph wires vibrated to such cheery messages as ' . . . am delayed three weeks longer.' "

Finally, she concludes, "But I shouldn't dream of doing another play with him for anything in this world—not, that is, unless he asked me."

Katharine, born in 1891, wrote for magazines and newspapers, discussing contemporary political topics in a sharp and witty style. She wrote a series entitled "Mrs. Democrat and Mrs. Republican" for the *Saturday Evening Post* and was a Washington correspondent for the North American Newspaper Alliance. Her only other venture into drama was a play entitled *Save Me the Waltz*, which opened at the Martin Beck Theatre in February 1938 and ran for only a week.[52]

Katharine died in 1945 at the age of fifty-four after a brief illness.

I do not want to sell my right of way or give any agreement in regard to the road across my property. As you know, I objected to having a road built in the first place as I did not want the public able to go through there, and I still feel the same about this. Of course, you went ahead and built this road without obtaining permission from me. You blasted rocks which went through my roof, broke windows, etc. You cut down trees, and all of this without my permission. I did not want to make any objection because I saw that it would be a benefit to your hotel and, therefore, said nothing about it, but I can not consider selling my right of way or making any agreement about a road across my property.[52]

This irate response did not prevent the road from being further developed, and eventually a three-car shed garage was built on the hill above the camp. However, Mr. Gamble's granddaughter writes, "Grandfather developed heart trouble and the doctor would not allow him to climb up and down the hill, so a small shed garage was placed by the camp. His was the only car allowed down the hill."[53]

Grace Gamble was the only one of the six Gamble children to retain an interest in the lake, her brothers and sisters having found other interests in the St. Lawrence and Lake Ontario areas. Grace married Howard Quimby in 1930. They had two children, Howard, Jr., and Grace. J. Munson Gamble died in 1942, and his wife, Blanche, died in 1959. Mrs. Gamble had ceased to come to the camp at some point after 1946. Grace Gamble Quimby reopened the camp in 1949 and continued to spend her summers at the lake. She became an active member of the community and of the Big Moose Community Chapel in particular. When it became unwise to leave the church building open at night, Grace would personally unlock the door in the morning and make sure it was secured at night. She was very talented at crafts and flower arranging, and for several years she chaired the annual church bazaar. Until about 1976, she spent much of her time at Big Moose, staying through until November to vote.

Grace's daughter, "Gracie," married Gilbert Flock in the Chapel in 1962. They had three children: Gilbert, Jr., Greg, and Jeni. The Flocks ran a flower shop and greenhouse in Clark Mills, New York, for fifteen years and spent as much time as possible at the lake during that time. Gracie's brother, Howard Quimby, now divorced, has three sons: William, Peter, and Michael.

When Grace Gamble Quimby died in 1988, the property passed to her children, Gracie and Howard. They sold parts of it to others outside the family. Bret and Beth Long of Greenwich, Connecticut, bought the original house and a large stretch of lakeside property that reaches up the hill beyond the road to state land (lots 335–44). Peter and Barbara Kelly and William and Kathleen Simpson each bought several lots to the east.

On the remaining land at the east end of the original parcel, Gracie Flock, now widowed, and Howard Quimby, grandchildren of Munson Gamble, have built year-round houses and become permanent Big Moose residents. Gracie's house is near the road but overlooking the lake; she has a floating boathouse and dock. Howard's house is just above the road at a spot where he sat as a boy and remarked what a great place it would be to build a home.

SIX EARLY CAMPS NEAR THE WALDHEIM

Five prewar camps stand to the west of the Waldheim property and one, now absorbed into the Waldheim itself, once stood on the east side. Wanda Kinne Martin has researched their history, tracking numerous changes of ownership through the deed books in the Herkimer County Courthouse. Many of these early families took their meals at the Waldheim and maintained close ties with the hotel.

DUN ROMIN (LOTS 322–25)

After Theodore Page died in 1916, his widow, Kate McCallum Page, sold much of their holdings. These three lots, 322–25, were purchased by the actress Minnie Maddern Fiske in 1921 when she bought Echo Island. In 1934, Harrison Fiske sold the property to Seward and Ethel Spoor. Mr. Spoor was the assistant district attorney for Nassau County at that time. They had two daughters, Doris and Caryl. Doris had a fine voice and gave generously of her time and talent to the fledgling choir at church. She married Gene Mather, a local boy from Old Forge. Gene served as a pilot during World War II and flew the Berlin Airlift during the Cold War that followed. Caryl married a young man from the Philippines.

In 1935, Seward Spoor hired Nelson Dunn, Sr., to build a camp for him using peeled logs from this area, from plans drawn up by Romaine Kinne. They named their place Dun Romin after the names of the two men involved with its construction. When they purchased a Chris-Craft, they maintained tradition and named it *Dun Rowin*.

When the Spoors sold the camp in 1954, the Steinhausens from Rochester, New York, who had been guests at the Waldheim for several years, and their friends, Bill and Eleanor Morris, bought the camp jointly. Bill Morris was a trial lawyer in Rochester. He and Eleanor had three children, twin girls Ann and Betsy, and a son, Thomas. At a later date, the Steinhausens bought the Morrises out and became sole owners.

Frame of the Roosevelt Camp, ca. 1910. Courtesy of Wanda K. Martin.

Childhood sweethearts, Theodore Behn "Pete" Steinhausen and Jane Wolcott were married in June 1940. Pete, a radiologist, and Jane, a registered nurse, both participated in Scouts during their children's younger years and were also active members of their church. At the time of Pete's death in June 1999, they had been married fifty-nine years.

THE CHARLES MARTIN HOUSE (LOTS 319–21)

The large house that stands along the shore in the shelter of the high cliff behind it belonged for most of its existence to E. J. Martin's brother, Charles. The two men were the builders, although it was originally constructed for someone else.

ROOSEVELT/INSLEY/TRAVERSE CAMP (LOTS 315–18)

On the land side of an enormous glacial erratic that sits at the water's edge is carved the name "J. Roosevelt" (See illustration on page 2). Near this site, John Ellis Roosevelt, a cousin of and personal secretary to President Theodore Roosevelt, camped for a time. In December 1899 he purchased four lots west of the Waldheim from the Ne-Ha-Sa-Ne Park Association. He then built Camp Roosevelt, a bare-bones, temporary structure consisting of several posts supporting a roof with no walls. (It is possible that canvas sides were used when the camp was inhabited.)

Teddy Roosevelt relied on his cousin John a great deal, as evidenced by a number of business letters now in the collection of Pennsylvania State University. But there was also a familial bond. Teddy Roosevelt called his cousin "Jack." When John married Nannie Vance in 1879, the future president was involved in the wedding. While there is no record of Teddy Roosevelt ever visiting Big Moose Lake, he was in the area several times while he was governor of New York, and it is hard to imagine the great outdoorsman passing up the hospitality of his cousin.

When Teddy Roosevelt became president, it seems that John's duties kept him away from his Big Moose property, and he decided to sell it. In a letter to E. J. Martin dated January 1903, John Roosevelt wrote, "As I am not able to use the property much I would sell the same and will, of course, pay a commission in case you could secure for me a purchaser. Before naming any price, I wish to know how property in that neighborhood is selling. If you can give me any information I shall be much obliged."[54]

Apparently, lakefront property did not move quickly in those days, and it did not change hands until Charles Williams bought the entire parcel in 1908. In 1911, Mr. Williams was able to sell lot 315 to Mrs. Clara B. Ogden, who had a camp next door. Not until 1929 were the remaining three lots sold to Mr. and Mrs. William H. Insley of Indianapolis, Indiana.

Mr. Insley, head of the Insley Manufacturing Company, was an industrialist who had invented the first small power shovels. Although he and his wife owned the nearby property, they stayed for many years in a cottage at the Waldheim, where Mr. Insley spent countless hours drawing up plans for the very compact cabin he intended to build.

At last, in 1952, the cabin was built. In the meantime, Mr. Insley and E. J. had developed a close relationship in which each had ample opportunity to exercise his wit. Even after the cabin was complete the Insleys continued to take their main meals at the hotel dining room. Mr. Insley never failed to invite the Waldheim staff to his lean-to for an evening of popcorn and marshmallows.

The property eventually passed to the Insleys' son Francis and his wife, Lois. They spent many summers enjoying the peace and quiet after the bustling pace of Indianapolis winters. They, too, took main meals at the Waldheim, where they found a large circle of friends with whom they hiked and played cards and chess. In their later years, their daughter, Elizabeth, accompanied them as chauffeur and cook. She and her husband, Alfred Traverse of Huntingdon, Pennsylvania, now own the property.

OGDEN/GRAUERT CAMP (LOTS 314–15)

As early as 1903, E. J. Martin was buying feed for his livestock from the Ogden Feed and Grain Company in Utica, and this may be how the Ogdens came to know Big Moose Lake.

In March 1907, E. J. and Hattie Martin sold a lot at the west edge of the Waldheim property to Clara B. Ogden, wife of F. C. Ogden. In April, E. J. and his crew began work on a camp that was nearly ready for occupancy on July 2. The Ogdens moved in for the summer on July 4, naming the camp Karyankoo. For many years, the Ogdens purchased most of their groceries from the Waldheim and dined there frequently as well. In 1911 they purchased the neighboring lot to the west from Charles Williams, owner of Lake View Lodge. Mrs. Ogden, perhaps a widow by then but obviously concerned with the lake environment, was part of the group that in 1914 hired the lawyer Theodore Cross to attempt (unsuccessfully) to block the Bissell and Yousey Lumber Company from building a sawmill on the North Shore. Some years after Mr. Ogden's death, Clara Ogden married a Mr. Putnam, and they continued to use the camp until 1929.

In that year, the property was sold to Mrs. Anna Marvin, who brought along not only her daughter but also her two lively grandsons. The boys, Charles and Marvin Langley, became friends with the Martin sons, Carl Otto, Jr., and the Bruyn brothers. Water sports were their specialty, and they kept things stirred up on the north side of the lake. The Langley family has maintained ties with the Waldheim for more than seventy years.

After Mrs. Marvin sold the property in 1950, a series of short-term owners followed. David Davis of Springwater, Massachusetts, bought the camp from Mrs. Marvin, selling it two years later to Barney and Betty Barnum. The cottage had seven bedrooms, and the Barnums rented rooms and ran it as a small hotel. Although the Barnums stayed only a short time, selling to Corson Castle in 1954, they remained on the lake and became active year-round residents. Castle owned the camp for the next ten years.

Dr. Hans J. Grauert from Rochester, New York, long-time guest in the 1950s and 1960s at both the Twitchell Lake Inn and Covewood Lodge, purchased the property from the Castles in 1964. Grauert changed the name of the camp to Camp Hamburg, after the name of his native city in Germany. An Adirondack enthusiast, he and his wife, Leila, enjoyed entertaining, often socializing with the founder of the Adirondack Museum, Harold Hochschild, who was Leila Grauert's high school classmate in New York City. Hans Grauert died in 1969, leaving the camp to his two sons, Chris and Alex.

Chris and Alex rented out the camp each summer until 1978, at which time Chris assumed full ownership of the property.

ROBY/KAISER CAMP (LOTS 312w–13)

Many families have come to Big Moose as guests at one of the lake's hotels, only to fall in love with the place and put down roots. Some of the earliest were three families who frequented the Waldheim.

William S. Roby of Rochester, New York, first signed the Waldheim register on July 26, 1906. One year later Roby had acquired a wife, and a Mr. and Mrs. William S. Roby signed in, as well as Mr. Clark Spoor of New York City (not related to the Spoors of Dun Romin).[55] Later, Mr. Henry Pagani and family joined the annual roster of friends who had met at the Waldheim. William Sterling Roby, Jr., was a newcomer in July 1913.

On July 18, 1918, Mr. Roby wrote to Mr. Martin confirming his reservation with these words: "We will be with you on the evening of July 26th, God and the Kaiser willing."[56] During the same summer, the three families arranged with E. J. Martin to lease one-half of his lot 312 and all of lot 313 for a period of ten years. These lots were part of the Martin property and stood next to the Waldheim. E. J. was to erect a cottage on this property for $2,900, and they would pay him $60 a year (to include upkeep and a water supply).

Construction began in October, and by July 4, 1919, a large camp was ready for occupancy. It contained four large bedrooms, a sizable living room with a massive fireplace, and a spacious verandah commanding a beautiful view of the lake. It was promptly named Mañana.

In 1923, Henry Pagani assigned his interest to Mr. Spoor. The Robys and the Spoors continued to eat their meals at the Waldheim, which kept separate accounts for each family and another separate account for Mañana.

In 1929, the Spoors and the Robys purchased the property from the Martins. In 1951, after the death of Mr. Spoor, Mrs. Spoor conveyed her interest in the camp to William Roby, Jr.

During World War II, there was an arrangement with E. J. Martin, whereby he could use the camp to accommodate some of his guests in July and August. In return he was to maintain the property.

After this, the young Roby family made good use of the camp during the 1950s and 1960s. During the '50s, the boathouse, with its charming apartment upstairs, was built for Mr. and Mrs. William Starr. Mrs. Starr was the widow of the elder William S. Roby. They found that the proximity of the Waldheim dining room made it easier for them to enjoy their summers there.

When the Starrs were no longer able to come to the lake, Bill Roby, Jr., and his wife, Mary, stayed in the boathouse and allowed their lively teenage children and their friends to use Mañana.

The Leslie W. Brown Camp, ca. 1910.
Courtesy of Wanda K. Martin.

In 1973, William S. Roby, Jr., sold the property to Albert D. Kaiser, Jr., of Rochester, New York, who, a year later, made his wife, Margaret, a joint owner. Since the Kaisers have owned it, many repairs and improvements have been made.

THE LESLIE WARNICK BROWN CAMP
(LOTS 262–302)

Leslie Warnick Brown, a prosperous tobacco dealer in Utica, New York, was among the very first to buy property on Big Moose Lake. Although he owned an extensive amount of land and put up an elaborate complex of buildings, his name is memorialized today only in Brown's Rock, the bald spot high above the lake reached by a trail from the Waldheim.

In 1900, Mr. Brown purchased forty lots that stretched from close to where the Waldheim beach is today (on the west side of the entrance to North Bay) all the way into the narrowest part of the bay where state land begins. The purchase included the tiny island at the entrance to the bay. Together, he and Dr. Retter owned most of the land around North Bay.

E. J. and Charles Martin built a very large camp for Leslie and Anne Brown and their five lively children. We know that the camp was in use as early as the summer of 1900, because Lena Retter mentions in her diary for that year exchanging visits with the family. Later, the Browns owned a large launch called the *Frances*.

Buildings on the land included not only the main house but also a boathouse on the main lake (called the "launch house") with a very long wooden dock, known for years at the Waldheim as the "Long Dock," that enabled the steamboat to deliver passengers and supplies. Another boathouse, now the Waldheim's Whipsaw Cottage, faced North Bay and was used for guideboats and canoes. Other buildings included a large woodshed (now Ivy Cottage), a playhouse for the children (now demolished but once the Waldheim's one-room Dream Cottage), and an icehouse. In addition, there must have been

The living room of the Leslie W. Brown Camp,
ca. 1901. Courtesy of Wanda K. Martin.

Mrs. Leslie W. Brown and family, ca. 1903.
Courtesy of Wanda K. Martin.

a shed or barn for the cow they kept to provide milk for the children.

The Browns' guide and handyman was Dan Ainsworth. The family enjoyed tramps in the woods, and an old photo shows them with pack baskets ready to start on a hike.

The idyllic days were not to last, however. Anne Brown died about 1917. Their son Randolph, age twenty-three, joined the army in World War I and was killed in action in France four days before the Armistice in 1918. After these tragedies, the Browns spent less time at the lake and in 1920 sold the property to Charles Williams of Lake View Lodge.

Williams lumbered the area behind North Bay in the winter of 1920–21, building the lumber camp shown on page 125. He retained the undeveloped land and continued to lumber it until 1938, hauling the logs for firewood across the ice to his hotel.

Late in 1921, Williams sold the residential area of the land to one Frederick Tipson, who held it for three years before selling it to Frank and Amelia Naporski in 1924. The Naporskis, once caretakers for Minnie Maddern Fiske, had operated the Fiskes' Camp Veery as a resort for two summers but had been asked to leave. They named their new camp Veery's Nest, changing their own names to Veery, but were never successful. (The story of the fire that destroyed the camp and the financial arrangements

that made the land part of the Waldheim are told elsewhere in this book.)

The Browns continued to visit the lake occasionally, registering at Camp Crag for four days of fishing in 1922. In September 1930, some of the family planned a hunting trip and arranged for their loyal guide Dan Ainsworth to meet them at the train. On September 20, they arrived at Big Moose Station but Dan was not there to meet them. He had left home at 4:30 or 5:00 in the morning, having eaten a big breakfast, to take two large pack baskets of supplies to Andes Creek. He rowed his guideboat up the lake in thick fog and was never heard from again. Searchers found his body in about eight feet of water near the mouth of the Inlet at about 8:00 that night. No one can be sure of what happened. Although Dan could swim, he was not a strong swimmer, and he was carrying a heavy load in a fragile boat. Some think that he may have hit one of the standing anchor logs that the lumber company had left in the lake to hold booms for confining cut logs. It was a tragedy that would never be explained.

Ann Brown Frost, the youngest of the children who had summered at the camp, often came to the lake for the day to swim, picnic, and visit her childhood friend, Grace Vander Veer McDonough. Anne died in 1996. Her obituary in the Utica newspaper read, "She loved sports and nature, especially her family camp in Big Moose."[57]

The North Shore

The North Shore of Big Moose Lake encompasses the land from the entrance to North Bay, stretching east to the marshes around the channel to the Inlet. Much of the shoreline boasts a sandy beach, and its orientation catches the morning sun. Privacy of the residents is enhanced by the lack of road access. Many of the current North Shore residents who roamed the woods as children know intimately the surrounding hills and hollows.

Some of the earliest camps on the lake stood on the North Shore, and a majority of them are still owned by descendants of the original families. Perhaps because of this fact, we have an unusual amount of material in the form of memoirs and reminiscences. The experiences of many residents parallel those of others, so we have included the accounts given to us without much concern about balancing the stories from other parts of the lake. We are particularly grateful to Henry Bruyn, whose long, unpublished memoir has given us a vivid picture not only of his own family but also of others on the North Shore and around the lake.

While electricity came to most of the lake in 1929, much of the North Shore depended on generators. Eventually, probably in the late 1930s, a group of residents persuaded the power company to extend an underwater line from the Waldheim property to the North Bay side of Turtle Point, as the west end of the North Shore is called. The line carried electricity as far as the Woodbury/Wertz camp. Telephone service was added even later, arriving in the late 1960s. Before telephones were available, family members or guests arriving at the property owners' dock near Higby's sat in their cars and blasted their horns (each camp had a different sequence of longs and shorts) until their hosts heard the signal and came by boat to fetch them. Four long blasts, for instance, brought a Wertz to the rescue. On days that the wind blew in the wrong direction or for those who were heading to the farthest end of the North Shore, the wait could be a long one. Olive Crawe Wertz remembers her mother, Grace Woodbury Crawe, who, when she thought she heard a horn, would cry, "Hark! Hark!"

In 1899, Arwed Retter bought a large stretch of land extending east from Turtle Point at the entrance to North Bay to the Totten and Crossfield Line (lots 241–49). He kept a generous amount for his own family and sold the remaining lots to six other families. The portion of the North Shore that extends beyond the Totten and Crossfield Line (lots 227–40) up to the wetlands near the Inlet was once owned by the Bissell and Yousey Lumber Company. Of the eight camps in this area, six were built before World War II but after World War I when the lumber company ceased operations.

NORTH SHORE, WEST END
ON-DA-WA (LOT 249)

The land on which stands the cluster of three camps at the eastern entrance to North Bay has been in the Retter family since 1900. The paterfamilias and builder of the first camp was Arwed Retter, a dentist in Utica, New York. His grandson writes,

> [Dr. Retter was] an immigrant from Germany to the United States by way of England . . . between 1870 and 1880. He came from a prominent family in the principality of Württemburg . . . According to [Mrs. Retter], Arwed and his brother were sent to England by their father to escape the political turmoil and persecution taking place under Prince Otto von Bismark, who later became the first Chancellor of the German Empire.
>
> . . . After a brief stay in England, Arwed immigrated into the United States where he decided to enter dental school.[58]

After graduating about 1880 from the University of Pennsylvania School of Dentistry in Philadelphia, Dr. Retter established his practice in Utica.

Dr. Retter, who retained his German accent all his life, was a tall, distinguished-looking man with high cheekbones. He dressed carefully in a collar and tie and wore elegant silk vests even in the woods. Highly successful in his dental practice, he was ahead of his time in stressing the importance of flossing. An article in the *New York State Dental Journal* in 1896 attests to his concern in an age when false teeth were common.[59]

The Hamlyn Camp on Turtle Point in 1899, the year it was purchased by Arwed Retter. In the picture are Hattie Retter, Jim Higby, and Arwed Retter. Courtesy of Peter Bruyn.

Arwed and Hattie Retter, ca. 1901. Courtesy of Peter Bruyn.

Family recollections state that one of his patients, Charles C. Snyder, introduced Dr. Retter to Big Moose Lake. Snyder, Webb's agent who lived at Cascade Lake and handled local transactions, was probably the person who told him about the land available at Big Moose.[60]

Dr. Retter was an astute businessman. The first lots he bought were among the most desirable on the lake, comprising a stretch of sand beach and a view of both the main lake and North Bay. Retter's main camp was built atop the foundations of a palisade-style structure (see illustration on page 183) erected by one Hugh Walter Hamlyn, about whom nothing is known but his name. Hamlyn had sold the building but not the land to H. H.

Covey on February 13, 1894, for $350.[61] Covey, in turn, sold to Dr. Retter on October 16, 1899, for an unrecorded amount. Only a week previously, on October 9, 1899, the fifty-two-year-old Dr. Retter had purchased from William Seward Webb's Ne-Ha-Sa-Ne Association the land extending from the end of Turtle Point all the way east to the Totten and Crossfield Line.

Dr. Retter tore down the Hamlyn camp and contracted with E. J. Martin to build another house in the half-log style; it was occupied for the first time in the summer of 1900. It was named On-Da-Wa, which in the Algonquin Indian language means "coming again." E. J. Martin, along with his brother Charles, organized not only the construction of the Retter camp but also that of several additional camps originally owned by the Woodburys, the Allbrights, and the Swancotts. Another family, the Pinkneys, chose to live in a tent, selling their land in 1903 to E. S. Woodbury. All of these properties were occupied in 1900 as shown by Lena Retter's mention in her diary of visits to nearby families.

Arwed and Hattie Hollingsworth Retter had two daughters, Lena Martina (1882–1983), sometimes called Peggy, and Mary Jeannette (1884–1982), called Janet or Matie. (The island in North Bay was, and still occasionally is, called Peggy's Island.)

Among the family papers are some diaries that Lena

On-Da-Wa, the new Retter camp, 1906. Note the rock, showing that it was built on the foundations of the Hamlyn Camp. Courtesy of Peter Bruyn.

The On-Da-Wa boathouse in its original position, accessible from both the main lake and North Bay, ca. 1910. Courtesy of Wanda K. Martin.

kept in the early years. In the first summer the camp was occupied, when Lena was seventeen and Janet was fifteen, Lena began her account on the day of their arrival, Saturday, July 7, 1900:

> We arrived this morning at "camp" about 8 o'clock. We started from home [Utica] about 12 o'clock Friday night and took the last [trolley] car to the station. The train for the Adirondacks was supposed to leave about 1:40 but the second section was blocked at Albany and we had to wait over 3 hours for it to arrive. We came up [the lake] on the steamer *Zilpha* and were over-pleased when we arrived in sight of the cottage. Papa seemed very much disappointed to think the boat-house was not started but we had so much unpacking and other things to do that he soon forgot all his troubles and was hard at work. Matie and I had a very exciting time choosing our rooms, but did not take long to select. Our two boats are beautiful and everybody says they are two of the handsomest boats on the lake. Nobody came to see us today and I am very glad of it.

Arwed Retter must have lost no time in arranging for the boathouse, because by Monday morning the work was under way. He returned to Utica at noon on the same day, leaving his wife, two daughters, and the cook in the cottage until his return the following Saturday.

Relationships between the family and the men who constructed the boathouse were very cordial. Charlie Martin was a particular favorite and often took the girls or

their guests on trips in the guideboats when the lake was rough and the rowing difficult. On July 25, Lena wrote, "The boathouse is nearly completed and both the lake and North-bay dock are completed." No doubt the reason that the boathouse was located at the narrowest part of the point was so that there could be a dock on either side. In 1925, E. J. Martin moved the boathouse to its present location east of the house. Later in the same summer, the Retters commissioned a long pier located farther to the east that extended into water deep enough to accommodate the steamer. On August 28, Lena notes that "Grandma was the first to leave on the steamer from the new dock."

Lena and Janet spent the following summers at On-Da-Wa. Lena had complained in her diary about having to translate Caesar: "but Papa does not want me to study at all."[62] However, she finished secondary school and went on to the Pratt Institute in New York. In due course, Janet followed her sister to the same institution. Both girls were talented and spent their time at Big Moose in such artistic activities as making blueprints of flowers and fashioning decorative table centerpieces out of natural materials. Later, they were each active in designing their own camps. Evidence of their careful planning and sensitivity to their environment is still obvious today both inside the houses and in the landscape surrounding them.

Both Retter daughters were married at Big Moose. Lena met her husband, Carl Ludwig Otto, a New York architect also of German descent, while he was a guest at Higby's. They were married at Big Moose on September 14, 1908, and their son, Carl, Jr., was born June 22, 1909, in Brooklyn, New York.

Janet and Lena Retter and a friend (center) in "tramping clothes," ca. 1903. Courtesy of Peter Bruyn.

Janet's wedding to Henry Bicker Bruyn took place in 1914. Janet's reception, and possibly Lena's as well, was catered by Hattie Martin, E. J.'s wife, who ran the Waldheim hotel. Charlie Martin, who had helped the family from the very beginning and who was especially fond of Janet, provided a whole canoe load of water lilies as bridal bouquet and as decoration for the wedding ceremony.[63]

In 1912 the Retters had renovated the main house and replaced the half-log siding with cedar shingles. Outbuildings by this time included an icehouse, a laundry and tool shed, and the original boathouse that sat on the narrowest part of the point.

In 1912, Lena's architect husband Carl Otto designed and built a house for his small family close to the end of the point and named it Turtle Point Cabin. Trees planted along the sand spit between the main house and the cabin provided shelter and privacy.

Lena was very proud of her German heritage. However, a great-grandson writes, "During World War I, Dr. Retter, who of course had immigrated directly from Germany, aroused suspicions with the authorities here in the United States. He was by no means a supporter of his native country before the war, but he did have some friends and relatives in Germany. He wrote letters to them . . . that were occasionally opened before he got them and he believed (never confirmed) he was sometimes being watched."[64]

Arwed Retter died in 1918 after taking an active part in affairs around the lake, including the Bissell and Yousey sawmill controversy. His wife, Hattie, died in 1934 at the age of seventy-five years, outliving her husband by sixteen years.

Until Hattie Retter's death, the Ottos occupied Turtle Point Cabin while Hattie shared On-Da-Wa with Janet Retter and her husband, Henry Bicker Bruyn, along with their two boys, Henry (1918–) and Arwed (Ned) (1920–85). In her will Hattie Retter left several specific bequests and concluded, "as for the rest, it shall be share and share alike between my two daughters."[65] As Henry Bruyn notes, "Janet and Lena were two very different personalities and the concept of sharing without direction was most unrealistic. Lena immediately took control and declared that she would hold everything in custody for a carefully planned division."[66] Three years of discussions brought no agreement between the strong-minded Lena and her younger sister. Finally, in 1937 they agreed that the existing houses, On-Da-Wa and Turtle Point Cabin, would be given to the Otto family. Janet would receive, in

return, approximately 10.6 acres of land extending eastward from the base of the pier, which served the Retter camp as a landing for passengers and supplies. This land also included the island in North Bay. Janet accepted this allocation and after much exploration, chose the site of the Bruyn Camp (at the eastern side of lot 249, now designated lot 249.2) for construction the next year. In 1938, the Ottos took over On-Da-Wa and enlarged, re-sided, and renovated it once again, adding the apse-shaped living room to the west end, which looks out on both the bay and the lake.[67]

Carl and Lena's only child, Carl Ludwig Otto, Jr., attended medical school but left near the end of his last year. His true interests lay in physics and engineering, particularly rocketry. Young Carl married and worked during World War II for the Douglas Aircraft Company, developing many patented devices. He later moved to an island in Puget Sound off the coast of the state of Washington. He continued to develop electronic instrumentation but eventually was diagnosed with amyotrophic lateral sclerosis (Lou Gehrig's disease) and died, widowed and childless, in 1974. Her son's death left Lena without descendants. Lena (always known affectionately as Tante, the German word for aunt) took a special interest in her nephews, Janet's sons, Henry and Arwed "Ned" Bruyn.

BRUYN CAMP (LOT 249.2)

Henry Bruyn recalls in his memoirs some of the many aspects of life at Big Moose in the 1920s and 1930s.[68] A graduate of Yale medical school, he had a long and distinguished career as a pediatrician, much of it in California, where he retired as head of medical services at the University of California at Berkeley. His parents shared On-Da-Wa with his widowed grandmother, Hattie Retter.

Henry recalls the trip from Long Island to Big Moose in the 1920s, before automobile travel was common. Quite a few families traveled in a similar fashion.

The trip started with a very early morning automobile ride provided by a livery service from Hempstead to Grand Central Station in New York City. . . . The trip from our home to Grand Central Station took from two to three hours, and I remember that it started out in darkness.

At the spectacular Grand Central Station in New York, we would bring our luggage down to the train and take our seats. . . . We detrained at Utica to transfer to the Adirondack Division, which ended in Montreal. As far as Ned and I were concerned, it ended at Big Moose. This was a smaller train and we were always able to walk quickly to the rear and stand on the platform, watching the rails come rolling out from under the train to the clicking of the wheels over the rail junctions. There was one spot, very shortly before arrival at Big Moose Station, where we could catch our first glimpse through the trees of Big Moose Lake. This was always a great thrill and source of excitement.

Upon arrival at the Station, we loaded our luggage onto a large limousine, often with its roof down, and took the approximately half-hour ride down the dirt road to the western end of Big Moose Lake. Here we were met by one of our childhood heroes, Mr. Romaine Kinne. He ran the boat livery which would carry us on our final link to grandmother's house. In later times, as highways improved, our father undertook to drive from Long Island to Big Moose, which again, required an extremely early rising and as much as twelve hours of time on the road.

In 1938, Janet Bruyn, working closely with Charlie Martin, planned and built a camp on the eastern part of the Retter property. The house features a living room with a curved wall overlooking the lake and a fireplace that reaches the full height of the two-story room. Charlie's brother Frank, as well as Walt and Charlie Dunn, helped in the work.

Henry, with his younger brother, Ned, took a keen interest in activities around the lake and has been willing to share his lively recollections. Henry describes the first day of construction.

On a beautiful spring morning in the year 1938, in a glade of birch trees and large brake ferns, a group of three men and two young men are crouched behind trees, watching intently down a trail leading toward the lake, which can be seen shimmering in the distance. Soon down this trail slowly walks a striking figure of a man. He is wearing a felt peaked hat, a khaki flannel shirt, and black denim pants. He is slowly lighting his pipe. His face is ruddy and framed by a classical Vandyke white beard with white shaggy hair coming out from under his hat. The back of his head is graced by a large bun of hair done up in the style very familiar to women with long hair, although he fastens it with a bone. As he walks down the trail, his pipe begins to smoke, and he suddenly steps behind a tree. At that instant there is a thunderous explosive roar and the rattle through the trees of flying rocks. With that explosion, the first day of construction of Bruyn Camp is undertaken. Frank Martin has just set off a "mud blast." The men and boys hasten back up the trail toward the lake to find that a large granite rock has been shattered and the digging of the foundations of the house can now proceed.

. . . Frank Martin, the dynamite expert and master carpenter, bears a striking and deliberate resemblance to the famous Buffalo Bill Cody of the "Wild West Show" fame in the early part of the twentieth century.

All the materials for the house were hauled from the Glennmore landing to the site on a scow towed by Charlie Martin's launch, powered by a one-cylinder engine.

The beams in the main room of the house were cut from carefully selected white pine found somewhere on the north shore of the lake by Charlie Martin in extensive expeditions on foot. Naturally, with trees of the size required for the beams, the nearer to water the tree was cut, the better, for they had to be hand-hauled down to the water's edge and loaded into the scow.

. . . Excavation into the lake shore and hillside for the boathouse required more dynamiting. This time, . . . holes were drilled into the rock and dynamite placed at the bottom of them to cut off large slabs. . . . These holes were drilled by steel "star drills" and for the most part were held in place by either Henry or Ned Bruyn, while Charlie Martin swung a 16-pound sledge

Frank Martin in his Buffalo Bill mode, ca. 1925. Courtesy of Wanda K. Martin.

past their face into the head of the drill. It was a measure of our worship of Charlie Martin that we never doubted for a moment where the sledgehammer was going. When the head of the star drill got hot, Charlie would spit from a chewing tobacco-filled mouth, accurately depositing a cooling dottle on top of the drill.

Eventually both Henry and Ned Bruyn went off to college, although they continued to return to Big Moose during the summers. Ned became a stockbroker and married Frances Shane, a student from Syracuse University who was working at Higby's for the summer. Ned and Fran shared many years with the widowed Janet in her cottage. Henry established himself on the west coast and spent his medical career in California, returning to Big Moose only occasionally.

JUDSON CAMP (LOT 248)

The neighboring lot on the North Shore immediately east of the Otto-Bruyn cottages changed hands several times after Arwed Retter first sold it[69] before it found a longterm owner, Marguerite Judson. E. J. Martin's record books tell us that there was a house that he maintained on the land.[70] It is likely that E. J. built the camp, although no direct record exists.

Marguerite Judson found Big Moose purely by chance. She was traveling by train from Toledo, Ohio, back to her home in Englewood, New Jersey, when she happened to meet an engaging gentleman named Walter Colpitts. When she told him she was looking for a place to take her children to spend summers, Mr. Colpitts (who had recently purchased property on the North Shore) told her about Big Moose. She was so pleased with his de-

THE FIRE AT THE JUDSON CAMP | *Bill Lux*

When Mrs. Judson's camp burned, I was out in my sailboat, becalmed, near the South Shore. I could see the smoke, and knew it was a serious fire. I shouted and shouted and tried to skull home, but eventually someone from the Higby Club saw it and the fireboat went over. They were able to save that camp.

scription that she got off the train at Utica and went with him to the lake. She rented Rockshire, the Shropshire camp on the east side of the Wightmans, during the summer of 1922. The summer after that she bought the camp on the opposite side of the Wightmans.[71]

The Judson family retained the camp until 1980. Marguerite and Frederick Allen Judson had three sons, David, John, and William, and one daughter, Ann, who spent summers there for many years. Frederick Judson was a stockbroker in New York. He commuted regularly by train to Big Moose in the summer, often with his neighbor, Walter Colpitts. The two men arrived at Big Moose Station and proceeded to the Glennmore, where Joe Thompson, the Colpitts's chauffeur, caretaker, and boat maintenance man, would meet them. They would be at Big Moose by 8:00 Saturday morning. In later years, the Judsons had an amicable separation, and Marguerite spent most of the summer at the camp with the children. Frederick Judson died in 1962.

Two Judson sons married women whom they met at the lake. Jack wed Connie Olhoff, who was working at the Waldheim. They lived in New Jersey but spent summers with their family at the lake until 1980. Connie died in 1990. Jack's children are Cynthia, Christopher, Katherine, and Kimberly. Bill Judson married Roy Higby's daughter, Patricia, and lived at Big Moose year-round. They both worked at the Higby Club for many years. Bill also built camps and developed land along the Judson Road on the southeastern lakeshore.

Marguerite's son Jack describes coming to the lake for the summer:

In the 1920s and 1930s we'd arrive at Big Moose Station, ride down to the big dock at the Glennmore and soon fill Romaine Kinne's launch with people, baggage and precious food shipped up from Macy's in New York City. Then off to camp. Once we were settled in, the big event of each day was the arrival of the "pickle boat" bringing mail, milk in five gallon cans from Remsen, New York, and fresh fruits and vegetables. I can still recall the wonderful aroma of the pickle boat.

We had an icehouse, and lugging one of those five gallon cans of milk up our trail was a chore but a celebration once it was buried in the ice cakes and mostly covered with sawdust. Even so, many a heavy thunderstorm gave us slightly turned milk.

Jack relates a nearly disastrous incident that occurred in the early 1950s:

I was alone in the camp heating water with our kerosene heater. It caught fire. Very shortly Roy Higby led a crew of firefighters in the fireboat to our dock. As the boat neared the dock, Roy instructed a young man holding a big and heavy brass nozzle to jump overboard. He did—into about 10 feet of water—and promptly sank. Nevertheless, their valiant efforts limited the damage to gutting the interior but left the outside untouched.

On one occasion in the 1960s, Marguerite Judson's car rolled completely over in a ditch on the Eagle Bay road near the entrance to Stag's Leap (the Newmans' camp near South Bay). Marguerite was left hanging upside down in her seat belt. Someone stopped to help her, and she went on with them to the party where she had been headed. The accident made wonderful cocktail conversation. In her later years, the independent and strong-minded Marguerite stayed at the Waldheim during the summer and late into the fall. She continued to drive her small aluminum boat, which was equipped with a steering wheel, around the lake until shortly before she died at the age of 103.

In 1980 the Judson family sold the camp to Michael and Ellen Wilcox of Old Forge. However, the Judsons returned, twenty-seven strong, for a reunion at the lake in 1995.

ALNWICK (LOT 247)

Dr. Percy Wightman first came to Big Moose and bought an empty lot from Emily Wright of Orange, Connecticut, in 1916. (Miss Wright had purchased the property from Dr. Retter in 1908 but never erected a camp.) The Wightman family, children and grandchildren, has remained at the lake for many years and owns additional camps in various locations.

Percy Wightman (1871–1958) was a prominent minister in New York (see illustrations above and on page xv), spending nearly his entire career as pastor of the rapidly expanding University Heights Presbyterian Church. The family history, compiled by Dr. Wightman's granddaughter, Elizabeth Singleton, gives us a picture of the early days.

So why did the Wightmans come to Big Moose Lake? Before becoming pastor of the University Heights Presbyterian Church, Grandy had a ministry [1901–04] in Fayetteville, New York. His brother, Robert Stillman Wightman, had a mission church in the Adirondacks at

Percy B. Wightman, ca. 1930. Courtesy of Elizabeth K. Singleton.

Wanakena. So he was acquainted with the area. But probably most important were his years spent as a member of the "Clerical Anglers"—eight graduates of Auburn Seminary who . . . fished and camped together in the Adirondacks, first in 1898, and then every year until at least 1928. "The Clerical Anglers" [came] to fish on the Independence River, Stillwater and other spots. . . . Three small booklets published by the group survive, "The Romance of the River," dated 1916; "The Romance of the Camp," dated 1920; and "Lyrics of the Camp," dated 1928.[72]

By 1900, Percy Wightman had married Edith Lewis Booth (1872–1924), who bore him four children, Henry "Pete" Booth (1901–80), Katherine Hartley (later Hadden) (1904–87), Elizabeth Leavitt (later Grafton, still later Selander) (1907–88), and Edith Abigail (later Kreitler) (1913–2002). Before building their own camp the Wightmans had vacationed at Higby's. When their last baby was born, the family stayed at Dart's; Bill Dart kept a cow and therefore had fresh milk available.

Kay Wightman Hadden recalls that "Ma and Pa" Dart had a device that

The family of Dr. Percy and Mrs. Edith B. Wightman, ca. 1910.
From left to right: their daughter Edith Wightman Kreitler,
nephew Orrin Wightman, niece Julia Wightman, daughters
Elizabeth Wightman Grafton and Katharine Wightman
Hadden, son Henry "Pete" B. Wightman, and sister-in-law
Purl Parker Wightman, with Mrs. Wightman and Dr.
Wightman themselves. Courtesy of Elizabeth K. Singleton.

wasn't heard of then, called a wireless. [Pa Dart] was proud to death of the wireless. . . . And one night everybody was standing around, waiting for dinner, and this wireless announced that Kaiser Wilhelm had marched into Denmark and it was the beginning of the First World War. And that was the first week of August, 1914. So, I can remember as a kid being worried about what was going to happen. "Are we all going to go to war?" He said, "Oh no, that's way across the Atlantic Ocean." [73]

In 1916, Percy Wightman, working hard to establish his church, found his health beginning to suffer; he was urged to take a long leave from work to rest. In that year the Wightmans bought land east of the Retters at Big Moose and commissioned a house to be built by Frank Koster, E. J. Martin, Frank Martin, and a Mr. Marleau.[74] E. J. Martin's ledgers record charges in March and April 1916 for board for Mr. and Mrs. Wightman as well as for Frank Koster, who also purchased building supplies from E. J.[75] Dr. Wightman himself came to Big Moose and worked all summer with his son, Henry "Pete" Wightman, alongside the other workmen. (Pete was paid a small sum, which he later used to purchase an Old Town canoe.) The camp was called Alnwick after the family seat in Scotland.

Dr. Wightman was one of the early leaders of the lake community. He was a founder and longtime president of the Big Moose Property Owners Association, organized in 1926. As far back as the 1840s, Joel T. Headley, a

Protestant minister and a popular historian, expressed the growing romanticism about the Adirondacks when he wrote that an "attack on the brain . . . drove me from the haunts of men to seek mental repose and physical strength in the woods." [76] Dr. Wightman obviously had similar feelings, and during his tenure he wrote letters to the members that expressed his love for the lake and the feeling most residents had for their summer homes. This passage, written in 1930, was read at his funeral in 1958:

There they are as they have always been, are now and will ever be, waiting for us. It is great to have a pleasant expectancy, something to look forward to with certainty. They have never failed and will not this season. The mountains about Big Moose call. The lake invites you on its hospitable waters. The trees are sending forth their new growth to give shade and beauty. The flowers and ferns are carpeting the forest floor. Hermit thrush, Canada white throat, blue jay, vireo and grossbeak are tuning up for their summer symphony. All are preparing to welcome the lovers of forest, lake and stream to their joy-lit homes by the wave-lapped shores.

Not only so, but Mr. Kinne has his boats in commission; the Transportation Company its cars tuned up; and the Supply Company, its shelves stocked to the ceiling; and the public camps ready and waiting—all to make easy and pleasant the stay of campers and guest at Big Moose this summer.

It is time to see to your rod and raquette, to set aside the things needful, to mend that trunk, to make one more journey; but more important still, to prepare oneself spiritually by allowing the joys of other years to flame anew, to dream of the pleasure to be in donning the old clothes that are so comfortable, in the feel of the oar and paddle, in meeting again friends tried and true. They it is who enjoy to the most, that bring their good times with them.[77]

Dr. Wightman and Dr. Albert Vander Veer, his neighbor across the lake, were responsible for bringing Sunday worship to the lake. Services were held in the Vander Veer boathouse, as well as in other locations. People gathered in their boats from all around the lake. Romaine Kinne would pick up children in his boat to take them to Sunday School. Dr. Wightman was also a prime mover in raising money for erecting the Chapel building and establishing the Chapel with its own minister. Although the Chapel had its own summer minister, Dr. Wightman regularly preached on Memorial Sunday, held every year in August.

Percy Wightman found great satisfaction and relaxation in doing things with his hands. He made furniture (chests, desks, and the like) for his camp, and for his children and their families; for the Chapel he made a pulpit and a communion table decorated with cutwork depicting pine trees.[78] His workshop, still filled with tools, remains standing today behind Alnwick.

All four Wightman children built or purchased camps at Big Moose, and many of their children, grandchildren, and even great-grandchildren continue to enjoy the lake. In 1999 more than eighty members of the family, including Haddens, Graftons, Kreitlers, Singletons, and others, gathered to renew family ties and to celebrate their close relationship.

ROCKSHIRE (LOT 246)

The colorful and sometimes obscure history of the three camps that stand today on the Menand property reaches into North Bay as well as the main lake. In 1902, Dr. Retter had sold the land closest to the Wightman camp, lot 246, to Sopho P. B. Shropshire and Ralph F. Shropshire. A short note to E. J. Martin shows on its letterhead that R. F. Shropshire dealt in mortgages and had a business address at 6 Wall Street, New York City.[79] Mr. Shropshire notes in the 1903 letter that he is glad to hear that the work (presumably construction) is progressing well. That this refers to a camp that E. J. Martin was building is shown by a copy of "Articles of Agreement" on a form provided by George Palliser, Architect, 32 Park Place, New York City.[80] The contract is between Shropshire and Martin and outlines the construction of a camp at Big Moose for one thousand dollars, to be paid in six installments, each due when certain phases were completed.

There were at least two Shropshire children, a son and a daughter. Legend around the lake tells us that at some point Ralph Shropshire, Jr., shocked the neighbors and created a scandal by swimming without the top of his bathing suit. The younger Shropshires were also notorious for the noisy parties that took place at the house.

Early in January 1928, Eliza "Lila" Welsh Steele, the aunt of Ralph, Jr., wrote a letter from her home in New York City to E. J. Martin referring to young Ralph. "The 'female' reported to be with him is not his wife," she wrote, "for Ruth [his wife] called at my apartment, with her boy, yesterday. Is it possible," she continues, "that such conduct as his is tolerated in your neck of the woods? Thank you for writing me fully."[81] Henry Bruyn, a neighbor on the North Shore, tells us that this kind of escapade

Rockshire (built in 1903), ca. 1920, with Aunt Lila Steele on the porch and Frank Day, E. J. Martin, and probably Buddy Capek below. Courtesy of Wanda K. Martin.

was entirely in character for Ralph.[82] At the end of 1928, Miss Steele wrote that a buyer for the camp had been found and that a Mr. Colpitts was to buy the camp soon after the first of the year.[83] Perhaps Ralph, Jr., sold the camp because he was preparing to leave for Antarctica with Admiral Byrd.

An article in the *New York Times* of June 23, 1933, announced the wedding of Mary Steele Shropshire, daughter of the late Captain and Mrs. Ralph F. Shropshire. The bride was escorted by her brother, Ralph F. Shropshire, "hydrographer[84] to the Byrd expedition to Antarctica." During the expedition, undertaken in 1928–30, Rear Admiral Richard E. Byrd made the first flight over the South Pole and accomplished for the United States the first aerial exploration. In the book published by the admiral soon after his return, Byrd mentions Shropshire twice. First, he refers to him as an "assistant to the scientific staff."[85] Second, Ralph F. Shropshire appears, listed as "hydrographer," in the roster of officers and crew of the ship, *The City of New York,* which made a round trip from Dunedin, New Zealand, to Antarctica in February 1930 to embark the winter party.[86] Although Shropshire was on this ship and was a part of the crew essential to the Byrd exploration, he was not one of the forty-two-man team that remained at Little America through the rugged months of the southern hemisphere's winter until the expedition's return later in 1930.

In 1929, the Shropshires' next-door neighbor, Walter

Cabellsdale facing North Bay, 1921.
Courtesy of Wanda K. Martin.

Colpitts, bought the camp to use as a guest house, reportedly because he was tired of the rowdy parties that took place there. It seems likely that the younger generation was responsible for the noise, and perhaps only the adventurous Ralph, Jr.

CABELLSDALE (LOT 244N)

On the North Bay side of the Shropshire property is a small camp built for Eliza Welsh Steele, who was often called Aunt Lila. The land was conveyed to Miss Steele in 1908, and the camp probably was erected shortly thereafter. The house, known as Cabellsdale, may have been built by one of the Martin brothers, although there is no firm record. It is said to be named after James Branch Cabell (rhymes with "rabble"), a prolific and sometimes controversial American novelist whose career extended from about 1907 to the 1940s. His books concerned the history of an imaginary medieval count and his family, whom he traced down to the twentieth century. Perhaps the books were favorites of Lila Steele.

Aunt Lila was the aunt of Ralph Shropshire, Jr., probably Sopho Shropshire's sister. She was a wonderful storyteller and a magnet for all the children on the North Shore. Olive Wertz and Henry Bruyn remember visiting her. She was a rather plump lady who, in later years, wore her white hair in a topknot. She was active in lake affairs and is frequently mentioned in the minutes of the Property Owners Association.

In 1941, Lila Steele sold Cabellsdale to Frank Martin,

brother of E. J. and Charles Martin. Late in life, "Uncle" Frank became a recluse and lived for many summers in the camp. He amused himself and controlled the population of mice by laying a trail of bread crumbs across one end of the porch. Sitting at the other end of the porch, he waited until the mice came out for the bait and then picked them off with his rifle. While Frank was at Cabellsdale, his nephew, Howard Martin, made weekly trips to check on his welfare and to take him the supplies that he asked for, including whiskey. Much later, Frank spent his summers in the old lumber camp on the Martin Road extension and his winters in Boonville, where he died in a nursing home in 1961.

When Frank was still at Cabellsdale, Walter Colpitts's children wanted to buy the property, but they found that, for obscure legal reasons, the title was not clear. The lawyer hired by the children conducted a long search and finally located Ralph Shropshire, Jr., who still had a lien on the land, in a jail in Florida. He had no heirs, his wife and son having apparently disappeared from his life. He signed over the property without protest.

THE COLPITTS CAMP (LOT 245)

Just east of the Shropshire property was a parcel of land that Dr. Retter sold in 1901 to two brothers from Utica, Benjamin and Frederick Swancott, who together owned a livery stable. Their business was not only a livery but also "Boarding, Sale and Exchange Stables," located at 76–80 Washington Street in Utica. In 1905, E. J. Martin con-

Walter Colpitts in the Bluenose, *ca. 1925.*
Courtesy of Nelle Menand Knox.

structed a camp for them. A letter from Benjamin Swancott to E. J. Martin states, "I want to start on my camp just as soon as weather will permit. Will you please let me know when ice goes out."[87] The Swancotts named their camp Witch-Hopple Lodge and used it until Walter and Florence Colpitts of New York City bought it in 1919.

Harry Swancott, son of one of the brothers, was the boy who introduced Fordyce Lux of Utica to Big Moose. The two fished, hunted, and got into a lot of mischief together. They would borrow a car from the livery and go racing, or drive in to Inlet before the road was meant for cars to see what the cornering limits of a vehicle were before the car tipped over. Ford Lux eventually bought property on the North Shore, and many members of the family are still at the lake.

By 1922, Harry Swancott was married. He and his wife, Edith, built a small camp just across the lake on lot 174, transferring the name Witch-Hopple Lodge to it. This camp was sold to William and Marlene Humphrey in 1967.

The elder Swancotts' successors were Walter and Florence Colpitts. Walter Colpitts, grandfather of the Menand families, came from a rather poor Canadian farm family. His father was very strict. When he was sixteen years old, his mother took him aside one night, gave him some money she had saved, and told him to go and make something of himself. He went off to McGill University in Montreal and became a civil engineer. He designed and built railroads, primarily in New York City, was highly successful and eventually became a United States citizen. When he bought the North Shore camp in 1919, he expanded the building substantially both to the east and to the west. He also added the sun porch with its magnifi-

cent plate glass windows. Much of the construction material was transported across the ice in the winter.

Among Walter Colpitts's inventions was a building material called "Cemestos," designed to have excellent insulating qualities and to be easy to handle. The material was used to build a house, now the manse for the Chapel, which stands on the site of the old Fern Spring camp and has taken over its name.

Walter Colpitts was also a gifted designer whose hobby was wrought iron work. He created many beautiful iron decorations such as sconces, latticework, and fireplace screens not only for the camp but also for the Big Moose Chapel. The camp also has many examples of imaginative decorative pieces made from native materials: fungi, driftwood, bark, bird feathers, and the like.

Walter Colpitts enlarged the boathouse that came with the property to accommodate the *Bluenose,* a large and powerful Hacker Craft built in the 1920s to his design. The boat was once the fastest in the Adirondacks. A twenty-six-foot-long, smooth-sided wooden vessel, it was made in 1925 in Detroit by an aero-marine company that went out of business in about 1940. Walter Colpitts had been on the board of directors of a company that built airplane engines during World War I. He obtained one of these engines after the war and designed the boat to accommodate it. The boat may have been modeled after powerful boats that were used on the Great Lakes to smuggle booze from Canada during the days of Prohibition.

The original engine had twelve cylinders and was a two hundred-horsepower motor, an incredible amount of power in the days when a ten-horsepower motor was considered dangerously fast. The boat was said to travel fifty-six miles per hour, faster than many automobiles of the time. The motor was placed somewhat forward of the center of the boat, which had a single cockpit and a very long covered bow. As E. J. Martin said in his diary for 1925 when he records being present at the first trial of the boat on the lake, it was probably too much power for either the boat or the lake. The airplane motor remained in the boat for only two years. It was delicately tuned and really needed a full-time mechanic to take care of its idiosyncrasies. It was also inefficient. The third problem, and the one that perhaps ultimately sealed its fate, was the noise it made. Complaints came from many people on the lake, led by Roy Higby, who was concerned about the disruption to the peace and quiet of his guests.

After two years the motor was replaced with a 50-horsepower motor. The Menand family, descendants of Walter Colpitts, is unsure whether only the second motor was a Liberty Motor or whether both engines were made under the Liberty name. In any case one or both motors were consigned to the bottom of the lake, a fate suffered at Big Moose by many unwieldy objects. The latest—and currently used—motor is a 150-horsepower Chrysler. However, the boat is in storage at this time awaiting renovations.

The Menands tell us that Governor Al Smith of New York State, during his 1928 campaign for president, heard of the high-speed boat during a stay at Higby's and requested a ride. Mr. Colpitts was accommodating (though in total disagreement politically) and off they went, with the governor continually asking for more speed. Apparently fifty-six miles per hour in the fastest boat in the Adirondacks was not enough.

The Colpitts, who lived in Princeton, New Jersey, had two children: daughter Lucy and son Jeremy. Lucy received a letter from Jeremy telling her that there was a Princeton man on the lake working as a counselor at the Boy Scout Pioneer Camp. Lucy set out to look for him and found Howard Menand, who was on a blind date with one of Roy Higby's daughters, at a dance at the Higby boathouse. The friendship developed rapidly. Howard would have the Boy Scouts paddle him over to the North Shore to visit Lucy. The two became engaged, and they married in 1936 in the first wedding to be performed in the Big Moose Community Chapel. Lucy and Howard had four children: Molly, Walter, Nelle, and Howard III, all of whom use the properties every summer.

EDILGRA (LOTS 241W–44E)

Edwin S. Woodbury of Boston was no stranger to Big Moose Lake when he bought three lots of land next to the Totten and Crossfield Line from Arwed Retter in late 1899 and early 1900. He was an enthusiastic hunter and fisherman and had stayed at Pancake Hall, presumably with Jim Higby as his guide, early in the 1890s.[88] Family stories tell us that his wife, Ilione Marcy, was "sickly." When Ilione first came to Big Moose, Earl Covey and Tom Rose carried her from the train in a rocking chair that was balanced on two poles to make a sedan chair. On the back of the photograph, her daughter wrote, "Mother had pneumonia so was carried in. The rest of us walked in. Our baggage and trunks were left in an old freight car that stood as a station." Bill Marleau believes

Ilione Woodbury (Mrs. E. S. Woodbury) being carried from Big Moose Station, probably to Club Camp, by Earl Covey and Tom Rose, ca. 1893. Courtesy of Richard Widdicombe.

Edilgra, built in 1900. Undated photograph courtesy of Richard Widdicombe.

that the destination on this trip was Club Camp on Big Moose Lake, by this time a roomy and reasonably comfortable place for a family and an invalid.[89]

Edwin Woodbury headed a firm in Boston that manufactured shoes. He fell in love with Big Moose Lake and at first coveted the property later occupied by Lake View Lodge. Finding it had been sold to Charles Williams, he turned to the North Shore and bought several lots from Dr. Retter. We know from Lena Retter's diary for 1900 that the Woodbury camp was occupied by that summer. Edwin and Ilione Woodbury had two daughters, Ilione and Grace. The name of the camp they built, Edilgra, is composed of the first few letters of the three names in the family.

E. J. Martin and his crew built the camp of logs that were harvested from the property. The style was the local vertical half-log or palisade construction. In front of the house was a long stone and wood dock that reached out into the lake so that the steamboat had enough depth to land. In April 1905, Mr. Woodbury wrote to E. J. Martin because he was concerned that the water level in the lake might rise in the spring runoff. He asked E. J. to "please see that the dock and run is sawed out, so the ice will not lift it from the foundation."[90]

Ellis Denio, son of John Denio who lived at Big Moose Station, was a live-in caretaker for the Woodbury family for a number of summers. In an interview shortly before he died in 1985, he described Mrs. Woodbury as a very good employer, someone who was considerate and who would on occasion ask him to join friends or family to make a fourth at bridge or some other game. He was always introduced as "our guide."[91]

Denio, who lived over the boathouse, was responsible for such chores as taking care of the boats, ferrying the family around the lake, chopping wood for fireplaces and stoves, and maintaining the icehouse. He also took care of the gas lights in the house. Mrs. Woodbury had a lighting plant up on top of the hill. The carbide for it came in twenty-five-pound cans, and, Denio said, "one of my jobs, was to fill that tank with water, pour the carbide in to make the gas."[92] Filling the tank with water was a major project in itself. A temperamental one-cylinder pump at the front of the camp ran by steam, so before operations could begin a fire had to be built and the leather bellows soaked so that the pump would work. The gas used for lighting was in fact acetylene, used mostly for welding today, which gave a hot, bright white light. Explosions were not uncommon, so the system had to be handled carefully.

Denio recalled that the Woodburys enjoyed fishing. "There was a spot in the corner [of the living room] and every fish they got, . . .the boy [a college boy who took care of their boats] . . . took this brown paper and cut a [silhouette] of the fish, and it told how much it weighed, the length of it, who was the fisherman, who was the guide and the whole thing, and you could go and get the whole history right in the corner by the fireplace."[93] The family still maintains this tradition, although the number of fish has declined dramatically in recent years.

Mrs. Woodbury's daughter, Grace, who is mentioned in Lena Retter's diary for 1900, graduated from Wellesley in 1904 and later married Edwin Paddock Crawe from Watertown, Massachusetts. Grace followed the family tradition and liked to fish and hunt. She and her husband had one daughter, Olive.

Among the Woodbury descendants' possessions is a locomotive headlight of the type invented by Irvin A. Williams, whose camp was on Old Pine Point. Irvin Williams kept the light on his own rocky promontory (Headlight Point then), and the Wertzes installed it on their own dock after the Williams family left the lake.

Olive Crawe first came to Big Moose in a pack basket carried by a guide when she was one year old. She was an avid outdoorswoman, having spent every summer of her life at Big Moose. When she was a teenager she attended Moss Lake Camp and made trips by horseback through the Cedar River Flow area. Later she became a regular participant in the Big Moose Canoe Crew trips and was active in that group until a stroke in 1998 limited her mobility.

Olive met Robert R. Wertz when she was a student at Wellesley and was attending summer school at Radcliffe in Cambridge. Bob, who was manager of the Harvard Glee Club, was also attending summer school. One afternoon Olive was rowing a guideboat on the Charles River. Bob had noticed Olive, an attractive athletic girl with long chestnut hair who had won trophies in horseback riding and diving. In a perhaps unique act of courtship, Bob jumped off the Anderson Bridge into the water near her. The acquaintance developed into a romance, and marriage soon followed.

Bob became an attorney in Pittsburgh. He also became very active around the lake. He was a trustee of the Big Moose Community Chapel starting in 1948, president of the Chapel board of trustees from 1951 to 1955, and served in various other capacities for many years thereafter. In addition, Bob Wertz was president of the Big Moose Property Owners Association from 1963 to 1967 as well as from 1972 to 1978, serving that organization in many different roles over the years. Olive and Bob had four children, Faith, Joy, Marcy, and Robert, all of whom still visit the lake regularly.

BRIGHTWOOD CAMP (LOTS 240–41)

Brightwood, the camp just east of the Woodbury-Wertz camp, is a mirror image of Edilgra and was also built very early in the history of the lake. Mr. Edwin Woodbury conveyed the land to his friend and minister from Boston, the Reverend William Hervey Allbright, in October 1900, less than a year after he had purchased lot 241 from Dr. Retter in December 1899. E. J. Martin was again the contractor. The palisade-style building, probably erected in

Brightwood, built in 1901. Undated photograph courtesy of Richard Widdicombe.

the winter of 1903, stood on the lot next to the Totten and Crossfield Line, the limit of Dr. Retter's purchase. It is the last lot on the North Shore that extends all the way through the peninsula to North Bay.

William Allbright's wife, Mary, never liked living there. In the hope of pleasing her, Mr. Allbright enlarged the kitchen and added a bay window that extended to the porch from the living room. The window had curved glass, an elegant and probably expensive feature. The window is still in place, although one of the three panels that was accidentally broken has been replaced by durable plexiglass.

In the meantime, Allbright had bought neighboring land (lot 240), which lay across the Totten and Crossfield Line in Township 41. This parcel, purchased from Theodore and Kate McCallum Page, included one hundred feet of shoreline and about two and one-half acres that did not go through to North Bay.

The Allbrights and their four children, Manley, Elizabeth, Eunice, and Amy, used the camp for only a few years before Mr. Allbright died late in 1907. However, his family retained ownership until the end of 1911.

In 1911 the Allbrights sold the property to Samuel J. Saunders, a professor of physics at Hamilton College in Clinton, New York. Professor Saunders died in 1950, and in 1952 his children, Jean S. Thompson and Stewart S. Saunders, sold the property.

The new owners were Eldon K. Ralston and his wife, Virginia, of Cleveland, Ohio. They and their sons, Douglas and Bruce, came to the lake for about a month each summer. The Ralstons later purchased a camp on South Bay and sold the North Shore camp to William and Annette Lux of Utica, New York, in 1959. The Luxes, along with their children Deborah, Karen, and Bill, Jr., have spent every summer since then in residence, Bill on weekends and vacations and all summer after retirement. Annette founded and still leads a weekly canoe group, which ranges along other lakes and rivers throughout the Adirondacks.

NORTH SHORE, EAST END

The history of the early camps at the east end of the North Shore begins after the Bissell and Yousey sawmill burned in 1918 and the company closed its operations. Most of the company's land along the shore was conveyed to Arthur Simmers of Elverson, Pennsylvania (near Philadelphia), who then sold the lakeside lots that had been marked out by Webb to various purchasers. Included in the property were two buildings that were part of the original lumber company complex. Four additional camps were built from lumber reused from company structures. The two remaining camps at this end of the North Shore, built after the war, are mentioned in Appendix A.

At the time he learned about Big Moose, Simmers worked in Niagara Falls at the Hooker Electro-Chemical Company, where two of his colleagues were Romaine Kinne and George Stone. (In 1919, Stone had just purchased a camp at Big Moose. Kinne, later the owner of Kinne's Boat Line, was looking for a house in the mountains where he could recover from the Spanish flu.) Simmers apparently saw the available land as a good investment. Stone's recommendation to Kinne and to Simmers was the means of bringing two important people to the lake.

Simmers built or renovated most of the camps at this end of the North Shore. Nelson Dunn, Sr., helped with some of the work. His son, Bill Dunn, tells a story about the relationship between the two men: "One of my father's customers on Big Moose Lake was Arthur L. Simmers . . . The only spectator sport my father had any interest in at all was prize fighting. When a Dempsey-Tunney fight was featured in Philadelphia back in those days, Mr. Simmers gifted Father with an all-expenses-paid trip to Philadelphia. My father talked about this for many, many years." [94]

Simmers's charm and good nature must have helped him sell the camps and property that were part of the original lumber company complex.

BIRCH KNOLL (LOT 239)

This camp, which stands next to Brightwood, was built about 1919 with lumber that came from one of the Bissell and Yousey buildings, perhaps the boardinghouse, just down the shore to the east. The builder was George Casler, who, with his brother, Hobe, owned a camp opposite this property on the southeastern shore near the outlet of Big Chief Pond. (The Caslers had been guides and caretakers for various camps, including, the Vander Veers, who had given them the land for their southeastern shore cabin.) In 1928, Fordyce and Anna Lux of Utica, New York, purchased the North Shore camp from Hobe Casler, who had recently inherited it from his brother. The original camp consisted of two rooms separated by hanging blankets and a loft accessible only by ladder. The new owners, who had four boys, added a living room, a fireplace with a birchbark log mantle, two bedrooms, and porches.

Fordyce Lux's son, Donald, who now occupies the building with his wife, Gloria, added a combination boathouse and workroom and also a wooden deck for plants and chairs.

WOOD HAVEN (LOT 238)

Wood Haven was built from lumber from the Bissell boardinghouse, which served the lumberjacks and sawmill employees. This camp is also now owned by Donald Lux of Utica, who rents it—often to people who have been there year after year.

The basic design of Wood Haven and Squirrel's Nook (two lots to the east) is the same. Arthur Simmers built both camps and sold them to Henry Wewerka of Brooklyn, New York, who rented Wood Haven to visitors until World War II, when Fordyce Lux purchased the property.

SQUIRREL'S NOOK (LOT 235w–36)

Squirrel's Nook was built about 1920 for Arthur Simmers. A duplicate of Wood Haven cottage, Simmers used it as rental property until he sold it to Henry and Emma Wewerka in 1928. The Wewerkas owned it for many years, at one point purchasing an extra fifty feet (lakeside) of land to accommodate a workshop that Arthur Burtch put up shortly after the boathouse was built. Later they added a dining room, a back porch with a modern bathroom, and a studio for their daughter, Gretchen (called "The Wee Camp"). Gretchen never married and occupied the property long after her parents died. She kept a piano and was organist, choir director, and soloist at the Chapel. She was also treasurer of the Chapel for many years. Her Chris-Craft, the *Flying Squirrel,* now belongs to Bill and Annette Lux.

Gretchen Wewerka sold the house to Henry Walters of Ithaca, New York, in 1960. Bill and Ford Lux owned the house briefly in 1963 and then sold it to the present owners, Theodore and Phyllis Strack Dietze of Schenectady in 1964. Phyllis is the daughter of Lora Higby Strack and the niece of Roy Higby; she spent much of her life on the lake at the Higby compound.

TWIN PINES (LOT 230)

Twin Pines goes back to about 1913, when it was built as a year-round residence for Dana Bissell, manager of the Bissell and Yousey Lumber Company. Tom Hartz, the current owner of the camp, discovered during repairs that its construction is unique: "The studs of the cabin's exterior walls extend the entire height [two stories] from the bottom floor to the roof rafters. This method, called balloon framing, was popular during the period 1850–1920."[95] (See illustration on page 123.)

However, exceptions to standard practice betray the concern of the builder for haste and his ingenuity in insulation. Wall studs are set on top of the subfloor rather than being nailed along its edge, and bracing between the studs is lacking. The entire building is wrapped by two horizontal layers of one-inch by six-inch hardwood boards lined with two further layers of black felt paper to keep out the winter winds. The exterior is covered with slab siding.[96] A front porch provides views across the lake.

The paneled interior of the camp includes the original impressive corner stone fireplace and also two wood stoves. A big wood cookstove dominated the small kitchen, and a hand pump at the sink brought water from the well. A woodshed and outhouse (the latter long gone) completed the buildings.

When the enterprising Arthur Simmers took ownership of this building, he named it Ardomar.[97] After renting the camp on and off, Simmers sold it to Lawrence W. Hill from Long Island, who, a few years later, sold it to Herbert Daiker, Sr., of Utica, New York. Daiker held the camp briefly and then sold to James and Gail Monk of Newburyport, Massachusetts, who, with their four children, spent many summers there. In 1971, when business took the Monks west, they sold to Thomas and Doris Hartz of Wyomissing, Pennsylvania. The Hartzes have improved and modernized the camp and added a fine wildflower garden.

BIRCHWOOD CAMP (LOT 229)

This camp, third from the east end of the North Shore, started life in 1913 as the store built by the Bissell and Yousey Lumber Company for their lumberjacks and other employees. The house was a simple box built of rough-sawn lumber from the neighboring sawmill. Behind the downstairs room was an addition that served as an office for both the store and the lumber company. At one time, Charlie Dunn worked there as a bookkeeper. A woodshed served for storage. An outside stairway led from the front porch to a single large room on the second floor.

Birchwood, which was originally the store for Bissell and Yousey's lumber company, ca. 1920. George Stone added the porch soon after he bought it in 1919. Courtesy of Janet S. Holmes.

George Stone (Janet Holmes's father) of Niagara Falls, New York, bought the camp in 1919 for $750. When Arthur Simmers, who owned the land on both sides, announced that the woodshed was two feet over the property line to the east and would have to be moved, George Stone did just that. Using rollers and a car jack as well as some family help, he turned it ninety degrees while moving it, so that its narrow end faced the lake. Hobnail marks from the lumbermen's boots on the unfinished floor of the structure are still visible.

When Stone bought the camp, only one door and one window were on the first floor. He added windows and a new front door and brought the stairs with their worn softwood treads inside. At that time there was no road to Higby's, and the family rowed nearly four miles all the way from the Glennmore, or they were transported by the Boat Line. The men in the family built a scow, which they rowed to carry building materials. Many of the neighbors used the scow, eventually towing it by motorboat and still later attaching a motor directly to its stern. The property owners' dock, built in 1933 and less than a mile away, was a very welcome convenience.

In later years, Bill Holmes, Janet Stone's husband, made extensive improvements to the camp, including adding a picture window and, when electricity arrived in 1950, a master bedroom and bathroom on the first floor. Before that time, there was only an outhouse, a hand pump with lake water in the kitchen, and a dug well outside for drinking water. A door in the cover of the well gave access to a shelf where food was kept cool. It was wonderful, said Janet, to put away the oil lamps (except for emergencies), flip light switches, turn on a faucet, and flush a toilet. All this is not to mention refrigeration and the washing machine that replaced washtubs, scrub boards, and the hand-cranked wringer.

A sturdy one-hundred-foot dock was left from lumbering days. It was made of boards twelve feet long, two inches thick, and eight inches wide so that it could accommodate heavy loads of lumber. Occasional bits of coal or sharp pieces of cinders from the lumber camp steamboat still are found on the lake bottom. Other reminders of early days that have turned up include quantities of bottles—whiskey, beer, medicine—all evidence of the life of the lumberjacks.

After the sawmill fire in 1918, raspberries and blueberries appeared in the clearings where the lumber camp buildings had stood. Children loved to play in the area where there were remains of foundations, cribs, and the old iron smokestack that helped the sand to pile up and made a wonderful beach.

TRAIL'S END (LOT 227)

In 1924, Herbert Daiker, Sr., of Utica built the original Daiker camp on the easternmost lot owned by Arthur Simmers, adjacent to state land. Bill Lux tells the story of a fire in 1938 at Trail's End:

> Herb, Sr., [and other hunters] came back from a day's hunting to find the camp on fire. They were able to go in and bring out all the furniture and other things that were smoking. Luckily, the fire had triggered an old fashioned, probably homemade, fire extinguisher (said to have been developed by George Stone). It was made from a large light bulb from which the brass end and the center part were removed. Then it was filled with carbon tetrachloride and hung from the ceiling by a wire of low melting point. When heat melted the wire the bulb fell to the floor, smashed and spread carbon tetrachloride fumes throughout the room, which put out the fire.[98]

Later, in the early 1970s, another fire occurred at the camp while the men were out hunting:

> They were over by Merriam [Lake] having lunch when they heard the fire siren. The theory is that mice had built a nest against the stovepipe where it passed through the wall, and the nest caught fire. This time the camp burned to the ground and no one knew it until the men came in from hunting at dark. Only the piers and fireplace and chimney were standing. Coincidentally, while the fire burned, Herb Daiker, Jr., was flying over the lake and tried in every way to draw someone's attention to the fire, but to no avail.[99]

The men spent hours trying unsuccessfully to find their car keys in the ashes.

However, the next summer, all the hunters and their families and neighbors built Dick Daiker's new precut camp in just one week. They even incorporated the wonderful old stone fireplace, which remained standing.[100]

6 *Major Events on the Lake*

A FEW EVENTS at Big Moose Lake have continued to echo through the years. Some, such as the 1906 incident that inspired Theodore Dreiser's *An American Tragedy,* have become emblematic. Half of those who take the boat tour around the lake ask about the location of Grace Brown's murder. The narrative here is confined to the parts played by local residents, many of whom entertained visitors for years with tales of the part they themselves played in the original event.

Natural disasters—forest fires and storms—have affected the surrounding land and also left permanent impressions on the minds of those who experienced them.

In 1974 a group of Indians occupied the former Moss Lake Camp for Girls, which straddled the road to nearby towns where schools and stores essential to life at the lake were located. For three years, residents were hindered in their travel and apprehensive about their safety and that of their children.

These incidents have been woven into Big Moose history.

An American Tragedy and Big Moose Lake

Big Moose Lake's chief claim to fame is that it was the setting for the murder that formed the basis for Theodore Dreiser's 1925 book, *An American Tragedy.*[1] One of America's greatest novels, Dreiser's tale paints a picture not only of a murderer's mind but also of class struggles and ambition among various representative types in American society—urban and rural characters, male and female, rich and poor, and working-class laborers and industrial entrepreneurs. All are depicted with acute insight and sympathy. The story, which Dreiser chose after much

searching of newspapers, was based on a murder that took place at Big Moose Lake in 1906. His accurate descriptions of the setting evoke a strong emotional response among all familiar with the lake.

In the early summer of 1906, Chester Gillette, a stockroom clerk in his uncle's skirt factory in Cortland, New York, met Grace Brown, a young employee in the same factory. The two fell in love, and Grace soon found herself pregnant. At the same time, Chester began traveling in the higher social circles of his uncle's friends. In spite of Grace's pleas that he marry her, Chester determined to rid himself of this encumbrance to his aspirations. He took Grace on a trip to the Adirondacks and, after registering at the Glennmore Hotel, rented a boat, which he rowed into South Bay (not Punky Bay, a secluded inlet off South Bay that is often named as the scene of the murder). There, out of sight of all witnesses, he allegedly struck Grace with an oar or a tennis racket, knocking her out of the boat and leaving her to drown. He then swam to shore, changed into dry clothes, which he had brought along in a suitcase left at their picnic spot, and made his way to the Arrowhead Hotel at Inlet. Within a few days, the law caught up with him and he was taken to the Herkimer County Courthouse. The trial in Herkimer received sensational publicity, especially in the New York City tabloids, and was a 1906 parallel to the 1996 O. J. Simpson trial.

Dreiser, of course, fictionalized the story. Chester Gillette became Clyde Griffiths, and Grace Brown became Roberta Alden. Many other details were changed, and the story was fleshed out with conversation, extra characters, and additional incidents. In 1931, Paramount Studios released a black and white movie with the same

Glennmore Hotel with steamboat Zilpha, *ca. 1906. Courtesy of Wanda K. Martin.*

name as the novel. Actors included Phillips Holmes, Sylvia Sidney, Frances Dee as a girl of a higher social class, and Irving Pichel as the district attorney. A second movie version, also by Paramount and also in black and white, appeared in 1951. The title was changed to *A Place in the Sun,* and the film starred Shelley Winters, Montgomery Clift, Elizabeth Taylor, and Raymond Burr. In the second film, the setting was contemporary California.

Various versions of the tale, fiction and nonfiction, occupy reams of paper. However, only recently has anyone attempted to determine the hard facts. Craig Brandon, a newspaper journalist from Utica, New York, published in 1986 a meticulously researched account called *Murder in the Adirondacks: An American Tragedy Revisited.*[2] His book offers a broad context and describes in detail many of the peripheral characters as well as the principals. The author combed newspaper and court records, searched libraries and historical societies, dug through private correspondence, traveled to distant locations in Ohio and Illinois, and produced an accurate and readable account of the conflicts between fact and fiction. Brandon includes an extensive comparison of the actual events with Dreiser's fiction. He also gives an account of Dreiser's hostility to the producer of the 1931 film and the reluctance of local residents to discuss the case.

Another book, *Adirondack Tragedy: The Gillette Murder Case of 1906* by Joseph W. Brownell and Patricia Wawrzaszek,[3] appeared in the same year. This book omits most of the literary comparisons, but its endnotes provide documented sources for the true tale.

A well-researched play by Glenn Allen Smith, *Chester and Grace,* depicts the emotional struggles not only of

Chester and Grace but also of the families involved and even of the judge in the case. The play was presented at the Old Forge Arts Center by the Ilion Little Theatre on July 15 and 16, 2001.

Because so much has been written about the incident, our account is limited to the Big Moose Lake residents who figure in the story.

Jim McAllister, then a young employee of D. B. Sperry, owner of the Big Moose Transportation Company, drove Chester and Grace from the Station to the Glennmore Hotel. McAllister testified at the trial that on the day of the murder he waited long past the couple's scheduled departure time and finally drove the stage back to Big Moose Station without them.[4] McAllister was also a justice of the peace, and he traveled to the Old Forge House, where Chester had been taken from the Arrowhead Hotel in Inlet, for the arraignment.[5]

Andrew Morrison, proprietor of the Glennmore, recounted at the trial the arrival of the couple; his father, Robert Morrison, described Gillette's renting a rowboat from the hotel boat livery.[6]

Marjorie Carey, daughter of Edward O. Stanley, who owned Fern Spring Camp just north of the present site of Covewood, also testified. The district attorney promised in the newspapers that he would produce a witness to Grace's death cry. In fact, Marjorie had heard a scream at about the noon dinner hour, but she had seen nothing.[7] Her testimony probably generated publicity but did not actually add crucial evidence. There was also some confusion later about her name. At the time she heard the scream, her name was Marjorie Stanley. By the time she appeared before the court, however, she was married and

If the Name of the People of the State of New York

To *Marjorie Stanley*

YOU ARE COMMANDED to appear before the Supreme Court of the State of New York at a trail term thereof at the Court House, in the Village and County of Herkimer, on the *11th*

................day of *November* 1906, at 10 o'clock in the forenoon, as a witness in a Criminal Action, prosecuted by the People of the State of New York, against CHESTER GILLETTE.

Dated at the Town of Herkimer, N. Y., the 27 day of August 1906.

GEO. W. WARD, *District Attorney of Herkimer Co.*

A court summons that Marjorie Stanley received to appear at the trial of Chester Gillette, 1906. Courtesy of Frank Carey.

had become Marjorie Carey.[8] Her grandson, Francis "Frank" E. Carey Jr., still visits Big Moose regularly.

Roy Higby, owner of the Higby Club, traded for years on his tale of spotting the body of Grace Brown under the water of South Bay. Roy was a well-known raconteur. However, some people, including family members, report that Roy was not on the rescue boat and never told the dramatic story that follows until the other witnesses were dead. Nevertheless, Roy gives a detailed account of the story from his point of view in his book, *A Man from the Past*.[9]

Thirteen years old at the time, Roy was on the steamboat *Zilpha*, which belonged to his uncle, D. B. Sperry. The steamer was used to tow several small boats and a crew of men to South Bay to search for the bodies of the two missing persons. Roy was left on the large boat along with Frank Crabbe, the engineer. While waiting for the men in the smaller boats to drag the bottom for the body of Grace Brown, Roy spotted a white blur resting in about eight feet of water. The engineer, he said,

> took a long pike pole off the roof of the cabin and began prodding at the object. These pike poles were capped with a heavy, pointed iron shoe and used by lumbermen for poling logs in the water to keep them away from rocks, thereby preventing jams of timber in rivers. On the boat we used ours for easing into the dock in windy weather or poling out of shallow water. Frank used this pike for several minutes until he became convinced it [the white blur] was a body. He called in the boats, and by letting down a hook which attached to some article of clothing, they brought the girl's body to the surface.[10]

Roy recalled that the girl "had a deep cut diagonally across her forehead from the edge of her hair across one eyebrow and blood oozed from the cut."[11] (Roy does not explain what any mystery story fan knows, which is that dead bodies do not bleed.)

When the time came for the trial, Roy was staying at the family home in Utica so he could attend school. His father took him to two days of the trial. "Because of my age, father had arranged with local men that my name should not be brought into the case and I was never subpoenaed by either side, and I was not permitted to talk about it in any way, even with my school friends."[12]

Although Roy's account states that "Experts testified that Grace had no water in her lungs,"[13] the autopsy, as reported in Brownell and Warwzaszek's book, was sketchy and unprofessional even by the standards of the time. The book by Craig Brandon gives a more detailed account of the confusion surrounding the autopsy.[14] The coroner had allowed an undertaker to inject the body with embalming fluid before the autopsy took place. Of the five doctors involved, none was a specialist in forensic medicine. One of the doctors even admitted that "there had been evidence of drowning found during the autopsy, but that it had been left out of the official report."[15] In addition, "the physicians who had made the autopsy met on at least three separate occasions to go over their testimony to make sure they all told the same version."[16] The conclusion of the report was a single line stating that the cause of death was "Primarily concussion, followed by syncope [a swoon] and then asphyxiation."[17] It seemed clear to the jury that Grace was unconscious or dead when she entered the water.

However, Gillette insisted that Grace, who could not swim, felt unable to face her parents with the fact of her pregnancy. She had, he testified, jumped out of the boat without warning, and he had been unable to save her.[18] In spite of the clamor from the press for a confession, Gillette refused.[19] Rumors surfaced later that he had in fact confessed to his spiritual advisors,[20] but this claim was never verified.

The hysterical atmosphere generated by the press undoubtedly contributed to the jurors' speedy verdict. The jury found Gillette guilty of murder in the first degree, and the judge sentenced him to death by electrocution at Auburn prison. An appeal failed, and the sentence was carried out on March 30, 1908.

Controversy over Gillette's guilt continued even after his death. Roy Higby never tired of recounting his part in the story. He always ended with the account of a visit that the prosecuting district attorney of Herkimer County, George Ward, had made to his father after Gillette's death. Making a case for Grace Brown's suicide in her despair over Gillette's refusal to marry her, "Mr. Ward told father . . . 'Jim, if the defense had got this boy on the stand we would never have convicted Chester Gillette.' They would have impressed the jury with the fact that the injury to the girl's head came about as a result of the engineer's using a sharp iron-pointed pole while trying to identify the body on the lake bottom."[21] If young Roy had testified, as Higby said Ward believed, the jury would not have found Chester guilty.

Natural Disasters

We have very few accounts of the major storms and other disasters that have affected Big Moose Lake over the years. The first was a forest fire that occurred in 1903, recorded only because its effects were serious enough to warrant an appeal for help from New York State. This fire was followed by a hurricane in 1938, a blowdown in 1950 and, most recently, a microburst in 1995.

THE FOREST FIRE OF 1903

The desperate efforts of Jim Higby may have saved Big Moose from serious damage by fire in the summer of 1903. The season was particularly dry. Between the first week of April and the second week of June, no rain fell except for light local showers.

> May had been by most accounts the driest month since 1826. . . . [O]n May 27 . . . it was eighty-five degrees [at Saranac Lake] with wind out of the south; and on the seventh of June the thermometer read ninety degrees in the shade. Signs and portents were not good. With alarming frequency, fires appeared in April. Along the right-of-ways [*sic*] of the New York Central, the New York and Ottawa, the Chateaugay and the Saranac and Lake Placid railroads, fires followed in the wake of every train that passed by.[22]

The charred area—often referred to as the "burnt ground"—left after the forest fire of 1903, near the Sisters Lakes looking west over the Inlet and Big Moose Lake. Courtesy of Wanda K. Martin.

Moreover, in the early spring the trees had not yet leafed out, and the sun dried out the forest floor. Loggers did not customarily cut the small branches from the tops of trees, so huge tangles of brushwood were exposed to the sun and wind to become tinder for any spark.

In that disastrous summer, 377 forest fires occurred in the Adirondacks. These devastated nearly one-half million acres.[23] It was the worst year for fires in the history of the Adirondacks. Five years later, in 1908, almost 300,000 acres burned, but 1903 surpassed all records.[24]

Railroads were one culprit, but not the only one. Careless fishermen and hunters as well as lightning also started fires. Big Moose may have been particularly lucky. The author of the New York State report on forest fires for 1903 remarked, "The New York Central, from Fulton Chain to Mountain View, was bordered with smoke and flames, except on the eight-mile stretch through the private preserve [presumably around Lake Lila] of Dr. W. Seward Webb, where a large number of patrols were employed at his expense to follow each train, night or day, and extinguish the locomotive sparks that fell along the road." [25]

Fires in the woods were particularly dangerous, not only because of timber slashes but also because of the thick layer of decayed leaves and other mulch that tends to accumulate on the forest floor. Those familiar with the woods refer to it as the "duff." A fire that takes hold in the duff, which can be two or three feet thick in some places, can burn underground and pop up in unexpected places. The only real defense is to dig a wide swath that goes all the way down to the true soil. In the days before bulldozers, this was a huge job. The state provided money to pay firefighters, although the pay was kept low so that the unemployed would not be inspired to make jobs for themselves.

The 1903 fire was the biggest that Big Moose ever experienced. Roy Higby, ten years old at the time, recollects:

> For weeks the sun was a ball of red in the sky and we breathed smoke day and night. My father had been assigned to supervise fire fighting in the Big Moose area and at one time, he had more than 400 men in his crew. Most of them were French Canadian lumberjacks from nearby camps. One fire, about two miles from Big Moose [in the area near Sisters Lakes] and fortunately our only bad one, covered 2,000 acres. . . . It was my job to carry water and food to some of the fire fighters. I vividly remember seeing several deer running from the burned areas with their backs on fire. . . . The loss of animal life was heavy. Bodies of rabbits, fox and deer were found in the burned area. [26]

This fire was near Burnt Mountain not far from the two Sisters Lakes, and, although its cause was unknown, it was not the result of sparks from the railroad. Perhaps the most vivid account comes from Roy's father, Jim Higby, who was in charge of the operation. He wrote a report to the Forest, Fish, and Game Commission pleading for official authorization and indicating his problems in recruiting men to work when he had no funds to pay them immediately.

> 1903 We have a bad fire at Sisters Ponds in TWP [Township] 41. I put on about forty men yesterday and some thirty more last night. The belt is about $1/2$ mile wide by 1 mile long but is burning like a furnace. The temperature in one pool on Big Moose lake inlet became so high, the surface of the pool was covered with dead trout. The smoke and heat are intense but we have held it on the West and South. I have got a tough proposition. The men say I have no right to order them to fight fire in Hamilton County. If you will do so, please send me a written order that I may show them. That is not all, there are a lot of men that refuse to go, not knowing where the pay is to come from. You know there is no provision to pay before next winter. You see I am handicapped all around. I am sending 7 men that I will pay myself and the other hotels are sending in some men also. These floating chaps [probably the lumberjacks] demand their pay at once but I am unable to advance the money.

Higby continues with a description that indicates how hard the work was and the responsibilities he was taking on.

> I have no idea how the fire started nor can I find out anything about it. I have now 60 men on the ground, night and day. We are doing all we can and we'll save every rod of timber possible. I go around the fire line myself and direct the men where the work is most

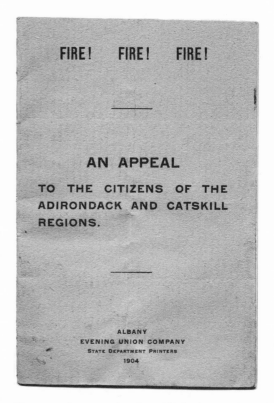

The cover of an appeal to the public by the superintendent of the state forests to help prevent forest fires in the Adirondack Park, 1904. Courtesy of Wanda K. Martin.

needed. I was not on the ground this A.M. but I put my son [Elmer Higby] in charge in my absence. He was up day before yesterday, night before last, and all day yesterday, without sleep or rest. The men have worked in heat and smoke. I think I can handle affairs now. I have taken up blankets and put in boats, tools and provisions. I haven't weighed out anything as yet because time has been so much taken up. But I will make an offer to board the men at $4.00 per week to save the bother of weighing provisions. Now another thing, how many hours is a day's work? The men say 8 hrs. I don't know what to think about it but am keeping time by the hour.

James Higby[27]

The letter was effective. The commission approved Higby's request and gave him the right to hire as many men as he wished to fight the fire.[28]

As a result of the fires in the early 1900s, the state began to build fire towers as observation posts. The first one was put up in 1909.[29] Others soon followed, although observers could not do much more than give early warning. Railroads switched to the use of petroleum fuel during the summer season. Eventually, helicopter inspections at particularly dangerous times superseded the towers. A few of the towers remain and, although they went out of use in the 1980s, some are being restored as part of Adirondack history.[30]

THE HURRICANE OF 1938

Occurring when weather forecasting was in its infancy, the hurricane of 1938 swooped down on the eastern part of the country from the northeast on September 20, 1938. It came without warning, and the trees, which all had developed root systems that would brace them against the prevailing west winds, fell on all sides, their tops snapped off. Romaine Kinne found himself caught in his boat, the *Big Moose,* at the east end of the lake with a full load of passengers. The only thing he could do was to lower the canvas curtains, keep the boat headed into the wind, and try to avoid the rocks that dot the bottom of the lake in that area. It was skillful seamanship that brought him and his frightened passengers home safely that day.[31]

Bill Dunn recalls walking up the Martin Road to deliver a magazine to Alice Martin. By the time he and his brother Nelson neared the house, the wind was really blowing and tree limbs were falling everywhere. Alice urged the two boys to sit the storm out on her porch,

which was on the sheltered side of the house. So Bill and Nelson Dunn sat out the famous hurricane of 1938 on Alice Martin's porch.

THE BLOWDOWN OF 1950

Richard "Bud" Brownell, a son of Ronald Brownell (then owner of the property where the Boy Scout Pioneer Camp had stood), recalls being in the woods near Russian Lake during the big blowdown of 1950. Then a youth of sixteen, Bud, his father, and his uncle were on a hunting trip on Saturday, November 25. The great storm roared down upon them from the east around noon, felling huge trees that had survived for centuries.

The party had separated before the beginning of the storm, and Bud was by himself. He remembers cowering alone under a large tree for what seemed like an eternity while the wind howled and trees all around were snapping like matchsticks, flying through the air. Winds during the storm approached 100 miles an hour. When it finally abated late in the day, Bud was relieved to hear his name being called, and he was finally reunited, unhurt, with his father and uncle. It seemed a miracle!

The path back to Big Moose Lake was obliterated, and it took many hours to climb over and through the devastation. Even in retrospect, Bud shudders as he recalls the scene. "It was horrible! Such a mess—and it remained so for many, many years."

THE MICROBURST OF 1995

We have no direct personal accounts of the windstorm that swept through Big Moose Lake in the early morning of July 15, 1995. It was called a *derecho,* close kin to a hurricane except that it traveled in a straight line rather than whirling. The storm flattened trees on 430,000 acres throughout the Adirondack Park and affected much more territory. The Five Ponds area north of Big Moose was particularly hard hit, and two people, one in the Five Ponds area, were killed when trees fell on them or on their tents.

At Big Moose Lake, a huge swath of trees along the trail to Gull Lakes was torn up by the roots. The trail was obliterated and the cliff on its west side exposed. At 6:00 A.M. the wind shrieked across the water, tearing up trees on the Mawhinney property on Crag Point and damaging the porch. The ten-minute blast of wind left a clear path of downed trees between the Mawhinneys' place and the

Charles Smith cottage to the east, where more property damage occurred. Other property on the south side of the lake also felt the blast. Tenants in the Hostages' Higby Point cottage were awakened by the noise of the wind and rain, leapt out of bed, and rushed to close the windows on the lake side of the house. By the time they reached the kitchen, the rain had drenched the opposite wall some ten feet away. A tree that stood three feet from the house and one foot from the parking spot was uprooted, missing in its fall both the camp and the car that stood next to it. Trees along the southeastern shore also came down, many simply torn up by the roots. In front of the Chapel a falling tree broke a window in the building, allowing rainwater to flood the vestibule and part of the sanctuary. Campers showed up with pails and mops to clean up and prevent permanent damage. A four-day power outage throughout the area followed, but fortunately nobody at Big Moose was injured.

Moss Lake and the Indian Occupation

The news swept through the Big Moose community on May 13, 1974: a group of Indians had taken over the former Moss Lake Camp for Girls on Big Moose Road. The group had seized a 612-acre tract of land and more than fifty-three buildings. They had blocked the foot trails that led into the area, and they now controlled the ground on both sides of the only direct road to Eagle Bay and the outside world. Most alarming, a rumor had begun to circulate that the Indians were armed.

This turn of events was surprising but not without precedent. In the year before the Indians arrived at Moss Lake, there had been a number of confrontations between the federal government, represented by the Bureau of Indian Affairs, and midwestern Indian tribes. The issues involved a variety of economic and civil-liberty questions. But in February 1973, tensions between the government and the Indians rose when an Indian was killed in Custer, South Dakota.[32] Shortly afterwards there was a confrontation between government troops and Indians at Wounded Knee,[33] site of a massacre of Indians by the federal government in 1890.[34]

Adding to the apprehension of the Big Moose residents was a letter written by Louis Hall, secretary of the Caughnawaga (Quebec) Branch of the Six Nations Confederacy,[35] to Dennis Banks, leader of the American Indian Movement and a chief spokesman at Wounded Knee. Many of the occupants of Moss Lake were Mohawks and had come from the Caughnawaga reservation. The F.B.I. had obtained the letter secretly, circulating it as a warning. In it the Indians outlined their plans to take over five million acres in New York State and Vermont by moving in and squatting on the land. Urging other Indians to join them, they stated that they would establish "a land base for [the] A.I.M. [American Indian Movement] where their Vietnam veterans may train young warriors in the art of defending their homeland and where they may settle with their families."[36]

The Indians called the settlement Ganienkeh or Land of the Flint and stated that they intended to live like their forefathers. Calling themselves Traditional Indians, they "sought to establish the life style of their ancestors, separate from white society—and separate from the elective Indian system which, in their view, is too closely tied to white man's ways."[37] According to their spokesman, Art Montour (a Mohawk Indian also known as Kakwirakeron), they wanted the coming generation to "have a clear-cut choice of living on the reservation, being assimilated or taking up the traditional life."[38] Despite these peaceful plans, and the fact that women and children were among the sixty or so occupants of the camp, tensions at Big Moose ran high.

Although the road between Eagle Bay and Big Moose was not cut off, a few cars were stopped at gunpoint by Indians. Police records showed two reports of shots fired in the vicinity. However, there was never any evidence that the training ground for militant young warriors was established.

But on October 28, 1974, events took a more serious turn. Two unarmed young men, residents of Inlet, who were driving to Big Moose, had a verbal confrontation with some of the Moss Lake Indians. When the two men were returning to Inlet, Indians fired six bullets into their car, wounding one of the men. On the same day, a car carrying a family of four from Geneva, New York, was struck by bullets and shotgun pellets. One of the occupants, nine-year-old April Madigan, sustained two wounds in her back, requiring a two-week hospital stay and at least two rounds of surgery.

Soon afterward, New York State police set up a checkpoint just outside Eagle Bay and established a second checkpoint near the Higby Road. During the early days of the occupation, cars traveling the road were escorted past the Ganienkeh property in groups. Later, police checked license plates and communicated by telephone to be certain that residents' cars passed the Indian encampment safely.

But local residents were still very much concerned. Children traveled regularly past the encampment in order to get to school. The road was also the only access to workplaces, stores, and medical facilities and was in constant use. Letters of complaint appeared in newspapers all around the Adirondacks, and in Utica, Syracuse, and Albany.

When the occupation first took place, Republican Malcolm Wilson was governor of New York, but, with an election coming up, was reluctant to take any action. In November 1974, Democrat Hugh Carey was elected. He, too, was wary of touching off a bloody confrontation by sending in police to remove the Indians. Also, neither governor did anything significant to inform local residents of possible courses of action, of the legal status of either group, or of attempts at negotiation.

In response, Big Moose residents formed an organization called Concerned Persons of the Central Adirondacks. They published a newsletter called *COPCA* and solicited support from people outside the immediate area. They also tried to arouse the interest of New York State officials.

At the same time, citizens who sympathized with the Indians began to appear. An organization called RAIN (Rights for American Indians Now) sprang up and found support from other groups around the country. Church organizations also contributed food, clothing, and money in answer to the Indians' plea that they needed help until they could become self-supporting. One of these groups was part of the national office of the Presby-

Environmental Conservation Commissioner Ogden Reid talking with Art Montour, spokesman for the Indians at Moss Lake, 1975. Courtesy of John Isley.

The "Walk-By" past the Moss Lake Indian encampment, May 11, 1976. Courtesy of Barbara K. Wheeler.

terian Church, and a bumper sticker soon appeared that read, "Indians, don't shoot! I'm a Presbyterian!"

Late in the fall of 1974, the Big Moose Property Owners Association held two special meetings at a motel just off the New York State Thruway in Syracuse. The meetings were well attended, and the group decided to appeal to the courts.

Early in the summer of 1975, five members of the Big Moose Lake community, Charles T. Beeching Jr., William P. Burrows, Donald F. Dew, Howard Martin, and Dennis McAllister, instituted a lawsuit against the supreme court of the state of New York, County of Oneida. They requested that the state issue a court order for the Indians to vacate the land, charging that environmental laws were being violated.

On July 15, 1975, Ogden Reid, then environmental conservation commissioner and acting as the emissary of Governor Hugh Carey, spoke to more than 150 people at the Big Moose Community Chapel. He said that area residents "could expect a settlement of the Indian occupation at nearby Moss Lake within two months."[39] Reid also paid a call at Moss Lake and conversed with Indian leader Art Montour.

However, state efforts at resolving the situation were slow, and Big Moose residents, who knew little of what was going on, were impatient. After watching two years of inaction on the part of the state, COPCA organized a protest, a "Walk-By" that took place on Sunday, May 11, 1976 (Mother's Day), in an attempt to attract the attention of the authorities. State troopers were on hand to ensure order. Some 200 people walked silently past the Moss Lake property. Participant Barbara Kinne Wheeler described the eerie stillness, broken only by the sound of one unseen Indian chanting in the distance. The marchers carried signs such as "Delayed Law is No Law" and "Justice for All." State senator James H. Donovan and assemblyman William R. Sears, frustrated by Carey's inaction, both participated. The Indians and their supporters countered with signs that read "Stop the Genocide Now" and "Honor U.S. Indian Treaties." Ironically, both groups expressed anger with the government rather than with one another.

Just before the protest, on April 28, 1976, Ogden Reid had resigned, citing "very serious external pressures." Peter A. A. Berle was appointed in his place.[40] Berle noted extensive dissension within the Department of Environmental Conservation and many vacancies in upper-level staff jobs. Whether the march and the change in personnel made a difference is unknown, but apparently serious negotiations to resolve the matter soon began.

Nearly three years after the initial occupation, New York State, with Mario Cuomo (then secretary of state) acting as broker, arranged an agreement to exchange the Moss Lake property for a much larger tract of land near the St. Lawrence River in the northeastern corner of New York State. The new site was Miner Lake State Park in Clinton County, to be leased to the Indians along with a portion of the Macomb Reservation in the town of Schuyler Falls, also in Clinton County. In addition, a private trust was to be established that would acquire private property in the county for the Indians. The Indians were also to pay "rent" through the establishment of a cultural resource—a model village that would demonstrate to the public the Mohawk way of life.

Michael Tarbell, a Mohawk Indian who is museum educator at the Iroquois Indian Museum near Cobleskill, told us that the Ganienkeh community, which follows the warrior tradition, still existed in 2002. Tarbell had no knowledge of a model village but reported that the group was supporting itself by logging and by operating a bingo business.[41]

October 31, 1977, was the deadline for the Indians' departure from Moss Lake. Twenty-five to thirty Indian families moved to the new location. A few Indians lingered at Moss Lake through the winter of 1977–78 until they could arrange for living quarters at the new location. However, Big Moose residents were satisfied that the problems were over. William Marleau, the local forest ranger for about thirty years, said, "For all practical purposes, the Indians are out of there."[42]

However, litigation on the larger question of additional land claimed by this group of Indians continued until 1982. In fact, Big Moose Lake was part of the Oneida Indian aboriginal lands, which were conveyed to the State of New York in the 1788 Treaty of Fort Schuyler. While the Oneidas sought to invalidate the treaty and to regain possession of the land, the courts held that the treaty was in fact valid, because New York State had had authority to enter into it, even though the United States Constitution was not ratified until 1789.[43] Therefore, although other parts of New York State are still in dispute, Big Moose is not part of the current legal entanglements.

7 Recreation

THE FIRST SETTLERS in the Adirondacks never expected that the local economy would thrive on recreation and not on agriculture or mining. Even before railroads provided access to the wilderness, sportsmen came to fish and hunt. However, it was ease of travel that started the influx of vacationers in the late nineteenth century.

Webb completed his railroad about the time that paid vacations began to enter the picture for workers, at least for those in the higher echelons of business. Cities were hot, humid, and smelly —good places to get away from in the summer. Air conditioning and even comfortable light clothing were far in the future. Although the upper classes might escape to Newport, Rhode Island, or even Europe, it began to be possible for a prosperous segment of the middle class to enjoy cool weather and fresh air closer to home.

As hotels sprang up, much of the appeal was simply to enjoy the fresh air (as tents and sleeping balconies attest) or to participate in social activities and view the scenery from hotel porches. Indeed, many hotels advertised in their brochures the extent of their porches, which of course offered an opportunity for promenades without the inconvenience of mud or rain.

When families began to come to the woods, often the wives were, or learned to be, fishermen along with the husbands. A surprising number of early photographs show women displaying the results of their prowess with a fishing pole. Hunting was largely confined to men, perhaps in part because suitable clothing for women was not available.

More intrepid individuals went for so-called tramps in the woods. Frank Carey has gleaned from old maps information about early trails and how they changed over the years.

Men and women alike rowed guideboats. The camp log at Big Moose Lodge in West Bay mentions a regatta at Higby's as early as 1910. Guideboat races of all kinds (single, double, men's, women's, and others) were a main

Group socializing on the porch of the Glennmore Hotel, ca. 1910. Courtesy of Richard Widdicombe.

209

Camp Crag female guest fishing, ca. 1920. Courtesy of Robert and Elizabeth Smith.

Spectators watching a guideboat regatta from the dock at Burdick's Camp, ca. 1910. Courtesy of Wanda K. Martin.

Canoe jousting off the dock of the Higby Club, ca. 1930s. Courtesy of Richard Widdicombe.

feature of these events. Messages on postcards attest to the simple pleasure of being in the woods. In her diary for 1900, Lena Retter mentions rowing. Also, photographs of boats on the water indicate the popularity of this pastime.

Youngsters found their own amusements, as Henry Bruyn's and Joy Hostage's accounts testify. In the 1920s and 1930s, the advent of motors for boats changed the picture. New varieties of boats appeared, making possible

sports that involved towing athletic young people upon the water. Motors evolved, and Big Moose Lake saw not only airplanes that could take passengers to distant lakes but also boats with ten-, fifteen-, or twenty-five-horsepower motors that ran at speeds considered dangerous.

After World War II, waterskiing became an obsession with some of the lake residents. Later, jet skis roared in, to the dismay of many on the lake. Still later, history came full circle and muscle power in the form of sailing, wind-surfing, canoeing, and kayaking entered the scene again.

Square dancing was popular, and Earl Covey's daughter, Mary Alden Williams, offers her reminiscences.

The voices and accounts in this section on recreation capture the atmosphere of many of these pursuits.

Early Amusements

ACTIVITIES AT PRIVATE CAMPS

We have a glimpse of life on the lake in 1900 in Lena Retter's diary for that year. She clearly implies that she, an attractive seventeen-year-old girl, anticipated an active social life at the family's new camp on Turtle Point.[1] The expected stream of callers soon began. She records frequent visitors including the Leslie Browns, whose camp was across the channel leading into North Bay, as well as Grace Woodbury of Edilgra Camp, the Swancotts of Witch-Hopple Lodge, and the Allbrights of Brightwood Lodge, all of the latter on the North Shore. There was also a parade of young men, most of whom seem to have been guests at Higby's hotel across the lake. Lena decorously refers to them all as "Mr.," as was the custom of the day. They enjoyed such pastimes as rowing, quoits, target-shooting contests (in preparation for hunting), card games, and numerous campfires that were usually enhanced with popcorn or fudge. There were frequent trips by guideboat to Higby's for milk and for mail. Higby's evidently held regular campfires where guests sat around a fire, told stories, sang, and ate popcorn or other treats. On August 14, Lena writes, "This evening . . . while Matie [Lena's sister, Janet] and I were sitting on the rocks

Mr. Porter and Mr. Hawkins came over and took us over to the campfire. They had a dandy one. We had fudge and danced afterwards. We met Grace Woodbury. She is very nice and sings beautifully." A few days later "Matie and I took Miss Woodbury [Grace] out, at least we went over to hear a gramaphone [no doubt then a novelty] and everybody was out on the water listening to it, so we went out and Miss Woodbury paddled. She paddles perfectly fine and does not make a sound."

Swimming does not appear to have been a regular activity, although in one instance Lena writes, "Matie went in bathing this morning but she is such a coward that she doesn't seem to have much fun."

Groups also went on "tramps" to Twitchell, Mays, and Dart's Lakes and down the Outlet. An interesting excursion occurred on August 11:

> Mr. Crapsey [evidently a guest at Higby's] came over early this morning and asked us if we would like to take a trip to Fourth lake and go through the chain to Old Forge. It was very rough and Mr. Crapsey rowed us over to Darts where we took the stage to Eagle Bay. The roads were simply terrible. Mr. and Mrs. Williams, Mr. and Mrs. Boller, Mr. Price, Matie and I comprised the last buckboard. 3 wagons in all. There were a party of twenty. I was very much disappointed to find that Mr. Crapsey was not going—He is a fine fellow. The trip through the chain was perfectly fine. The lake was very rough. We saw ex-president Harrison's camp. It is nothing extra. We reached home about 7 o'clock . . . Mr. Crapsey is ever so sincere and quite attractive.

It would be interesting to know what Lena would have considered a noteworthy camp. President Harrison's

Sailing on Big Moose Lake, ca. 1930.
Courtesy of Diane Ritz.

house was perhaps too much like the camps at Big Moose for her taste and not grand enough to impress her.

On August 4, Lena writes, "The Indian called about half past ten this morning and we bought quite a number of things from him. Papa ordered some large birch bark picture frames."

Later, on August 23, she adds, "The Indian brought the frame I ordered and it is sweet." This is surely a reference to Julian Dennis, an Abenaki Indian living in Old Forge, who made regular canoe trips around the lakes in the area selling pack baskets, snowshoes, and other items.

There are notes of visits to hotels other than Higby's. About Lake View she says, "Everything is perfectly lovely there—much prettier than I expected." She also mentions the Glennmore and "Camp Covey" [Camp Crag]. Lena records no actual visits to the latter two.

FISHING

The fishing that had brought the earliest visitors to the lake continued, but perhaps more decorously. In a photograph preserved in the Wightman family, Dr. Wightman is shown teaching his nephew, Orrin Wightman Jr., to fish while his niece, Julia Wightman, looks on (see illustration below). The picture was made (probably in the early 1920s) by Orrin's father, Dr. Orrin S. Wightman, who was a gifted amateur photographer and who spent many summers at the lake with his two children.

SOCIAL ACTIVITIES IN THE 1930s

In the 1920s and 1930s, the Colpitts camp on the North Shore was the center of much social activity. A tennis court, built to the east of the house, was used not only for many memorable tennis matches but also for plays and even for a "circus." The circus, held in 1933, raised money for the Chapel at a time when its budget was very low. Ellie Reed Koppe gives a vivid description of it in her history of the Big Moose Community Chapel. "It started with a parade, music provided by an 'orchestra' from Higby's (which never did get together on the same tune!). There was a chariot race (with wheelbarrows) [featuring Ben Hur and Ben Him]. Lucy Colpitts [Walter's daughter, later Mrs. Howard Menand Jr.] walked the tight rope. The Judson boys did acrobatics. There were many other events, a marvelous time was had by all, and the Chapel income was augmented."[2] The circus was written up at great length in the *Adirondack Arrow*[3] and has attained legendary status. There were also a barely controllable trained two-part elephant named G.O.P. who had lost all but a very few friends the previous November, a Mademoiselle Samson who lifted a 2,000-pound block of iron, King Keng (relative of King Kong), several clowns, and many other acts, all presided over by Walter Colpitts. The circus raised a generous $105 for the Chapel. Home movies of the event, which were run both forward and backward, provided entertainment at the Colpittses' house on many occasions.

Percy Wightman fishing with a niece and nephew, ca. 1910. Courtesy of Elizabeth K. Singleton.

Jack Judson recalls that the Colpitts camp was

> a beehive of activity . . . on a Saturday night. Walter Colpitts had a big slide on the dock. It was watered so you could slide down easily—and fast. He also had a cart built to go down the slide on wheels on rails. Pictures of those doings plus aquaplane activity were shown, and then reversed, on Saturday night accompanied by cookies and punch. Boats from most parts of the lake brought people to the dock. Mr. Colpitts had a friend who came up in his own seaplane, and I think a good portion of Big Moose people got a ride.[4]

A variety of social activities took place during the 1930s, when the Bruyn boys became teenagers and eventually college students. Henry remembers square dances held on the upper floor of the boathouse at Higby's. These were finally discontinued because of concern that the aging floor would no longer hold the crowds. Square dances also took place at Covewood about every two weeks. In addition, there were gatherings at the Colpittses' guest house, the former Shropshire house, where, according to Henry Bruyn, "The favorite game was 'murder.' This involved drawing cards with the person holding the ace of spades being the murderer. The lights were turned out and everyone circulated throughout the house, trying to avoid contact with the unknown murderer. This circulation involved teaming up girls and boys with much timid physical contact."[5]

All in all, the amusements of the day showed a creativity and a sense of fun not dependent on outside influences.

Hiking Trails

THE ONLY ROUTE TO THE LAKE

The earliest visitors to Big Moose Lake must have cut their own trails to reach the lake, because there is no record of any trails made by Native Americans or the seasonal trappers who were known to have passed through the area before settlers arrived.

These early settlers and sportsmen came from the Fulton Chain of Lakes via a series of carries between lakes. The oldest-known route began as a footpath between Fourth Lake and Bub Lake, on to Moss Lake, then Dart's, and finally up the Outlet to Big Moose. An early account of Big Moose settlers describes hand carrying building materials over this route.[6] Another route began with a carry from Third Lake to Rondaxe Lake and proceeded from there to Dart's and the Inlet, using the same final trail segment as the Fourth Lake route.

The opening of the railroad in 1892 caused the early trails from the Fulton Chain to fall into disuse. However, the last segment of the early trails from Dart's to Big Moose Lake continued as part of a new route for travelers to reach Dart's Lake. With the commencement of rail service to Big Moose, a carriage road was opened from the Station to the lake, and steamboat service on the lake began. A steamboat stop known as "Dart's Landing" was established at the old trail terminus slightly west of the Outlet on property later owned by the Ayer family. At this time, travelers to Dart's could go by train to Big Moose Station, travel to the lake on the new carriage road, take the steamboat to Dart's Landing, and then take the old trail to Dart's Lake.[7]

EARLY RECREATIONAL TRAILS

In the early years most trails were travel routes, and as such they were strictly utilitarian. Trails tended to follow the easiest path from one place to another. But recreational trails leading to scenic views, good fishing spots, and other areas of interest also existed almost from the beginning of the settlement. The earliest is the trail to Billy's Bald Spot from the West Bay's northern shore.

Early residents maintained trails to remote hunting camps, and the hotels and public camps began publishing trail maps for their guests. A 1903 map[8] shows hiking trails originating from the shores of Big Moose Lake to the following lakes and wilderness ponds:

Mays Pond. This trail originated from the Higby Camp and continued past Mays Pond to Queer Lake. The Ainsworth family maintained a hunting camp on Queer Lake at the site of the present Department of Environmental Conservation (DEC) shelter.

Twitchell Lake. This trail originated from the midpoint of the north shore of North Bay and ended at the Twitchell Lake Inn.

Merriam Lake. This trail also originated from the midpoint of the North Bay north shore and was, therefore, not the same as the current Merriam Lake trail, which begins near the end of North Bay.

Gull Lakes. The trail originated in the Marsh (Big Moose Lake Inlet) at the same point as the current trail, but continued past Gull Lakes to Andes Creek,[9] which is navigable (with some carries over beaver dams) for sev-

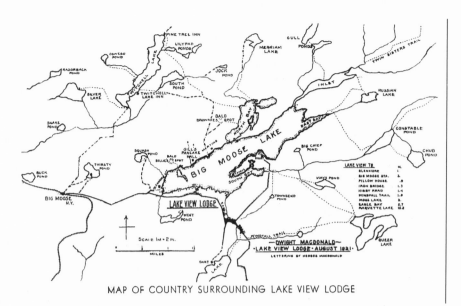

MAP OF COUNTRY SURROUNDING LAKE VIEW LODGE

Lake View Lodge map of trails around Big Moose Lake, 1921. Courtesy of Wanda K. Martin.

eral miles in that area. The trail followed Andes Creek north to a carry to Terror Lake. This suggests that guideboats could have been used by sportsmen going to Terror Lake. Howard Martin once demonstrated the feasibility of this[10] by traveling this route from Big Moose Lake to Terror Lake. This navigable portion of Andes Creek was also the site of the hunting camp of Carson Conkey, brother of Dave Conkey, area guide and ranger at Beaver River.

Russian Lake. This early trail originated from the south shore of the Marsh. The current trail to Russian Lake from East Bay came many years later. Charlie Martin once had a hunting camp on Russian Lake near its inlet.

Constable Pond. The trail began at the end of East Bay. At Constable Pond it divided. One branch went to Chub Pond and the other to Pigeon Lake, once known as Crooked Pond.[11]

Sisters Lakes. The trail originated from the eastern end of the marsh. A quarter mile from the trailhead, a side trail led to Andes Creek, the site of attractive rapids and an open camp later donated to the Big Moose Property Owners Association by Kay Young, a longtime guest at Lake View Lodge. A DEC shelter stands at this location today. The Martin family's hunting camp at Lower Sisters Lake was in existence in 1903 and was burned under state orders in the late 1930s or early 1940s.

GROWTH AND CHANGE

As the community grew, new trails were blazed and older trails rerouted. Generally, there was a trend to provide trail access from roads as they were built, and in some instances the lakeshore access was abandoned.

The trail to Billy's Bald Spot was extended to Squash Pond, and two different trails to Squash Pond were created from different points on the Martin Road. Bill Dunn and Gordon Kellogg built one of these in the late 1930s. In addition, a trail was made from Squash Pond to Thirsty Pond near the Twitchell Lake Road.

The trail to Twitchell Lake changed in several ways. The original trail was relocated to pass close to South Pond, also once known as Sunshine Pond.[12] Both the old and new routes seem to have been maintained, because they appeared on a cross-country ski trail map[13] from the 1970s. Later, a connection to the original Twitchell Lake trail was created from the end of the Martin Road; a 1941 hiking map[14] shows a trail from this new connection to Brown's Rock. Near South Pond, a new branch was opened to Lone Pine Camp at the northeastern end of Twitchell Lake.

Two trails to Townsend Pond were created by persons unknown. An early trail originated from South Bay, while a later trail started from the Higby Camp. This later trail was still appearing on hiking maps in the 1940s.

West Pond was also the destination of several trails. An early trail originated from Nelson Dunn's camp on the West Bay shore near the Chapel. When the road from Eagle Bay was completed, it crossed the trail. The trail segment from the shore to the road was abandoned, and the trail then began at Nelson Dunn's garage on the road. Some time later, this trail was extended to Safford Pond. When the current trail to West Pond from the Glennmore corner was created, it joined the original trail in a small clearing near the falls on the West Pond outlet. The remainder of the original trail—from the road to this intersection—was then abandoned.[15]

Three different trails led to Big Chief Pond at various times. The earliest was from the Higby Camp.[16] A second trail[17] came from the West Mountain trail and originated about halfway between the Higby Road and Constable Pond. The third trail[18] originated from Camp Alkmaar, the Vander Veer family's camp on the southeastern shore.

The trails in the area surrounding Constable Pond, Mays Pond, and Queer Lake changed considerably over the years. By 1941 the West Mountain trail had been created, and it followed a path very close to what is there today. Individual trails then branched off to the various area ponds and to Williams's New Wood Lumber Camp.[19] This camp was about a quarter mile northwest of Mays Pond on land purchased from Guy Harry by Charles and Fred Williams of Lake View Lodge. The Williamses used the land to cut firewood for Lake View Lodge and constructed the small camp to support their woodcutting operations there. From this woodlot, the Williamses transported their firewood to Lake View Lodge by creating a route that crossed the Mays Pond property of C. O. Nichols. However, they had not obtained permission, and litigation ensued. An out-of-court settlement was eventually reached through the intercession of Nelson Dunn, caretaker of Nichols's property.[20]

By this time, the Windfall Trail from the Big Moose Road into Queer Lake had also been opened. These changes left only two trails into the area from the lakeshore—the Camp Alkmaar trail via Big Chief Pond and the original Constable Pond trail from East Bay, starting from the location occupied for many years by the Boy Scout Camp. With these changes, there were then three trails originating from the Higby Road: the West Mountain trail, the Townsend Pond trail, and a trail up Sugar Loaf Mountain. Change in this area has continued, and DEC trails today are significantly different in the areas of Mays Pond and Queer Lake.

EVOLUTION AND REVOLUTION

During the gradual expansion and evolution of the trails, there were two instances of violent disruption and destruction. The first was on November 25, 1950. East winds of 100 miles per hour obliterated many trails. The destruction was immense. The Adirondack Park con-

tracted with logging companies to remove downed trees, because to let them remain on the forest floor was deemed an unacceptable fire hazard.[21] Decisions regarding the reopening of trails were influenced by the trends away from water access and toward road access, and the trail from East Bay to Constable Pond was abandoned.

The second violent disruption of trails was the microburst on July 15, 1995. This anomalous event created tornado-like destruction, at times extremely localized. The privately maintained trail from Twitchell Lake to Terror Lake was obliterated, and as of this writing it has not been reopened. The trail to Gull Lakes from the Marsh was rendered impassable, and it was several days before campers at the DEC shelter there could get out. Their entries in the shelter's log book (now lost) are chilling.

THE PRESENT

Trails today are of two types: those maintained by the DEC and those privately maintained. The Adirondack Mountain Club publishes maps that include both kinds of trails, although it is admittedly difficult for the club to keep current with privately maintained trails. The club's current maps show the private Billy's Bald Spot trail but not the Brown's Rock trail on Waldheim property. And they continue to show the private trail to Squash Pond, although field visits disclose that it is barely discernible and heavily overgrown.

Recollections of Hunting and Fishing in the 1930s | *William Lux*

HUNTING

As kids we would go to Big Moose in the winter to hunt rabbits. Dad would load the toboggan—boy, that was a miserable thing to pull—and his pack basket, and off we'd go across the ice to camp.

Dad let me hunt for two years before I was old enough to have a license. I think you could get a license at sixteen. At that time, Dad, Herb Daiker, Gordon Wood, Harry Latus, Harry Swancott, and my brother Jim hunted just about every weekend.

We used to get quite a few rabbits, especially if we had a good dog. The best dog was Dick Daiker's, named

Bill Lux has summered on the North Shore since he was a child.

Brooker. He was a crackerjack. He never barked unless he was on a hot rabbit trail, and he never left that trail until one of us had seen the rabbit. That was great fun.

Gordon Wood was an officer at the Savage Arms Company [in Utica], and in the mid-1930s he would bring up some experimental guns that had a new load [a different amount of powder or a new bullet] or some new gadget they were trying out. Everybody would shoot them to see how they liked them. He used to bring up guns for me to use, before I owned my own. Besides the regulars, Bill Holmes and his son, Hap, hunted sometimes. Later, when they were old enough, Herb Daiker Jr., Dick Daiker, and my brother Don joined the party.

We all slept at Herb Daiker's camp—the one that burned down just after Dick took it over. We'd go up Friday nights—and this seems silly now—we'd stay through a huge dinner on Sunday evening and then go home, sometimes after midnight. We hunted right up until the last weekend of deer season, or as long as we could get across the lake. Several times we had to break ice to get out, and sometimes we left on Saturday instead of Sunday because the ice was forming fast. One time, Herb, Jr., and I took the kicker [small outboard motor] across the lake, and had to break ice well over half an inch thick. We broke a channel across, and then went back for the others. Starting back through our channel, we had to break ice all over again. It was a really cold night.

There were a lot of deer in those days before World War II. It was nothing to see fifteen or twenty deer when we were out hunting during the day, and we used to get quite a few. I remember one year when we had ten deer lined up at one time. We'd drive the deer in the morning and still-hunt in the afternoon. When I first started hunting, I did mostly driving—I think they thought I was better at that. The first buck I ever shot is the one that's hanging up in our living room.

A typical hunting day started before daylight, when Dad would get up and make a huge breakfast of pancakes, bacon, and sausage. Then we'd go out and drive the point first, from Otto's to Daiker's. Sometimes we'd hunt Mount Tom and sometimes the ridges behind Mount Tom, going up by the trail behind George Stone's.

Once, when an old friend of Dad's, Harold Lyman, was hunting, Dad said to him, "Harold, you always draw the drives and seldom the watches. I'll take your place driving today and you can stand watch." Well, Harold was very pleased and off they went. But Dad hadn't gone 200 yards down the trail when he spotted a nice six-point buck standing between the trail and the shore. He shot it, and later, when the drive was finished, he took Harold over there and showed him the buck. Harold was not happy. One other thing I remember about Harold: he always wanted to use leftover pancakes in place of bread for his sandwiches, which was usually corned beef with a slice of cheese.

Another time, Dad, Don, and I were with Dad's good friend and super fly fisherman, Lee Spinning. We were over near Woodbury's, and spotted a doe lying in deep snow. She was so weak she could hardly stand, but she finally got up and walked a few feet. We knew she was starving. We went and got an axe at camp, and returned and cut down a three-inch birch tree near the doe. When we went back a couple of weeks later, there were deer tracks all around the birch, which had been stripped clean. I know we saved that deer's life.

Deer hunters at Covewood Lodge, ca. 1930. Courtesy of Frank Carey.

FISHING

This is one of the first fishing experiences I had as a kid. It was either 1929 or 1930. One day, Hobe Casler brought over an eighteen-pound lake trout he'd caught to show to my Dad (Fordyce G. Lux, Sr.). It was a rather impressive fish.

When I was probably eight years old, around 1930, Dad and my honorary Uncle Harry (Harry Swancott) and I went to Chub Pond to fish for brook trout. Harry had a small—probably fourteen foot—guideboat they called a "Raider." We rowed that down to the Scout Camp, and Dad or Harry carried it up and over to Constable. Then we rowed it up Constable and carried it into Chub. That was the first time that I ever had coffee in my life. Dad had brought an old five-pound honey pail with egg shells and coffee in it, and we boiled up some coffee for lunch. We caught a few trout. I don't remember how many or how big, but it was a big day for me to go fishing with Dad and Uncle Harry.

In the spring we'd catch trout off the docks, the best luck being on Woodbury's and Saunder's. I remember one morning back in 1930 or 1931. Mom was getting breakfast and she said, "Billy, go over to Saunder's dock and catch some fish for breakfast." I said, "How many do you want, Mom?" She answered, "Well, there are seven of us, why don't you get seven." So I caught seven brook trout, eight or nine inches each, and it didn't take me twenty minutes before I was back with them. Cleaned.

We also used to fish at Andes Creek and Sister's outlet. One day, Dad and either my brother Jim or Don and I were at Sister's, and we found a boat sunk in the water. I later saw a boat just like it at the Adirondack Museum that had been found in some other nearby lake. This was a steel boat, badly rusted and very leaky. It was made in three sections and had a beam of about four feet. The sections were bolted together. We bailed it out and fished in it that day, but I never saw it again.

We caught a lot of fish in Andes Creek from the landing up to the bridge. In the riffles above the bridge there was good spring fishing. The upper stillwaters, a mile or so above the lean-to at Andes, were also good fishing. We went up there as kids, and if we didn't have any more worms we'd catch grasshoppers and hook them in the back. Then we'd lie in the grass and toss out the hook. We got some nice fish that way. I remember catching one trout in a little pool just above the waterfall near the open camp.

String of fish on the dock of Brown Gables Camp, ca. 1935. Courtesy of Harrison Bicknell, Jr.

We had a bait trap up in the marsh made out of hardware cloth. It was a pretty good-sized trap, and it was my brother Jim's and my job to go up to that bait trap every morning and take all the fish out and rebait it with stale bread. The fish would be chubs and horned ace and shiners. We'd also catch a lot of suckers and some bullheads. The bullheads went into the frying pan the next morning.

The rest of them we kept in a bait car tied to the dock. It was made of wood and hardware cloth, and maybe two to three feet long and a foot square. Every morning we'd take a few fish out, depending on how many we had, and chop them up into small pieces about an inch long. Then we'd get in the boat and take them out to the buoy, which was in eighty feet of water and three or four hundred feet off Aras Williams's point (now owned by Tom Clark). We'd tie the boat to the buoy and dump out the chopped-up pieces of shiner, sucker, or chubs. The bait would sink to the bottom and attract the fish.

When Dad would come up on Friday nights, we'd fish if he'd gotten in on time. But we always fished on Saturday mornings. We'd catch whitefish and lake trout. Sometimes we'd catch some great big suckers, but usually it was whitefish or lake trout.

If we had a sucker eight or nine inches long, we'd use that as live bait. Dad would run the hook and the snell through the skin along the sucker's back. He had a five-foot rod with a level-winding reel with silk line, and he'd cast that fish out twenty or thirty feet from the boat. He had a sinker—maybe a piece of lead the diameter of a pencil and one and one-half inches long—and he'd put the sinker about three feet from the bait. The sucker would swim down to the bottom, and a big lake trout would take that fish. He'd grab it by the back and run with it and the reel would sing. It was beautiful to hear. When the reel stopped singing, that meant that the laker had stopped. The fish would turn the sucker around in his mouth and swallow it headfirst. Then, when he started to swim again, he'd swim slowly and the line would slowly go out. That's when Dad would set the hook. It was a lot of years before he let us set the hook.

Dad had a butt of a fly rod to which he added a brass pulley about an inch in diameter to the end. He used copper wire for line, and it ran over that pulley without kinking. It was wound on a regular reel, probably not a level-winding reel, but the same size. He used this to troll for lake trout. This rig also had a spoon but did not need a sinker, the theory being that the wire would bounce off the bottom as the boat moved along. He'd often catch lakers, but if he kinked the wire he was out of business.

In the spring we'd fish at a buoy in shallower water about a hundred yards off Wewerka's dock. Dad used to say there was a spring hole right off there that would attract the lake trout. We'd also troll nearer shore from a guideboat. We'd use a Lake Clear spoon followed by two treble hooks. We'd skin a sucker and take a few strips of skin, about four or five inches long, and hook two of them with the dark side on the outside and one with the white side on the outside. This was supposed to look like a fish. That trailed the spinner by a foot. Two feet ahead of that, we'd have a three-way swivel. We'd tie the silk line that led to the hooks to one part of the swivel, and then attach a tear-drop shaped lead sinker to the second part. The third part of the treble swivel was left for your line. We'd use a hand line to troll with this rig for lake trout. We used to go up and down the North Shore between Otto's and Stone's.

We also trolled closer to shore to catch brook trout using a little silver Pfleuger lure on a swivel with a worm on the hook. We'd troll using a fly rod and a Martin reel.

One time when just Dad and me went out, we caught two lakers—one of them was ten pounds and the other eight pounds. I don't know how old I was, but it was all I could do to keep the tails of those fish off the ground when I held them up. That was a great day.

I remember Grandpa Lux (Arthur J. Lux) loved to cast for smallmouth bass. He would start fishing along the southeastern shore near Harry Swancott's and fish along to Rasbach's. We'd row the "kicker" down, and Gramp would cast his big old plugs in there and catch some nice smallmouth bass. He really enjoyed that. We also used to catch them off our dock once in a while. The bass would spawn in North Bay and probably elsewhere in the lake. We'd see them on their spawning beds.

We caught whitefish at the buoy with hand lines. We had two types. One was a heavy cotton line that was wound on a piece of rectangular shingle or wood that was carved concave on all four sides. You'd wind the line on the shingle in a figure eight on each side. On the end we'd have a big hook—there'd be about an inch of space between the hook's point and the shank.

The other line we had was silk, and it also was wound on a shingle. We used two hooks on it about two feet apart, one large and the other small—maybe a number eight or so. On the big one we'd have a piece of sucker or other bait, about a one-inch cube. On the little one, which was the lower one, we'd have a cube of bait about one-half that size. The little one was for whitefish, and the big one was for lake trout. The big one was always higher because lake trout don't swim as close to the bottom as whitefish.

The sinkers we used were heavy. They would take the hook down quickly. We always put them down so that the lower hook was just off the bottom and the large hook about two feet higher.

Dad also used to buy sprung cans of corn (probably from the Olney and Floyd Canning Company), which was no good for people but okay for fish. So if we had corn it would be on the bottom hook, and we'd also dump the contents of a can when we first got there and that would draw the fish in.

When you got a bite with those hand lines, it was not easy to determine if you really had a bite or if it was just the sinker on the bottom. You also had to determine whether you had a whitefish or a lake trout. If we got a strong bite we'd set the hook with a real sharp jerk. A lake trout has a tough mouth, and that would do a good job of sinking that hook. But when a whitefish bit, it was just a gentle little tug, and if you set that hook too hard on a whitefish you'd pull it right through his mouth and you'd have nothing. We probably lost a few lake trout and pulled the hook through some whitefish mouths, but over all we got quite a few of both of them.

We sometimes caught four or five whitefish in one morning—that was a good morning. The whitefish we caught ran about three to four pounds, up to twenty-four inches. My mother always considered the whitefish to be the best eating.

Through the 1930s, we used to catch fish at the buoy almost every time we went out. We did very well fishing right up until the 1940s. Since then, we haven't seen lake trout and very few brook trout.

Boyhood Amusements | *Henry B. Bruyn*

What did boys do in the 1920s and 1930s when they had all summer to amuse themselves? No planned programs. No television. Nothing but the wilderness around them. These excerpts are taken from Henry Bruyn's memoir, *Big Moose Memories and the Beginnings of the Bruyn Family Presence*.[22] Henry and his younger brother Ned explored the lake and its inhabitants, both animal and human.

TURTLES

Throughout our childhood at Big Moose, Ned and I were frequently regaled with stories about the much-dreaded snapping turtle. We heard about one that was so large that it carried Charlie Martin on its back as it walked along the beach. We heard about one that grabbed a broomstick and broke it in two with its powerful jaws. Our early boyhood concept of this creature was that of something as long as five feet with a long neck and tail. The truth, of course, is that the snapping turtle may weigh as much as twenty or thirty pounds, with a shell as long as four feet. . . . To the best of my memory, Ned and I were never able to see an adult snapping turtle. We did, however, learn a great deal about their reproductive habits.

The snapping turtle comes ashore on sandy beaches to dig a hole and lay about thirty round eggs, looking like a small ping-pong ball. Foxes and coons sometimes found these nests and dug up the eggs to eat them. Ned and I would observe carefully for snapping turtle tracks on the beach to the west of the original boat house at On-Da-Wa [our camp]. Upon finding a suspicious area in the sand, we would dig in far enough to find a few eggs and then cover the spot with a large wire net with strong stakes driven around it to prevent invasion by coons or foxes.

In late August, we would be rewarded by the hatching of the young turtles, which would make their way to the surface of the sand. Instead of crawling to the safety of the lake, they would find themselves in containers of water, in which we kept them until they were set free or sold for twenty-five cents each. We often kept one or two to take back to Long Island for the winter and fed them pieces of hamburger. We usually brought them back to the mountains the next spring and let them loose. On at least one occasion, my brother kept one in an aquarium at home for several years, and it grew to about eight inches in length.

FISHING ADVENTURES

This first event took place at the Upper Gull Lake, in front of the open camp and fireplace at the end of the trail from Big Moose Lake. As I vividly recall, the clear water on this occasion revealed several trout swimming about a large rock.

At the suggestion of our mother, I went to a nearby meadow and caught several grasshoppers and rigged a line with a bent pin. A freshly cut maple pole completed the equipment, and within a remarkably few minutes, I had beached a five and one-half-inch eastern brook trout, to be photographed for posterity and eaten for dinner that night back at Big Moose Lake.

Another fishing adventure resulted from a bit of advice given us by Charlie Martin: there were large eastern brook trout to be caught at the upper end of the Upper Sister Lake. Ned and I took off with our wonderful Old Town carrying canoe (sixty-nine pounds), probably in the early summer of 1937. The expedition involved a long hike to the Lower Sister Lake, paddling its length and then through a narrow stream inlet to the Upper Sister Lake. We trolled lures across the upper end of the lake and on each trip across, we each caught a two and one-half to three and one-half-pound brook trout.

We came back again to this lake in 1938 with equal success, accompanied by my college roommate, Bob Bartholomew. Some time that year, we made a mistake that neither Ned nor I ever made again. We shared our secret with a guest at the Martin's Waldheim resort. Some time in 1939, a young man from Fourth Lake with a pontoon airplane flew into the Upper Sister and gill netted the lake on several occasions, selling the fish to hotels in the area. A third trip by Ned and me produced no fish.

In these early years before the days of acid rain, Big Moose Lake sustained a population of lake trout, which during the summer were caught by trolling with a copper line to carry the bait as deep as 90–100 feet. Our dear friend Walter Dunn caught one of the fish weighing twenty pounds in 1939.

ACTIVITIES AT THE WALDHEIM

Howard Martin was the younger son of Edward Martin, proprietor of the Waldheim [located just across the entrance to North Bay from the Retter/Bruyn camp]. In our earliest years, Howard's mother would bring him up to play with Ned and me on our beach in front of the house. As Howard grew older, he used to walk up to our place from his home. This trip included wading across the Inlet between the lake and North Bay, which sometimes got as deep as four feet. Howard, Ned and I spent many hours together in the early years of childhood, building rafts, constructing toy boats, and exploring the vicinity. I have notes in my diary about a period of time when we were making maps of all sorts of areas, including a detailed map of Retter Island in North Bay, which was done in 1930.

Ned and I often went down to Howard's home, which was not only a resort for guests living in individual cabins but also included a large barn with a herd of pigs and a busy lumber mill that Ed Martin used to produce the material for building cottages as well as for sale to construction projects on the lake. As we grew into our early teens, we worked at this mill, helping to pile the cut timbers and to roll the logs onto the carriages that carried them into the saws.

Another fascinating activity that we three boys undertook was to herd the pigs into a large area of forest that was fenced in, and which provided a large amount of vegetation for the pigs to eat. Ed Martin believed that this improved the meat, but he did not depend upon such natural food as a sole source of nutrition for the year. The pigs would be kept in the forest for about a month and then herded together, counted, and returned to their pens for more extensive fattening. One of our activities in the role of pig wrangling required us to produce an accurate count of the herd.

Howard's mother put up concord grapes in quart jars to be made into pies during the year. We discovered a way to sneak into the cellar and make off with one of these quart jars of grape juice and grapes. This enabled us to mark the pigs that we had counted by spitting a grape skin at them as we herded them through a funnel fence. A marked pig had a large purple stain somewhere on its back.

WATER ACTIVITIES

The first outboard motor that Ned and I were allowed control of was a three-quarter-horsepower Sears Roebuck, which moved us around very slowly in our Cape Cod-made flatboat. . . . In 1930, Father Bruyn bought from the Old Town Canoe Company a large outboard motor launch with a natural wood deck, which held about six people. This required a twelve-horsepower Johnson

engine, which was about as big as outboard motors came in those times. We also rigged a steering wheel opposite the front seat so we could sit far from the engine once it was started and up to speed.

The great water sport was riding on the aquaplane. This board was fastened to a boat with a long line and had two ropes coming up that the rider grasped and leaned back. The rider had no control over the board and followed the boat wherever it went. Our neighbors to the east, the Colpitts, had a spectacular, natural wood speedboat named the *Bluenose* . . . This boat developed extremely high speed and behind it the aquaplane was truly a thrill ride.

In about 1934, Carl Otto, Jr., introduced the freeboard, which had been invented in Europe. He and his friend Everett Martin [Howard's older brother] made one from white pine planks that were thinned down to about one-inch thick and formed around two hand-cut ribs to make a slightly V bottom and curved front. Naturally, Ned and I copied this activity and created a board of our own that lasted many years. These boards were about three and one-half to four feet wide and four to five feet long. The connection to the boat was a long line with a handle on the end. The rider on the board could control its course by leaning one side or the other to jump the wake and swing out beside the towing boat. We took to this sport with great enthusiasm and became quite skilled at it.

One of our favorite tricks was to have a wooden kitchen chair thrown overboard from the boat and then picked up by the rider who then sat upon it. The ultimate from this beginning was to pass the rider a flotation cushion from the boat, upon which was placed a magazine and a lighted pipe. The rider would pick this up, sit on the cushion, smoke the pipe and pretend to read the magazine as we flashed by the hotel docks where the visitors were struggling to get up on these boards.

HIKING AND CAMPING

Together with Howard Martin and Don Salisbury, Ned and I took many trips into the lakes around Big Moose, using topographical maps and compasses to find our way to where there were no trails. In retrospect, it is most surprising to me to realize that our otherwise concerned and worried mother would accept our departure on these trips without a promised return date. We would come back when we ran out of food. And this would be three or four days after departure. We ate fish that we caught on these trips, and on two occasions, we roasted red squirrels over our campfire. A favorite staple to be carried on these expeditions was rice and raisins mixed together and carried in bags at the bottom of our pack baskets. This mix we boiled up with water and ate at breakfast, lunch, and dinner.

One of our most ambitious expeditions was to hike to Terror Lake and from there over the ridge to Beaver River. This trip involved carrying our canoe up to the Upper Gull lake, paddling its length, and carrying through the woods to the headwaters of Andes Creek. . . . The beaver activity had produced large amounts of meadowland, through which the stream flowed slowly and deeply. This enabled us to paddle upstream for almost two miles toward Beaver River.

On the great adventure to Beaver River, we left our canoe at the head of navigable water on the creek and climbed over a high ridge to go down into the Beaver River watershed. We then hiked across the railroad and down into the little village. I think this was probably about 1934 or 1935. At the village, we found it mostly inhabited by French Canadian loggers, who were passing the summer before starting the extensive logging operations in the winter. I remember that we had both had some French in school by this time, and upon attempting to speak to these men, we were greeted with much laughter. The French "canuk patois" is quite different from Parisian French, and we were most embarrassed.

The Big Moose Lake Motor Regatta of 1941

The summer before the United States entered World War II, Phil Ellsworth, owner of Adirondack Air Service and an avid motorboat racer, organized an event that was to spread both joy and dismay among lake residents. The occasion was a gathering of professional and amateur racers of so-called mosquito boats.

Phil Ellsworth himself had established a world record in 1931. He was the first amateur driver to exceed fifty miles an hour. However, in this race he was the chairman and not an entrant. Fred Jacoby of North Bergen, New Jersey, was the "Number 1 U.S. Outboard Driver," and his photograph was on the cover of the program.

The boats were tiny one-man affairs designed to skim the water with the help of a bulky motor that had its working mechanism entirely exposed. The motors were powerful for the time, about twenty-five horsepower, and

Program cover for the First Annual Motor Boat Regatta, 1941. Courtesy of Peter Bruyn.

were innocent of mufflers. Most drivers tinkered with their motors to coax the maximum power from them, and some people thought that the louder the noise the greater the power.

Twenty-three drivers registered to race. Of these, ten were amateurs. They came from New Jersey, Massachusetts, Connecticut, and various locations in New York State. Three, all professionals, were from Poughkeepsie, where races had been held on the Hudson River. All the drivers wore helmets and life jackets, and they leaned forward as they drove in order to minimize the drag of the air.

The race took place on August 2, 1941. Because daylight savings time was a local option at the time, the program carefully specified that the appointed hour was 2:00 P.M. DST. The course was set up in West Bay, and the racers were divided into four classes according to the size of the boat. There were two heats in each class, and the winner was determined by the best total time in both heats.

Spectators at the First Annual Motor Boat Regatta, 1941. Courtesy of Barbara K. Wheeler.

The officials were all local and included, besides Phil Ellsworth, Everett Martin, H. E. Bicknell, Ned Bruyn, Seward Spoor, Fred Brack, and Joe Thompson. The announcer was Joe Grady, the author of the well-known history of the Fulton Chain-Big Moose region.

Crowds gathered at the dock in front of the Glennmore to watch the excitement. Others roundly condemned the disturbance to the peace of the lake. Unfortunately, we have no knowledge of the winners. The Big Moose Property Owners Association expressed its displeasure in an official vote. However, by the next year World War II had started, gasoline was rationed, and such frivolous pursuits were impossible.

Square Dancing at Covewood | *Mary C. Williams*

Of all my memories of Covewood, I recall the square dances with the most delight. Those dances were always a summertime activity and, although they were also held at Twitchell Lake and at the Glennmore, the best ones were at Covewood.

No matter where the location, the music was always the same: Mr. Germain Mitchell played the piano and his son played the violin. All those wonderful tunes had names but I don't remember ever seeing any sheet music. Those two men had the rhythm and the notes in their heads. Mr. Mitchell was tall and very thin and his son was his mirror image. They both wore plain black suits and I thought them to be very solemn, although they invariably had a smile for me. I often wondered how our old piano stood up under the workout Mr. Mitchell gave it—he could make the whole room vibrate.

Taken from *Growing Up in the Woods*, the memoirs of Mary Alden Covey Williams, written in the spring of 1996 and dedicated to her mother and father, Frances and Earl Covey.

The day of the square dance was such a long one for me! How could everybody go about their business with such calm when we all knew what wonderful things would be happening that evening? Soon after supper serious preparations for the dance started. Dad had disappeared: he had gone down to Forestport to pick up the musicians. While he was gone, the big couches and chairs from the living rooms were lined up around the edges of the two rooms, and extra chairs from the dining room were brought in to fill the gaps. The rugs were rolled up and those beautiful hardwood floors were perfect for dancing with just a touch of wax at the last minute.

By 8:00 Mr. Mitchell had arrived and run a few scales on the piano while his son tuned his violin. As the clock struck the hour, Dad called out "Four more couples," and to the tune of "Turkey in the Straw" the dancing began. Oh, those marvelous dances! My heart still leaps at the thought of my Dad calling out, "Eight hands around," as that wonderful circle of neighbors, guests, and friends, stepping to the music, joined their hands for another wonderful evening.

There was always a pattern of three figures with a moment's pause in between for the dancers to catch their breath. The first figure was a quadrille: a stately dance with a slow tempo. The two following were faster—often

BARNEY LEPPER

Barney Lepper has been immortalized in Harold Thompson's book, *Body, Boots & Britches*: "He is the favorite 'prompter,' directing the quadrilles all the way from 'Join hands and circle left' to 'All promenade—you know where and I don't care.' The gods of the mountain and the gods of the plain are one when Barney 'winds the clock' or orders his dancers to 'Swing your Ma, now your Pa; don't forget old Arkansaw.' He mingles prose with verse; one of his 'second changes' runs:

> Join hands and circle left.
> First couple lead out to the right.
> Join hands and circle four.
> Ladies join your lily-white hands—
> The gents, the black and tan.
> Ladies bow, gents know how,
> And hippety-hop and around you go.[51]

creating a complex pattern of bowing and swinging that left dancers breathless at the end of the third round. Dad taught me the schottische, a dance halfway between a waltz and a polka; one, two, three, hop . . . I still remember.

Barney Lepper, the stationmaster at Big Moose Station, was often present at our dances. He was the only other person who called at the squares. Barney didn't look like a dancer. He was a stout, balding man with a red face and a hearty laugh, but oh how Barney could swing.

After a couple of hours of dancing, Dad would disappear again—this time into the kitchen and soon thereafter a parade of young people would emerge with trays heaped with dishes of ice cream for everyone. At midnight, Dad had called out the last set, and we reluctantly danced the last round before bidding our goodbyes until the next time.

The Early Days of Waterskiing | *Charles Adams*

My waterskiing experience began in 1940 or 1941, when Gordon Kinne asked me if I wanted to get on his freeboard behind his outboard motorboat. The boat was a Thompson runabout made in 1934, and on it he had either a twenty-two or twenty-five-horsepower Evinrude motor.

For the unknowing, a freeboard was made out of wood, normally light pine, and was approximately five to six feet long with a rounded nose, a bevel rising from keel level, and usually a rubber mat near the back where you stood. The rope came directly from the boat to the person riding the board—it was not attached to the board, like on an aquaplane—and that gave you a great deal of freedom to move the board with your feet as you went

Everett Martin sitting on a chair on an aquaplane, 1930.

George "Joe" Dunn on a chair on a freeboard, ca. 1945. Courtesy of Ann Dunn Hall.

over the wake and made turns. Interestingly enough, the rope from the boat had a handle, which was nothing but a piece of rubber cut out of an old tire. Why there was not a normal wooden handle with a yoke in front of it is beyond me, but anyhow that is the way it all began.

When Gordon suggested I try it, he explained how to get up on it. I lay on the board in the water, and the boat idled out until the rope became taut. Then, when the boat accelerated, I got up on my hands and knees, while holding the rope handle in one hand. I then got on my feet in a squatting position, and eventually stood up. The first cut or turn that I tried to make took the board right out from under me, and I learned the hard way that it was a very touchy operation if you wanted to stay dry. That was my first experience riding on the water in something other than a boat. I was eleven.

When you were done with a run, one of the fun parts was letting go of the rope quite a long ways out and gliding into the dock and stopping "dry" by either sitting down on the dock or stepping off on it, if you were really agile.

My first time up on water skis was in 1944 or 1945. I was working at Dunn's Hotel with Joe and Bud Dunn and Dick Rivett, and Walt Dunn would let us use the boats. He didn't complain about the gas we were using as long as we did our work during the day. As a result, we did the vast majority of our skiing between suppertime and dark, and often after dark.

The skis were heavy things that had thin strips of

wood on the bottom for keels, and the first slalom ski had virtually no keel at all on it. The large metal keels came later.

We soon progressed from two skis to the slalom ski, then to trick skis (both normal size and smaller), and eventually we moved on to doing all sorts of things on skis. Ultimately, we had to have our own jump.

At that time we subscribed to a couple of water-ski magazines, and often saw pictures of jumps but never saw any dimensions. So we guessed at the height of the people in the pictures, and tried to estimate the size of the jump. From that exercise, we concluded that our jump had to be twenty-four feet long, ten to twelve feet wide, and six feet high on the high end. For strength, we decided to build it out of two-by-sixes, used some pretty stout lumber for the framework underneath, and built the whole thing on two great big logs with a platform between the logs. Under the jump the ballast was made up of stone.

After we managed to raise enough money to buy the lumber from the mill over in Limekiln, we three boys—plus Harold McEdward (a carpenter) and Dick Rivett—built the jump one Sunday afternoon. It was the middle of the summer, and Dunn's had some guests who, as I remember, came along to see the activity. As Hank Wightman would say, it was probably a four- or five-beer job by the time we finished, but we got it finished just before dark.

Naturally we couldn't wait to try it, but we didn't know how it worked at all. So we decided to use the biggest, heaviest skis we had, and someone would draw the short straw and go over the jump before dark closed everything down.

I remember Bert Dunn coming down to the dock, looking at it and saying "that wood will be awful sticky when you hit it—you'd better do something about greasing it."

She then donated a box of Ivory Soap Flakes, and when we had moved the jump out into the lake and were all ready, we threw water on it and spread the soap flakes over it to make it slippery.

Bud Dunn had drawn the short straw, so he was going over first. Joe Dunn drove the boat, and Dick Rivett and I were underneath the jump, one on each side, with paddles trying to keep it straight. We pointed the jump toward the big lake beyond the island.

The first time Joe Dunn went by, Bud didn't go over the jump. He just rode alongside of it to see what it looked like. Then they made their circle for the next pass,

which turned out to be the inaugural ski jump on Big Moose Lake.

Rivett and I had a great deal of trouble keeping the thing straight, but we did the best we could. The next thing we saw was the boat going by, and then we heard the skis hit the jump, and in less than a second he was over it and he came off the jump upside down and backwards. Those Ivory soap flakes worked fine.

When he hit the water it was exciting for everybody, and I suppose more so for him, but he came up laughing. When he tried it the second time he fell again, but on the third time he made it, so our day's activity was a success, and everybody on the dock cheered. We then towed the jump back and tied it up to the dock.

On many Sundays thereafter, we had the thing anchored out in the lake between Dunn's dock and what is now Bill Keener's, and after lunch Walt would let us jump for a while, which was entertainment for the people who were staying at the hotel.

The Dunns had three different-sized boats, and they were all used at one time or another to ski behind, but mostly we used what was called the *Stub*, which was identical to the Chris-Craft that Hank Wightman now has. We also used the larger *Renée* boat, which ultimately went to John Ditmas when Walt had finished with it. The *Renée* had the biggest wake, and jumping it was a challenge. But Joe finally conquered it on a slalom ski by jumping from one side of the wake and catching the first wave roll on the other side, which we measured as a darned good jump of more than twenty feet. Joe did this many times if he could get the height to pull it off, which he frequently did.

The third boat, the *PJ*, was an even larger Chris-Craft with a wide beam. The two larger boats were more fun to ski behind, but they also used a lot more gas and Walt rather frowned on that, so we stuck pretty much to the *Stub*.

I can remember Joe trying various tricks that we saw in the magazines or heard about, and among those were 360's and 180's, which we learned to do with our regular skis before we actually got any real trick skis. This made it much harder because the regular skis were longer and narrower than trick skis, but we'd take the keels off of them so they'd skid better.

Joe always claimed that it had to be possible to start backwards on skis, and although he did try it a few times from off the dock—and was never successful—he did learn to do it from the water. However, starting this way out of the water meant that your head was down, and this was a little more than one bargained for with respect to the sinuses. One time, Joe was in bad shape for a couple of days, so we gave this up.

We had many other tricks, though. Two or three of us would get behind the boat on slalom skis with different length ropes, and we'd cross over and under the ropes. We'd also have a skier with a shorter rope passing under another skier who was in the air coming off the jump, as well as various pyramids and other tricks we could think of or that we saw in magazines.

I guess it was during all this activity that we conjured up the idea of having our own water-ski show. After a while it became something of a business for us, so we rigged up some racks on the side of Walt Dunn's truck so we could carry all of our equipment with us. We'd load it up with ski ropes and skis and all of the other things we needed, including our boat with its heavy outboard motor, so we could put on our show even in places like White Lake and Indian Lake, where they didn't have powerboats like we had on Big Moose.

Jim Ottoway was in the show as part of the three-person pyramid, and Howard Martin used to ride a free-board with a stepladder or a chair on it, and do a hand stand while holding on to the rope with one hand. I can remember one time at the Glennmore when we were practicing before we went down to Old Forge, Howard came around by the dock and picked the stepladder up right off the dock without slowing down. He also did the same thing with chairs. Another time, Howard was doing a handstand on a chair on the freeboard, when some guy drove by in a boat ahead of him. Howard went through the wake of that other boat, never as much as swayed in the wrong direction, and came back down dry on the board without a problem. Whenever his act was over, Howard would come roaring into the dock or the beach on the freeboard, dump the rope, and set the stepladder or chair down on the dock just before he stepped off the freeboard on the dock itself. Those people down at Cypress Gardens didn't have anything on us.

My specialty was juggling croquet balls while wearing a top hat and a frock-tailed coat. At first I tried it with tennis balls, but they blew right over my head back into the wake. Eventually, we settled on croquet balls, which were heavy enough so I could throw them out into the wind and they'd come back to me pretty well. I wore a net in front of my chest where I'd keep the croquet balls until I was ready. The old frock-tailed coat was always a problem,

as it was wool and after it got wet it would shrink. We did, however, come up with a solution to one big problem—how to hold onto the rope. Originally, I'd put the handle of the rope behind my knees, but this made it difficult to go over a wave and not end up in the lake. But some fellow who worked for NIMO [Niagara Mohawk Power Company] as a pole climber, and who watched us ski one afternoon, suggested to Bud Dunn that I needed a belt. Bud got me a pole climber's belt with these big rings on it. Then we made a special handle with snaps on some extension ropes that I'd snap on to my belt once I got out into the water and all set up the right way. This arrangement freed up both my hands, and I could then reach into the net for the croquet balls and start juggling. This worked pretty well, and the show went on well for a while until one day when I fell down in Old Forge, and the belt came up under my arms and took me straight down to the bottom.

That was a close one, so we decided something better had to be devised. We eventually managed to find, through a man in the Utica cattle business named John Sullivan, a special mechanism that cowboys used to release the lariat from around a steer. They had a little button on the clamp of their saddle horn, and they could quickly get free by just pushing the button.

We fixed one up for us by welding an arm on it and hooking it up so it was connected to the back of the boat, and then connecting a ski rope to it. I remember hiring

Charles Adams juggling on waterskis, ca. 1950s.

Chuckie Deis to sit in the back of the boat with his fingers lightly on that arm, and telling him if I fell he was to yank the arm as fast as he could. Twice this contraption saved me from a very unpleasant affair—one time at the Mohawk Hotel on Fourth Lake, and another time on Blue Mountain Lake, when the wind was blowing badly during a ski show.

Now that we'd found a way not to get dragged down to the bottom of the lake, we did all sorts of things. We tried everything we could think of, including skiing behind Bud Dunn's Piper Cub airplane. We did that a few times, but gave up after Bud's extensive fall one night. He was going down the lake behind the plane, and he fell and skipped across the top of the water for probably 200 yards. When it was all over he had lost his bathing suit, had red welts all over him, and had decided that this wasn't such a good idea.

Apparently, it was very hard to hold on to the rope as the plane accelerated, and it became almost impossible as soon as the floats lifted up a little and you were suddenly going along at about seventy miles per hour. At this point, the friction on the skis was so great that they just went out behind you. But the thing that did you in was when the airplane lifted off the water: the airspeed automatically jumped about ten or fifteen miles per hour, and that was more than we could handle.

We had great fun back in those days, met a lot of nice people, and performed tricks on skis that I'm sure were never performed anywhere else. All things considered, we were extraordinarily lucky that no one ever became seriously injured.

We did some foolish things as well, such as the time we skied around the island the day the ice went out of the lake, and we all had frozen feet for hours. Just think if one of us had fallen. We really weren't too smart.

We also skied at night with railroad flares, and we thought that was great sport. One night, three of us skied with flares from Dunn's dock and around the island, through the narrows, and back down the north shore of West Bay. I was on the right of the three skiers, or closest to the shore. I knew that there were some people on the Days's dock (which today is owned by the Singletons), and as we came down the shoreline I could see them sitting on the dock from the light above them on the boathouse, and I decided to swing in and give them a little thrill as I went by.

I came in close, but about thirty feet after I had passed the dock, my right foot began to go backwards on me,

and I had a terrible time holding on to the ski. Something was dragging it under the water. Fortunately, I was skiing on the right side of the group, and was scheduled to get off first when we went by the dock at Dunn's. When I let go of the rope to slow down, I stopped very quickly—well before I got to the dock. I then swam in quickly and pulled the skis up on the dock to get out of the way for the next skier who was coming around, and it was then that I learned that a fishing line had lodged itself between the wooden keel on the bottom of my ski and the ski board itself. Pulling that in, I brought in none other than the fellow's fishing rod that I had snapped out of his hands as I went by the Days's dock. It was an expensive night, because I had to buy him a new reel. It was embarrassing having to go over and apologize for what we had done.

One time we conjured up the idea of a new trick—Dick Rivett and I would play cards on a table and chairs that we'd set on top of a big ping-pong table. In other words, we'd have a huge aquaplane that we were going to ride on in chairs. We actually tried it from Dunn's dock and started across the bay. Bud Dunn was driving the boat, and he knew that he was supposed to make a very slow circle while Dick and I pretended to have cards as we sat on our chairs with a small table between us. However, it soon became clear that we had forgotten to make any type of a keel for the ping pong table, and as the boat began to turn the table began to skid to the right, and it just kept skidding, went on over the wake, and as we came down the other side the ping-pong table tipped over. It was at that point that I learned that Rivett did not swim very well, and it was truly an unpleasant experience.

Much later, in the 1960s, there was an annual "Can You Top This?" competition between the people on the west end of the lake and the people down on the big lake. The routine was to have a show at Covewood at 10:00 A.M. followed by a show at Dunn's at 2:00 P.M. Jim Marble, a regular guest at Covewood who owned Marble Dairy Farms in Syracuse, loved the competition. We always tried to surpass the feats of bravery exhibited by Jim Marble and all of his people at Covewood, such as the time they got painted up like Indians, climbed into a flotilla of canoes, and came down into West Bay and "attacked" Dunn's dock and captured Joe Dunn.

In 1968, the last year that I participated in the competition, we were putting the show on at Covewood, and we decided on a couple of very special acts. First, I would come out of retirement and juggle again on skis, which I hadn't done for some years. I'd bought a new boat from

Joe Dunn, and my son Douglas drove the boat while son Arthur was ready to release the rope if there was a problem. With Major Bowes's permission, we practiced in the bay in front of Covewood while I showed Douglas the path to take through the rocks hidden on the bottom of the lake. I never juggled on those practice runs so as not to give the show away to all those Covewood guests who sat on the dock and wondered why that white boat kept running back and forth. The act was a big hit.

Second, we rigged up about 400 feet of rope that we "buried" on the bottom of the lake with some weights, and it went from the church manse dock all the way over to the boathouse (formerly Milligan's) in the Outlet where Jim Marble stayed. The boathouse door was hinged at the top and was folded up against the building during the summer. A few nights before the competition, we had let it down and painted "CAN YOU TOP THIS?" on it, and then folded it back up. We then brought the rope into the boathouse, built some shives through which it passed, and attached the other end to a Volkswagen. The whole idea was to drive the Volkswagen up the driveway, around the corner, and right up the Covewood Road until the rope became slack.

I think Joe Hameline was the skier, and on the day of the competition he sat on the manse dock while all the spectators were focused on the other water-ski acts being performed out in front of the Covewood dock. Earl Brady was the announcer in the show, and when this act was set to begin, he said to all of the people on the dock at Covewood that they should turn their attention to the manse dock on the right, because they were going to see the world's first water-skier without a boat.

They all turned, I fired a blank pistol, which told the driver of the Volkswagen (and someone we had posted on Marble's dock to yell at the Volkswagen driver) to hit the gas. Everybody looked and all of a sudden there was a guy on water skis with a rope down in the water ahead of him coming straight across the bay toward Marble's boathouse, and as he passed the Covewood dock he waved at everybody, and they cheered and thought it was wonderful, and just before he got to the dock at Marble's he let go of the rope and glided into the boathouse slip, at which point another person pulled the rope on the boathouse door and it came down with great big letters that said "CAN YOU TOP THIS?"

This last episode, which took place the following year, has nothing to do with water skis, but it was great fun. We had gotten John Sullivan to get us a cow from Utica,

which we then put on a pontoon party boat (after building an enclosed structure painted to look like a Marble Dairy Farms truck) and then ran the boat down to the Covewood dock. As we pulled up to the dock, we said that we were going to give a gift to Jim Marble for all he had done over the years with the "Can You Top This?" competition. Joe Dunn presented Jim with a trophy, and with that we opened the side doors on the "truck" we had built on the boat, and out came the cow right onto Covewood's dock. The look on Major Bowes's face was worth the whole episode, and Marble had no idea what the hell to do with the cow standing there on that dock.

Following our era, my own children and many other kids started doing the same types of things, but they soon graduated to kites, large pyramids, special slalom skis, and trick skis that we never saw.

I was always very pleased and proud of Joe Dunn and what he did to lead the young people into the water-ski shows that were put on at Dunn's long after we quit. Thousands of hours of preparation time went into getting those kids ready, and because I was the announcer on top of the boathouse for several years, I look back with great pride on those shows we put on. Some of them had pretty sizeable crowds that came from near and far to see what we had put together. I still have a picture of Joe Dunn standing up in the boat, going by the dock with five kids on skis behind it, and I think it was just a great era in Big Moose watersport history.

Later Waterskiing

Although Charlie Adams, Joe and Bud Dunn, Everett and Howard Martin, Jim Ottaway, Chuck Deis, and others were pioneers in waterskiing on the lake, new skiers soon came along. In the 1960s, another generation of water-skiers appeared. Joe Dunn, then teaching at the Old Forge School and coaching winter skiing, was running Dunn's Boat Service in the summer as his father, Walt Dunn, eased into retirement. Boats were faster (up to at least 150 horsepower), skis were better and more varied in design, and dazzling new feats were possible. Joe found himself leading the young people on the lake into creative new adventures. In fact, much of what Joe and his wife, Annie, did led directly to the wide-ranging recreation program sponsored by the Big Moose Property Owners Association.

There were many athletically talented children on the lake who were eager to learn new skills. In addition to

Joe and Ann Dunn, ca. 1975. Courtesy of Diane Ritz.

those who lived on the lake, young Hank Kashiwa from Old Forge (later an alpine skier in the 1972 Olympics at Sapporo and also the World Pro Ski Champion in 1974–75) was working at the Dunn marina. Joe began coaching many of the youngsters informally and soon decided that an annual ski show would give the participants a chance to display their skills and also provide an incentive to continue to improve.

In the mid-1960s, the Big Moose Fire Company needed a new jeep, so Joe Dunn suggested doing a ski show and donating the proceeds to the Fire Company. A generous lake resident told Joe he would match whatever amount the show brought in, and thus the Fire Company

Pyramid on an aquaplane, with Peter Cowie on the shoulders of Tom Dew and Cindy Munsell, middle to late 1960s. Courtesy of Ann Dunn Hall.

received a very sizeable donation. This was the first ski show, and it subsequently became an annual event. The ski shows were usually held in early August.

Beginning skiers started out on two skis, soon moved to a single slalom ski, and learned to jump wakes and to maneuver through a slalom course. Before long, two skiers behind one boat would crisscross back and forth with one skier using a shorter rope than the other. Pyramids, when youngsters climbed on the shoulders of two others, both on aquaplanes and on skis, were also featured. Some of the children were as young as four years old. A new ski jump in front of the marina inspired longer and more complex jumps (requiring careful timing and skillful driving) and further tricks. Annie Dunn helped with costumes and props, which made the shows ever more colorful and amusing.

A little later, the "Can You Top This?" contests between Dunn's and Covewood took place, always on the Saturday of Labor Day weekend. These contests were often imaginatively directed by and sometimes participated in by the pioneers. Big Moose Lake became known as the center of creative waterskiing, and audiences gath-

Tom Cowie crossing under ski jumper Taro Alps, middle to late 1960s. Courtesy of Ann Dunn Hall.

Don Dew, Dave Munsell, Cindy Munsell, and Tom Cowie stepping out of water skis to go "barefooting," middle to late 1960s. Courtesy of Ann Dunn Hall.

ered from all around the area. At one contest, the Covewood group appeared towing just one skier behind eight boats. This act was much more difficult than it looked because the ropes were not fastened together and the skier had to manage the pull of different forces.

Pioneers like Joe Dunn had learned to ski with one foot on a ski and one hand on the other ski, while the second foot extended out in front and the second hand held the rope. Later came barefooting, when skiers stepped off their skis and skimmed along the water on their bare feet. This feat called for not only a high-speed boat but also strong legs and tough soles. A crowning achievement, and probably the most difficult act ever, was a three-person pyramid supported by barefooters.

Hank Kashiwa, Joe Dunn, and young Don Dew, brave souls and all outstanding athletes, learned to take off and land on the water using a special kite towed behind a powerful boat. The kite could be maneuvered to

rise and fall, tip and glide, and was usually the climax for the ski shows.

Toward the end of this era, a Big Moose Waterski Club was founded that nurtured talent. The activities at Big Moose Lake were unusual enough to come to the attention of the Public Broadcasting System. Martha Hanlon worked hard to coordinate the crews that came to film a segment in which a chosen few of the younger children appeared on national television on a PBS show called *Kids' World.*

The Big Moose Canoe Crew

Every Wednesday morning at 8:00 from June to October, a group of cars with canoes lashed on top gathers at the foot of the Higby Road. There may be four cars or there may be twelve or fifteen, depending on the time of year and the weather. This is the Big Moose Canoe Crew. It is a group, if such a loose organization can be called a group, of enthusiastic paddlers who have, over the last thirty or thirty-five years, explored nearly all of the waterways in the Adirondack Park.

In the early days, Annette Lux and three women friends decided it would be fun to get acquainted with lakes outside the immediate area. On those first few trips, the women had such a good time that others soon joined them. There were many women on the lake whose husbands came mostly on weekends and whose teenage children were busy with summer jobs. Eventually, a slowly expanding female group was making weekly trips to all corners of the Adirondack Park. The women would help each other to lift the canoes onto the car roofs, to master the art of tying them down, and to learn paddling skills.

Kite-skiing, middle to late 1960s. Courtesy of Ann Dunn Hall.

*The Big Moose Canoe Crew in 1997.
Left to right by canoe and bow to stern
in each canoe, the crews were Shelly
Thompson and Carol Wheeler; Merle
Binyon and Annette Lux; Gail
Mawhinney and Jeanne Taylor; Lois
Murphy and Betty Peters; Olga Adams
and Lucy Craske; Betty York and Mary
Ann Simpson; and Jane Hanlon and
Kathy Sardino. Photograph copyright ©
Nancie Battaglia.*

At destination points and at portages, the same spirit prevailed.

The all-day trips usually began with a stop for coffee and a breakfast snack. At the put-in point there was often a pause while two or three cars were driven to the take-out spot. This arrangement ensured that the territory covered was always new. Some of the favorite routes were along the Raquette River, through the Marion River, and along Eagle and Utowana Lakes to Blue Mountain, Saranac Lake, and Stillwater Reservoir.

As time went on, the husbands of the women began to retire and spend more time at Big Moose. The men joined in as "associate" members, even though they were heavily outnumbered, and still are, by women. Annette continues to be commodore and to choose the routes, with suggestions from her fellow travelers. If a last-minute change of plans is necessary, perhaps because of high winds, Annette always knows of a sheltered river or an alternate route. Janet Holmes, an expert botanist, has shared her knowledge of common and rare flowers and shrubs. Jeanne Taylor has recorded nearly every trip with her camera. Bird-watchers help to identify species that may appear. Camaraderie prevails, and the tradition of the Wednesday trips continues.[23]

8 *The Big Moose Lake Community*

EVERY COMMUNITY has its organizations. At Big Moose Lake, the local school was the earliest. Other groups concerned with fire protection, medical matters, religious life, and socializing soon followed. The Big Moose Property Owners Association has dealt with many of these matters and has also acted as a link to local township and county entities.

Barbara Kinne Wheeler, who was herself a pupil at the Big Moose Lake School, has researched and written about the schools over the years. Others who helped with the summaries of various community groups are mentioned later in the text. Mary Ann Simpson has condensed and summarized the lengthy files of correspondence and minutes of the Big Moose Property Owners Association that stretch over seventy-five years between 1926 and 2001.

The Big Moose Lake Schools

The education of the children at Big Moose Lake was an early concern. Although a grade school was established at Big Moose Station in 1896,[1] pupils from the lake were obliged to walk as much as three or more miles from their homes to attend. In the winter, that often meant three well-below-zero, bone-chilling miles, because no public transportation was provided. A plan for the school district to build new schoolhouses in Old Forge and Fulton Chain (Thendara) aroused the indignation of the residents of Big Moose Lake. Their anger is reflected in a letter written to the Town of Webb School Board by E. J. Martin on August 29, 1905.

Gentlemen:

Your petitioners who are taxpayers in School District No. 1 respectfully protest against any action on the part of your honorable body in relation to the accepting of site for new school building at Fulton Chain or raising the sum of $8000.00 for a new school building at Old Forge.

The taxpayers and citizens of Fulton Chain, Old Forge and up the chain of lakes seem to be bent on furnishing themselves with new school houses at the expense of the taxpayers of Big Moose and adjacent territory, while the old log school building is entirely satisfactory to the residents of this part of the district.

In case the proposition to build two new schoolhouses goes into effect, that part of the district consisting of Big Moose Lake and surrounding territory will make application to withdraw and become a district by itself.

Yours truly,
Edward J. Martin[2]

We do not know whether the two new schools were built, but Big Moose Lake did not in fact become a separate district. It was eight years later, in 1913, that the first school building on the lake opened its doors.[3]

This new building stood on land donated by Charles Williams, owner of Lake View Lodge, on the hill above the Big Moose/Eagle Bay road, not far from Burdick's Camp. It cost $1,068.[4] No longer did students have to walk or be transported to the Station school. Charles's son Fred, who sat for many years on the Town of Webb

Big Moose Lake School, ca. 1920s. Built in the early 1920s, it was the second schoolhouse on the lake. Courtesy of Barbara K. Wheeler.

School Board, was influential in supporting education at the lake and in insuring access to the high school at Old Forge by making certain that transportation was available.

The first teacher at this early school was Katherine Barry from Talbots Corners, and the first student roster included children whose parents had played an important part in lake history, or who themselves would later become key figures: George Bissell; Charles, Nelson, and Walter Dunn; Maynard LaClair; Aletha Saunders; Vera Sperry; and Everett, Harold, and Thelma Stevens.

In about 1918, after just a few years of operation, the schoolhouse burned to the ground,[5] but a number of local people stepped forward so that no classes would be missed. Florence Martin, a summer resident and retired teacher, taught school for three months at her camp, Shawondasee, on West Bay, until lack of heat and other problems forced her to give up. Then a building near the McAllister home on the lake housed the classes until the new school was ready in 1920.[6] The new school building was erected on a lot on the Big Moose Road, close to the Glennmore Corner. The Hotel Glennmore Corporation donated the land. Frank Lesure, a grandson of Bill Dart, attended the school in the 1930s. He describes the building in detail:

> There were rather steep cement steps up to a small cement stoop with an iron-pipe railing on each side. Inside the front door was a hallway, and just inside the door to the right in a corner was a large crock with drinking water. One of the chores of the older kids was to fetch a pail of water from the springhouse near the store at the Glennmore.
>
> To the right was a girls' cloakroom and beyond that in a smaller room, the flush toilet. To the left was a boys' cloakroom and adjacent to it in a smaller room, a chemical toilet for emergency winter use when the water froze. There was a large hot-air register in the floor in the hallway, and there we dried boots and wet coats in the winter. There was a sink in the corner near the register. The classroom was straight ahead beyond a large doorway. A bank of windows was on the right side as one entered, and two more windows were at the far end of the room. Slate blackboards lined the wall of each side of the doorway and along part of the left side of the room. The teacher's desk was on the right side as one entered. Students' desks were scattered and sometimes lined up. There were several sizes: small, blond oak ones with space for books below the seat and larger dark wood and metal ones with tops that lifted up to allow space for books and papers underneath. Those also generally had inkwells and a groove for pencils. All were typical of late nineteenth—or very early twentiety-century schools.
>
> A glass-fronted bookcase at the far end of the room held a few children's books, some reference books and a miscellaneous bunch of magazines and New York State Museum pamphlets. Some of these were about Paleozoic fossils found in areas south of the mountains. I remember looking at the pictures of the fossils and wishing that we could find things like that around the school.
>
> In the cellar was a large coal-burning furnace that kept the school quite warm in the winter. Sometimes we were a bit cold on Monday mornings until the room warmed up from being colder on the weekends. As we grew older our chores were to stoke the furnace and put on coal.[7]

In front of the school was a steep slope that curved down toward the swamp. In the winter, the children used it as a toboggan run. On the other side of the school was a cleared flat area, which was used as a playground. Large enough for a small baseball diamond, the clearing was the scene of many hotly contested softball games.

One of the trees on the far side of the clearing had a swing slung from a high branch. Because of the unusually long ropes, it was the "mother" of all swings. A child could pump his way to a pretty good height, but the greatest thrill of all was when the teacher would not only stand there and push, but also follow through by running behind, pushing the swing as he or she ran. One final thrust threw the rider skyward, giving the child an aerial view of the playground, the road, and the trees beyond! (Any self-respecting OSHA official would have had a heart attack.)

Some of the teachers who served at the Big Moose Lake schools included, at various times, Katherine Barry, Edward Manning, Mabel Means, Jack Morton, Ralph Osgood, Edna Judd (Scouten), and Ethel Sears. Early classes included such students as Gordon Kinne, Everett Martin, Katherine Martin, Bob McAllister, Elizabeth "Nibs" Williams, and Mary Williams. According to Bob McAllister, one winter Gordon Kinne was the only student in attendance, and he was taught by Ralph Osgood.

Conspicuously absent from the lists of students were the names of Roy and Frieda Higby's three daughters, Letha, Allison, and Patricia. Roy had established a special school for his girls, building a small schoolhouse west of the automobile driveway entrance to the Higby Club. Some say that the teacher (a Miss McIlhenny for at least part of the time in the early 1930s) was paid by New York State, just like the teachers at the other Big Moose schools. Most people in the community attributed this privileged situation to Roy's influence within the local Republican Party. Others were convinced that the teacher was a private tutor. Vernon Harry (son of Robert Guy Harry, who had purchased large tracts of land from Edward P. Morse) lived at the end of the roadless Crag Point during the winter of 1933–34 and remembers attending school with the Higby daughters when it was unsafe for him to cross the ice to meet the school bus on the Covewood Road.[8]

Except in the very early days of the school, there were six grades taught in the school's one room. On attaining seventh grade, students attended the school in Old Forge, where they could continue until the twelfth grade.

Many student memories of the lake school during the early 1930s center on Ted Manning, a teacher well known as a stickler for discipline. Manning had a house on Thirsty Pond on the Twitchell Road, where he lived with his wife and two young daughters. Not infrequently, his car would not start on cold mornings, and he would have to walk the three miles to school. The students would be waiting outside the door when he came trudging down the road with his lunch bucket in hand, close to frozen from the long, cold walk. These days did not bode well for the students. Already sorely tried, he would have little patience left, and the ruler might be brought out if students did not have their lessons prepared or did not live up to his expectations in some way.

Bill Dunn recollects:

What I remember most is, of course, our teacher, Edward (Ted) Manning. He was the teacher for all of my six years at BMLS. Manning was, without question, a very, very strict disciplinarian—at times, as a student, I disliked, and sometimes even feared Manning's dictatorial strictness. But now I can reflect back to those years and say to myself, "For Bill Dunn, Manning was the correct teacher 65 years ago." I have a learning dysfunction called "dyslexia." In the 1930s hardly anybody knew about this problem in reading and arithmetic, and he probably had no idea whatsoever that he was teaching a dyslexic.

Manning gets a resounding vote of approval from Gordon Kellogg:

I remember our teacher Mr. Manning fondly. He taught a few years there and worked at the store in the summer. As I remember the story, he had a sickly wife and [two] children. At the end of the year his expenses outweighed his income. He used to tell us ghost stories. One of these so upset little [me] that Lawrence [Potter] had to walk me home. A favorite character of his was the "man with the golden arm." One story concerned a dream he had where Junior [Nelson] Dunn shot him three times in the leg. The explanation was that Junior's paper was the last he had corrected, and he went to bed after removing a garter that pressured his leg in three different spots!

Joy Waldau Hostage writes from the perspective of a city girl who spent her summers at Big Moose:

The mailboat dropped the mailbag on our dock on Big Moose Lake. Out of the bag my mother took a letter from my father. With no telephone in camp we received much mail. That day mother's face was serious. "Your father writes, 'there is a polio epidemic at home. Helen Mizwa from Joy's Girl Scout troop is in Grasslands Hospital—paralyzed. Best keep the children in the mountains. Send them to school there until it's safe here at home.' "

Hence started a memorable part of my education. Home was Scarsdale, New York, where I attended Edgemont School. Progressive Edgemont taught woodworking and manual arts to young girls. Music, art, and physical education had separate departments and teachers, and we went there to be taught. Otherwise our class of twenty students worked every minute with our own class teacher.

That September morning I felt confident and prepared to start fourth grade in the one-room Big Moose school. My friend, Barbara Kinne, stopped by on her way and we happily ran along the lakeside trail to school.

Mr. Manning was the teacher who greeted us. He had black wavy hair with some specks of gray. Behind the spectacles, his eyes were lively. He was thin and seemed very tall to me, although I believe he was of only average height for a man. He arranged the twenty children in rows. First graders were close to his desk in front, sixth graders had their desks in back of the medium-sized room. Only two or three others were in my grade. Gordon Kellogg may have been one. Each class was called in turn to gather around Mr. Manning's desk for a lesson. When it was my turn I marched right up with confidence. Mr. Manning seemed pleasant enough, but next to his right hand I saw a ruler. I had heard about that ruler. The session ended uneventfully and we were given an assignment and told what the next lesson would be. Back at my desk I listened entranced to the other lessons. Fifth grade had math and sixth grade had geography and so on. After a brown bag lunch in the sunny yard, classes resumed. I listened all afternoon enraptured with all I was learning. Next day when my class was called, I was not prepared. I had not done my desk work. I had spent my time listening in. I had no idea of how to work independently—how to study alone. I learned how that day. No more listening until my work was done.

Next day I received another rude awakening. My class was briskly reviewed through their solid knowledge of roman numerals and me none. My ignorance was total in roman numerals. I was embarrassed.[9]

Barbara Kinne Wheeler welcomes a new teacher:

In 1936 Mrs. Judd took Ted Manning's place. Her manner of teaching was much different from Manning's. Pe-

tite—not much taller than the tallest sixth-grader and slight of build, she asserted her authority in a way we hardly noticed, but definitely understood. The ruler was retired, except for measuring and ruling purposes. She bullied the school district into getting a piano for us, and she played well enough so that we were able to have music in our "curriculum." The students all enjoyed standing around the piano and singing while she played. She encouraged us to write, and we published a little newspaper that was typed and mimeographed by the business students in Old Forge. She loved to read, and would have us put our books away at 3 o'clock and read to us the last period. I remember *The Virginian* and *Penrod and Sam* in particular. She was an excellent teacher and she made learning fun.

When Mrs. Judd assumed the teaching position, the school district hired Ray Sanderson as custodian to run the furnace and do the cleaning, thus lightening the chores for both teacher and students.

Of Mr. Manning, Mary Alden Covey Williams recalls, "I am sure he would have preferred a more academic situation and a less rowdy student body. However, in fairness, I think he generated some of that hostility by his own precise and rigid discipline." And of Mrs. Judd, Williams says, "She encouraged us to enjoy life and to learn." Of the little one-room school itself, she recalls that it

seems very old fashioned now—but we lived in a simpler time then. Only the radio and an occasional newspaper brought the universe into our sheltered world. We had to devise our own entertainment—and we did. We had to rely on our own abilities and establish our own credibility—and we did. When we left Big Moose Lake School and went into the seventh grade in Old Forge where we encountered things like a gymnasium and a separate lunchroom, we were as prepared as we could be for new friends, new teachers, and new experiences in a different kind of school because we had learned how to manage ourselves at a basic level. We were established persons by then and ready to take on whatever Old Forge could throw at us —and we did.

For about thirty-four years, Walt Dunn drove the school bus that took the students to the Old Forge school. His first vehicle was an eight-passenger 1928 Packard car, purchased from P. E. Crowley, president of the New York Central Railroad and a regular guest at Lake View Lodge. Walt, a cautious driver, seldom missed a day, even when the roads were glare ice. In some winters

Town of Webb school bus with pupils from Big Moose Lake on their way to a picnic, ca. 1937. Left to right: bus driver Walter Dunn, Mary and Jeannie Potter, Eleanor and Helen Strife, Larry Potter, Jackie Strife, Joyce Potter, William and Bud Dunn, Mary Covey, Barbara Kinne, Joe Dunn, Nelson Dunn, Jr., Gordon Kellogg (?), Frank LeSure (?), and Mary Strife. On the reverse is a note to the driver Walt Dunn: "With sincere appreciation of the many kindnesses shown to the pupils of the Big Moose Lake School and myself. [Signed] E. H. Manning." Courtesy of Barbara K. Wheeler.

when the snow was deep and the roads not regularly plowed or sanded, Walt would put chains on the car in the fall and not take them off again until spring.[10] Later, he bought a small bus to accommodate the growing number of children. Walt tolerated no mischief, but he earned the respect and affection of the students.

A list of the students who regularly attended the Big Moose Lake School through the 1930s includes Elizabeth, Helen, James, Jeanne, and Ruth Brownell; Mary Alden Covey; George "Joe", Nelson, Walter "Bud," and William Dunn; Barbara and Wanda Kinne; Frank, John, and William Lesure; Willard McAllister; James, Jean, Joyce, Lawrence, and Mary Potter; and Eleanor, Helen, Jack, Mary, and Virginia Strife.

The lake school finally closed its doors in l939. Thereafter, students were bussed from Big Moose to Old Forge. However, in 1953 parents from both the lake and the Station requested that the school at Big Moose Station be reopened for the very young students so they would not have to make the long trip to Old Forge. The teacher was Mary E. Timmerman. This school closed again, for good, in 1957. The final year's enrollment included only three children from the lake (Jon, Nancy, and Philip Martin) and three Marleau children from the Station. After that, Big Moose-area children were taken to Old Forge.

The old lake school building itself stood unoccupied for several years and was heavily vandalized. LaVerne Orvis, the lawyer who represented the Kellogg sisters, acquired the lot in 1942 for services rendered during the Glennmore Hotel case. He eventually turned the property over to the Department of Environmental Conserva-

tion (DEC), which made the land into a trailhead for the West Pond-Safford Pond trail. A sign that reads "Orvis School House, Trailhead Parking" is actually a misnomer. The schoolhouse was long defunct when Orvis received the land, so he had nothing whatever to do with the school.

When Nelson Dunn, Jr., won the contract from the DEC to tear down the old schoolhouse, the building was razed and the resulting rubble trucked away. The concrete steps, apparently too cumbersome to be transported, were bulldozed over the bank and into the small adjacent swamp, where they rest today, atilt among the cattails.

Community Groups

A variety of organizations exist within the Big Moose community. Membership in all of them includes both year-round and summer residents, although it is the year-rounders who in most cases have provided the initiative and the sustaining power and who have shouldered the major responsibility. We have received help from John Vander Veer, Jon Martin, and Barney Barnum in writing about the safety organizations and from Charles Adams and others about the Fish and Game Club. Other contributors are mentioned under the appropriate sections.

BIG MOOSE FIRE COMPANY

No one knows for sure how long the Big Moose Fire Company has been in existence, but the earliest recorded evidence turned up in a letter written a little more than two weeks after the Big Moose Community Chapel went up in flames on July 19, 1930. R. H. Alton, who identified himself as chief of the Big Moose Volunteer Fire Department, wrote a letter on Hotel Glennmore stationery to the Property Owners of Big Moose suggesting that "there be a portable pump for auto or boat stationed at a favorable position on the lake to insure immediate protection and action in case of a fire. As Big Moose Station is to receive the benefits of a fire pump, it is felt that the Glennmore should be the place to keep the pump."[11] Alton asked for donations from property owners, noted that a firemen's dance had been held at the Glennmore at which more than $50 was raised toward such protection. We have no record of whether such a pump was ever purchased. It is possible the lake was without proper fire protection for another eleven years.

When the Big Moose Volunteer Fire Company was officially organized in February of 1941, its officers were all men. Walt Dunn was the deputy chief, Everett Martin president, Roy Higby vice-president, George Deis secretary, and Fred Williams treasurer. Although all the members were men drawn from the community, late in that year the United States entered World War II, and many of the men were called into the armed services or left for war work in other places. The women stepped in unofficially to help. Frieda Higby, for instance, drove the fire truck to a fire at the Higby Club, and other women helped with the hoses and took over other tasks that freed the men to enter the burning buildings.

The fire hall was built in 1942 to house a pumper truck and to provide space in an upstairs room for meetings and other events.

After World War II, the Big Moose Property Owners Association raised money to buy a fireboat—an open boat with two powerful pumps that was owned and maintained by the BMPOA (and stored in a special boathouse at the Higby Club) but operated by the Fire Company. The boat made it possible for the firefighters to reach camps that did not have road access, and it also provided protection for other camps and structures not easily accessible by land.

The Fire Company now averages about twenty-five to thirty members. Barney Barnum was fire chief for some thirty years. The company was the first to take women as official members, of which Betty Barnum was the first. Other female members have included, at different times, Wanda Martin, Pat Judson, Jenny Martin, and Linda Martin. The women's first official active participation was at the practice burning of the Higby Club in 1978.

All members must have approximately twenty-five hours of basic training and an additional eight hours of training annually. The training includes methods of not only fighting fires but also search and rescue, arson detection, and OSHA (Occupational Safety and Health Act) standards. Much emphasis is placed on safety. Several members are trained Emergency Medical Technicians. In the case of a fire, firefighters communicate the location and other information through the 911 center of Herkimer

Big Moose Lake's first fire truck, far right, with spectators on Glennmore dock at Motor Boat Regatta, 1941. Courtesy of Wanda K. Martin.

County, using two-way radios on an assigned frequency. The radios are also used for on-scene communication.

The Town of Webb Fire District tax now pays for the fire company, and it owns not only the equipment but also the fire hall. Even the fireboat, which was owned by the Big Moose Property Owners Association until 1985, is now owned by the town. The Town of Webb has five fire commissioners, one from Big Moose (currently Jon Martin), one from Eagle Bay, and three from Old Forge. The commissioners oversee the training of volunteers, maintenance of the equipment and property, and the purchase of insurance.

Big Moose has had several serious fires. Club Camp, on the site of the present Tojenka property, was probably the earliest. The first school at the lake, located across the road from what is now the Big Moose Inn, burned in 1918. In 1921 both the old Higby Camp on Higby Point and the Vander Veer camp, on the south shore of the eastern end of the lake, burned to the ground. The main building at Camp Crag was destroyed, perhaps by fire, some time between 1924 and 1930. The Chapel fire occurred on the eve of its dedication in 1930. In early September of 1950, the Glennmore Hotel suffered a spectacular conflagration. Deerlands, the historic camp at the entrance to the Inlet, went up in flames in the fall of 1964, when the ice was too thick for the fireboat but too thin for a truck or other vehicle. (Old Forge now has a hovercraft for use on Fourth Lake that can deal with just such situations.) The fire hall itself was hit by lightning at 4:00 A.M. one summer day in the 1960s, confusing the community by the insistent but senseless signals of the siren. Fortunately, the damage was quickly contained. When they repaired the building, the firefighters added a kitchen and storage room. The most recent major fire, in July of 2001, destroyed the large and lovingly built home of retired forest ranger Terry Perkins, located on an island in Stillwater Reservoir. Although the Big Moose Fire Company truck, among others, rushed to the scene, it was helpless because the reservoir had been drained for dam repairs. The trucks were unable to get close enough to the house to save it.

BIG MOOSE AMBULANCE COMPANY

Big Moose Lake is more than seventy miles from the nearest hospitals, which are in Utica. Although there is a health center in Old Forge staffed by dedicated doctors and nurses, it is not equipped to help in a serious medical emergency. For many years, the community managed its medical problems with the help of a few physicians, Dr. Robert S. Lindsey and his father, Dr. Robert N. Lindsey. These doctors maintained an office in Old Forge, made annual visits to remote communities where residents gathered for consultations or inoculations, and in the early days made house calls either by horse and buggy or by train. Later, patients requiring hospital attention were taken to Utica by station wagon. As late as the 1960s, pregnant women routinely traveled to stay with friends or relatives in Mohawk Valley cities a few weeks before the expected birth.

The Big Moose Ambulance Company was organized in the early 1970s. With money raised by donations, the company bought a secondhand Cadillac ambulance. The vehicle was shaped very much like a station wagon, and, although it was up-to-date for its time, attendants could not stand up inside it, nor was it equipped with the life-saving equipment we expect today. In 2001, the community raised $90,000 for a new ambulance that provides much more space for attendants as well as for state-of-the-art technical devices.

The Big Moose Ambulance Company has no membership list, but its members are drawn from the Fire Company members, who are covered by the Volunteer Firemen's Benefit Law (similar to Workmen's Compensation). The Town of Webb Board of Fire Commissioners carries additional insurance. There is also separate liability insurance for the ambulance company, paid entirely by the company.

In order to function, the Big Moose Ambulance Company requires trained Emergency Medical Technicians. Among the first were Betty and Barney Barnum, Keith Johnson, Bill Judson, Jenny Martin, Jon and Linda Martin, and Dennis McAllister. EMT training is long (180 hours) and complicated, and it must be updated every three years. The first courses were taught in Utica. Later, Barney Barnum trained EMTs in Old Forge, serving as the instructor for twenty-seven years. There are three different levels of Emergency Medical Technicians, leading up to certification as a paramedic. A special act of the New York State Legislature, known informally as the Good Samaritan Act, protects EMTs from liability.

Becoming an EMT requires not only arduous training and frequent renewals of the license, but also a willingness to answer calls at any time of the day or night, even in severe weather. The Big Moose Ambulance Company covers not only Big Moose Lake and the Station but also the remote communities of Twitchell Lake, Stillwater, and Beaver River. Snowmobile accidents account for much of the activity in the winter.

The company owns two snowmobiles and a rescue sled for patient transport. EMTs may be called upon to travel by snowmobile, pulling a sled for the victim, out the rough road to Stillwater or along the railroad tracks to Beaver River. These volunteers evacuate the patient to a point where they can meet the ambulance, and then they accompany the patient to the hospital. In some years when the snow conditions bring in many tourists, there are many sleepless winter weekends for the EMTs. Recently it has become more and more difficult to recruit volunteers. The possibility of hiring paid EMTs has been considered.

In addition to donations from residents, in the last few years the Big Moose Ambulance Company has been able to receive funds from a private company hired to bill the patients' insurance companies and reimburse the company. As a volunteer organization, the Big Moose Ambulance Company is prohibited by state law from billing directly, but the private company set up for the purpose can provide this vital service. No money from taxpayers is available.

In the case of a life-threatening emergency, a medical helicopter can be called in from Camp Drum, near Watertown, along with highly trained EMTs to assist. Although the helicopters are theoretically on stand-by, they cannot always be reached, or take-off or landing conditions may not permit them to reach the patient. Also, the medical helicopters cannot be called in for a person who becomes lost in the woods. If a person is reported missing, the state police will send a helicopter from Albany or Syracuse to conduct the search.

BIG MOOSE FISH AND GAME CLUB

Old pictures of proud men and women with catches of lake trout, brook trout, bass, and other fish testify to the abundant species in the waters of Big Moose and nearby lakes and ponds. Similar pictures of hunters standing beside impressive numbers of deer show the wealth of trophies that stalked the surrounding woods.

Karl A. Adams, a summer resident of West Bay and an avid fisherman, became aware in the 1940s that the population of game fish in the lake had been declining over a number of years. Roy Higby, among others, was also con-

cerned. In an effort to do something about the problem, Adams in 1950 founded the Big Moose Fish and Game Club, a group with the motto "Promote Fishing. Protect Game. Preserve Forest." His charismatic personality soon helped him gather many members (for dues of two dollars per year that still stand). Many prominent lake residents joined and proudly wore the badge that identified them as members. Many also contributed extra funds. The group established a relationship with the New York State Conservation Department, working with the state conservation staff for many years.

One of the first steps was to initiate a program of rehabilitating nearby ponds where Big Moose residents fished. Under this plan, all the fish in a small lake were eliminated by chemical means and the lake was closed to fishing for about two years. When it was reopened, the state stocked the lake with desirable species and prohibited fishing with live bait. Merriam Pond, Bubb Lake, Cascade, and others were reclaimed under this program.

At Big Moose Lake itself, another early step intended to improve fishing was the perch removal program designed to provide suitable conditions for the survival of stocked brook trout fingerlings. In the early 1960s, club members put out trap nets in North Bay and caught huge numbers of perch. Barney Barnum recalls filling four fifty-gallon barrels on one occasion, the weight of which left only five or six inches of freeboard on the boat.

Over the years, the Fish and Game Club worked with the state conservation staff to stock various species of fish on an experimental basis. In addition to brook trout, lake trout, smallmouth bass, and largemouth bass were deposited, often by plane, in lakes and ponds. Stockings of rainbow trout, salmon, and smelt proved less successful.

In the mid-1970s, the problem of acid rain caused by nitrates and sulfates spewed out by industrial smokestacks to the west came to national attention. Cornell University conducted extensive studies on Big Moose waters and found that the acidity of the lake had increased markedly since the early 1930s, when the New York State Conservation Department had made detailed studies. The later studies established that acid conditions, over which local people had no real control, were responsible for killing off many species of fish.

In spite of this setback, the Fish and Game Club has continued, and in the last few years lake conditions have improved. In the summer of 2001, reports of catches of brook trout and even lake trout began to surface. Loons, which feed on fish (albeit not game fish), have returned after an absence of some years. Herons continue to inhabit the marsh, and the occasional osprey (also a fish consumer) is spotted.

Over time, leadership of the Fish and Game Club passed from Karl Adams to Barney Barnum. Roy Higby and Bill Judson were also active for many years, as were Lena Otto, Edith Milligan, Howard Martin, Bill Marleau, Ford Lux, and many others.

As a fund-raising effort, the club has sponsored the "ice out" contest, whereby residents pay a small amount to guess the date and hour when the ice will go out of the lake. The time is determined by the moment at which a barrel placed on the ice disappears from view. The person whose guess comes closest wins a substantial amount of money.

The Fish and Game Club has also worked with the state conservation staff to maintain a reasonable deer population. Early in the twentieth century, deer remained deep in the woods. (In her diary for 1900, Lena Retter noted with excitement that her family had seen two deer during the summer.) Recently, as the size of the herd has increased, there are more and more tame deer, and, hunters say, fewer in the woods. The club, along with private donors and (until recently) the Big Moose Property Owners Association, helps to pay for a game protector to patrol the roads around the lake to see that deer are not shot within the protected zone near inhabited areas.

For several years the club owned property along the road to Big Moose Station that was once the dump for the area. A rifle range for the benefit of members was established on the land.

The Fish and Game Club continues its monthly meetings, usually held after the meetings of the Big Moose Fire Company and the Big Moose Ambulance Company, and works under increasingly difficult conditions to maintain the sports that have historically attracted visitors to Big Moose Lake.

THE BIG MOOSE COMMUNITY CHAPEL

Ellie Reed Koppe has written an excellent history of the Big Moose Community Chapel's first fifty years.[12] The Reverend Percy B. Wightman and Dr. Albert Vander Veer, both summer residents, were the moving spirits in establishing the Chapel, although many year-round residents were also active. We do not intend to take up the story where Ellie Reed Koppe left it, but a few short supplementary notes belong in this history. Ida Ainsworth Winter has contributed the piece on the Willing Workers and the Jolly Moosers.

THE CHAPEL FIRE OF 1930

In the course of gathering recollections from Big Moose residents for this history, we came across two members of the community who remembered the fire that consumed the Big Moose Community Chapel on the night before the first service was to be held. Rumors of arson have circulated for years but without any firm evidence.

Wanda Kinne Martin, Barbara Kinne Wheeler, and Joy Waldau Hostage, all longtime Big Moosers, interviewed Bob McAllister in July 1999. Bob, then in his late eighties and now deceased, had been part of a team of men who were finishing last-minute jobs on the new Chapel to prepare it for the dedication the next day. One of the chores was to rub down the paneling with linseed oil. According to Bob, when they finished, it was late at night and all were tired and eager to get home. Without thought of possible consequences, they left the oily rags in a closet under the stairs. Spontaneous combustion did the rest.

The story is confirmed by Bill Dunn, whose father, Nelson, was also there. Why rumors of darker causes have persisted is a mystery. However, as is now common knowledge, pledges of funds for rebuilding the Chapel came pouring in, and the new structure opened the following summer.

THE WILLING WORKERS AND THE JOLLY MOOSERS | *Ida Ainsworth Winter*

The Willing Workers. In 1929, while the construction of the Big Moose Community Chapel was still in the planning stages in the mind of Earl Covey, a group of local women gathered to form an organization that would toil summer and winter to raise money that would be necessary beyond the building expenses. They foresaw the need for equipment for social events and for other general purposes. The ladies met in each other's homes to make handmade items to sell at the church fair. The articles for sale included beautiful aprons of all sizes and colors, pot holders, luncheon sets, pajama bags and pillows, crocheted and knitted children's clothing, doilies, and once in a while a crocheted tablecloth that had taken the maker all winter to complete or an occasional special item such as a quilt.

This was the time when the traditional balsam pillows came into their own. During the winter the women sewed by machine small pillow covers, stitching up three sides and part of a fourth. Often the pillow covers had a picture of the Chapel stamped on them. Before the sale, the men of the community would go into the woods to cut balsam branches. On a designated date, usually a week or so before the sale, the community came together to assemble the pillows. The men supervised chopping the balsam in a corn-cutting machine that was usually of great interest to the children. Others stuffed the pillows tightly with the fragrant needles while the women stitched together the openings in the pillow cases. The result was a woodsy sachet that could perfume a drawer or a couch for months. The balsam bees are still annual events, and the pillows are best-sellers.

In the early years church fairs were held in boathouses of the various hotels on the lake. The first meeting of the Willing Workers inside the Chapel was on September 9, 1931. Two weeks later they served the first of many church suppers in the basement, which was the social room of the Chapel. In about 1933 this group provided gifts for all of the community children at the Chapel's Christmas party. A huge balsam Christmas tree presided over those gathered. Students from both the lake school and the village school at Big Moose Station presented pageants, after which refreshments were served. The Willing Workers also began the tradition, still carried on today, of sending Christmas greetings with a calendar and a newsy letter to all Chapel friends.

During the days of World War II, there were no fairs or suppers at the Chapel. In the late 1940s and early 1950s, these were reintroduced. The Guides' Suppers were held on the Chapel lawn by the lake. As the name suggests, the local guides cooked, and the women and young people served. The menu consisted of steak or chicken, corn on the cob, home-fried potatoes, rolls, tossed salad, gallons of coffee, and for dessert, pancakes or flapjacks (as they were called) with real maple syrup. Occasionally cake and ice cream were available also. What feasts they were! Lots of work, but the money raised made it all worthwhile. Everyone volunteered in some way, and it was the social event of the summer.

As the members of original women's group grew older and were unable to participate, daughters, sisters, or cousins took their places. But after the war, times were rapidly changing and new ideas came along.

For many years now the Chapel has held a bazaar, which is always the first Saturday in August. Although many new items have been added, the balsam pillows remain a sell-out attraction. Various committees under the leadership of bazaar chairpersons now accomplish the work, and this proves to be very successful.

The Willing Workers, now only a memory, served the Big Moose Community Chapel with many, many hours of dedicated service, and they will be remembered as a vital asset to the Big Moose community and to our history.

The Jolly Moosers. Although the Jolly Moosers are descendants of the Willing Workers, they are an independent organization no longer affiliated with the Chapel.

In the mid-1950s a handful of local women wanted to have an organized group through which they could socialize and do creative and helpful work that would benefit the community.

A proper organizational meeting was held at the Big Moose Fire Hall on October 4, 1956, and officers were elected and installed. The Reverend Lyle Buck of Old Forge officiated. This was the beginning of the Jolly Moosers.

For a few years, the Jolly Moosers tried to carry on the work of the Willing Workers, but with lifestyles rapidly changing, those plans were abandoned. An important new activity was the Jolly Mooser Bake Sale in July, to which craftspeople both from the local area and from nearby communities were invited. Other activities such as teas, card parties, and dinners helped to raise money for good causes. The Chapel concentrated on the annual bazaar held in August. This arrangement has worked out well for all concerned. The community has grown considerably and can well support both activities.

The Jolly Moosers are not affiliated with any group, but they contribute to many local causes. The Big Moose Fire Hall, centrally located and accessible even in the winter, is the location for meetings and activities. With income from dues and proceeds from bake sales, craft sales, and other functions, the group supports local organizations such as the fire and ambulance companies, the Town of Webb School's scholarship fund, and individual local students. The traditional Christmas party, initiated by the Willing Workers, takes place in mid-December with a dinner at the fire hall. The Chapel still provides the gifts for the local children and also purchases the meat for the dinner. The Jolly Moosers and the firefighters cooperate to make the occasion a happy and fun-filled evening for everyone. Santa attends, adding joy for the little ones.

Membership includes those who live at Big Moose year-round, those who spend their summers at the lake, and those who may simply vacation in this area. The group maintains an average of one hundred members at this time. All in all, the Jolly Moosers have become a very active organization in this Adirondack community.

The Chapel Choir. The first choir at the Big Moose Community Chapel was organized by Frances Covey, whose love of music was well known. For many years, Mrs. Covey drove weekly to Utica in all weather to sing in a community choral society. In the 1930s she directed a young people's choir that sang at the services. The youngsters, who caught their enthusiasm for music from Mrs. Covey, wore green robes and soft hats.

In 1984, Maureen Van Slyke became the organist at the Big Moose Community Chapel. A few people in the congregation who loved to sing initiated a choir, which Maureen agreed to direct. The choir grew gradually over the years and became an important part of the Sunday service, drawing many people from nearby areas. A new organ, dedicated on August 11, 1991, further enhanced the services.

Chapel Ministers, Loss and Renewal. The Reverend Frederick C. Mathias of the Westminster Presbyterian Church in Wilmington, Delaware, became the summer minister at the Chapel in 1973. After ten years he was called to the Northminster Presbyterian Church in Indianapolis, Indiana, but he and his family continued to return to Big Moose. He was a popular preacher and a valuable addition to the choir. In December of 1996, he and his wife, Cleta, were brutally killed when they returned home from a Christmas service to find their house being robbed. The two young men responsible were prosecuted and imprisoned. The Chapel established a music fund in memory of the Mathiases, and Joy Hostage published a book of Cleta's recipes, sales of which help to swell the fund. Fred Mathias served the Chapel for twenty-three summers, longer than any previous minister.

After two summers of temporary pastors, the Chapel trustees called the Reverend Richard McCaughey of Canandaigua, New York. Also a Presbyterian, he has served the Chapel since 1999.

The Big Moose Property Owners Association, 1926–2001[13]

PART 1: BEGINNINGS, 1926–1942

On September 4, 1926, the Reverend Percy B. Wightman invited a few interested people to meet at Dr. Albert Vander Veer's boathouse to consider forming an association of property owners on Big Moose Lake. The purpose of the association would be "to stimulate interest in the natural attractions of the region and to preserve them as far as possible, to cooperate with the Conservation Commission, to maintain trails, to stock waters with fish, to

The cover of a booklet published by the Big Moose Property Owners Association, 1927. Courtesy of the Big Moose Property Owners Association.

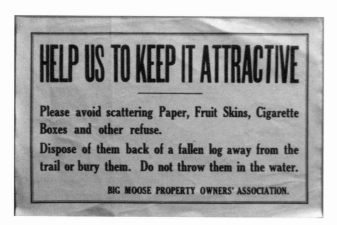

Reminders posted at various approaches to the lake, ca. early 1930s. Note the suggested location for disposing of litter. Courtesy of Richard Widdicombe.

promote social relations among its members, and to concern itself with matters touching their interests on Big Moose Lake."

The name "Big Moose Property Owners Association" was adopted at this meeting. Dr. Wightman was named temporary chairman, and Aras Williams the temporary secretary. The new officers were charged with inviting membership from property owners and with framing bylaws. They also were to prepare material for a pamphlet of local history, "natural life," and suggestions for "the proper use of the woods." It was thought that visitors would be coming in increasing numbers because of the "new road," the road in from Eagle Bay.

By November 15, Dr. Wightman sent a letter to "Friends and Neighbors on Big Moose Lake," in which he announced, "A chic and promising debutante made her bow to the world on September 4th in the boathouse of Dr. Albert Vander Veer. Her name is Big Moose Property Owners Association."

As long as he was chairman, Percy Wightman would continue to write eloquent and delightful letters to his "Friends and Neighbors on Big Moose Lake." These letters would report on the snow and ice, fishing, black flies, and birds, reminding all that the late winter "takes us nearer to the realization of our dreams, another summer on the shore of the lake, where rest and recreation, fellowship and freedom stand to welcome."

And so the first formal meeting of the association was held on August 19, 1927, at the Vander Veer boathouse. The association's name, bylaws, and purpose were all adopted, and dues were set at three dollars per year. Matters under discussion included the clearing of trails, keep-

ing open camps (called "lean-tos" by some) in proper condition, constructing floats at the trailhead to Russian Lake and at the entrance to the marsh, and building open camps at Upper Gull and Russian lakes. There were complaints about barking dogs and speedboats, and mention was made of "throwing a low dam" across the Outlet to raise the water level of the lake.

This last matter was serious indeed, and it would prove quite controversial. On June 1, 1928, the New York State Conservation Department granted permission to build a low dam across the Outlet of Big Moose Lake (on property owned by Earl Covey) in order to provide "sufficient depth for motor boats and generally improve navigation." The dam was to be a sill with flashboards. The open space in the spillway of the dam would have a series of boards placed in grooves; the boards could be added or removed to adjust the level of the water.

At the annual meeting on August 3 of that year, association secretary Aras Williams urged the members to incorporate the association to protect it from liability for any damage caused by the dam. Incorporation took place on August 29, 1928, and with this arrangement in place, Earl Covey agreed to have the dam placed on his land. This matter of the dam then led to special meetings of the directors and the membership. However, there was so much disagreement over the need for a dam, as well as over the procedure to obtain it, that the matter was not resolved, even temporarily, until 1933.

In the period between 1928 and 1933, the association heard many other matters of concern. Tax reduction was called for, as was the elimination of blackflies. There was talk of a fireboat and much disapproval of boats with their "cutouts" open, running without lights after dark, and speeding. Dr. Wightman wrote, "Muffle the exhausts on your boats if you would retain the affection of your neighbors." In 1930 an unusual neighbor appeared from Albany—the Big Moose Pioneer Camp of the Fort Orange Council of the Boy Scouts. These Scouts, under the supervision of George Sparkes, the camp director, agreed to clear trails and attend to the open camps—valuable services to the people on the lake.

In 1933 the association reached several important decisions. The annual meeting elected new officers: Joseph Greenwood as president, James Griffin as treasurer, and Robert M. Jeffress as secretary. At last, the dam at the lake's outlet was approved, and W. W. Colpitts, a resident of the North Shore, was chosen to supervise its construction. Finally, a special meeting was called on September 5 to change significantly the purposes and powers of the corporation, as follows: "(2) . . . to purchase, lease or otherwise acquire and to hold and own and to sell, mortgage, lease or otherwise dispose of real property, whether improved or unimproved, or any interest therein in the State of New York or in any State or territory of the United States, all in accordance with the laws of the State of New York."

The year 1933 was busy. By the end of that year, the Big Moose Property Owners Association (BMPOA) had overseen the start of the dam; the building of open camps at Andes Creek, Upper Gull Lake, Russian Lake, and Billy's Bald Spot; the construction and maintenance of floats at the head of the Russian Lake trail and the entrance to the marsh; the clearing of trails; and the publishing of a guidebook. This book, incidentally, is a prized possession of those who have one today. Finally, a dock was completed at the "end of the state road" (the Higby Road).

Mr. Colpitts built this new dock and gave it to the BMPOA with the understanding the association would maintain it. In an amusing letter to Dr. Wightman, he wrote, "I beg to hand you herewith one boatlanding at the end of the Higby Road with all rights and titles of use and misuse and the privilege and entertainment to be gotten from maintaining it and removing it in Fall and setting it out in the Spring—to have and to hold at no expense to the Association except as aforesaid."

In March 1934, Joseph Greenwood, BMPOA president, died, and Dr. Wightman agreed to step in temporarily. Also in that year the tradition of a hobby exhibit, now called the Chapel bazaar, was begun. Mr. Colpitts also completed the dam at the Outlet, and immediately there were misunderstandings. From time to time, the lake level was lowered for individual purposes without notice, which inconvenienced some residents.

In his spring letter of 1935, Dr. Wightman announced a proposed state road between McKeever and Port Leyden, and another between Big Moose and Spillwater [sic]. These were of great concern, because they would affect the seclusion of the lake. A "fill-in" at the dock landing was also proposed, so that automobiles would have a place to park.

Attendees of the annual meeting of the Big Moose Property Owners Association, 1934.
Left to right in first row: Joseph Greenwood, Everett Martin, Charles Dunn, Arthur Burtch,
Peter Masson (of the Hotel Glennmore), and Frank Naporski; in second row: Ilione Woodbury,
Francena Higby, Roy Higby, E. J. Martin, Donald Salisbury, Robert Jeffress, Percy Wightman,
and Henry Milligan; in third row: Nelson Dunn, Albert Vander Veer, Jr., Janet Bruyn, Ruth
Greenwood, Mrs. Vander Veer, Florence Phillips, Marguerite Judson, Elizabeth Kreitler, Florence
Colpitts, George Sparkes (director of the Boy Scout camp), and unknown; and in fourth row, Robert
Wertz, Olive Wertz, Va Scruggs, Elizabeth Jeffress, Gretchen Wewerka, Mary Eustis Wightman,
Mrs. Jack MacAffrey, Walter Colpitts, and the Reverend Hillis Miller. Courtesy of Diane Ritz.

About 1935, a period of unusually high water damaged the dam, and repairs were made in 1936 under the direction of Mr. Colpitts. Arthur Burtch was employed to put in and take out the property owners' dock and to make any necessary repairs.

In the spring of 1937, Dr. Wightman wrote to his fellow members on Big Moose Lake: "King George VI has been crowned. With his exalted position goes wealth, castles, hunting lodges, horses and motorcars, and an income which staggers the imagination. But, and here is the point, not a camper who has enjoyed the beauty, freedom, and fellowship of Big Moose for a few years, envies him."

By 1938, the purposes for which the association had been organized were accomplished. The tasks now were the maintenance of the docks, the dam, and the trails; and the preservation of the four open camps. The newly established Big Moose Fish and Game Club also invited the association's cooperation in stocking fish, posting property, and donating funds to patrol for poachers.

On September 1, 1939, the German army invaded Poland, and World War II began. But the United States did not enter the war until 1941, and so the people of Big Moose Lake had time to take care of a few things before everyone's attention turned elsewhere. Dr. Edgar Vander Veer was elected president of the BMPOA in 1939, and Gretchen Wewerka was elected secretary. Also, the Boy Scouts celebrated their tenth season at Big Moose Lake by hosting the annual meeting of 1939. The Scouts not only continued to clear trails and clean up East Bay, but they also invited association members to their songfests. In 1941 boat noise again became an issue when a "Big Moose Sports Association" (organized by Phil Ellsworth) held a motorboat race, attracted fifty entrants, and won the "unanimous" disapproval of the property owners.

The Japanese bombed Pearl Harbor on December 7, 1941. The association held its annual meeting on August 7, 1942, and decided not to meet again until the war ended.

PART 2: TRADITION AND GROWTH, 1946–2001

In 1946, at the first meeting in four years of the Big Moose Property Owners Association, Duncan M. Dayton was elected president. Auspiciously, the secretary, Gretchen Wewerka, wrote, "The war years, which brought numerous calls for service both civilian and in the armed forces, anxieties and losses, gasoline and food rationing, prevented our meeting together in 1943, 1944, and 1945. The summer of 1945 saw us facing a happier future, however, and now in this year of grace, 1946, we hope to resume our community activities with renewed vigor and vision."

For a time, life at Big Moose appeared to be a continuation of things as they had been before the war. The property owners' dock needed to be rebuilt, but donated logs were used because commercial lumber was hard to obtain in those first postwar years. The dam also faced rebuilding, having been damaged by storms and neglect.

In addition, fire protection was needed, and a fireboat, which had been long discussed, was finally bought. The boat was owned and maintained by the association but operated by the Big Moose Volunteer Fire Company. The association decided to erect a building for the boat and its equipment on land offered by Roy Higby, and a "frolic" was held at the Higby Playhouse to raise money.

PRESIDENTS OF BIG MOOSE PROPERTY OWNERS ASSOCIATION

1926	The Reverend Percy B. Wightman (temporary chairman)
1927	Percy B. Wightman
1933	Joseph Greenwood (d. March 1934)
1934	Percy B. Wightman
1939	Dr. Edgar Vander Veer
No meetings after August 7, 1942	
1946	Duncan M. Dayton
1954	Alexander Hadden (d. April 1957)
1957	E. Winslow Kane
1963	Robert Wertz
1967	Albert W. Schenck
1970	Edwin H. Lederer
1972	Robert Wertz
1978	Arthur Knorr
1982	Donald F. Dew
1987	Jane Wilson
1991	Edgar C. Kenna
1995	George Schunck
1996	Alfred W. Popkess
1999	Donald H. Dew
2003	H. Thomas Clark, Jr.

In 1949 the Fire Company bought a Jeep squad car, and again the Playhouse was the scene of a fund-raiser, a rendition of *High Jinks*.

The roots that people had put down still held, but the nation—and Big Moose Lake—had been changed by the war. The nation's long period of peace and growth after 1945 challenged the people of Big Moose Lake in new directions—some welcomed, some resisted, some accepted.

"GOOD FISH" VERSUS ACID RAIN

In 1950 the Big Moose Property Owners Association became the first organization in New York State to form a partnership with the State Conservation Department. In order to improve fishing, perch spawn was removed from feeder streams and beaver dams were cleared. The lake was then stocked with lake trout, sockeye salmon, and brook trout.

Hopes for a resumption of the fishing of prewar days were soon dashed as awareness of acid rain grew. In the mid-1970s, studies by Cornell University for the state showed Big Moose Lake to be too acid to support trout. In 1977 the state stopped regular stocking. In 1980, BMPOA experimented with dropping limestone into North Bay and South Bay in order to reduce the acidity. However, after a few years the results were deemed short-lived and expensive, and the project was discontinued.

"THAT DAMN DAM"

If the property owners thought the debates over the dam and water levels were behind them, they were mistaken. In 1952 there was another discussion over "desirable" water levels and the use of flashboards. In 1965 a new "rock dam" was reported, located above the bridge between Covewood Lodge and Buzz Point at the entrance to the Outlet. More rocks and cobbles were noted in 1985, sufficient to raise the lake level by a foot.

The Waldheim, among others, objected to the damming, saying the continued high water had submerged the main dock where mail was delivered, that smaller docks for guests were useless, and that the beach area had been reduced by 40 percent. In August, the state Department of Environmental Conservation was informed by letter of this new dam. The letter noted that, while the dam was in good shape, its flashboards needed renewing because of their accidental destruction when a front-end loader went off the bridge above the dam. In

the end, the issue died down when some rocks were removed from the dam, allowing water to move more freely.

FROM "A NATIONAL PARK?" TO THE APA

After World War II, New York State was faced with a myriad of questions, all stemming from the rapid growth of the nation's population and its economy. It began to appear, some time after 1950, that the BMPOA was going to have to deal with questions of use, regulation of use, and the state's new approach to the Adirondack Park. Under the activist governor Nelson Rockefeller, the question of whether to make a national park of the Adirondacks arose. BMPOA was one of many organizations adamantly opposed to the proposal, and in the end the state rejected the idea.

The decision against a national park led to the state Study Commission on the Adirondack Park and eventually, in the 1970s, to the creation of the Adirondack Park Agency (APA). BMPOA viewed the APA with suspicion, fearing that state lands in the park would be opened to "undesirable recreational, commercial, and amusement purposes."

Also of concern to BMPOA members was the questioning in the 1990s by the state Attorney General's Office of the legality of private telephone and electric cables resting on the bottom of a public lake. In 1996, BMPOA came to understand that, although the cables were not lawful, they would not have to be removed. However, new applications for such use of the lake bottom might be denied. So, at present, the issue, like the cables, has been put to rest.

MOHAWKS, MOSS LAKE, AND THE ASSOCIATION

Just before the Memorial Day weekend of 1974, a group of Mohawk Indians moved into the former girls' camp at Moss Lake, claiming sovereignty and ownership of the land. Moss Lake sits between Eagle Bay and Big Moose Lake. Many BMPOA members, who were coming to spend the holiday weekend at their camps, found their arrival punctuated by a police escort down the road.

BMPOA first expressed its deep concern by sending a letter to Governor Hugh Carey, and two special meetings were held in late fall in Syracuse. BMPOA also retained counsel in order to play a role in any forthcoming legal action to gain evacuation of the "trespassers at Moss Lake." To reassure the owners, Department of Environmental Conservation Commissioner Ogden Reid spoke to the membership in mid-July of 1975. He said that the matter would be settled diplomatically, without violence, and that the Adirondack Forest Preserve and the "forever wild" clause would be maintained.

At long last the governor's representative, Mario Cuomo, brokered an agreement in 1977, and the last Indians left Moss Lake in the spring of 1978.

ZONING, TAX EXEMPTION, AND AN END TO WASHBOARD ROADS

In 1953 growth in the use of Adirondack Park lands and lakes prompted a call by BMPOA for zoning regulations that would preserve the "character and personality" of Big Moose Lake. However, many owners opposed zoning, wanting to guard against undue restrictions upon their property. In the face of opposition, E. Winslow Kane of Crag Point worked hard to promote long-range planning. However, he was disappointed when a planning committee's work was discontinued in August of 1957 because only a minority of owners was willing to sign an agreement.

Interest in zoning arose again in 1959 over concern that the subdivisions of large tracts of land at the Hotel Glennmore and Lake View Lodge would result in the building of "shacks." The association urged the Town of Webb to have an overall zoning plan that would be fair to hotels and camp owners alike. An ordinance was passed in 1965—supported by BMPOA—that called for "strict" zoning for Big Moose Lake but "relaxed" zoning for the rest of the Town of Webb. In spite of this ordinance, trailers appeared near the Glennmore, and docks and boathouses encroached into the lake. BMPOA complained, but the zoning officer said he had no power to intervene.

In 1961 an improved road from Eagle Bay to Big Moose was proposed in order to straighten curves and expand the right-of-way. As in the past, the association opposed this proposal, arguing that expansion would interfere with the seclusion of the lake. The Higby Club wanted the road for the greater ease of its guests, and the road became a hot issue.

But as the road continued to deteriorate, the association's opposition eventually changed to support. In 1970 association president Edwin Lederer wrote to the Herkimer County Legislature that the failure for ten years

to build a better road amounted to taxation without benefit, and the association threatened legal action. The Town of Webb eventually agreed with BMPOA, rebuilding the road in 1978. BMPOA expressed thanks to the highway superintendent for the new Big Moose Road, deeming the change "very good."

FIREBOAT, WATERS, DUMPS, AND DOCKS

Over the years, BMPOA has provided property owners with a consistent, yet ever modified, number of services. The fireboat, for example, was purchased and maintained for many years by the association, but in 1985 it was turned over to the Town of Webb Fire District.

Clean water has continued to be a vitally important issue. Originally, the association expected each camp to monitor and regulate its drinking water. But recently, a vigorous program of lake-water testing has been enacted in order to uncover any problem areas. The result of these tests is that today, drinking untreated lake water is no longer considered wise because of the high count of disease-causing bacteria in some parts of the lake.

When the Big Moose dump closed in 1975, the bears that had frequented it soon spread out to everyone's backyard. BMPOA came to the rescue by providing dumpsters, but the bears quickly learned to open them. The association then came up with a solution, which was to build a bear-proof house for garbage. This "Bear Hut" on the Higby Road has worked well under the watchful eye of the hut keeper and his or her helpers.

While the property owners' dock at the end of the Higby Road has never changed its position, its physical condition has, over the years, varied greatly between solidity and decrepitude. The association and some individuals have done their best to maintain it, because members who do not have road access need this dock to get to their camps, and canoes and kayaks are regularly launched there by the public and by various boys' and girls' camps. Also, local "leaf peepers" appreciate the beautiful views from the dock in the fall.

The association's boating committee has had buoys placed where there are hazards and where speed limits need to be observed. It has continued to admonish boaters who drive on the lake at night to display running lights, to remind water-skiers to have spotters in their boats, and to urge all to drive their boats under five miles per hour when less than 100 feet from shore. The annoyance of noise made by boats with their "cut-outs" open in the 1930s has become the annoyance of noise made by jet skis in the twenty-first century.

BOATHOUSE FROLICS, PICNICS, AND THE LAKE SWIM

From its earliest days, the BMPOA has been charged with promoting "social relations among its members," and in the years after World War II, there were two "frolics" and a rendition of *High Jinks* to raise money for the purchase of a fireboat. August 17, 1963, saw the first picnic, later an annual event, and on August 2, 1976, BMPOA celebrated its fiftieth anniversary with the annual meeting and a family picnic served by the Youth Committee.

In 1965, Donald F. Dew and others proposed to start a youth program for the lake. All children would have an opportunity to engage in activities. Teenagers especially would be included in the planned activities, because some had been drinking alcohol and speeding around the lake at night without boat lights.

As the program got under way, the youngsters engaged in work projects, athletics, and entertainment. By 1969 the association hired a part-time instructor to teach swimming, and by 1970 the program included movies at the Higby Club Playhouse. There were also informal gatherings on Tuesday and Thursday nights. As time went on, the program held sailing races, swimming and lifesaving lessons, volleyball, tennis, badminton, water-skiing with the Ski Club, dances, softball, and soccer. Given all of this, the recreation director's position became full-time. Bill and Linda Keener spent several years in this job and eventually became Big Moose residents. Terry Yardley has been the program director since 1986. Each summer brings a new and comprehensive schedule, mailed early to families so that all can get ready for the summer.

Early in the 1970s a lake swim was added to the program. Participants entered the water at the Hotel Glennmore and swam, each accompanied by a person in a boat, the length of the lake. For many years, lake swims were held in late August early in the morning, often a time of thick fog. Because of this, some swimmers got lost and went around the island, while others beached in South Bay. But those adept with a compass arrived at Clark's Point. More recent swims have been held earlier in the summer.

Sustaining the program's many activities soon became expensive, and members initiated a chicken barbeque (using the famous Cornell recipe), along with a raffle, with spectacular results. The program also has been supported in large part by donations from parents and other members. In the summer of 2000, some 130 children participated. The program was further expanded in 1996 with a focus on activities for adults. The Adirondack Discovery program, first established in Inlet in the early 1980s, has visited Big Moose with a number of interesting regional programs, and the Conservation Committee has brought in local forest rangers to speak. In 1999 the Big Moose Lake History Project Committee held an evening of reminiscences with six speakers who had all been students in the one-room lake schoolhouse in the 1930s. In 2000 a course in the making of pack baskets was well received.

THE ASSOCIATION CENTER

Perhaps no undertaking by BMPOA in the last part of the twentieth century was more important than the Association Center. The Association Center's building was originally the Higby Club garage and now includes a number of large spaces, bathrooms, a handsome fireplace, and an area for a kitchen. The impetus for the Association Center came from a small number of dedicated camp owners who felt strongly that the people of Big Moose Lake needed a place to congregate for the programs of the association to flourish.

At a general meeting on May 28, 1977, a group of eleven association members led by Arthur Knorr reported that they had set up a trust and had purchased four lots on the Higby Club property, and that they would hold the land to ensure its availability for community use. However, there were those who felt that the Big Moose Property Owners Association should stay out of the real estate business.

In the fall of 1979, a committee met to consider the appropriateness of buying the Higby Playhouse, renovating the garage, or constructing a new building for the association's use. At the annual meeting of 1981, purchase prices were presented for consideration—$40,000 for the garage and $35,000 for the adjoining Strack House, which would be used as a residence for the recreation director. These figures would also allow for repairs.

Members, however, were concerned about the association's keeping its nonprofit status and its ability to meet long-range costs. Nearby Higby Point residents were worried about traffic on their road and about a septic system threatening their drinking water. However, in 1981 the BMPOA accepted the trust's donation of the four lots and the garage.

When the BMPOA took ownership of the donated property, New York State considered the association a nonprofit group. At that time the Town of Webb did not levy taxes on property held by the association (the Association Center, the Strack House, and Billy's Bald Spot). However, in 1995 the Town of Webb reversed itself and began to tax the property, but this did not affect the BMPOA's nonprofit status.

In 1983 the board of directors decided to go ahead with improvements to the Association Center. The next year's meeting saw the presentation of an augmented plan that increased the size of the center from 2,400 to 6,000 square feet. At this point, the lake community became strongly polarized, and some longtime members withdrew from the association.

A report of the executive committee of August 30, 1985, stated that "it appears that funds from somewhere between three and six interested BMPOA members would make it possible to substantially improve the condition of the garage." Eventually, a certificate of occupancy from the Adirondack Park Agency was granted, and a septic system and water supply were approved. In 1989 a fireplace dedicated to the memory of Joe Dunn was added. Insulation and knotty pine paneling were installed. Members, who as children had enjoyed the Rec Program, were asked to donate windows and doors. Finally, at the annual meeting in July of 2000, it was proposed that the association finish the kitchen in the Association Center.

The annual picnic is now held at the Association Center on Labor Day weekend. It is always preceded by the great boat parade. This procession of boats, both large and small, is led by the fireboat blowing its whistle and spraying its hoses high into the air. The picnic draws many people, and the sight of children running around, groups gathered to talk, and the sky darkening to night is cherished by the lake community.

The Big Moose Property Owners Association has acted as a beacon to its members, both year-round and summer residents, steering them in ways sometimes harmonious and sometimes fractious. It has been independent, perhaps impatient and quick to litigate, but it has always fostered a great pride in Big Moose Lake. It has a history of hardworking leaders and generous persons expediting its projects. The hope is that the Big Moose Property Owners Association will continue to lead for the good of the community for many years to come.

Big Moose Lake at the Beginning of the Twenty-First Century

THIS APPENDIX is a roster of the residents of the lake in the year 2002. The list uses the original survey lot numbers established by William Seward Webb in 1892. It starts with lots 376 and 1 at the end of West Bay (west of the Glenmore Road and near the Big Moose Community Chapel) and progresses counterclockwise around the shore of the lake and into each bay. Exceptions to the sequence occur in the subdivisions of the sites of former hotels, Lake View Lodge, Higby Club, and the Hotel Glennmore. In these cases, where cottages were built close together and do not always face the lake, Town of Webb tax office numbering is used.

The listing includes each lot that contains a camp, with the exception of camps on the south side of the Big Moose Road in the Lake View subdivision. Information about camps comes from survey questionnaires, telephone calls, and visits to residents and neighbors, as well as records at the Herkimer County and Hamilton County courthouses.

In spite of these efforts, there are some properties about which we have gathered little or no information. Please note that this is a roster of *occupants* rather than owners. Some camps are owned by family trusts or have been put in the names of children. For the early history of some of these camps, readers may consult the index. Appendix A itself is not indexed.

We have attempted to indicate the marital status of the children of primary occupants by placing (m) after the names of those who are married. In some cases, information was incomplete.

376. Balsam Rest. George and Barbara Schunck. Jamesville, N.Y. The Schuncks bought the camp in 1985.

Children: James (m), Lawrence (m), and Lorraine. The Schunck sons married twin sisters. Grandchildren: four.

1. Scott and Roberta Bennett. Big Moose Lake, N.Y. Children: Zachary and Alexandra. The Bennetts own the garage and apartment bordering the Big Moose Road that Nelson and Ada Dunn built in 1923.

Rocco and Mary Maggiore, New Hartford, N.Y., own the house close to the lake that the Dunns built.

2–3W. Big Moose Community Chapel. (See index.)

3E–4. David Ames. Clinton, N.Y. In 1921, Dr. Charles W. Walker bought the camp and had it moved closer to the lake. In 1951, James Jackson purchased it. In 1961, the Chapel bought the land, subdivided it to expand Chapel property, and sold the remainder to David Ames. (See index: Rockefeller.)

5. Paul and Linda Sugrue. Coral Gables, Fla. Children: one daughter. The lot was originally sold to Dwight Sperry in 1900. Sperry sold it to Jim McAllister in 1916.

6. Timothy and Jeanne Brown. Oswego, N.Y. Children: Michael and Melissa. This lakefront property does not extend to the road; the Big Moose Inn wraps around the back. There are two camps, originally parts of Burdick's Camp. Tim's parents, Robert and Elizabeth Brown, bought the camp nearer to the Big Moose Inn in 1956. The other camp, which had been purchased by William Rowland at the same time, was bought by the Browns in 1972. Both camps are now owned by the younger Browns. (See index: Burdick's Camp)

7–8. Big Moose Inn. (See index.)

9–11. Dunn's Boat Service. (See index.)

12W. Ann and Kathleen Romer. Williamsville, N.Y. One of two camps originally associated with the New Burdick Camp.

12E. William and Linda Keener. Cape Coral, Fla. Children: Mary Jane Chambers and Jeffrey. An original cottage of New Burdick Camp, bought in 1978 from Robert McAllister.

13. Thomas Dunn et al. Owned by Thomas Dunn and his siblings: Diane Ritz, Laurie Baumbach, Barbara Harrington, and James, all children of George "Joe" and Ann Dunn. This property contains three buildings: one, now occupied by Tom Dunn, was the home of Walt and Bert Dunn on the Big Moose Road; one, a garage with apartment, is often used by Steve and Diane Ritz in the summer; the third, the original home on the lake built by the four Dunn brothers in the 1920s, is now shared by the entire Dunn family. (See index: Dunns.)

14–15. Robert and Maureen Van Slyke. Big Moose Lake, N.Y. Children: Debra Duffy, Michael, Mark, Barbara Hanlon (on Higby Point), Annette Mahoney, and Paul (m), owner of the Big Moose Station Restaurant. Grandchildren: thirteen. This property originally belonged to Arthur and Goldie Burtch and includes a lakefront cottage and a garage with apartment on the road. The Van Slykes bought it in 1989 and have remodeled the roadside building as their permanent residence.

LAKE VIEW LODGE SUBDIVISION
(TAX NUMBERS 22–68)

At the time of the auction of Lake View Lodge in 1957, there were eleven cottages along the shore, in addition to the main lodge and several outbuildings. At the auction much of the land was subdivided. Camps not on the lakeshore have lake rights and the use of the subdivision dock that lies immediately east of the Scalzo boathouse. Lake View subdivision camps are identified by their tax numbers, starting at the western end of Lake View property and progressing eastward.

22. Frances Knorr. Camillus, N.Y. Children: Jenny Engel, Karen Como, and Leslie Zinc. Grandchildren: eight. The late Arthur Knorr purchased the lot in 1965 from David Ames, who had bought the land at the auction. The camp was built shortly afterward. Arthur was a past president of the Big Moose Property Owners Association, a prime mover of the Association Center, and one of the initiators of the recreation program.

23. Harold Decker. Manlius, N.Y.

24. Edward and Emily Sullivan. Utica, N.Y. Children: Edward, Jr., Michael, and Kim McLaughlin. The Sullivans' camp was built in 1980 on a lot purchased at auction by Edward's father, Bernard Sullivan, who had been a partner with Charles Williams in the horse livery business in Utica.

25–27. Charles C. Michels. Fairport, N.Y. Family: mother, Lillian Michels (93 years old), who still sings in the Big Moose Chapel choir; siblings: Lillian A. Michels, James T. Michels, and Victoria. Charles Michels purchased the land from Mr. Fortunato of New York City in 1962. Fortunato had bought it from Paul Pierce of Syracuse, who had bought it at the 1957 auction.

28. Richard and Dorothy Carter. Stillwater, Pa. Children: Richard C. III and Mark. Grandchildren: four. After renting at Goldie Burtch's, the Carters bought this Lake View cottage in 1963 from Ruth and Harry Walker.

29. The Bungalow. Robert and Merle Binyon. Cedar Grove, N.J. Children: Jill Kurtz and Gail Tobin. Grandchildren: three. Bob Binyon, who had been coming to Lake View Lodge since 1947, bought this camp (also known as Honeymoon Cottage because of its small size) at the 1957 auction. The walls of the original camp consisted of mosquito netting and canvas awnings. It was later enclosed. A winterized house behind this original one is under construction.

30. Steven and Diane Baker. Big Moose Lake, N.Y. This property was purchased from Diane's parents, Donald and Gail Mawhinney, who bought it in 1964 from Floyd Bennett and Harry Walker, who had themselves purchased it at the 1957 auction. A larger, winterized house has been built behind this original camp.

31. William and Maureen Tomeny. Baldwinsville, N.Y. Children: Jennifer Staccini. Bill and Maureen's siblings own Lake View property to the west. This camp was purchased in 2000.

32. Cook Cottage. Bernt and Mary Hoppert. Santa Rosa, Calif. This was the first of three camps built privately on Lake View property. It was built in 1904 for Charles S. Cook. Family records indicate that Minnie Maddern Fiske was a frequent visitor and sometimes brought along her guest, Diamond Jim Brady. The Cooks' daughter Katherine is the great-grandmother of Laura McSweeney and Hamilton White (lots 47–49). The camp was sold in 1957 to Joseph Straub from Pittsburgh, in about 1975 to Richard Graef, in 1979 to Robert and Maureen Van Slyke, and in 1989 to Nick Curri. The Hopperts bought it in 1999.

33. Crowley. James and Glenda Uvanni. Penn Yan, N.Y. Children: James, Heather, and Michael. This, the second of the private camps at Lake View Lodge, was built for Patrick E. Crowley, president of the New York Central Railroad. The camp was sold at auction to Mr. Blake and then to Roger and the late Joan Munsell. The Uvannis purchased it from the Munsells in 1976.

34. Pratt. Trainham and Helen Herskind. Ticonderoga, N.Y. Children: Curtis, Mary-Lou Armstrong, and Helen. Grandchildren: two. This camp, the third to be privately built on Lake View property, was originally owned by Arabella Pratt. It was sold at the 1957 auction.

35. Timber Lodge. Philip and Linda Kurtz. Big Moose Lake, N.Y. This was an original Lake View camp bought from Mr. Hazlet in the late 1970s.

36. Bear Lodge. Robert and Jane Wilson. Bridgeport, N.Y. The Wilsons bought this camp in 1961 from Paul Pierce of Syracuse, who bought it at auction; local history indicates that Charles and Fred Williams may have lived here year-round. The Wilsons have now totally winterized it for their retirement. Jane is a past president of the Big Moose Property Owners Association and a descendant of the Harvey family, who owned Echo Island.

37. Rustic. Charles and Maureen Moynihan. Fayetteville, N.Y. Children: Charles, Jr., and John. This camp was originally the Rustic Dining Room for Lake View Lodge, connected to the Lodge by walkways on both the first and second floors. Because the second floor was used for staff quarters, the cottage originally had no inside stairway. The camp was bought from Judy Herron in 1986.

38. Lake View Lodge. Edward and Janice Legere. Scotia, N.Y. The Lodge was bought in the winter of 1968–69 from Orville Hubbell. Legere and a friend anticipated using the building as two private camps. Soon after, the Legeres bought their partner's share. The western section was razed.

42–43. Barns and Stables. The red barn on the road between Big Moose Road and Lake View Lodge was once a garage with staff quarters on the second floor. It is now jointly owned. The stables collapsed in 1960. A second red barn, farther east on the road, is owned by Philip Kurtz.

45. Gary and Patrick Pfluke. New Hartford, N.Y. This building was the laundry for the old hotel.

46. The Boat House. Connie Scalzo. Clifton, Va. Children: Laurie Beaucham and twins Janice Wojciechowski and Janet Turk. Grandchildren: eight. Connie's late husband Louis once worked at Covewood and liked to recall the old days when staff from the various hotels would congregate at the old boathouse. It had a hardwood floor, good for dancing. Before the Scalzos purchased the building in 1982, it had been turned 90 degrees by a former owner. The Scalzos had hoped to restore it, but that proved impossible. They replaced it with a new building in the same location.

47–48. Windfall A. Terence and Laura McSweeney, West Granby, Conn. This was an original Lake View camp, purchased at auction by William Wildman and sold in 1968 to Hamilton White, Sr., father of Laura McSweeney and Hamilton White, Jr. They are descendants of Charles Cook, owner of the first private camp at Lake View. Children: Terence McSweeney, Jr. (m), and Jennifer Rothamel. Grandchildren: two.

49. Windfall B. Mary and Hamilton White, Jr. This camp was formerly owned by Robert and Barbara Licking. Children: Andrew.

50. Robert and Margaret Tomeny. Cicero, N.Y. Children: Jill and Robert. (Siblings of William and Maureen Tomeny, who own lot 31.) The Tomenys bought the camp in 1994 from Laddie Martin.

51. Andrew and Regi Scarafile. Sauquoit, N.Y. The cottage, often referred to as the Owners Cottage, was bought in 1984 from Fred and Olive Williams.

53. Phyllis Tipper. Baldwinsville, N.Y. This log cabin on the Big Moose Road was bought in the mid-1990s from Mr. Ravello.

54–55. Carol Kolar and Michael Stuhler, a brother and sister from Long Island, purchased this log cabin on the Big Moose Road in 2001 from Phillip Downs.

57–59. Vincent D'Arrigo. Skaneateles, N.Y. Children: Joseph and Sandy. Grandchildren: two. The lot on the Big Moose Road was purchased from Mr. Randel in 1975.

60. Tim and Linda Goff. Big Moose Lake, N.Y. The building was once the tool shed for the Lake View gardens.

61. Wayne and Rosemary Kort. Orchard Park, N.Y. **Lora Constantia.** Sterling, N.Y. **James M. Purington.** Auburn, N.Y.

WEBB LOT NUMBERS 35–106

35–36. Cindabar. Roger Munsell. Surfside Beach, S.C. Children: David and Cynthia. Grandchildren: one. The Munsells' camp is built on land bought from Fred Brack in 1982 that had been a part of Tojenka.

37–43. Tojenka. Spartacus and Marie DeLia. Freeport, Bahamas. Children: Barbara Bennett, Janice Martinez, Jean DeLia, Phyllis Connors, and Elis. Grandchildren: nine. Great-grandchildren: one. (See index: Tojenka.)

44. Robert and Bonnie Hubbell. Washington Mills, N.Y. Children: Robert, Jr., Andrew, and Elizabeth. The camp was built on the site of the old Tojenka boathouse.

45. Richard and Colleen Zogby. Manlius, N.Y. Bought from Celia Hubbell in 2000. (See index: Tojenka.)

46–48. James Hubbell and Janet H. Knapp (brother and sister). Vero Beach, Fla. Children: Hubbell Knapp and Stephanie Knapp. (See index: Tojenka.)

49–55. Stag's Leap. Robert and Lucy Craske. Boca Raton, Fla. Children: Katherine Beltz and Alice Waxman. Grandchildren: four. Also, nephew Robert Youngs and niece Elizabeth Stunkel. (See index.)

56. Allison Hackney. Atlanta, Ga. Land originally part of Milligan's Buzz Point.

57. Omar and Tania Bailey. West Chester, Pa. The land was part of Milligan's Buzz Point.

58, 60–68. Covewood Lodge. C. V. "Major" and Diane Bowes. Big Moose, N.Y. Children: Kimberley and Rebecca (m.).

59. Section on the road from Covewood to the Big Moose Road: at the corner. **Troy and Joyce Whitfield.** Originally the Rodney Ainsworth lot. Between the Whitfield house and Covewood. **John Vander Veer.** Big Moose Lake, N.Y. Children: Patricia Zamperlin and Barbara Walter. Grandchildren: two. House built in 1994.

69. The Manse (of the Big Moose Community Chapel). (See index.)

70–72W. Brown Gables. Eugene and Christine Lozner. Manlius, N.Y. Children: Alison and Charles.

72E–73W. Harrison and Jane Bicknell. Lexington, Ky. Children: Catherine Crabtree, Elizabeth Cyr, Harrison (m), David (m), Bruce (m). Grandchildren: six. (See index: Fern Spring Camp.)

73E–74W. Donald Blair and Janet Owens. Children: Donald, Robert, and Bruce Blair; Douglas and Donald Owens. The camp was built in 1962 by their father, Dr. Jackson Blair, on land from one-half a Hadden lot and one-half a Harvey lot. (See index: Bicknell.)

74E–76. Hadden Camp. Robert and Alexander Hadden and Edith Hadden Matthew (grandchildren of the late Percy Wightman). Children: Debbie, Jeff, Betsy; Christopher, Hartley, and Gerald Hadden; Thomas, James, William, Terrence, and Katharine Matthew. Grandchildren: twenty-one.

77. Kenneth and Anne Korby. Colrain, Mass. Camp bought in 2002.

78. Beulah R. Swain (died in August 2002). Now owned by sons Richard and John, both from Mentor, Ohio. Children: Erik, Jill Kilpeck, and Adam. Grandchildren: four. House built by Earl Covey in 1936.

79. Harold and Katherine Lutz, Agnes Walsh, and Margaret Walsh. The three women are sisters. Children: Janice and John Lutz, Marianne Monahan. Grandchildren: seven. Great-grandchildren: four. The camp was built in 1947. Doug is brother of Bruce.

80–81. Douglas and Corabel Ralston. Novelty, Ohio. Children: Sarah and Griffin. The camp, once owned by Walter Mathers, was bought in 1979. The Ralstons have been renovating since then.

82–83E. William and Patricia Irish. Fairport, N.Y. Children: Catherine, Peter, and Amanda.

83W–84. Fred and Stella Gibbs.

85–86. Douglas and Bruce Ralston. Children of Bruce: Scott and Heather. Grandchildren: two. The camp was formerly owned by their parents, Eldon and Virginia Ralston, who at one time owned Brightwood on the North Shore. They moved to this South Bay camp about 1950.

87. Philip Hardy. Ausable Forks, N.Y.

88. Charles and Mary Ann Hartman. Central Square, N.Y.

89. Edward and Eleanor Wandro. Utica, N.Y.

90W. John and Jeannine Surgent. Children: Deborah Wu and Shannon Schaeffer, both on Crag Point. Grandchildren: two.

90E. Co-owners Peter and Diane Adams and Charles Burns. Simsbury, Conn., and Yorktown, N.Y., respectively. Children (of Adamses): Karl and Abigail Adams.

91. Lynne Kingsley. Pittsford, N.Y. The camp was built in 1971 on land purchased from Roy Higby.

92. Arthur and Madeline Kanerviko. Syracuse, N.Y. The camp was built in 1968 on land purchased from Roy Higby.

93. Herbert and Louise Munk. East Amherst, N.Y.

94. Stephen and Sharon Seitz. Robbinsville, N.J. Son: Scott.

95. Edwin and Patricia Bogan.

96. Anthony and Donna Baratta. Hampton, N.H. Children: Allison and Kristan. This hunting camp was purchased in 1977 from Mr. Wright, who bought the land from Roy Higby. A winterized camp has recently been built closer to the lake.

97. Ronald and Mary Benjamin. Solvay, N.Y. Six children and one grandchild. Camp built in 1971 on land bought from Roy Higby.

98. Doris and John F. Williams. Syracuse, N.Y. Children: Patricia, John A., David, and Wendy Scheening. Grandchildren: four. The land was bought in 1973 from Mr. Lamphear of Rochester, N.Y. On July 4, 1976, a liveable, but unfinished, camp was first occupied.

99. C. Samuel Beardsley. LaFayette, N.Y.

100–06. The Ledges. Donna Watkins Zorge and Frederick Watkins. Children: Christopher, Timothy, and Anna Watkins. A boathouse was built in 1928 by Earl Covey for D. W. Salisbury, president of Sun Oil and Gas. Donaldson and Alice Watkins, parents of Donna and Frederick, bought the camp in 1955. (See index.)

CRAG POINT (LOT NUMBERS 107–39)

The Crag Point development started after Ross Paltz from Syracuse, N.Y., bought land in 1951 and in 1953 built a dirt road from the Higby Road to Crag Point along the main lake. Later he built an extension of the road on the South Bay side. These two roads are not connected; the deeds in one or more properties prohibit a connection. Paltz incorporated many other restrictions in the deeds. Residents on Crag Point have an association to maintain the private road that serves the Point.

107–108. Irad and Janet Ingraham. New Berlin, N.Y. Children: John, Richard, and Laura Ann Welch. Grandchildren: four. The camp was built in 1969 for George Hebard. The Ingrahams bought it in 1973.

109–110. John and Sara Burrows. Simsbury, Conn. Children: Alison and Jay. Bought in 2002 from Bruce and Karen Barber, who built the camp in 1968.

111–14. William and Anne Burrows. Manlius, N.Y. Children: William, John (lots 109, 110), and Sarah B. Winch. Grandchildren: six. The camp was built in 1971.

115–116. Suzanne Beeching. Syracuse, N.Y. Children: Barbara and Victoria. The camp was built in 1972.

117–19. Robert Hankey. Villanova, Pa. Children: Bruce and Kevin. The camp was built in 1988.

120. Lakeside. Richard and Donna Shindell. Furlong, Pa. Richard Shindell's children: Richard, Scott, Caroline, and Colburn. Grandchildren: five. Donna Shindell's children: Maria, Christopher, and Heidi. Grandchildren: three. This was an original Camp Crag cottage bought in 1978 from Doris and Edwin Lederer. A winterized camp away from the lake was built in 1996. (See index: Minnie Maddern Fiske.)

121.41. Robert and Elizabeth Smith. Newtonville, Mass. Children: Matthew, Molly, and Thomas. The camp was originally a garage and staff building for Camp Crag. It was bought in 1981 from Cameron Jameson, who had purchased it from Nan Paltz shortly after the death of her husband, Ross.

121.42 Townsend. Brian and Judith Farranto. De-Witt, N.Y. Children: Margo, Amy, Molly Roth, Emily, Brian, Joseph, and John. The camp was bought from Cameron Jameson in 1985. He had bought from Walter and Barbara Cowie, who had bought the camp in 1960. At one point Jameson also owned lot 121.41. Before sell-ing to Smith, he attached the boathouse to the Townsend lot.

121.43. Summit. Mark and Jane Barlow. Shutesbury, Mass. Children: Andrew, Sarah (m), and Elizabeth (m). Grandchildren: four. The Barlows bought the camp from Paltz in 1961. Built in the late 1880s, it is arguably the oldest extant camp on the lake.

122–123. Trail's End. David and Patricia Hinkle. Pittsford, N.Y. Children: Caroline McCamant, Daniel (m), and Thomas (m). Grandchildren: one. Trail's End, sometimes called Harter Camp, was purchased in 1992 from Paul Edic, whose parents, Edward and Marie, had bought in 1961 from Ross Paltz's sister, Marian Hibbard. For many years, Edward Edic and son Paul, contractors, spent the summer months in restoration and maintenance projects at Camp Crag and around the lake.

123. Kevin and Denise Hanlon. Manlius, N.Y. Children: Lilly and Mark. The camp was built in 1995 on a lot originally owned by the Edics.

124–26. Andrew and Barbara Getty. Old Forge, N.Y. Children: Andrew, Jr., Jennifer, Alexander, and Elizabeth. Andrew's father, Clinton Getty, was a land surveyor who surveyed all of Crag Point for Ross Paltz. He originally constructed a simple camp close to the shore, but in 1986 son Andrew built a new and larger camp and razed the original building. Clinton's deceased wife, Mary, was the daughter of Dr. Charles Walker from West Bay.

127. Regis and Shannon Schaefer. Cohasset, Mass. The Schaefers bought in 2002 from Jeffrey Bartel, who built the camp in 1996.

128–30. Deborah and David Wu. Phoenix, Ariz. The camp was originally built in 1954 by Willis and Rose Burdick and has been extensively renovated.

131–34. Robert and Elizabeth Scher. Chagrin Falls, Ohio. Children: Robert, Barbara Patton, Katherine Brown, Martha Clizbe. Grandchildren: seven. The camp was purchased from John and Jeanne Taylor in 1999. (See index: Polaris Lodge.)

135. Nordlys. Jeanne Taylor. Yorktown Heights, N.Y. Son: John (Jay)(m). Grandchildren: one. Jeanne and the late John "Jack" Taylor built this camp in 1991 on a lot adjacent to their former camp, Polaris Lodge.

136. Donald F. and Joy Dew. Fayetteville, N.Y. Children: Donald H. and Thomas. The Dews bought two lots in 1959 and built soon thereafter. In 1980, they built a second camp to the west, where they now reside. Donald F. Dew was president of the Big Moose Property Owners Association and the Board of Trustees of the Big Moose Community Chapel.

137. Donald H. and Sarah Judson Dew (granddaughter of Roy Higby). Oneida, N.Y. Children: Donald W. and David M. They now own the original Dew camp.

138–139. Donald and Gail Mawhinney. Fayetteville, N.Y. Children: Diane Baker, Bruce, Joyce MacKnight, and Carol Canne. Grandchildren: eight. After residing at Lake View for some years in a camp now owned by daughter Diane Baker and her husband, the senior Mawhinneys bought the camp from Max and Clara Kleinert. The Kleinerts had built a substantial, almost self-contained, camp at the time of the Russian nuclear bomb scare, when many Americans were building bomb shelters in their backyards.

HIGBY SUBDIVISION (TAX NUMBERS 01–36)

1. Hobbit Hole. Charles and Ann Smith. Wilmington, Del. Children: Charles, Gene, Becky, and Debbie. Grandchildren: two. The lot was bought from Mr. Searle in 1977 and the camp was built the same year. Previously, the area had been used by the Higby Club as a picnic/party gathering location.

2. Newstead. Arthur and Joy Hostage. Cheshire, Conn. Children: Basil, David, Eric, and Mark. Grandchildren: five. The camp was bought from Walter and Gertrude West in 1980. The Wests had purchased from the Searles. Originally part of the Higby Club, the camp had been built for the exclusive use of a young Englishman.

3. Larch. Paul and Betsy McMahon. Palmyra, N.Y. Children: Kevin and Brian. The camp was purchased from Richard and Marcia Osmer in 1988.

4–5. William and Phyllis Reidt. Grosse Point Farms, Mich. Children: Paul, Diana Berlin, Laura Reidt, and Linda Reidt-Critschfield. Grandchildren: six. There were two original Higby Club camps on the property, one on the lake front and the other, called Hemlock, away from the lake. The latter was razed and a new camp built.

6. Lora. Robert and Joan Derrenbacker. Fayetteville, N.Y. Children: Robert, Jr., Peter, and Susan Gnade. Grandchildren: six. Originally there were three Higby Club camps on this lot, which was bought by Dr. Lee Bartholomew. Unable to winterize any of the camps, Bartholomew built a winterized camp called Lora. The Derrenbackers bought the camp in 1991.

7. Comfort. Helen Weltman. Burlington, Vt. The camp was allegedly called Comfort because it originally had a two-seat outhouse. It is the only remaining camp that Jim Higby built. In 1972, Roy Higby sold it to Mrs. Carugan, who in turn sold it to Helen Weltman in 1978. There is also a lakeshore cabin on the property. Restoration of the camp's original features has been recognized by Adirondack Architectural Heritage.

8.1. Harold and Pamela Williams, Delmar, N.Y., and **Carman and Patricia Mastroianni,** Sayville, N.Y., joint owners since 1992. The Williams's children: Gillian, Jeremy, Jessica, Benjamin, and Denise. Grandchildren: one. The Mastroiannis' children: Daniel, Alyssa, and Jillian. The Williams family occupies West Lodge, Roy Higby's home until his death in 1991. The Mastroiannis have adapted the former Higby Club laundry.

8.2. Christopher and Barbara Hanlon. Loudonville, N.Y. This structure was once the maintenance shop for the Higby Club. Upstairs were sleeping quarters for staff. The cabin next to it was the chef's cabin.

8.3. Kenneth and Patricia Raymond. Loudonville, N.Y. This camp was built in 1997 on the spot where the Higby Playhouse had stood.

8.4. East Lodge. Howard and Arline Littman. Niskayuna, N.Y. Children: Paul (See index: Echo Island), Susan, and Vicki. The Littmans were joint owners with Allan and Mary Barduhn and Marie and William Gill, but they are now the sole owners. The building was one of the Higby Club cottages.

9. Edgar and Joan Kenna. Poughkeepsie, N.Y. Children: Kevin, Timothy, and Kathleen Thoburn. Grandchildren: three. An original Higby Cottage.

10. The Hutch. Barrie S. Woods. Manhasset, N.Y. Children: Gail W. Johnson and Beatrix. Grandchildren: two. Barrie's late husband, W. C. Wood, came as a child from Fourth Lake to the Higby Club for Sunday dinner and fondly remembered Big Moose Lake. He bought the camp in 1974.

11. Higby Point Association Common Beach.

12. The Beeches. Stephen and Susan Vaisey. Thonotosassa, Fla. Susan's parents, Anthony and Josephine Augello from Rochester, N.Y., had bought the camp, an original one-room Higby cottage, in 1974 from Thomas Dowling. Anthony Augello renovated it and added a second story.

13–14. Roger and Margaret Lind. Big Moose Lake, N.Y. Children: Taylor and Roger. The Linds built in 1976. They now own Inlet Golf Club.

15. Anthony and Mary Louise Kordziel. North Syracuse, N.Y. The lot had been part of the beach and picnic area and was bought from Roy Higby in 1968. The camp was built in 1974.

16. Robert and Pamela Cox. Manlius, N.Y.

17–18. John and Mary Hodson. Williamsville, N.Y. The camp was built by William Judson in 1980 as a year-round home for himself and his wife, Patricia Higby Judson. The Hodsons bought the camp in 1995.

19–21. William and Mary Lou O'Connell. Webster, N.Y. The O'Connells bought the camp in 1970 from Roy Higby. In 1988 an extension to the house and a garage were added.

26. Margaret Ervin. Rochester, N.Y. Children: Christine, Kathleen, Susan, Elizabeth, Mark, and Patricia. In 1978, the Ervins bought the camp from Fred Burch, who had purchased it in 1970.

27.1. Strack House. Had been owned by Roy Higby's brother-in-law, Eric Strack. After a succession of short-term owners, the Big Moose Property Owners Association purchased it for use by the summer recreation program director.

27.2. Big Moose Property Owners Association (BMPOA) Center.

28–29. Roadside. Richard and Jacqueline Crispin. Liverpool, N.Y. Children: Frank, Shawn, Kelly, and Wendy. Grandchildren: five. The Crispins bought this original Higby Cottage in 1984.

30. Raymond and Jane Hanlon. Barrington, R.I. Children: Mary Fingar, Patricia Raymond, Christopher, John, Joseph, and Martha. Grandchildren: seven. Ray Hanlon was the waterfront director at the Higby Club for many years.

31. William, Jr., and Diane Lux. Westernville, N.Y. Children: William III and Jacob. The camp was built in 1999.

33. Big Moose Tennis Club Courts.

34. Brian and Anna Johnston. Big Moose, N.Y. The house was built in 1986.

35. Paul and Mary Traverse. Vestal, N.Y. Children: Ben, Nick, and Hannah. This property was sold by Roy Higby to Albert and Hazel Schenk in 1955. It was then sold in 1969 to Carsten and Margaret Borglum, who resold it four years later to Keith and Heather Watson. Over the next thirty years, the Watsons acquired many of the adjacent lots, planted trees and wildflowers, built trails, and erected bluebird boxes, creating a nature preserve surrounding Constable Creek. They sold the camp to the Traverses in 2001. Paul's family has been on and around the lake since his great-grandfather's days.

36. Margaret Miller. Scottsville, N.Y.

SOUTHEAST SHORE (WEBB LOT NUMBERS 146–85)

By the turn of the twentieth century, Jim Higby owned land from the end of Crag Point to the Totten and Crossfield line, lots 140–62. In 1916, Roy Higby and Dr. Albert Vander Veer jointly bought land along the southeast shore to the eastern end of the lake (lots 163–97). The land had been owned by Theodore Page and the Herkimer Lumber Company. Higby and Vander Veer divided this property in 1919, and they later conveyed parcels to other parties. Many of these lots remained undeveloped for years. In 1960, Roy and Frieda Higby deeded lots 177–85 to their daughter, Patricia Judson. Her husband, William, put in the Judson Road in 1961 and brought in electricity. He constructed two camps that they initially used for themselves. Roy Higby retained lots adjacent to the property owners' dock until the early 1970s.

146S. Dean Siegenthaler. Oneida Castle, N.Y. Dean and his late wife, Jackie, bought undeveloped land on the Higby Road from Dr. Lee Bartholomew and built a small camp with a large garage for snowmobiling and rental. He also owns a camp on the Judson Road in East Bay.

149–51. Janet Straley. Rockville Center, N.Y. Children: Michael, David, Peter, and Pamela. Grandchildren: six. Janet's parents, Loueda and Albert McIntosh, had vacationed at the Higby Club from the 1940s until 1953. They bought lots 149 and 150 from Roy Higby in 1954. A pie-shaped piece of lot 151 was deeded to them by the neighboring Rutherfords to facilitate the building of their camp. In 1960 the cottage was enlarged to accommodate Janet's growing family. Janet inherited the property in 1986 and in 1998–99 added a guest camp.

151–55.1. Greyrocks. Lawson and Jerry Rutherford. Penn Yan, N.Y. (See index: Greyrocks.)

155.2–57. Alkmaar. John Vander Veer, Big Moose, N.Y., **Edgar Vander Veer III,** Old Forge, N.Y., and **Elizabeth Casscells,** West Winfield, N.Y. Children: John's: Patricia Zamperlin and Barbara Walter. Edgar's: Valerie Baldes and Margaerite. Elizabeth's: Kathaleen Hanlon and Debra McCartney. The old caretaker's house, repeatedly modified, remains a family camp for the grandchildren and great-grandchildren of Dr. Albert Vander Veer. (See index: Alkmaar.)

158–62. Marianne and Clarence McDonough III. Williamstown, Mass. Children: Garth and Clarence J. McDonough IV. This property was originally included in the Vander Veer family tract. In 1987, Grace Vander Veer McDonough deeded her cottage to her son Clarence McDonough and his wife, Marianne.

167–68. David and Elizabeth Casscells. West Winfield, N.Y. Children: Kathaleen Hanlon and Debra McCartney. Grandchildren: five. Elizabeth is the sister of John and Edgar Vander Veer III. She and David acquired this property from her uncle, Albert Vander Veer, and built a camp without road access in 1991.

171–73. David and Marjorie Lee. Ithaca, N.Y. The Lees' chalet-style camp was purchased from Norman and Betty Pesch in 2001. It was erected by Joe Dunn without any architectural drawings after the Pesches had drawn an interior layout on a piece of paper. One distinctive feature of this hillside camp is a small funicular that carries supplies from the dock up to the front porch. It can also take an occasional passenger.

The Pesch family bought lots 172 and 173 in 1986 from Joseph and Elizabeth Belser. In 1995 they added Lot 171, purchased from Marjorie Donnelly of Albany. This land includes frontage on Big Chief Pond, which is not accessible by road.

172.1–75.1. Steven and Carol Mackintosh. Deansboro, N.Y. Children: Will and Hollis. They are the sole residents at Big Chief Pond. Although other lakeshore properties back up to the pond and draw water from it, no other owners use their pond shorelines. The Mackintoshes bought the Big Chief Pond property from Bill Judson in 1970. In 1971, they built a lean-to on its eastern shore and camped there for several years without road access. They started building a cottage in 1989.

174. Witchhobble Lodge. William and Marlene Humphrey. Elliston, S.C. Children: Susan, Cheryl, and Shawn. The Humphreys bought this property from the Swancotts. (See index: Swancott.)

175. Camp Thibault. Gary and Norrine Thibault. Skaneateles, N.Y. Children: Jacob, Seth, and Samantha. The camp, purchased from Liz and John Jaenike in 1999, was originally a part of the Vander Veer tract. The camp previously had been owned by "Dutch" Ray and his wife, Dorothy. After her husband's death in 1984, Dorothy married Donald Murphy. Many Big Moosers will remember the Irish flag that would fly at the waterfront when the Murphys were in camp.

176. Michael and Kathy Birke. Ridgefield, Conn. Daughter: Kimberly. This is one of the camps Bill Judson built in 1969. The Judsons lived here for thirteen summers, until they moved to a more accessible year-round cottage next to the property owners' dock.

177–78. David Kreitler. Haverford, Pa. Children: David, Elizabeth Singleton (in West Bay), Robert, and Charles. Grandchildren: six. This camp, built by Bill Judson, was started in 1966. Bill originally planned to locate it farther up the hillside, but the rocky cliff proved impossible for building. The Judsons lived here for two summers before building the neighboring camp. The late Edith Wightman Kreitler and her sister, Elizabeth Wightman Grafton Selander, daughters of Percy Wightman, bought the camp in 1968. The Selanders sold their share to the Kreitlers in 1980.

179–80. Robert and Betty York. Hood River, Oreg. Children: Ben and Carol. Grandchildren: two. The Yorks bought their property in 1966. They have been active members of the Big Moose community; Bob served as treasurer of the Property Owners Association for thirteen years; both have been directors of the association and trustees of the Big Moose Community Chapel.

181–82. Steven and Catherine Chambers. Milford, N.H. Children: Jason and April. This property was acquired in 1956 by Donald Lux and his first wife, Marylou Strack Lux, a niece of Roy and Frieda Higby. Because Don has a family camp on the North Shore, the land had remained undeveloped until Don recently ceded it to his daughter, Catherine, and her husband.

183. Sugarloaf Lodge. René and Karin Kress. Media, Pa. Children: Steven, Michelle, and Michael. Grandchildren: four. Sugarloaf Lodge was built in 1962 for Stanley and Marion Damulis. Mrs. Damulis was the daughter of George Casler. (See index: Casler.) Stanley Damulis died after only a few years of ownership, and Marion used the camp only occasionally. René and Karin, who had been vacationing on the lake in rental cottages since 1979, persuaded Mrs. Damulis to sell to them in 1985.

René has chaired the water safety committee of the Big Moose Property Owners Association for many years, taking water samples from around the lake to be tested for contamination. He has reported at the annual meeting each year.

184. Andrew and Sharon Petrides. Raleigh, N.C. Children: Alex and Eleni. Grandchildren: two. Sharon's family has summered at Big Moose Station since 1919. The Petrides bought this property from Bill Judson in 1965. In 1968–69 their A-frame camp was erected. Their grandchildren are a fifth generation of Big Moosers.

185.2–85.3 Walpert-Fanning Family. Danbury, Conn. This twelve-sided house, which appears round when seen from a distance, was built between 1981 and 1984. It is anchored by a huge masonry fireplace in the middle. The unusual rooflines were designed to shed heavy snow loads and add an aesthetically distinctive crown to the building. The steep waterfront area has slowly been tamed by a succession of steps and docks, facilitating boating, swimming, and sunning. The camp's two floors now provide independent living accommodations for George's children, Mark and Sally, and their families.

185.4–85.5. George and Betty Peters. Rochester, N.Y. Children: Eric and Marge. Grandchildren: two. The Peters and George's brother Donald bought land in 1965. During the summers of 1968 and 1969, George and Don erected the camp from a Vermont Log Homes kit. Eventually, George purchased his brother's interest in the property. In 1973 rocks were blasted by the lakeshore to accommodate a boathouse and dock, including a system of rails to hoist the boat inside. The multistage staircase was built in 1976. A studio was built in the summer of 1998 to accommodate George's hobby, wood carvings of birds. Many have been on display in the Old Forge Art Center and some have won major awards.

185.6. Richard and Barbara Lester. Orchard Park, N.Y. Children: Mark, Paul, and Jean Marie. The Lester family purchased this camp in December 2000. The original, very small, cabin on this lot was built in 1966 by Nancy Langham and Natalie Smith and later sold to Leo and Evelyn Van Leeuwen, from whom the Lesters bought. The Lesters retain their camp on West Bay.

EAST BAY (WEBB LOT NUMBERS 186–97)

The end of East Bay lies in Hamilton County, Township 41, Town of Long Lake. Most of the north shore of East Bay is state-owned and has never been lumbered. It is part of the Pigeon Lake Wilderness, which extends eastward to Raquette Lake. Theodore Page was the first land owner at this end of the lake after William Seward Webb (see index: Page, Echo Island, and Lumbering). After Page's death in 1916, his widow sold all the lots to Dana Bissell, another lumberman. Bissell retained them for only a few days before selling the property to Roy Higby and Dr. Albert Vander Veer jointly. Three years later, the two men divided the property between them, Higby taking the eastern end (lots 176–97) and Vander Veer lots 163–75.

In 1922, Roy Higby sold his East Bay lots to Edward P. Morse, who died in 1925. In 1930 his widow, Ada Morse, hired Ford Rasbach to survey and subdivide the tract. The following year, Ada Morse sold the entire parcel to realtor Robert G. Harry, who also owned Crag Point and other area tracts at that time. (See index.)

185.7. Back O' Beyond. Barbara and Len Partelow. Loudonville, N.Y. Children: Len, Jr., Linda (m), Patricia (m), and Laura (m). Grandchildren: nine. In 1967 this westernmost lot in Hamilton County was purchased by Dan and Joycee Gaines (Barbara Partelow's sister and brother-in-law). The camp was built between 1968 and 1970. They deeded the property to the Partelows in 1985.

186–91. Richard and Jean Rasbach Scholet. Richmondville, N.Y. Children: Art, Tom, and Cosy. Grandchildren: four. (See index: Rasbach camp.)

192–193. Dean Siegenthaler, Oneida Castle, N.Y., and his sister, **Joanne Williamson,** Fairport, N.Y. Joanne's children: Peter, Rob, and Susan. Grandchildren: nine. Frank Siegenthaler, their father, bought these lots in 1952 from the Fort Orange Boy Scout Council. In the earliest year, while building the first camp in 1952, they stayed in the Boy Scout dining hall at the end of the lake. The first camp was built in 1952. Because there was no road, all building materials and furnishings were brought in on a homemade sixteen-foot flat-bottomed scow.

194. Sammons Camp. Kathleen Sardino, Liverpool, N.Y.; and her sisters, **Patricia Crosby,** Harvey, Illinois; **Sharon Crenshaw,** Hewitt, N.J.; and **Judy Humeniuk,** Jamesville, N.Y. Children: Kathleen's: Audrey and Abigail Sardino, Sheila Sardino-Procopio; Patricia's: Jim, Jr., David, John, Tricia Shanahan; Sharon's: Valerie Skinner, Michael, Diana Tully, Bethany, Marcia Ayer; Judy's: Timothy, Robbie, Cassie. Grandchildren: fifteen. Great-

grandchildren: seventeen (collectively). Jack Sammons, father of the four sisters, purchased lot 194 in 1953 from Ronald Brownell and Edward G. Hendrick. While building the camp, they, too, stayed in the old Boy Scout dining hall.

195. Alexander and Mary Ann Simpson. Pittsford, N.Y. Children: Betsy Keim, Timothy (m), and Katie Tortorello. Grandchildren: seven. The Simpson family first saw Big Moose in 1967, purchasing the lot three years later. They started with a bunkhouse with a loft by the lake, which was followed by a complete camp in 1973. Indoor plumbing and a shower were added in 1992. In 1999 the camp was expanded and a composting toilet was installed.

196–197, 197A. V. Ennis and Edith Pilcher. Schenectady, N.Y. Children: Steven and Dorothy. Grandchildren: five. In 1967 and 1968, the Pilchers bought lots 196 and 197 from LeRoy Hodge and Ronald Brownell. Lot 197A was added in 1983. They declined road access at the time the Judson Road was being extended. The cabin's profile and roofline are similar to that of an Adirondack lean-to.

EASTERN HEAD OF THE LAKE
(LOT NUMBERS 215–19)

215–216. Old Pine Point. H. Thomas and Carroll Clark. Fayetteville, N.Y. Children: H. Thomas III, Robert, Christopher Clark, Merritt Locke, and Jane Amico. Tom has been active in the Big Moose Property Owners Association, serving as its vice president, president, and chair of the recreation program. (See index: Old Pine Point.)

214–217. Lucy Clark Popkess and Alfred Popkess. Marcellus, N.Y. Children: John, Megan, and Sara. The camp was built in 1981. Al is a past president of the Big Moose Property Owners Association and together he and Lucy served for several years as chairs of the recreation program.

213. Timothy and Sue Dowling. Schenectady, N.Y. Children: Dan and Kristen. In 1972 they bought a small Higby cottage, which they sold the following year when they purchased this lot from Tom Clark.

219. Deerlands. Ann Dunn Hall and Bob Hall. Big Moose Lake, N.Y. Children: Ann's: Thomas, Diane Ritz, Laurie Baumbach, Barbara Harrington, and James; Bob's: Melissa Glisson, Daniel, Frederick. Grandchildren: fourteen. In 1986, Ann and Joe Dunn bought Deerlands from Edward Dunn's heirs. They had started to renovate the guest house when Joe Dunn became critically ill with a brain tumor. A community workday was organized that fall by many friends and family to expedite the renovation, but Joe died in 1988 without seeing his dream fulfilled. The *Natty Bumppo*, the Chris-Craft once owned by the Greenwoods, has been restored by Tom Dunn. (See index: Deerlands, Edward Dunn.)

NORTH SHORE: INLET TO THE ENTRANCE TO NORTH BAY (LOT NUMBERS 227–49)

227. Trail's End. Richard and Jean Daiker. Sodus, N.Y. Children: Diane, David, Gail, Elizabeth (Beth), and Alison. (See index: Trail's End.)

228. Plywood Lodge. Edwin "Bert" and Jean Daiker Johnson. Westbury, N.Y. Children: Eric (m), Krissa, Daiker (m), and Kurt (m). Grandchildren: four.

229. Birchwood Camp. William and Janet Stone Holmes. Dewitt, N.Y. Children: Carlton "Hap" (m), Peter (m), and Rebecca H. Moran. Grandchildren: seven. (See index: Birchwood Camp.)

230. Twin Pines. Thomas and Doris Hartz. Wyomissing, Pa. Acquired in 1971 after several previous owners. (See index: Twin Pines.)

235W–36. Squirrel's Nook. Theodore Dietze. Niskayuna, N.Y. Children: Eric, Amy Yeager, Barbara Colose, and William. Grandchildren: eight. Theodore's late wife, Phyllis, who died in 2003, was the daughter of Lora Higby Strack and a niece of Roy Higby. She spent much of her early life on the lake at the Higby compound. (See index: Squirrel's Nook.)

237. Oak Lodge. Linda Danforth. Cortlandt Manor, N.Y. Children: Paul (m) and Virginia Angilello. Linda's husband, Byon "Dan" Danforth, died in 2002. The camp was built by Henry and Annadell Walters in the early 1970s and later sold to Annadell's sister and husband.

238. Woodhaven. Donald and Gloria Lux. Utica, N.Y. A rental camp belonging to Donald Lux. (See index: Woodhaven.)

239. Birch Knoll. Donald and Gloria Lux. Children of Donald and Mary Lou Strack Lux: Katherine Chambers, Kenneth (m), and Jessica Rush. Grandchildren: four. Children of Gloria from a previous marriage: Paul, Marcia, and David Armstrong; grandchildren: three. (See index: Birch Knoll.)

240–41E. Brightwood. William and Annette Lux. Westernville, N.Y. Children: Deborah Woltag, Karen Taussig-Lux, and William Lux, Jr. Grandchildren: six. (See index: Brightwood.)

241W–44E. Edilgra. Olive Crawe Wertz. Lexington, Ky. Children: Faith Eastwood, Joy Church, Marcy Thomas, and Robert Crawe Wertz (m). Grandchildren: eight. Great-grandchildren: one. Olive Wertz died in the summer of 2002. (See index: Edilgra.)

244W–46. There are three camps on the Colpitts/ Menand extended-family property: the Colpitts/Menand camp, Rockshire, and Cabellsdale.

Colpitts/Menand camp. Leslie and Nelle Menand Knox, Rochester, N.Y.; and **Molly Menand Jacobs,** Princeton, N.J. The Knox's children: Leslie III, Victoria "Tori" Reyner, and Rebecca Knox, Jacobs's children: Anne Weekes, Cynthia "Cricket," and Kimberly.

Rockshire. Walter and Constance Menand. Cleveland, Ohio. Children: Christine Cameron and Steven Menand. Grandchildren: two.

Cabellsdale. Howard and Heidi Menand III. Townsend, Mass. Children: Howard IV and Georgina. Grandchildren: one. This camp faces North Bay. (See index for these three camps.)

247. Alnwick. Henry B. "Hank," Jr., and Joyce Wightman. Camillus, N.Y. Children: Henry III, David (m), and Karen Bruyn. Hank Wightman is a grandson of the late Percy Wightman. (See index: Alnwick.)

248. Michael and Ellen Wilcox. Old Forge, N.Y. Children: David (m), Joshua (m), and Erica. Purchased in 1980 from Marguerite Judson. (See index: Judson.)

249E. P'Tauk-Seet-Tuft. Richard and Martha Bruyn Widdicombe. Hoboken, N.J. After Janet Bruyn died, the camp was left jointly to the Widdicombes and Frances Shane Bruyn Turner, widow of Ned Bruyn, Plymouth, Vt. Frances S. B. Turner died in November 2002. (See index: Bruyn.)

249. On-Da-Wa. Peter Bruyn and Sharon Gilley, Wakefield, Mass.; and **Christopher and Karen Wightman Bruyn,** Plymouth, Vt. Peter Bruyn and Gilley's children: Catrina and Eric. Christopher and Karen Bruyn's children: Jessica and Emily. (See index: Bruyn.)

249W. Turtle Point Cabin. David and Deborah Bruyn Sleeper. Bridgewater, Vt. Children: Amy and Molly. (See index: Bruyn.)

NORTH BAY TO WEST BAY
(LOT NUMBERS 262–368, 378)

262–311. Martin family and the Waldheim. (See index: Waldheim.)

279–81. Roger Pratt and Nancy Martin Pratt. Big Moose, N.Y. Children: Gayle Bennett and Jason (m). The Pratts built their house, which is partially solar heated, in 1985. Roger and Nancy, with the help of their son Jason and his wife, Kelly, operate the Waldheim.

287–90. Philip and Jennifer Martin. Big Moose, N.Y. Children: Craig, Kerriann, and Alison. Phil built this energy-efficient house in 1982. The Martins own and operate Big Moose Yamaha in Eagle Bay, N.Y.

291–93. Jon and Linda Martin. Big Moose, N.Y. Children: Howard (m) and Kristen Mariaca. Jon and Linda's house, built in 1980, is designed for maximum comfort during the cold winters. Jon is the owner of Martin Maintenance.

301. Wanda Kinne Martin. Big Moose, N.Y. Children: Jon (m), Nancy Pratt, and Philip (m). Grandchildren: seven. Great-grandchildren: two

312W–13. Margaret Kaiser. Rochester, N.Y. Children: David "Dick" (m), Jamie (m), Meg Kassel, and Andrew (m). Grandchildren: seven. (See index: Roby/Kaiser Camp.)

314–15. Camp Hamburg. Christopher and Deborah Grauert. Fairfax, Va. Children: Christopher and David. (See index: Ogden/Grauert Camp.)

316–18. Alfred and Elizabeth Traverse. Huntingdon, Pa. Children: Paul (m), Martha, John, and Celia Lerner. Grandchildren: seven. The camp was designed and built by William Insley, Elizabeth Traverse's grandfather, in 1952. (See index: Insley camp.)

319–21. Thomas W. and Sandra G. Witmer. Rochester, N.Y. Children: Elizabeth, Jonathan, Matthew, and Michael. In 1981 the Witmers bought from Katherine Martin Vollenweider the property that had belonged to her father, Charles Martin. They used the footprint of the boathouse to build a virtually new camp. (See index: Charles Martin.)

322–25. Dun Romin. Jane W. Steinhausen. Pittsford, N.Y. Children: Theodore B., Jr., Jane "Jae" Semich, and Ruth "Candy" Wachterman. Grandchildren: four. Great-grandchildren: two. (See index: Dun Romin.)

326W–29. Grace Quimby Flock. Big Moose, N.Y. Children: Gilbert, Jr., Greg, and Jeni. Grandchildren: two. (See index: Rowanwood.)

326W–35E. (above road) Howard Quimby, Jr. Big Moose, N.Y. Children: William, Peter, and Michael. Grandchildren: two. (See index: Rowanwood.)

330–31. Unoccupied camp.

332–34. Peter and Barbara Kelly. Big Moose, N.Y. Children: John, Peter Shawn, Mark, and Paul. Grandchildren: one. The Kellys first came to the Big Moose area as snowmobilers and built a vacation home on the Glenmore Road in 1990. In 1994, they bought the land on the main lake from Grace Flock and Howard Quimby. In 1998, having completed their house, they became permanent residents.

335W–44. Bret and Beth Long. Greenwich, Conn. Children: Garrett and Jack. The Longs bought the camp in 1995 from Grace Flock and her brother Howard Quimby. The Longs have extensively renovated the interior. Bret has been an officer in the Big Moose Property Owners Association and Beth has chaired the recreation program committee. Both have been active in the Big Moose Community Chapel. (See index: Rowanwood.)

345–49. Owl's Nest. Hunter W. and Frances Finch. Goldsboro, N.C. Children: Hunter "Jeff" J., Frances Mayo, and Jennifer. Grandchildren: four. (See index: Owl's Nest.)

350. Camp Vetti. Manuel and Bonnie Vetti. Stamford, Conn. Children: Tamara and Manuel III. They built their camp in 1997.

351. Paul Littman. Rexford, N.Y. This undeveloped lot contains an ancient sinkhole, called the "pug hole" by old-timers, catches the snow runoff and provides a home for peepers and other wildlife in the spring.

352. Pine Narrows. Ronald and Betty Hayes. Big Moose, N.Y. Children: Marsha Jaenke, Anne Howes, Alan (m), and Walter (m). Grandchildren: seven. Great-grandchildren: four. Nelson Dunn, Jr. built the camp in 1957. It was rented during the summers until 1972, when it was purchased by the Hayes. Both the Hayes have been active in Chapel affairs.

353. Douglas and Bonnie Bennett. Big Moose, N.Y. Children: Scott. Grandchildren: two. (See index: Big Moose Inn.)

354–55. C. Robert and Pamela McCoy. Webster, N.Y. Children: Robert and Michael. (See index: Dr. Herbert Williams.)

356. Thomas and Mary Moore. Clinton, N.Y. Children: Timothy. The Moores purchased the camp in 1995. Mary has taken on the supervision of the summer Sunday school program at the Chapel. (See index: Frank Day camps.)

357. Arthur "Pete" L. and Elizabeth "Libby" K. Singleton. Port Royal, Va. Children: Libby's children: Elizabeth "Lee" W. Kirkpatrick, Christopher K. Kirkpatrick (m); Pete's children: four. Grandchildren (Pete's): four. Libby Singleton is a granddaughter of the late Percy Wightman. (See index: Frank Day camps.)

358. Richard and Barbara Lester. Orchard Park, N.Y. Children: Jean Marie, Paul, and Mark. (See index: David Milne Camp.)

359–360. Barbara Kinne Wheeler. Apulia Station, N.Y. Children: Paul (m), Barbara Vendetti, Carol Rutherford, and Laura Rankin. Grandchildren: six. The Wheeler family occupies the upper part of these two lots on the Martin Road and a small part of lot 359 that extends to the lakeshore. Barbara is the daughter of Romaine and Lillian Kinne and grew up on the lake. Her father owned and operated Kinne's Boat Line. (See index: Kinne's Boat Line and Frank Day Camps.)

359–360. Charles and Olga Adams. Auburn, N.Y. Children: Douglas, Peter, Kathy, and Winnie. Grandchildren: seven. The Adams own the lower parts of these lots except a small section of 359, which is retained by Barbara Wheeler. The house was the first of the Frank Day building projects. Until 1943, the Kinne family occupied it. (See index: Frank Day camps.)

361. Crestwood. Charles and Olga Adams. (See index: Winona, Crestwood.)

362. Wilhelm's Cove. Bernard and Mildred Seavey Carney, Middleville, N.Y., and **William and Jean Seavey Humphrey,** Herkimer, N.Y. Children of the Humphreys: Linda, Jean, Barbara, and Harry. Mildred Carney and Jean Humphrey are granddaughters of William T. Autenrith. The cottage is named in memory of the Humphreys' son, Harry William, and his great-grandfather, William Autenrith. (See index: Crestwood.)

363. Wildwood. John Carney. Lake George, N.Y. Children: Ryan and Shawn. John Carney is a nephew of Bernard Carney, husband of Mildred Carney. (See index: Wildwood.)

364–365W. Big Moose Lodge. Roy and Alta Waldau. New York, N.Y. and **Arthur and Joy Waldau Hostage,** Cheshire, Conn. Children: Roy's children: Geoffrey, Christopher, and Peter. Roy and Alta's son: Alan. Joy and Arthur's children: Basil (m), David (m), Mark, and Eric (m). Grandchildren: five. (See index: Big Moose Lodge.)

365W. Giffarget. Jean Thoburn. Solon, Ohio. (See index: Giffarget.)

366. Shawondasee. Gregory and Patricia Mohr. Camillus, N.Y. This camp was recently purchased from

Henry and Janet Fearon, Lawrenceville, N.J. (See index: Shawondasee.)

367. The Cottage. Paul and Ingrid Van Slyke. Big Moose, N.Y. Children: Maris and Andrew. The Van Slykes tore down the old Brookside camp and erected a winterized home for year-round occupancy. Paul owns and operates the Big Moose Station Restaurant. (See index: Brookside.)

368. Jonneybrook. Alice Daye. Chittenango, N.Y. Children: John, Jr. (m), and Mary (m). Grandchildren: one. In 1957, Alice and her late husband, Jack, bought an undeveloped lot from the Hotel Glennmore Corporation. They built a cabin on the west side of the Squash Pond outlet and later an A-frame closer to the lake.

369. Dexter Estate. (See index: Phil Ellsworth.)

378. Camp Veery (Echo Island). Paul and Rainy Littman. Rexford, N.Y. Children: Mara and Madelyn. The Littmans are restoring the historic complex that was the home of Theodore Page, Minnie Maddern Fiske, and the Harvey family. (See index: Echo Island.)

GLENMORE SUBDIVISION
(TAX OFFICE LOT NUMBERS 5–44)

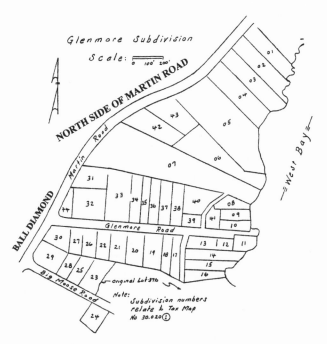

Glenmore subdivision map.

Like the mythical phoenix, the Hotel Glennmore rose from the ashes, but in a somewhat different form. For one thing, it shed an "n" from its name; it is now known as the Glenmore, short for Glenmore Bar and Grill.

Charles Vosburgh, an auctioneer from Cortland, New York, bought most of the Glennmore real estate on December 24, 1957. On July 5, 1958, he auctioned off the property in forty-nine very small parcels. According to George Rote, who purchased the boathouse, the Big Moose Supply Company building was sold to Norma A. Zinsmeyer for about $4500.

Walter and Alta Cole were the next owners of the Big Moose Supply Company building, buying in December 1961. They also owned the area behind the previous location of the old hotel, next to where the tennis courts, woodhouse, and waitress quarters had been. The Coles ran the Supply Company building as a restaurant and bar, assuming the name Glenmore Bar and Grill. The big plate-glass windows facing the lake, which were once part of Mr. Forkey's office, became perhaps the most scenic backbar in the Adirondack Park. The Coles served meals and rented out the bedrooms on the upper floors.

Alta had a small grocery store in the wing beyond the store's coolers. In 1966, Walter and Alta sold the hotel business to Donald E. Cole (no relation) from Baldwinsville. Shortly thereafter, Donald and Libby Morgan owned the hotel briefly, before Carlton G. and Marilyn Muller acquired it in 1970.

Carl and Marilyn set out to create a successful business, catering not only to summer customers but also to a new winter clientele, snowmobilers. They had three sons, Steve, Carlton, and Robert, all of whom grew up helping out in the hotel. Carl and Marilyn ran the business for nineteen years; at this point they decided to go south and sold the Glenmore to Ray Orsanti in 1989, opting to hold the mortgage. Carl died in Florida in September 1996.

Ray Orsanti was doing well in the business until, tragically, he was killed in a snowmobile accident on the Stillwater Road in 1996. Ownership of the Glenmore reverted to Marilyn Muller as the mortgage-holder. Her son Robert and his wife, Becky, have operated it since 1998.

The original Hotel Glennmore property consisted of lots 366–75. (See index: Hotel Glennmore.) However, by the time of the auction in 1958, the Glennmore Corporation had already sold lots 366–69. Hence the property that Vosburgh auctioned was lot 370 to a part of lot 375. The Town of Webb tax office renumbered the new parcels that are south of the Martin Road, 1–44. Lot numbers 1, 2, 3, and 4 coincide with Webb numbers 366, 367, 368, and 369, which have been described above. The next lot in the Glenmore subdivision, then, follows.

5. Hinman Cottage. Ian and Mary Ann Orvis Lucas. Kensington, Conn. Mary Ann is related to LaVerne Orvis, the lawyer who represented the Kellogg sisters during the financial difficulties of the Hotel Glennmore Corporation. He was given Hinman Cottage as compensation for his efforts. It remains in the possession of his family today.

6. Davis Cottage. Ralph and Donna Schmidt. Ancram, N.Y. The cottage was named after a Davis family who came yearly to the hotel during the 1930s. It was sold to Joe and Judy Smith at the auction. They broke up the lot by dividing off two pieces on the Martin Road at the back of the lot. The lakefront portion was sold to Peter Kelly and Jim Heitz. Later it was sold to the Schmidts.

7. Green Cottage. Al and Joan Serway. They purchased the cottage in 1987 from Joe and Sally Metzger, who had acquired it before the auction.

8. The White Cottage lot. William and Carolyn "Chi-Chi" Seamans. Big Moose Lake, N.Y. White Cottage was destroyed in the fire that consumed the hotel in 1950. In 1957, before the auction, Gilbert and Jean Stedman had built a small camp on the premises. Upon Gilbert's death in 1963, the property was sold to John and Alice Larson, who added a garage and an upper bedroom. In 1973 ownership passed to Dana and Shirley Poyer, who sold it to the Seamans in 1978. The Seamans have added a second story to the camp, which they have named "Bald Billy's Spot."

10. Dorothy O'Brien Rote and Lou. These two lots encompass the land upon which stood the original Hotel Glennmore. It was acquired by a Mr. Brownell, who constructed some small camps that he later resold. These properties are now held by Dorothy O'Brien Rote.

The Boathouse. George Rote. The father of Dorothy O'Brien Rote, with a partner, bought the boathouse at the Glennmore public landing at auction. They converted the former second-floor dance hall into two apartments.

Rote bought out his partner in 1972 and later sold to Robert Orsanti. The building is now owned by Marilyn Muller. Until some time after World War II, the dock was considered a public facility.

12–13. Glenmore Bar and Grill. (See index: Big Moose Supply Company.)

14–17. William and Anne Hameline. Clinton, N.Y. Children: Thomas, Joseph, John, and Robert. Grandchildren: seven. The Hameline family has been associated with Big Moose Lake since the early 1920s. Bill's great-uncle Fred was the Hameline who, with Pete Samson, owned lot 376 in 1921.(See index: Summit Club.) In 1955, Bill and Anne bought the Bell Cottage, one of the hotel cottages south of the Glennmore Road. In 1963, to protect their original purchase, they acquired the Fitzgerald Cottage, another of the Glennmore cottages. In 1981, when Helene Fidell, the owner of the third cottage, Walker Cottage, wished to sell, the Hamelines bought it. With the purchase of lot 17, along the other side of the service road that runs behind their camps, the Hameline family compound was protected.

With the exception of lots 12, 13, and 17, lots 1–16 all have lake frontage. Lots 18–41 are on one side or the other of the Glennmore Road.

18. Sar-a-len. Chris and Mary Guenther. Sodus, N.Y. The camp was built in 1959 and remodeled in 1989. It was originally named A Place in the Sun.

19. Joyce McQuillen. Vero Beach, Fla.

20. Peter Nichols. Canastota, N.Y.

21. Spruce Lodge. Paul and Deborah Rose. Ilion, N.Y. This was an early Glennmore camp, once owned by Henry and Mary Callahan, later by Willard and Jean McAllister, and then by Steve Muller before the Roses bought it.

22–23. David Rice. Syracuse, N.Y.

24. James Sweet. This is a year-round residence on the south side of the Big Moose Road, next to the West Pond trail head where the Big Moose Lake school once stood.

25–26. Irene Miller. LeRoy, N.Y.

27–28. **John and Mary Bell and John Mills.**

29. **Wayne and Tammy Norris.** Hopewell, N.J.

30. **Charles and Marion Woodward.** Frankfort, N.Y.

31. **Edward Hiscox.**

32. **Paul and Lynn Weckesser.** McGrath, Alaska. This is the old Transportation House, which the Big Moose Transportation Company constructed for its employees. (See index: Big Moose Transportation Company.)

33. **John and Mary King.**

34–35. **Gregory and Cynthia Johnston.** Greg is currently president of the Glenmore Property Owners Association. The camp was built in the 1960s on the site of the Hotel Glennmore garages, from which came the lumber.

36. **David Rockafellow.** The camp was built on the site of the Hotel Glennmore stables.

37. **Ron and Barbara Bickham.** Owego, N.Y.

38. **Henry La Fountain.**

39. **Dr. James Casper.** Utica, N.Y.

40. **Walter and Barbara Cole.**

41. **Louis and Siri Pardi.** Schenectady, N.Y.

Owners of the four camps located on the former site of the Hotel Glennmore baseball diamond, on the hill facing the entrance to the Glennmore Road, are (from left to right facing the hill) **Jim and Roseann Heitz, Jeff and Vicki Ossont, Susan Barduhn, and Andrew Scarafile.**

Lot owners along the north side of Martin Road (lots 58–43) from west to east are **Constance Moran, Sue and Martin Coughlin, William Hameline, Jr., Walter Ifflander, Alex and Lydia Maltzan, James Harder, Philip Card, Dorothy Lividas, and Greg and Patricia Mohr.** The Coughlins are currently building a home on their property, and Marty is the chef at Big Moose Station restaurant.

The Webb Covenant

THIS CONVEYANCE is made upon the following express terms and conditions, viz: That the party of the second part, his heirs, successors or assigns shall not start or permit to be started any forest fires upon the above described premises or any part thereof or upon said T.S. 8 John Brown's Tract or adjoining lands that the lands and premises above conveyed shall be used solely for permanent forestry, hotel, camp or cottage purposes and shall not be used for commercial, agriculture or manufacturing purposes; that all trails and ways of communication across and over the said lot and premises above conveyed shall forever remain free and open to the People of the State of New York. And in case said party of the second part shall start or permit to be started any forest fires upon the premises above described or upon any part thereof, or upon any part of said T.S. 8 or if said land above conveyed is not used for permanent forestry, hotel, camp or cottage purposes as aforesaid, or is used for commercial, agriculture or manufacturing purposes, or if trails and means of communication across or over said lands above conveyed are not forever open and free to the People of State of N.Y. so far as the acts of the party of the second part, his heirs or assigns are concerned, then and in either of the said events hereby created shall cease and be absolutely null and void and the party of the second part, his heirs, successor or assigns shall from thence forth be divested of all title to said premises and the party of the first part, its successors or assigns shall have the right to enter upon said premises and take possession thereof, and the said premises shall in that event belong to and be the property of the party of the first part, its successors or assigns, the same as if these presents had not been executed.

[The document goes on to describe a contract be-

tween William S. Webb and a John A. Dix, which has since expired. The document continues.] Also excepting and reserving to the party of the first part, its servants, agents, contractors, successors or assigns the right to float logs, timber and pulp wood down and through said lake and past said premises above described, the same as if this deed had not been made and executed, together with the rights to the party of the first part, its successors and assigns, to dam up the waters of said lake wherever desirable for the purpose of driving logs either above or below said lands, such damming, however, not to exceed the height of the natural highwater mark, doing no unnecessary damage. The parties hereto for themselves, their heirs successors and assigns mutually covenant and agree as follows: First, the parties of the second part covenant and agree to and with the party of the first part that the lands herein conveyed shall not be used or sold by the party of the second part, his successors or assigns for commercial, agriculture or manufacturing purposes but shall be used and sold exclusively for permanent forestry, hotel, camp or cottage purposes. It is understood that this covenant runs with the land and binds the land whether owned by the party of the second part or his heirs, successors or assigns. The party of the second part also covenants and agrees for himself, his heirs, successors or assigns to and with the party of the first part, its successors and assigns that all trails and ways of communication of every kind or nature either by land or by water across or over the land above described and conveyed shall forever remain open and free for the People of the State of New York so far as the acts of the party of the second part, his heirs, successors and assigns are concerned. It is understood and agreed that this covenant runs with the land and binds the

268

land whether owned by the party of the second part, his heirs, successors, and assigns owning land on the said Big Moose Lake shall have the right and privilege of using in a reasonable manner for domestic purposes the surplus water from any spring or stream upon the premises above conveyed. Such right however to be subordinate to the use thereof by the party of the second part and in the use thereof not to interfere with the reasonable use thereof by the party of the second part, his heirs, successors and assigns, the using of such water is not to be deemed a breach of the covenant of warranty hereinafter contained. Nothing herein contained shall be construed against the floating of timber down the said lakes and the inlets and outlets thereof by the party of the first part, its successors and assigns. Second: And the said Ne-ha-sa-ne Park Ass'n. covenants and agrees that the premises, thus conveyed in the quiet and peaceful possession of the party of the second part, his heirs, successors and assigns, it will forever warrant and defend against any persons whomsoever lawfully claiming the same or part thereof, except as to all mines, fossils and mineral rights are not owned by the party of the first part as to which this covenant of warrant shall not apply and excepting also all trails and highways and the use thereof by the public as to which the covenant of warranty shall not apply and excepting also the lumbering and timber rights of Lemon Thomson, John A. Dix and Edward Thomson Jr. under the contract of warranty shall not apply; and excepting also the reserved right of floating logs, timber and pulp wood and the right of erecting and maintaining dams as aforesaid as to which this covenant of warranty does not apply.

Big Moose Lake and the Adirondack Park Agency

THE ADIRONDACK PARK AGENCY (APA) was established in 1971 to respond to increasing land-usage threats to the integrity of the Park. It was charged with designing a master plan for the preservation of the Adirondacks that would include recommendations to prevent overdevelopment on both private and state-owned lands. The objective was to preserve the quality of the lakes, waterways, mountains, and forests, because at the time there were few zoning restrictions within the Park that governed the size of developments, waterfront setbacks, septic systems, and a host of other considerations that could affect the Adirondacks.

The recommendations were adopted in 1973 and have been amended several times since, most recently in 2001. These recommendations constitute the most stringent conditions of any zoning system anywhere in the world. Implementation has not been without controversy. Although vigorously supported by preservationist groups, the recommendations are just as vehemently opposed by many Park residents and organizations.

The entire Adirondack Park lands, both state and private, are divided into categories based on various characteristics and manner of use at the time. Each area has distinct regulations that must be followed. One category is the Wilderness Area; this designation applies only to state-owned land that is without improvement or permanent human habitation—land that is almost primeval in character. Such areas are protected and managed to enhance their wild state; anything motorized is banned. Big Moose Lake is fortunate that it is nearly surrounded by what is called the Pigeon Lake Wilderness Area. This area contains more than 50,000 acres of land, sixty-four bodies of water, and elevations varying from 1,680 feet to 2,900 feet (West Mountain). It has five lean-tos, 41.7 miles of foot trails, and many fine brook trout ponds and streams. The terrain is mainly low, rolling hills with a near-mature forest of mixed softwoods and hardwoods, along with some dense stands of balsam. Some of the interior forests have never been lumbered, and the virgin white pines are noteworthy.

Other categories include the Primitive Area, Canoe Area, Wild Forest, Intensive Use Area, and Historic Area. Primitive Areas are lands that are essentially wilderness but that contain structures or improvements that do not conform to the designation of Wilderness Area. Such areas will become Wilderness Areas when the nonconforming elements are eliminated. Canoe Areas have watercourses or bodies of water that allow canoe travel in a wilderness setting. Wild Forests are less fragile ecologically than Wilderness Areas; the Fulton Chain and the Moose River Plains are Wild Forests. Intensive Use Areas are managed to allow the public opportunities for intensive forms of outdoor recreation. Many have campgrounds. Historic Areas, such as the Crown Point Military Site and Great Camp Santanoni, are state-owned sites significant to the history of the region, state, or nation. Rivers are classified as Wild, Scenic, or Recreational, depending upon their degree of development and accessibility. In the Big Moose region, all three branches of the Moose River are considered Scenic; the region also includes the Independence, Indian, Marion, Raquette, Red, and Rock Rivers and West Canada Creek.

The APA has classified privately held lands according to the intensity of use. Each classification has specific conditions of use. Those that affect Big Moose Lake are:

- Moderate Intensity Use—All of West Bay.

- Low Intensity Use—South Bay, Crag Point, and Higby Bay to the southeast shoreline lots extending to and including Big Chief Pond.

- Rural Use—All lands abutting North Bay and the two peninsulas at the east end of the lake between the Inlet and East Bay.

- Natural Resource Area—Lands in East Bay east of lots abutting Big Chief Pond.

Most camp owners at Big Moose have not been much involved with the APA because their camps were built before 1974, and any nonconforming uses have been "grandfathered." A few residents have tangled with the rules and experienced inconsistent interpretation of regulations.

Barbara McMartin's recent book, *Perspectives on the Adirondacks: A Thirty-Year Struggle by People Protecting Their Treasure*,[1] describes the conflicts among the various local organizations and state agencies that strive to balance environmental preservation and economic interests. In particular, her last chapter, "Final Thoughts," synthesizes the difficulties, raises questions, and suggests methods for resolving questions of development now and in the future.

Notes

The *S* designation refers to notes found in the sidebars.

1 *The Intractable Wilderness*

1. William R. Marleau, *Big Moose Station* (Van Nuys, Calif.: Marleau Family Press, 1986), 42; Henry A. Harter, *Fairy Tale Railroad* (Utica, N.Y.: North Country Books, 1979), 50.

2. "History and Heritage," *Adirondack Express,* 22 Apr. 2003: 22; story confirmed by Ceil Buckley, granddaughter of Seth Rozon.

3. Alfred J. Donaldson, *A History of the Adirondacks,* (Port Washington, N.Y.: Ira J. Freedman, 1921), 21.

4. Jerold Pepper, "When Men and Mountains Meet: Mapping the Adirondacks" (unpublished lecture presented at the Adirondack Museum, Blue Mountain Lake, N.Y., 16 Aug. 1999), 5.

5. The 1906 annual report of the New York State Forest, Fish, and Game Commission estimated that there were at least one million beaver in northern New York when the white man came to America.

6. Joseph F. Grady, *The Story of a Wilderness: The Fulton Chain and Big Moose Region* (Old Forge, N.Y.: North Country Books, 1933), 13.

7. E. P. Wallace, *Descriptive Guide to the Adirondacks* (Syracuse, N.Y.: W. Gill, [1872] 1876), 20.

8. Edith Pilcher, *The Constables: First Family of the Adirondacks* (Utica, N.Y.: North Country Books, 1992).

9. Marleau, *Big Moose Station,* 7.

10. Grady, *Story of a Wilderness,* 129.

11. William H. H. Murray, *Adventures in the Wilderness or Camp-Life in the Adirondacks* (Boston: Fields, Osgood, and Co., 1869; reprint, Blue Mountain Lake, N.Y.: Adirondack Museum/Syracuse Univ. Press, 1970).

12. Philip G. Terrie, professor of English and American Studies at Bowling Green State University, who summers at Long Lake, has written two books on the social and cultural history of the Adirondacks: *Forever Wild* (1994) and *Contested Terrain* (1997), both published by Syracuse University Press.

13. Verplanck Colvin, *Topographical Survey of the Adirondack Region, Third to Seventh Report* (Albany, N.Y.: n.p., 1879), 141.

14. Wallace, *Guide to the Adirondacks,* 20.

15. Ibid., 73.

16. Herkimer County Court House, Herkimer, N.Y., *Book of Deeds,* vol. 98, 567.

17. Ibid. (newspaper clipping attached to the page).

18. Craig Gilborn, *Durant: The Fortunes and Woodland Camps of a Family in the Adirondacks* (Sylvan Beach, N.Y.: North Country Books, 1981).

19. Barbara McMartin, *The Great Forest of the Adirondacks* (Utica, N.Y.: North Country Books, 1994).

20. Emma J. Dart Lesure, "Tales of an Innkeeper's Daughter," 1977, (unpublished family memoir, copies deposited with Town of Webb Historical Association, Old Forge, N.Y., and with Adirondack Museum, Blue Mountain Lake, N.Y.), 11.

21. James Harland Higby (great-grandson of James Henry Higby), unpublished family genealogy, 1996.

22. Roy C. Higby, *A Man from the Past* (Big Moose, N.Y.: Big Moose Press, 1974), 17.

23. Committee for the 1992 Adirondack Park Centennial, *100-year Adirondack Park Roots* (Schenectady, N.Y.: n.p., 1992), 12, incorrectly states that it was James Higby's father who fought in the Civil War.

24. Higby, *Man from the Past,* 17.

25. Grady, *Story of a Wilderness,* 182–83.

26. Ibid., 183.

27. Ibid.

28. Ibid, 183–84. Frances Lepper once told Wanda Martin that she had always thought that "Billy's Bald Spot" was named after her grandfather, William Stevens, a very early resident of the lake.

29. Frances Alden Covey, *The Earl Covey Story* (New York: Exposition Press, 1964).

30. Lesure, "Tales of an Innkeeper's Daughter," 1.

31. Ibid., 1.

32. Ibid., 12.

33. Charles Brumley, *Guides of the Adirondacks: A History* (Utica, N.Y.: North Country Books, 1994), 158.

34. *Adirondack News,* 18 July 1900; files of Town of Webb Historical Association, Old Forge, N.Y.

35. Kenneth Sprague, "History and Heritage," *Adirondack Express,* 4 Apr. 2000: 17.

36. Brumley, *Guides of the Adirondacks,* 30–31.

37. Note given by William Judson (Roy Higby's son-in-law) to

Richard Widdicombe titled "1907. The Brown's Tract Guides' Association." The single sheet lists the game laws, members, and officers of the association. Higby family papers in possession of Sarah Judson Dew, Oneida, N.Y.

38. Roy C. Higby, typescript, "Big Moose Guides, 1870–1910," n.d., Higby family papers in possession of Sarah Judson Dew, Oneida, N.Y.

39. Brumley, *Guides of the Adirondacks,* 310–63.

40. Ibid., 45–46.

41. Ibid., 45.

42. Ibid.

43. Susan J. Smith, "An Old Guide's Campfire Tales." *Rochester Times-Union,* 1 July 1988.

44. Katherine Whited, *An Historical Sketch of Big Moose Lake* (Big Moose, N.Y.: Big Moose Property Owners Association, 1927).

45. Grady, *Story of a Wilderness,* 199.

46. Marleau, *Big Moose Station,* 267.

47. "An Interesting Camp," *Adirondack News,* 18 July 1900; article about Club Camp, which mentions Hamlyn's camp; files of Town of Webb Historical Association, Old Forge, N.Y.

48. John J. Walsh, "Locomotive Headlights," *Vignettes of Old Utica* (Utica, N.Y.: Dodge Graphic Press, 1982), 124.

49. Paul C. Willard, *Utica Daily Press,* 30 Mar. 1962; quoted in Walsh, "Locomotive Headlights," 124–25.

50. Walsh, "Locomotive Headlights," 125.

51. Charles H. Burnett, *Conquering the Wilderness* (privately printed, 1932), 8.

52. Ibid., 8.

53. Lesure, "Tales of an Innkeeper's Daughter," 1.

54. Information on the Peg-Leg Railroad from Peg Masters, Town of Webb Historian, Old Forge, N.Y., 31 Mar. 2003.

55. *New York Times,* 27 May 1891: 5.

56. Ibid.

57. Ibid.

58. Martin Burke, Letter to the editor, *New York Times,* 28 May 1891: 4.

59. *New York Times,* 28 May 1891: 5.

60. Burnett, *Conquering the Wilderness,* 50.

61. Harold K. Hochschild, *Adirondack Railroads, Real and Phantom* (Blue Mountain, N.Y.: Adirondack Museum, 1962), 13.

62. The Webb Covenant is reproduced in Appendix B.

JIM HIGBY'S FIRST FAMILY

S1. Higby, *Man from the Past.*

S2. Clinton David Higby, *Edward Higby and his Descendants* (Boston, Mass.: Privately printed by P. R. Marvin and Son, 1927), 344–55.

S3. James H. Higby, 1996, "Higby Family: From James Henry to Anne Hamilton," family memoir, Wilton, Conn., 3.

S4. Higby, "Higby Family," 3.

2 Hotels and the Birth of a Resort Community

1. William L. Scheffler and Frank Carey, *Big Moose Lake New York in Vintage Postcards* (Charleston, S.C.: Arcadia Publishing, 2000).

2. Higby, *Man from the Past,* 38.

3. Karen J. Taussig-Lux, 1995, "Diamonds in the Rough," *Adirondack Life* 26, no. 6: 31–37; an excellent description of the entire palisade style of architecture.

4. Covey, *Earl Covey Story,* 64.

5. George H. Longstaff, *From Heyday to Mayday* (St. Petersburg, Fla.: Valkyrie Press, 1983), 171.

6. *Utica Sunday Tribune,* 14 Aug. 1910; article in Camp Crag scrapbook in possession of Robert Smith, Crag Point and Newtonville, Mass.

7. The Camp Crag registers for 1907–13 are in the Adirondack Museum archives at Blue Mountain, N.Y. The last such record book, for April 1922 to May 1923, is in the possession of C. V. Bowes at Covewood Lodge, Big Moose, N.Y.

8. Newspaper clipping from Camp Crag register for 1922–23. No source given.

9. William S. Dunn, letter to Mark Barlow and Jane Barlow, 4 Nov. 2000.

10. F. A. Higby, "Life of F A H," n.d. [ca. 1938], handwritten document, family papers of Phyllis Strack Dietze, Niskayuna, N.Y.

11. Ibid., 1–2.

12. Ibid., 2.

13. Ibid., 2.

14. Ibid., 3.

15. Ibid., 3.

16. "Mrs. F. A. Higby, Central Adirondack Pioneer," *Adirondack Arrow,* 8 Aug. 1937; courtesy of Town of Webb Historical Association, Old Forge, N.Y.

17. Quoted in "Mrs. F. A. Higby, Central Adirondack Pioneer."

18. Higby, "Life of F A H," 3.

19. Higby, *Man from the Past,* 19.

20. Ibid., 31.

21. Higby, "Life of F A H," 4.

22. Personal communication from Sarah Judson to Jane Barlow, July 7, 1997.

23. Herkimer County Courthouse, Herkimer, N.Y., *Deed Book 202,* 259. I am grateful to Kathleen Decker of the staff of the Herkimer County Clerk's Office for help in locating this obscure information.

24. Phyllis Strack Dietze, letter to Jane Barlow, 10 Feb. 2002.

25. "Higby Club, Big Moose, N.Y.; F. A. Higby and Roy C. Higby, managing owners" (brochure), 1.

26. Phyllis S. Dietze, telephone interview with Jane Barlow, 12 Feb. 2002.

27. William S. Dunn, letter to Mark Barlow, 5 Sept. 2000.

28. *Adirondack Arrow,* 22 Aug. 1939; courtesy of Town of Webb Historical Association, Old Forge, N.Y.

29. Donald Mawhinney, personal communication to Jane Barlow, 7 Sept. 1998.

30. Gordon Kellogg, letter to Barbara Kinne Wheeler, 26 Aug. 2000.

31. Jean Seavey Humphrey, n.d., "1930–1940, The Way it Was," unpublished family paper.

32. Kellogg to Wheeler, 26 Aug. 2000, 2.

33. William S. Dunn, letter to Mark Barlow and Jane Barlow, 2 Nov. 1998, 4.

34. Kellogg to Wheeler, 26 Aug. 2000, 2.

35. Many of the stories about George Burdick are contained in let-

ters to the Big Moose Lake History Project Committee from William S. Dunn dated 6 Sept. 1998, 13 Oct. 1998, and 2 Feb. 1999.

36. William S. Dunn, letter to Mark Barlow, 13 Nov. 1998.

37. R. W. Wallace, 9 Apr. 1896 (letter of recommendation from Albany Business College), Martin family papers, Big Moose, N.Y.

38. Arwed Retter, letter to E. J. Martin, 17 Dec. 1904, Martin family papers, Big Moose, N.Y.

39. Muriel Groves, *Reminiscences of West Bay on Big Moose Lake in the Adirondack Mountains* (privately published, 1964), 18.

40. L. W. Brown, letter to Martin brothers, 31 May 1904, Martin family papers, Big Moose, N.Y.

41. Harriet Martin, letter to Everett Martin, 11 Apr. 1945, Martin family papers, Big Moose, N.Y.

42. Harriet Martin, letter to Everett Martin, 14 May 1945, Martin family papers, Big Moose, N.Y.

43. In 1996 the Waldheim received the Adirondack Architectural Heritage Award for a business, "In recognition of the remarkable way that four generations have lovingly cared for the Waldheim by preserving its wonderful structures, setting and ambience."

44. Wanda K. Martin, personal communication to Jane Barlow, Feb. 1999.

45. William S. Dunn, personal communication to Mark and Jane Barlow, 6 July 1999.

46. Copy of chattel mortgage filed at Herkimer County Courthouse, Herkimer, N.Y., 17 Oct. 1922, Martin family papers, Big Moose, N.Y.

47. Martin family papers, Big Moose, N.Y.

48. Harriet Martin, letter to Everett Martin, 7 Apr. 1929, Martin family papers, Big Moose, N.Y.

49. Information from Wanda Kinne Martin.

50. Reported in the annual spring letter of the Big Moose Property Owners Association, 1935.

51. Covey, *Earl Covey Story.*

52. Ibid., 87.

53. Ibid., 56.

54. From the brochure of Covewood Lodge on Big Moose Lake, 2000.

55. Katherine Wightman Hadden, interview by Karen Taussig-Lux, 7 Aug. 1984, Archives of Adirondack Museum, Blue Mountain Lake, N.Y.

56. Ellie Reed Koppe, *The Big Moose Community Chapel: The First Fifty Years* (Big Moose, N.Y.: Trustees of the Big Moose Community Chapel, 1981).

57. Mary Alden Covey Williams, letter to Mark Barlow, 17 Feb. 2002.

58. The nickname "Major" was given to Bowes while he was in college. A popular radio show at the time was "Major Bowes's Amateur Hour."

PATRICK CROWLEY

S1. Information about the wye from Jon Martin, Big Moose, N.Y., personal communication to Jane Barlow, 31 May 2000.

3 Making a Living at Big Moose Lake

1. Higby, *Man from the Past,* 19.

2. Ibid.

3. Bill of Sale. 3 Jan. 1916. D. B. Sperry to Hotel Glennmore Corporation. Harry Kellogg family papers, Old Forge, N.Y.

4. Article of Agreement. 12 Oct. 1916. Hotel Glennmore Corporation and Dana Bissell, et al. Harry Kellogg family papers, Old Forge, N.Y.

5. E. J. Martin, 23 Nov. 1929. Canceled check written to Big Moose Transportation Company. Martin family papers, Big Moose, N.Y.

6. *Adirondack Arrow,* 9 Jul. 1936.

7. Joyce Potter Hall, letter to Wanda Kinne Martin, 27 Aug. 2001. Martin family papers, Big Moose, N.Y.

8. Vera Bleckwell, letter to Everett Martin, 6 Aug. 1943. Martin family papers, Big Moose, N.Y.

9. Marleau, *Big Moose Station,* 156–57.

10. John Judson, letter to Jane Barlow, 11 Apr. 2000.

11. Henry B. Bruyn, "Big Moose Memories and the Beginnings of the Bruyn Family Presence," Bruyn family papers, Wakefield, Mass., 38.

12. Philip Martin, interview with Jane Barlow, 19 Aug. 1999.

13. Charles Adams, letter to Jane Barlow, 29 Nov. 2000.

GROWING UP AT BIG MOOSE LAKE

S1. Higby, "Higby Family," 19.

4 Ventures from Outside the Lake

1. James N. Vander Veer, M.D., letter to Nelson Dunn, 8 June 1930. Family files of William S. Dunn, Southport, N.C.

2. The Vander Veers were to continue their support of the Scouts. Edgar A. Vander Veer, James's brother, was elected president of the Fort Orange Council in 1940.

3. Eleanor Brown, *The Forest Preserve of New York State* (Glens Falls, N.Y.: The Adirondack Mountain Club, 1985), 22.

4. McMartin, *Great Forest,* 118–22.

5. Originally Article VII, Section 7, of the state constitution.

6. McMartin, *Great Forest,* 192–220.

7. Ibid., 38.

8. State of New York, *Sixth Annual Report of the Forest Fish and Game Commission* (Albany, N.Y.: J. B. Lyon, 1901), 15.

9. Ralph W. Hosmer and Eugene S. Bruce, Bureau of Foresters, U.S. Department of Agriculture, "Forest Working Plan for Townships 5, 6 and 41, Totten and Crossfield Purchase, Hamilton County. NYS Forest Preserve," in New York State Forest, Fish and Game Commission, *Eighth and Ninth Reports for 1902 and 1903* (Albany, N.Y.: J. B. Lyon, 1903, 1904), 436.

10. Hosmer and Bruce, "Forest Working Plan for Townships 5, 6, and 41," 437.

11. McMartin, *Great Forest,* 41.

12. Ibid., 86; note photograph of Koetteritz, 87.

13. John B. Koetteritz, letter to Hon. Thomas E. Benedict, deputy-comptroller, 31 Jan. 1886. Quoted in McMartin, *Great Forest,* 90.

14. McMartin, *Great Forest,* 90.

15. Norman J. VanValkenburgh, *The Adirondack Forest Preserve* (Blue Mountain Lake: The Adirondack Museum, 1979) 64–66.

16. Condensed from: Supreme Court of the State of New York, Appellate Division—Third Department, *The People of the State of New York against Herkimer Lumber Company, Plaintiff-Appellant, against The Herkimer Lumber Company, Theodore A. Page, George Harvey, Solomon Carnahan and George Raymond, Defendants-Respondents* (Albany, N.Y.: J. B. Lyon, 1909), 14–19. (Hereafter referred to as Supreme Court Case, 1909.)

17. *1896 New York State Fisheries, Game and Forest Commission Report*, 460.

18. William Marleau, personal communication to Ennis Pilcher and Edith Pilcher, ca. 1980.

19. See Irvin A. Williams (index) for details.

20. Marleau, map, *Big Moose Station*, 313.

21. Edward A. Bond, "Boundary Line Between the Counties of Herkimer and Hamilton," *Laws of the State of New York: Passed at the 123rd Session of the Legislature (1900)* (Albany, N.Y.: J. B. Lyon, 1900), vol. II, 280–308.

22. Supreme Court Case, 1909.

23. Herkimer County Court House, Herkimer, N.Y., records, vol. 214, p. 20; vol. 219, p. 493, respectively.

24. Herkimer County Court House records, vol. 230, p. 337.

25. Theodore L. Cross, letter to New York Conservation Committee, 17 Feb. 1913.

26. George Burdick, letter to Arwed Retter, 19 Feb. 1913.

27. Ibid.

28. Marleau, *Big Moose Station*, 293.

29. Arwed Retter, ca. 20 Feb. 1913. Copy of handwritten note attached to letter from Theodore L. Cross to Conservation Commission, State of New York, Albany, N.Y., 17 Feb. 1913. Family papers of E. S. Woodbury transmitted through descendants Olive Wertz and Faith Wertz. Eastwood, Lexington, Ky.

30. Edward H. Hall, "Report of the Secretary on Visit to Albany, February 25, 1913," *Archives of the Association for the Protection of the Adirondacks* (Adirondack Research Library, Schenectady, N.Y.), vol. 1913, 55–56.

31. Theodore L. Cross, letters to Dana Bissell, 27 Feb. and 3 Mar. 1913.

32. Theodore L. Cross, letter to Arwed Retter, 14 Mar. 1913.

33. Theodore L. Cross, letter to Arwed Retter describing Cross's visit to Big Moose Lake and his meeting with H. H. Covey, 23 Apr. 1913.

34. Dana Bissell and P. Yousey (transmitted by Frederick M. Boyeratty), 8 Apr. 1913, proposal to Hon. George E. Van Kennan, chairman, Conservation Commission of New York State. Copy in Adirondack Research Library, Schenectady, N.Y.

35. Theodore L. Cross, letter to Arwed Retter including copy of letter from John W. Norton, deputy attorney general of New York State, reporting that on 26 June 1913 the Conservation Commission had empowered the attorney general to commence and prosecute an action against Bissell and Yousey, 17 July 1913.

36. Theodore L. Cross, letter to Arwed Retter, 17 July 1913.

37. Thomas Hartz, "Adirondack Cabin." Unpublished paper, 2001. Wyomissing, Pa.

38. Hartz, "Adirondack Cabin," 1.

39. Karen Lux, transcript of conversation with Grace Vander Veer McDonough, 26 July 1984, McDonough transcript, tape 1, pp. 93–116, 99. Courtesy of Adirondack Museum, Blue Mountain Lake, N.Y.

40. Higby, *Man from the Past*, 52.

41. Marleau, *Big Moose Station*, 295.

42. Ibid., 339–43, passim.

43. McMartin, *Great Forest*, 144.

44. Ibid., 159.

45. Roy C. Higby, *Man from the Past*, 49–53.

46. Marleau, *Big Moose Station*, 293.

47. Peter Bruyn, e-mail correspondence with Jane Barlow, 15 Jan. 2001.

48. Marleau, *Big Moose Station*, 290.

49. Charles Adams, letter to Jane Barlow, 8 Dec. 2000.

50. John M. Judson, notes to Jane Barlow, Aug. 1999.

51. Higby, *Man from the Past*, 53–54.

5 *Private Homes and Camps Before World War II*

1. Frank Hameline was the grandfather of William Hameline, who today owns the parcels created in the 1958 auction south of the hotel.

2. For much of the following information, I am indebted to G. Clinton Getty, son-in-law of Dr. Charles Walker, to Andrew Getty, his grandson, and to Barbara Getty, Andrew's wife.

3. Paul Dodington et al., *The Greatest Little Motor Boat Afloat: The Legendary Disappearing Propeller Boat* (Ontario: The Boston Mills Press, 1983), 164.

4. Ibid., 149.

5. Ibid., 154.

6. Patsy Milne, ca. 1958, Unpublished Memoir in National Archives of Canada, Ottawa, p. 30. Quoted in David P. Silcox, *Painting Place: The Life and Work of David B. Milne* (Toronto: Univ. of Toronto Press, 1996), 175.

7. Silcox, *Painting Place*, 393, n. 24.

8. Charles Adams, note to Barbara Wheeler, 6 Aug. 2001.

9. Groves, *Reminiscences of West Bay*.

10. *Adirondack Arrow*, 22 June 1939, Annual Resort Edition; courtesy of Town of Webb Historical Association, Old Forge, N.Y.

11. Ibid.

12. Groves, *Reminiscences of West Bay*, 23.

13. This and the following information on sales comes from the property abstract of Paul Littman, Rexford, N.Y.

14. Ibid.

15. Ibid.

16. Ibid.

17. *An Electrifying Message Announcing Electri-Craft, the Modern Boat* (advertising brochure) [n.d.], Finch family papers, Goldsboro, N.C.

18. "Top 10 Costly Homes in Herkimer County," *Utica Observer-Dispatch*, 4 Oct. 1998.

19. Obituary for T. P. Kingsford, *Oswego Palladium-Times*, 6 Jan. 1932; Kingsford family papers, Sodus, N.Y.

20. Katherine S. Kingsford, telephone conversation with Jane Barlow, 21 Feb. 1999.

21. Herkimer County Court House, Herkimer, N.Y., *Deed Book*, vol. 180, p. 335 (lakefront lots 34–58).

22. Katherine S. Kingsford, telephone conversation with Jane Barlow, 26 Mar. 2001.

23. William S. Dunn, letter to Mark Barlow, 12 Feb. 1999.

24. Ibid.

25. Ibid.

26. Bonnie Hubbell, note to Jane Barlow, 20 Aug. 2001.

27. Ibid.

28. Obituary for Frederick Brack, *Adirondack Echo*, 25 Sept. 1981.

29. Marleau, *Big Moose Station*, 165.

30. Francis E. Carey, Sr., 1996. "Big Moose Anecdotes" (as told to Francis E. Carey, Jr.), Carey family papers, West Melbourne, Fla.

31. Waldheim ledger entries, E. O. Stanley account, 1906. Martin family papers, Big Moose, N.Y.

32. Carey, Sr., "Big Moose Anecdotes," 7.

33. Elizabeth Baldwin Tomlinson Kelsey, *A Biographical Sketch of Clarence Hill Kelsey* (privately published, ca. 1931).

34. Edward Comstock, Jr., *The Adirondack League Club, 1890–1990*, ed. Mark C. Webster (Old Forge, N.Y.: Privately published, 1990), 217.

35. Billy Powell, letter to Nelson Dunn stating that Kelsey agreed to sell the motor launch, 1929. W. S. Dunn family papers, Southport, N.C.

36. Count [Richard] Coudenhove-Kalergi, *An Idea Conquers the World* (New York: Roy Publishers, n.d. [1953]), 239.

37. Bruyn, "Big Moose Memories," 29.

38. Edward Winslow Kane, 1976, "Early History of Polaris Lodge," unpublished memoir.

39. Karen Lux, transcript of interview with Lawson Rutherford, 29 July 1984, recorded for the Adirondack Museum, Blue Mountain Lake, N.Y.

40. Karen Lux and Karen Creuziger, transcript of interview with Grace Vander Veer McDonough, 26 July 1984, recorded for the Adirondack Museum, Blue Mountain Lake, N.Y.

41. Grace Vander Veer McDonough, letter to William Judson, 11 Oct. 1989, 3–4.

42. Ibid., 4–5.

43. Karen Lux and Karen Creuziger, transcript of interview with Grace Vander Veer McDonough, 26 July 1984, recorded for the Adirondack Museum, Blue Mountain Lake, N.Y.

44. Ibid.

45. *The People of New York v. Herkimer Lumber Company & Theodore Page et al.*, New York State Supreme Court, Appellate Division, 3rd Dept., 1905–08, 20.

46. The indenture is noted in records of the legal suit brought by New York State against Page and the Herkimer Lumber Company in 1905, p. 20.

47. *Oswego Daily Palladium*, 18 Jul. 1906: 4. Information courtesy of Justin White, Historian of the Town of Oswego, Oswego County Records Center, Oswego, N.Y.

48. Marleau, *Big Moose Station*, 266.

49. Ibid., 267.

50. Gwendolyn Owens, *The Watercolors of David Milne: A Survey Exhibition Organized by Gwendolyn Owens* (Herbert F. Johnson Museum of Art, Cornell University, 1984), 39. Collection of the Art Gallery of Ontario, Gift of the Douglas M. Duncan Collection, 1970.

51. Silcox, *Painting Place*, "Painting Place I," 28 Aug. 1926, p. 1, in color; also other versions on dust jacket and p. 187.

52. J. M. Gamble, letter to E. J. Martin, 7 Dec. 1931. Martin family papers, Big Moose, N.Y.

53. Grace Q. Flock, note to Barbara Kinne Wheeler, 2 Oct. 2000.

54. John E. Roosevelt, letter to E. J. Martin, 1903. Martin family papers, Big Moose, N.Y.

55. Waldheim Hotel guest register.

56. William S. Roby, letter to E. J. Martin, 18 Jul. 1918. Martin family papers, Big Moose, N.Y.

57. *Utica Observer-Dispatch*, 9 Dec. 1996. Copy in Martin family papers, Big Moose, N.Y.

58. Bruyn, "Big Moose Memories," 7.

59. Ibid., 8.

60. Henry B. Bruyn, personal communication to Jane Barlow, 4 Aug. 1999.

61. This deed, recorded in Herkimer County, and the record of the following purchases are among the Bruyn family papers in Wakefield, Massachusetts.

62. Lena Retter, 13 July 1900, diary entry. Bruyn family papers, Wakefield, Mass.

63. Bruyn, "Big Moose Memories," 2.

64. Peter Bruyn, personal communication to Jane Barlow, 26 Feb. 2000.

65. Henry B. Bruyn, "Big Moose Memories," 9.

66. Ibid.

67. Ibid., 10.

68. All of the indented material and the other recollections in this section are taken from Henry B. Bruyn, "Big Moose Memories." The authors are very grateful to him for sharing his colorful reminiscences.

69. Lot 248. On February 16, 1900, Retter sold to E. C. Hare of Utica, N.Y., who in turn sold to A. P. Coonradt of Cold Brook, N.Y., on July 8, 1901. The property then passed to Jennie E. Burnham, who sold it to Marguerite Judson.

70. E. J. Martin, ledger 1907–17. Martin family papers, Big Moose, N.Y.

71. John Judson, telephone conversation with Jane Barlow, 11 Apr. 2000. Date confirmed in letter from Lila Steele (the owner at that time) to E. J. Martin, 20 Mar. 1923. Martin family papers, Big Moose, N.Y.

72. Elizabeth Wightman Singleton, *The Wightman Family History* (privately printed, 1999). Wightman family papers, Front Royal, Va.

73. Karen Lux, transcript of conversation with Katherine Wightman Hadden, 7 Aug. 1984, tape 1, p. 19. Adirondack Museum, Blue Mountain Lake, N.Y.

74. Information from Henry B. Wightman, Jr., 29 Sept. 2000. No first name for Marleau is recorded.

75. E. J. Martin, ledger for 1907–17. Martin family papers, Big Moose, N.Y.

76. Joel T. Headley, *The Adirondack; Or, Life in the Woods* (New York: Baker and Scribner, 1849), 1.

77. P. B. Wightman, 1930, spring letter to the members of the Big Moose Property Owners Association. BMPOA files, Big Moose, N.Y.

78. Karen Lux, transcript of conversation with Henry. Wightman, Jr., 7 Jul. 1984. Adirondack Museum, Blue Mountain Lake, N.Y.

79. R. F. Shropshire, letter to E. J. Martin, 9 Jan. 1903. Martin family papers, Big Moose, N.Y.

80. Martin family papers, Big Moose, N.Y.

81. Lila Steele, letter to E. J. Martin, 11 Jan. 1928. Martin family papers, Big Moose, N.Y.

82. Henry B. Bruyn, telephone conversation with Mark Barlow, 15 Apr. 2000.

83. Lila Steele, letter to E. J. Martin, 17 Dec. 1928. Martin family papers, Big Moose, N.Y.

84. A hydrographer is an expert in the surveying, sounding, and charting of bodies of water.

85. Richard Evelyn Byrd, *Little America: Aerial Exploration in the Antarctic, the Flight to the South Pole* (New York: G. P. Putnam's Sons, 1930), 38.

86. Ibid., 416.

87. B. L. Swancott, letter to E. J. Martin, 21 Apr. 1905. Martin family papers, Big Moose, N.Y.

88. Faith Wertz Eastwood, telephone conversation with Jane Barlow, 28 Feb. 2000.

89. Marleau, *Big Moose Station,* 117.

90. E. S. Woodbury, letter to E. J. Martin, 1 Apr. 1905. Martin family papers, Big Moose, N.Y.

91. Karen Lux, transcript of conversation with Ellis Denio, 21 June 1984, p. 53. Adirondack Museum, Blue Mountain Lake, N.Y.

92. Ibid., 56.

93. Ibid., 55.

94. William S. Dunn, letter to Mark Barlow, 25 Nov. 1998.

95. Thomas Hartz, 2001. Unpublished memoir, Wyomissing, Pa., 3.

96. I am very much indebted to Tom Hartz for this information.

97. William S. Dunn, letter to Mark Barlow, 25 Nov. 1998.

98. William Lux, 2001, "Recollections and Reminiscences of Bill Lux on Big Moose Lake," unpublished family paper, Westernville, N.Y.

99. Ibid.

100. Ibid.

DAVID MILNE: CANADA'S CELEBRATED PAINTER

S1. Barbara Fear, "A Glimpse into Genius," Huronia [Canada] Sunday newspaper, 1991. Martin family papers, Big Moose, N.Y., [dated by hand].

S2. Rosemarie L. Tovell, "Responding to Nature: David Milne's Adirondack Prints," in *Adirondack Prints and Printmakers: The Call of the Wild,* ed. Caroline Mastin Welsh (Syracuse, N.Y.: The Adirondack Museum/Syracuse University Press, 1998), 161.

S3. David Milne, letter to James Clarke written from Big Moose Lake, 23 Aug. 1925. National Archives of Canada, Ottawa. Excerpt published in *David Milne,* ed. Ian M. Thom (Vancouver, B.C.: The Vancouver Art Gallery, 1991), 107.

S4. Thom, *David Milne,* 122; also reproduced in Silcox, *Painting Place,* 157.

S5. Collection of M. F. Feheley. Reproduced in *The Watercolors of David Milne: A Survey Exhibition, Organized by Gwendolyn Owens* (Ithaca, N.Y.: Herbert F. Johnson Museum of Art, Cornell Univ., 1984), 35.

S6. Collection of the Art Gallery of Ontario, Toronto. Reproduced in Silcox, *Painting Place,* 193.

S7. Collection of the National Gallery of Canada, Ottawa, in watercolor. Reproduced in Silcox, *Painting Place,* 144.

S8. Collection of the National Gallery of Canada, Ottawa. Several versions reproduced in Silcox, *Painting Place,* 187 and on the dust jacket.

S9. Silcox, *Painting Place,* 169.

S10. Rosemarie L. Tovell, *David Milne: Painting Place: Un coin pour peindre,* Masterpieces in the National Gallery of Canada, no. 8 (Ottawa: The National Gallery of Canada, 1976).

S11. Thom, *David Milne,* 18.

S12. Silcox, *Painting Place,* 215.

S13. Ibid., 301 and n. 54, mentions Florence Martin's interest in numerology.

S14. Ibid., 250.

S15. Ibid., 304.

S16. Thom, *David Milne,* 19.

S17. Ibid., 20.

MINNIE MADDERN FISKE: AMERICA'S FAVORITE ACTRESS

S1. Alexander Woolcott, *Mrs. Fiske: Her Views on Actors, Acting and the Problems of Production* (New York: The Century Co.) 1917.

S2. Archie Binns in collaboration with Olive Kooken, *Mrs. Fiske and the American Theatre* (New York: Crown Publishers, 1955).

S3. Land deed for lot 378, Echo Island, in Deed Book, Vol. 169, p. 342, Herkimer County Courthouse, Herkimer, N.Y.; land deeds for lots 351–53, mainland around Big Moose Lake, in Deed Book, Vol. 252, p. 475, Herkimer County Courthouse, Herkimer, N.Y.

S4. Binns, *Mrs. Fiske and the American Theatre,* preface, n.p.

S5. Ibid., 24.

S6. Ibid., 46.

S7. Ibid.

S8. Woolcott, *Mrs. Fiske: Her Views,* 3–40.

S9. Ibid., 113.

S10. Ted Aber and Stella King, *History of Hamilton County* (Lake Pleasant, N.Y.: Great Wilderness Books, 1965), 689.

S11. Aber and King, *Hamilton County,* 689.

S12. Henry Covey, Journal for 1907 (unpublished manuscript), Library of Adirondack Museum, Blue Mountain Lake, N.Y.

S13. Binns, *Mrs. Fiske and the American Theatre,* 326.

S14. Silcox, *Painting Place,* 175.

S15. Wanda Kinne Martin and Barbara Kinne Wheeler, conversation with Jane Barlow, July 2000.

S16. William S. Dunn, letter to Mark and Jane Barlow, 25 Nov. 1998.

S17. Muriel Groves, *Reminiscences of West Bay on Big Moose Lake in the Adirondack Mountains* (privately printed, 1964), 5.

S18. Silcox, *Painting Place,* 175.

S19. Ibid.

S20. Wanda K. Martin, conversation with Jane Barlow, February 1999.

S21. Binns, *Mrs. Fiske and the American Theatre,* 326.

S22. William S. Dunn, letter to Mark Barlow, 21 Mar. 1998.

S23. Nelson Dunn, letter to Harrison Grey Fiske, 8 Oct. 1924, Martin family papers, Big Moose, N.Y.

S24. William S. Dunn, letter to Mark and Jane Barlow, 25 Nov. 1998.

S25. Note in possession of William S. Dunn, Southport, N.C., date unknown.

S26. Binns, *Mrs. Fiske and the American Theatre*, 395.

S27. "Mrs. Fiske Dies Here as Role Awaits Her," *New York Times*, 17 Feb. 1932, 23.

S28. Binns, *Mrs. Fiske and the American Theatre*, 396.

S29. William S. Dunn, letter to Mark and Jane Barlow, 19 June 1998.

"DEERLANDS" VERSES

S1. Dunn family papers, Southport, N.C.

KATHARINE DAYTON

S1. "It Must Be Such Fun to Work with Kaufman," *New York Times*, 8 Dec. 1935: 3.

S2. "Katharine Dayton, Wrote 'First Lady'; Co-Author of Hit Play Dies-Penned Sharp Commentaries on Washington Scene," *New York Times*, 6 Mar. 1945.

6 *Major Events on the Lake*

1. A readily available edition of the book is Theodore Dreiser, *An American Tragedy* (New York: Penguin Putnam, 2000). This edition includes a selected bibliography of biography and criticism.

2. Craig Brandon, *Murder in the Adirondacks: "An American Tragedy" Revisited* (Utica, N.Y.: North Country Books, 1986).

3. Joseph W. Brownell and Patricia A. Wawrzaszek, *Adirondack Tragedy: The Gillette Murder Case of 1906* (Interlaken, N.Y.: Heart of the Lakes Publishing, 1986).

4. "Gillette Slaying Key Witness Dies," *Syracuse Herald Journal*, 31 Oct. 1955. McAllister family papers in possession of Dennis McAllister (grandson of James), Big Moose, N.Y.

5. Brandon, *Murder in the Adirondacks*, 146–47.

6. Brownell and Wawrzaszek, *Adirondack Tragedy*, 127.

7. Ibid., 127–28.

8. Francis E. Carey Jr, 1997. "Fern Spring Camp: The Stanley-Carey Years, 1898–1938," unpublished family notes, West Melbourne, Fla.

9. Higby, *Man from the Past*, 137–41.

10. Ibid., 140.

11. Ibid.

12. Ibid., 142.

13. Ibid., 130.

14. Brandon, *Murder in the Adirondacks*, 195–99.

15. Ibid., 196.

16. Ibid.

17. Brownell and Wawrzaszek, *Adirondack Tragedy*, 131.

18. Ibid., 136.

19. Ibid., 142, 154.

20. Ibid., 157–58; Higby, *Man from the Past*, 142.

21. Higby, *Man from the Past*, 142–43.

22. Peter C. Welsh, *Jacks, Jobbers and Kings: Logging the Adirondacks 1850–1950* (Utica, N.Y.: North Country Books, 1995), 130.

23. New York State Forest, Fish;, and Game Commission, *Report of Superintendant of Forests, 1903* (Albany, N.Y.: J. B. Lyons, 1904), 111.

24. McMartin, *Great Forest*, 140–41.

25. New York State Forest, Fish, and Game Commission, *Eighth and Ninth Reports for 1902 and 1903* (Albany, N.Y.: J. B. Lyon, 1903, 1904), 102.

26. Higby, *Man from the Past*, 57–58.

27. New York State Forest, Fish, and Game Commission, *Eighth and Ninth Reports*, 129.

28. Marleau, *Big Moose Station*, 266.

29. Norman J. VanValkenburgh, *The Forest Preserve of New York State in the Adirondack and Catskill Mountains: A Short History* (Fleischmanns, N.Y.: Purple Mountain Press in cooperation with Adirondack Research Library of the Association for the Protection of the Adirondacks, Schenectady, N.Y., 1996), 25.

30. "Hadley Fire Tower Restoration Committee," *Adirondack Architectural Heritage Newsletter* 10, no. 2 (winter 2000–01): 8.

31. Story from Barbara Kinne Wheeler.

32. *New York Times*, 7 Feb. 1973: 31.

33. *New York Times*, 2 Mar. 1973: 1.

34. Dee Brown, *Bury My Heart at Wounded Knee: An Indian History of the American West* (New York: Holt, Rinehart, and Winston, 1970); "Massacre at Wounded Knee, 1890," EyeWitness—History through the eyes of those who lived it, 1998; available from www.ibiscom.com.

35. In 1980 the Iroquois of Caughnawaga changed the spelling of their name to conform more closely to the Mohawk language pronunciation. They are now known as the Kahnawake Band. Their headquarters are close to Montreal in the Kahnawake Mohawk Territory. Information from the Corporate Information Management Directorate, Indian and Northern Affairs, room 1415, 10 Wellington Street, Hull, P.Q. K1A OH4, Canada.

36. Louis Hall, letter to Dennis Banks (American Indian Movement, St. Paul, Minn.), 17 Feb. 1974. Published in *Concerned Persons of the Central Adirondacks* (Eagle Bay, N.Y.), Oct. 1975, no. 3: 3.

37. Edward Hale, "Ganienkeh," *Adirondack Life* 8, no. 3 (1977): 20–23, 42–46.

38. Hale, "Ganienkeh," 20.

39. Barbara Charzuk, "Reid Sees Moss Lake Settlement in 2 Months," *Utica Daily Press*, 16 July 1975: 1.

40. *Boonville Herald*, 5 May 1976: 10.

41. Michael Tarbell, museum educator, Iroquois Indian Museum, P.O. Box 7, Caverns Road, Howes Cave, N.Y. 12092; personal communication with Mark Barlow and Jane Barlow, 1 June 2002.

42. *Boonville Herald*, 3 May 1978.

43. *Oneida Indian Nation of New York et al. v. State of New York et al.*, U.S. Circuit Court of Appeals, 691 F.2d 1070 (2d Cir. 1982). This decision was not appealed to the Supreme Court of the United States; therefore, the Second Circuit decision is the final word on the subject. We are indebted for this information to G. Robert Witmer of the firm of Nixon Peabody LLP, Rochester, N.Y., which firm is counsel to the counties of Madison and Oneida in the current land claim litigation brought by the Oneida Indian Nation of New York.

7 Recreation

1. Lena Retter, 1900, Diary for Summer of 1900. Bruyn family papers, Wakefield, Mass.

2. Koppe, *Big Moose Community Chapel,* 34.

3. "Circus at Colpitts," *Adirondack Arrow,* 31 Aug. 1933. Menand family papers, Rochester, N.Y.

4. John M. Judson, notes to Jane Barlow, Aug. 1999.

5. Bruyn, "Big Moose Memories," 30.

6. Grady, *Story of a Wilderness,* 184.

7. Ibid., 195.

8. Dept. of the Interior, Geological Survey, Big Moose Quadrangle, July 1903. Frank Carey collection.

9. Current maps give the spelling as "Andy's." Origin of the name is unknown.

10. Wanda K. Martin, private communication to Frank Carey, Jr., 1998.

11. M. Myra Hamilton, n.d., *Trail Map,* Lone Pine Tea Room, Twitchell Lake. Frank Carey collection.

12. Ibid.

13. Jennifer Martin, 1979, *Hiking and Cross Country Skiing from Covewood Lodge* (map).

14. D. L. Darnell, 1941, *Trails from Lake View Lodge* (map), Big Moose, N.Y.

15. Information on West Pond trails is largely from William S. Dunn, private communication, 1998.

16. Higby Club Trail Map, n.d. Frank Carey collection.

17. Ibid.

18. Darnell map.

19. Ibid.

20. William S. Dunn, private communication with Frank Carey, 1998.

21. Robert K. Voll, private communication with Frank Carey, 1997.

22. Bruyn, "Big Moose Memories."

23. For more details, see Christine Jerome, "Group Therapy," *Adirondack Life: 1998 Annual Guide to the Adirondacks* 29, no. 4 (1998): 64–69.

BARNEY LEPPER

S1. Harold W. Thompson, *Body, Boots & Britches* (New York: Dover, 1962), 308–9. Harold Thompson was a son-in-law of Professor Samuel Saunders, owner of Brightwood on the North Shore for many years.

8 The Big Moose Lake Community

1. Marleau, *Big Moose Station,* 179.

2. E. J. Martin, letter to Town of Webb School Board, 1905, Martin Family Papers, Big Moose, N.Y.

3. Marleau, *Big Moose Station,* 174.

4. Judy Brownell, "Early Adirondack School Days," *Adirondack Tourist,* 20 April 1983, Old Forge, N.Y.; courtesy of Town of Webb Historical Association, Old Forge, N.Y.

5. Marleau, *Big Moose Station,* 181.

6. Brownell, "Early Adirondack School Days."

7. Frank G. Lesure, notes on memories of Big Moose Lake School between Sept. 1933 and June 1939 in letter to Barbara K. Wheeler, 25 Jan. 1999.

8. Vernon Harry, conversation with Jane Barlow, 15 Sept. 2001.

9. Joy Waldau Hostage, "Adirondack Reflections" (paper read at the Writer's Workshop, Old Forge Library, Old Forge, N.Y., 21 July 1999).

10. Brownell, "Early Adirondack School Days."

11. R. H. Alton, letter to property owners of Big Moose, 4 Aug. 1930, family papers of William S. Dunn, Southport, N.C.

12. Koppe, *Big Moose Community Chapel.*

13. All quotations in this chapter are taken from the records (minutes of meetings, correspondence, etc.) of the Big Moose Property Owners Association, which are kept in the custody of the current president of the association and stored in the Association Center, Big Moose, N.Y.

Appendix C Big Moose Lake and the Adirondack Park Agency

1. Barbara McMartin, 2002. *Perspectives on the Adirondacks: A Thirty-Year Struggle by People Protecting Their Treasure* (Syracuse, N.Y.: Syracuse University Press, 2002).

Selected Bibliography

Books

Aber, Ted, and Stella King. *History of Hamilton County*. Lake Pleasant, N.Y.: Great Wilderness Books, 1965.

Brandon, Craig. *Murder in the Adirondacks: "An American Tragedy" Revisited*. Utica, N.Y.: North Country Books, 1986.

Brown, Henry A. L. *John Brown's Tract*. Canaan, N.H.: Phoenix Publishing, 1988.

Brownell, Joseph W., and Patricia A. Wawrzaszek. *Adirondack Tragedy: The Gillette Murder Case of 1906*. Interlaken, N.Y.: Heart of the Lakes Publishing, 1986.

Burnett, Charles. H. *Conquering the Wilderness*. Norwood, Mass.: Plimpton Press, 1932.

Covey, Frances Alden. *The Earl Covey Story*. New York: Exposition Press, 1964.

Dodington, Paul, Joe Fossey, Paul Gockel, Ron Hill, Bill Ogilvie, and James L. Smith. *The Greatest Little Motor Boat Afloat: The Legendary Disappearing Propeller Boat*. Ontario: The Boston Mills Press, 1983.

Donaldson, Alfred J. *A History of the Adirondacks*. 2 vols. Port Washington, N.Y.: Ira J. Friedman, 1963.

Gilborn, Craig. *Durant*. Sylvan Beach, N.Y.: North Country Books, 1981.

Grady, Joseph F. *The Story of a Wilderness: The Fulton Chain and Big Moose Region*. Old Forge, N.Y.: North Country Books, 1933.

Harter, Henry A. *Fairy Tale Railroad*. Utica, N.Y.: North Country Books, 1979.

Higby, Roy C. *A Man from the Past*. Big Moose, N.Y.: Big Moose Press, 1974.

Koppe, Ellie Reed. *The Big Moose Community Chapel*. Big Moose, N.Y.: Big Moose Community Chapel, 1981.

Marleau, William R. *Big Moose Station*. Van Nuys, Calif.: Marleau Family Press, 1986.

McMartin, Barbara. *The Great Forest of the Adirondacks*. Utica, N.Y.: North Country Books, 1994.

———. *Perspectives on the Adirondacks: A Thirty-Year Struggle by People Protecting their Treasure*. Syracuse, N.Y.: Syracuse Univ. Press, 2002.

Pilcher, Edith. *The Constables: First Family of the Adirondacks*. Utica, N.Y.: North Country Books, 1992.

Scheffler, William L., and Frank Carey. *Big Moose Lake New York in Vintage Postcards*. Charleston, S.C.: Arcadia Publishing, 2000.

Schneider, Paul. *The Adirondacks*. New York: Henry Holt, 1997.

Terrie, Philip G. *Forever Wild*. Syracuse, N.Y.: Syracuse Univ. Press, 1994.

———. *Contested Terrain*. Blue Mountain, N.Y.: Adirondack Museum/Syracuse Univ. Press, 1999.

Articles

Taussig-Lux, Karen J. "Diamonds in the Rough." *Adirondack Life* 26, no. 6 (1995): 31–37.

Index

Related individuals are sometimes listed in the same entry. Italic page number denotes illustration.

Data in Appendix A, including ownership and lot numbers, are not indexed.

Our Big Moose Story